BEING IN SHADOW AND LIGHT

Being in Shadow and Light

Academics in Post/Conflict Higher Education

Edited by Dina Zoe Belluigi

OpenBook
Publishers

https://www.openbookpublishers.com

©2025 Dina Zoe Belluigi (ed.)
Copyright of individual chapters is maintained by the chapter's authors

ISBN Paperback 978-1-80511-404-8
ISBN Hardback 978-1-80511-405-5
ISBN PDF 978-1-80511-406-2
ISBN HTML 978-1-80511-408-6
ISBN EPUB 978-1-80511-407-9

DOI: 10.11647/OBP.0427

Cover concept: Brent Meistre
Cover image: Back of USA postcard stamp (1987). Photo by Brent Meistre (2022)
Cover design: Jeevanjot Kaur Nagpal

Contents

About the Editor and Contributors   vii

Acknowledgements   xv

Foreword   xix
Takyiwaa Manuh

Introduction: Evoking What It Is to Be in Shadow and Light   1
Dina Zoe Belluigi

PART I: PAST CONFLICTS AND THEIR LEGACIES   **23**

1. Truth and Reparations: A Conversation on the Participation of the Higher Education Sector in the Colombian Commission for the Clarification of Truth, Coexistence and Non-repetition   25
Natalia Maya Llano, Juan Camilo Domínguez Cardona, Juan Sebastián Flórez Herrera, Catalina Puerta Henao and Adriana Rudling

2. The Whiteboard: Reflections on a Personal Archive of Apartheid-era Items from the Security Police of a University Town   57
Brent Arthur Meistre

3. Academics of Post-war Sri Lanka: Traces of Experiences and Impact   91
Hemalatha Pradeepkumar

4. Being a Woman and a Researcher between Exile and Social Reconfiguration: An Interview with Hebe Vessuri   125
Guillermo López Franco, Nissa Yaing Torres-Soto, Alejandra Aray-Roa and Paulette Joseph

5. Hidden Legacies of the Troubles: Post-conflict Pedagogy as Resistance in Northern Irish Medical Education   161
Jenny Johnston, Mairead Corrigan and Helen Reid

PART II: CONFLICTS IN THE PRESENT   **191**

6. 'A Virtual Target Painted on my Back...': Contested Constitutionalism in a Post-conflict Society   193

Colin Harvey

7. (Her)story between Shadow and Light: A Displaced Syrian Woman Academic   217

Rida Anis

8. Home and Abroad: Exploring my Lived Experiences through Poetry and Narrative   241

Fadel Jobran-Alsawayfa

9. The Lone Voice in the Academic Wilderness: Nigerian Academics' Experiences in Industrial Conflicts   263

Gregory O. Ugbo and Henry Chigozie Duru

10. The Conflict of the Faculties, Again   287

Richard Hudson-Miles

List of Illustrations   339

Index   343

About the Editor and Contributors

Dina Zoe Belluigi is Professor of Authorship, Representation and Transformation in Academia and a Fellow of the Senator George J. Mitchell Institute for Global Peace, Security and Justice at Queen's University Belfast (Northern Ireland). She is a Visiting Professor at the Chair for the Critical Studies of Higher Education Transformation at Nelson Mandela University (South Africa). Her scholarship and practice revolve around comprehending oppression and inequalities within, and by, the university, and the ways in which these are negotiated by intellectuals (specifically academics and artists) of the Majority World. She is fortunate to have learnt from collaborations—particularly in South Africa, India and Northern Ireland—utilising a range of research methodologies, including the creative arts. She was also fortunate to have her intellectual formation—as an academic and artist—informed by commitments to transformative justice prevalent in post-Apartheid South Africa. Dina serves in editorial roles of journals and councils of learned societies in Higher Education Studies, the Social Sciences and Humanities, and Creative Arts Education. She contributes to the work of the Scholars at Risk Ireland Committee, as she did the Council for At-Risk Academics (UK) Syrian programme. She is co-editor of *Emancipatory Imaginations: Advancing Critical University Studies* (African Sun Media, 2024 [in press]). https://orcid.org/0000-0003-4005-0160

Rida Anis is currently an Assistant Professor in English at Hasan Kalyoncu University, Gaziantep, Türkiye. She studied English Literature at the University of Aleppo, Syria. She received Fulbright scholarships to study her MA in English Literature at Old Dominion University, Norfolk; and a Doctorate of Philosophy in Literature & Criticism from Indiana University of Pennsylvania, USA. Between 2006 and 2015, she was a lecturer at the University of Aleppo. She has collaborated with

Syrian, Turkish and UK-based colleagues on interdisciplinary research projects. She is currently working on an anthology of Syrian women's writing. https://orcid.org/0000-0001-7111-3502

Juan Camilo Domínguez Cardona holds a BA in Sociology and an MA in Socio-spatial Studies from the *Universidad de Antioquia*, in Colombia. He is currently doing his PhD in Socio-spatial Studies at the same university. He is a full-time Professor at the Regional Studies Institute at the Universidad de Antioquia, having previously been Coordinator of Post-graduate Studies, of the Master's in Socio-spatial Studies and of the Specialist Qualification in Theories, Methods and Techniques of Social Research. His research topics have been the comparative studies of the Colombian armed conflict, peacebuilding in Colombia, socio-spatial theory, and soccer and supporters studies. https://orcid.org/0000-0002-1330-6557

Mairead Corrigan is a Senior Lecturer (Education) and the Academic Lead for Equality, Diversity and Inclusion (EDI) in the Centre for Medical Education, Queen's University Belfast (Northern Ireland). She is a sociologist and educationalist, and a qualitative researcher. Her academic work focuses on social justice, inequalities and diversity. https://orcid.org/0000-0001-8941-0572

Henry Chigozie Duru currently teaches at the Department of Mass Communication, Nnamdi Azikiwe University, Awka, after having been active in the field as a full-time journalist. He holds a doctorate in Mass Communication with a specialisation in Political Communication and Journalism.

Colin Harvey is a Professor of Human Rights Law and a Fellow of the Senator George J. Mitchell Institute for Global Peace, Security and Justice at Queen's University Belfast. He has served as Head of the Law School, a member of Senate, and a Director of Research. Professor Harvey is a Commissioner on the Irish Human Rights and Equality Commission and a member of the Scientific Committee of the EU Agency for Fundamental Rights. He was a member of the REF2014 Law sub-panel and the REF2014 Equality and Diversity Advisory Panel. He served two terms as a Commissioner on the Northern Ireland Human Rights Commission and was a member of the Northern Ireland Higher

Education Council. He has written and taught extensively on human rights and constitutional law. https://orcid.org/0000-0002-2147-6580

Juan Sebastián Flórez Herrera holds a BA in History from the *Universidad Nacional de Colombia*. He centres the history of social movements and armed conflict in Colombia. Between 2019 and 2022 he was a researcher with the Colombian Commission for Clarification of Truth, Coexistence and Non-Repetition. Part of this body's Bogotá-Soacha-Sumapaz territorial team, he was also the rapporteur for *Case 52 / Universities and Armed Conflict*, which outlines the history of the violence, activism and victimisation of the higher education sector during the Colombian armed conflict. https://orcid.org/0000-0002-6968-6042

Richard Hudson-Miles is an interdisciplinary researcher, currently working as Senior Lecturer in Critical and Contextual Studies at Leeds School of Arts, Leeds Beckett University. His research operates at the intersections of the history of art and design, radical social theory and the sociology of education. He is the editor of a forthcoming monograph on alternative art schools titled *Cooperative Education, Politics, and Art* (Routledge, 2024 [in press]). He sits on the editorial boards of the Journal of Writing in Creative Practice, and the Journal of Design, Business and Society. He also writes fashion and music criticism for ASBO magazine. https://orcid.org/0000-0002-1055-4459

Fadel Jobran-Alsawayfa is an Assistant Professor of Education at Bethlehem University, Palestine. He is a pedagogue and a poet. He is the Chairperson of the Early Childhood Education Department and the Coordinator of the Master's Programme in Creative Pedagogies and Community Practices. He completed his Doctor of Education (EdD) at the University of Chester. Prior to the completion of the EdD, Fadel had attained an MA in Comparative Education from the Institute of Education, University of London. He teaches courses in drama in education, storytelling, theatre, play and creativity, arts-based research and creativity in practice. Jobran-Alsawayfa is interested in self-reflexive methodologies that allow individuals to narrate their stories and lived experience evocatively and authentically. He also hopes that poetic inquiry and drama performance will be widely adopted as creative pedagogies and arts-based research approaches, emphasising their potential to foster creativity and give voice to participants through the development of arts-based participatory research. https://orcid.org/0000-0002-3635-7736

Jenny Johnston is a critical medical educationalist and an experienced general practitioner (GP) working in deprived areas of Belfast. Her academic work focuses on social justice issues and is informed by diverse theoretical perspectives drawn from social science. Her prize-winning PhD work has been published as a monograph exploring power structures in medical cultures from the viewpoint of GP trainees. She directs a vibrant and progressive research programme in medical education. https://orcid.org/0000-0002-3999-8774

Paulette Joseph has a doctorate in Health Psychology, Universidad Miguel Herrera (Spain). She is an industrial psychologist with postgraduate studies in Physical Activity and Health, and currently works with disabled mentally ill patients. She has experience working with women with fibromyalgia as well as patients subjected to high levels of stress in Germany and Spain. She has always been interested in the studies of gender, physical activity and personal integral health, well-being and self-determination.

Guillermo López Franco is based at the Universidad Kino A.C. and has a PhD in Social Sciences from the Universidad de Sonora (México). His research interests include academic profession, public policies, internationalisation of higher education and science communication. He acts as an adviser for the regional event EXPO CIENCIAS 2020 of science popularisation. In his current position at Universidad Kino A.C., he is a registered advisor for the Delfin Research Program and also a member of the National Research System (SNI) of México. https://orcid.org/0000-0002-3441-0361

Natalia Maya Llano is a journalist and a specialist in theories, methods and techniques of social investigation, holding a Master's in Political Science from the *Universidad de Antioquia*, Colombia. She is a member of the research group Conflicts, Violence and Human Security of the Faculty of Law and Political Sciences of the same university. She worked at the Colombian Commission for Clarification of Truth, Coexistence and Non-Repetition as a researcher for the Urban Dynamics team of the

Territories Directorate. Her research interests are in general topics such as armed conflict, peace building and transitional processes. https://orcid.org/0000-0002-9005-7101.

Brent Arthur Meistre is a South African artist, curator and independent scholar. He has created numerous one-person exhibitions, including photography and film installations exhibited internationally, and is a recipient of prestigious awards such as the inaugural *Nelson Mandela Biennale Award*. He is the founder and curator of *Analogue Eye*, a mobile drive-in and pop-up cinema that showcases African video artworks to rural audiences. He was previously a Senior Lecturer at Rhodes University, South Africa, and is currently based in Belfast, Northern Ireland, undertaking his PhD independently. https://vimeo.com/brentmeistre and https://counternarrativefilm.wixsite.com/analogueye

Hemalatha Pradeepkumar is the Head of Academic Affairs at Ambiga College of Arts and Science for Women, affiliated with Madurai Kamaraj University, India. She has worked as a teacher-trainer, educational planner and lecturer in South Asia. She holds a Master's degree in computer network management from Middlesex University, England, and a doctorate in Higher Education at the University of Liverpool, England. Her research interests lie in social justice issues, gender studies, higher education policy and practice. https://orcid.org/0009-0001-3960-8465

Catalina Puerta Henao is a Professor of Political Science at the Universidad de Antioquia, Colombia. She holds a BA in Law from the same university and an MA and PhD in History from the Universidad Nacional de Colombia in Medellín, Colombia. She has held coordination and research positions in public institutions dedicated to the care and reparation of victims and the construction of memory and truth in Medellín. She has also worked as an expert in the Justice and Peace Chamber of the Superior Court of Medellín. Her research focuses on the understanding of the victim subject in a historical, legal and political sense, the definition of the internal enemy and the processes of clarification and truth (re)construction in the Colombian armed conflict. https://orcid.org/0000-0002-6429-3557

Helen Reid is a clinical academic based at Queen's University Belfast in Northern Ireland. She is passionate about general practice and the importance of high-quality community healthcare in effective health systems. She holds an MPhil and PhD in medical education and continues to research and publish alongside her clinical and curricular responsibilities. Her expertise lies in critically oriented qualitative research in areas ranging from rural health inequalities to domestic abuse. https://orcid.org/0000-0001-8530-1766

María Alejandra Aray Roa holds a PhD in Science Education from the Universidad Nacional Experimental Simón Rodríguez (Venezuela). She is a sociologist interested in gender studies, higher education, science education management, citizenship and education in natural science. She participated in the project *Transversalidad de la perspectiva en el estado de Sonora* [Gender perspective in Sonora state], and is engaged in social studies in science processes and education in natural science. She currently lives and works in Sonora, México. https://orcid.org/0000-0002-8341-908X

Adriana Rudling is a GRI Post-Doctoral Fellow—Transitional Justice at William & Mary, in the USA. She holds a PhD in Politics from the University of Sheffield, UK. She has held research positions at various academic institutions in Sweden, the UK, Colombia and Norway. She has also worked as a consultant specialising in monitoring, learning and evaluation with (I)NGOs and international aid. Her research interests centre on the interactions between victims of massive and systematic human rights violations and measures and state bureaucracies established in (post-)transitional societies to respond to their harms. https://orcid.org/0000-0002-5758-0531

Nissa Yaing Torres Soto holds a PhD in Social Sciences from the Universidad de Sonora, México, and is based at *Universidad Autónoma del Estado de Quintana Roo*, México. She is a social psychologist with postgraduate studies in Educational Innovation and Social Sciences. She is interested in positive environments, mental health, education, public health and vulnerable social groups. She was the recipient of an award at the Arizona Student Energy Conferences (AzSEC) in the Grand Challenge Competition by University of Arizona, for 'Testing a Tridimensional Model of Sustainable Behavior: Self-care, Caring for Others and Caring for the Planet'. She is a member of the International

Honor Society in Psychology and National Researchers System (SNI) of México. https://orcid.org/0000-0003-3646-6649

Gregory Obinna Ugbo lectures in the Department of Mass Communication at Federal University, Oye-Ekiti, Nigeria. He is an avid researcher with specific interests in journalism and media studies, conflict communication, health communication, and gender studies. He is a member of several academic associations including the International Association for Media and Communication Research (IAMCR), the African Council for Communication Education (ACCE) and the Association of Communication Scholars and Practitioners of Nigeria (ACSPN). https://orcid.org/0000-0001-6088-9794

Acknowledgements

This book was produced during, and in the aftermath of, a period of international disruption with the COVID-19 pandemic and its restrictions. For many of the chapter authors, this was amidst periods of personal, professional and public instability and change.

Writing during such conditions is made possible through the support of others, in our immediate vicinity and at a distance. Within the individual chapters—either in the acknowledgement sections or within the main text—the authors have exercised their own approaches to recognising those whose investments enabled and deepened their work and their practice. For the book as a whole, as the editor there are a number of people and organisations I would like to acknowledge for enabling this project to come to fruition.

Firstly, the authors of this book are the substance of its making. Each of you—as individuals and intellectuals—and your contributions on these pages are very much appreciated. The process of making this book has not been quick nor easy. I thank you for patience when fellow contributors needed longer, or could not continue and pulled out; I thank you for responding graciously to my continued requests and detours. I also appreciate your investment in your fellow contributors' work and thinking. Each of the chapters in this book underwent a number of cycles of peer review, undertaken by fellow chapter authors. Additionally, my gratitude to my colleague Dr Yecid Ortega, of Queen's University Belfast, who undertook a review of the Spanish version of Chapter 1.

This endeavour was catalysed by the participants of a roundtable event hosted by the Council of At-Risk Academics (Cara) in Istanbul in 2019. My hope is that the book begins to touch upon some of the silences and omissions that were raised there as problematic. Thank you to those individuals who cannot be named who have since contacted me and encouraged the continuation of this project. My thanks to Dr Tom Parkinson, who was the primary investigator for that Cara initiative, for directly contacting all participants when this book project began, and for your input and support of the original concept note that went out with the call for chapters. None of this would have been imaginable if you had not reached out at the Society for Research in Higher Education (SRHE) conference in 2018 and invited me to become involved in Cara's Syrian Programme. Your openness and trust are rare, Tom. Related is my appreciation of Kate Robinson, the Director of the Cara Syrian Academic Skills Programme, and Dr Cath Camps, as role models of service to our counterparts in exile.

As an unfunded endeavour undertaken during neoliberal times, it was a pleasant surprise that my agency to persist in this project was not constrained nor interrupted by my employing organisation, Queen's University Belfast. For that I am grateful to my colleagues at the School of Social Sciences, Education and Social Work. Events and discussions hosted by colleagues at The Senator George J. Mitchell Institute for Global Peace, Security and Justice, and by those of the Scholars at Risk Ireland committee, have enriched my thinking around this project. At its very end, a number of authors connected to me via networks of Critical University Studies, particularly the Advancing Critical University in Africa (ACUSAfrica) collectives, engaged with the final chapters and provided feedback. In particular my thanks to Roxana Chiappa, Sol Gamsu, Savo Heleta, Chris Knaus, Premesh Lalu, Dalene Swanson and Roja Fazaeli. My thanks to the Queen's University Belfast open access library staff who persevered in securing funding for the book publication costs.

I am humbled by the commitments to academic publishing of the Open Book Publishers, in the midst of such a monstrously capitalist system. Your horizontal ethos within this working relationship, Alessandra Tosi, was lovely. My thanks for the attention of the team in their care of this work, specifically Adèle Kreager for language editing, Jeevanjot Nagpal for the cover design, and Raegan Allen for marketing material. These were the people with whom I engaged directly—my thanks too to those behind the scenes of OBP who are acknowledged by name at the end of this book.

Takyiwaa Manuh responded with grace to the invitation to compose the foreword of this book. Early on, I knew with a deep sense of certainty I would ask her, and no other, to make that contribution to this book. The integrity of your work is your legacy to the world, Takyiwaa, and it is humbling. It was a privilege to witness, and to learn from, moments of your intellectual force in South Africa in 2023 and then later in Ghana in 2024. Thank you for taking the time to read this work and invest your words in its beginning, when so many fires are burning.

Thank you to Brent Meistre for our many discussions over the years deliberating the central questions of this book, which remain unanswerable. My hope is that those of the generations to come may come to a deeper understanding of what drives many like us, what we have experienced and what blinkers we continue to have, despite wrestling with shadows. For now, thank you to my children, for being gracious about the late hours away to bring this to fruition.

Foreword

Takyiwaa Manuh[1]

Universities and higher education institutions around the globe are sites of knowledge-making and dissemination, of debate, and of vigorous expression. Often conceptualised as 'protected' spaces somewhat standing above politics and society with their usual messiness, the institutions are not usually seen as implicated or complicit in conflict; images of academics and students bent over books or in their laboratories and libraries, exercising their academic freedoms, dominate our thinking. Such comforting assumptions are shattered in this volume that presents readers with realities that at first sight may appear different from what we are accustomed to, but then begin to feel somewhat familiar, depending on where we are located. As we turn the pages, we read about the close associations and accommodations between universities in many locations with power and authority, and their roles in stifling and punishing protest.

Being in Shadow and Light: *Academics in Post/Conflict Higher Education* is a powerful but troubling volume that highlights the gendered experiences, subjectivities, (re)tellings and withholdings, and the place of memory of academics and scholars in countries and contexts as far apart as Colombia and Sri Lanka, with many stops along the way, including through the UK, Nigeria, South Africa and Palestine. The common elements are those of conflict in its different sites and forms that also challenge the possibilities for academic freedom on which scholarly work and expression are hinged, and the resulting responsibilities and accountabilities of scholars to themselves, their

---

1   Emerita Professor of Africa Studies, University of Ghana, Legon/Honorary Professor, Nelson Mandela University, Gqeberha, South Africa.

   https://doi.org/10.11647/OBP.0427.12

colleagues and families, and to the societies in which they are located. The search for truth and reparation/reconciliation, for repair and rebuilding of trust in post-conflict societies and institutions also reveal the complexities, complicities and resistances that confront such efforts, including uncomfortable discoveries about close kin and associates and their participation in atrocities, silencing and repression of scholars.

The necessity and importance of solidarity and networks of support from academics, students and publics, both local and global, is poignantly revealed in the '(Her)story between Shadow and Light' of the displaced Syrian woman academic (Chapter 7). Similarly, in 'A Virtual Target Painted on my Back' (Chapter 6), Colin Harvey captures the feeling of being avoided with his phrase the 'shuffling sideways when they see you coming'. This experience is strikingly familiar for me. These accounts reveal the challenges scholars in such situations face and highlight the critical role of support in breaking that isolation. As an academic who has experienced some of such silencing and threat in the culture wars invading our campuses, churches and societies with the rise of anti-democratic and authoritarian forces, and their discourses and practices, I cannot reiterate enough the importance of solidarity. The power and warmth of solidarity are invaluable as we, as scholars and academics embedded in our communities, continue to resolutely do our work.

The resonance and poignancy of this volume is enhanced by the mixed methods approaches, diverse methodologies and sensitivity that the editor adopts. The book blends heavy academic writing with more reader-friendly styles as most of the authors are not, as noted in the Introduction, 'primarily scholars of the university, of higher education, or even of conflict'. There are conversations, interviews, transcribed WhatsApp exchanges and podcasts, the retellings of creative artists and memory activists and practitioners, alongside more scholarly renderings. These different modes succeed in presenting in their own words the difficult contexts, content and choices that the authors experienced. The stories and chapters are necessary but uneasy retellings, and we deserve to know, to lift the veil on our institutions and create spaces for reflection, further debate and meaningful solidarities. By doing so, we can enlarge the meanings and practices of academic freedoms in our societies. The volume will resonate with critical scholars, practitioners and activists working for social transformation, democratic rights and space, and peace around the world.

Introduction: Evoking What It Is to Be in Shadow and Light

Dina Zoe Belluigi

Weighing... Wanting... Waiting...

Thus begins a homage to the moments of remembrance, desire and melancholia which have lodged themselves, festered and demanded a reckoning. 'Waiting as a site of subject formation' (Debele, 2020) is part of the title of an academic paper about the prayers of Ethiopians seeking asylum in Europe. I read it within months of interacting with academics[1] who bore the personal-professional scars of violent political conflict and oppression, at a formal gathering of atypical academic development at the Swedish Embassy in Istanbul (Belluigi and Parkinson, 2020).[2] As a

---

[1] Throughout this introduction the term 'academics' is utilised as an umbrella term for intellectuals who have practiced within the university. As this book has been published in the United Kingdom, that terminology has been adopted; 'professors' or 'teachers' of higher education are used elsewhere. I have avoided the additional term 'staff' because this would suggest current employment within an institution, which would exclude many academics in exile or displaced, those working on precarious contracts and those who are currently independent. The terminology used within other chapters of this book may differ, reflective of variations of situated usage.

[2] This event of roundtables and workshops was organised by the Council of At-Risk Academics (Cara), as part of the Syrian Academic Programme in Türkiye, funded through the efforts of Dr Tom Parkinson. It sought to respond to 'a pressing need' of Syrians within the Türkiye-based Academic Skills Programme 'to seek input from academics with comparable, complex experiences, and/or whose work has involved reckoning with the legacies of conflict, oppression or displacement in other parts of the world. It was hoped, too, that international colleagues would themselves value an opportunity to share their experiences and reflect on these complex issues' (Belluigi and Parkinson, 2020, p. 17). Participants included those from (or working in) Belarus, Bosnia-Herzegovina, Kenya, Northern Ireland, Palestine, Serbia, Syria and South Africa. Dr Parkinson informed the

   https://doi.org/10.11647/OBP.0427.00

member of the generation entering academia after the cessation of state oppression, I uttered a promise there: to archive, somehow, the quotidian quandaries and endurances of academic life affected by conflict. The desire was to disrupt the free fall into cycles of hostilities and allegiances that encase universities and its citizens 'post' such conflict.

There was a sense we were waiting, with crushed hopes (Inayatullah, 2017), for our countries and leaders, including fellow intellectuals, to bring that which was disregarded and in the shadows to the fore. In the aftermath of devastation, the intense scrutiny of the spotlight cast from inquisitors, commissions and investment in 'development' does not lead to controlled burning within academia. Indefinite delays to the relief of the catharsis that comes from bringing truth to the light, and deferred reckoning with justice, impose detours away from healing and the possibilities of the rebirth of the university. After a 'crisis', academia is strategically deprioritised from that spotlight, and pragmatically operationalised for the business of repairing public trust in the institution's capacity and partiality to perform its role of stewardship of education and knowledge-making for the public good.[3] The many reasons and effects of such diverted attention is not the subject of this book. Rather, it is a response to the experience of wanting, felt by academics experiencing oppression in the present, due to omissions made by similarly-placed intellectuals, and the dearth of representations of what they endure/d (Abdulateef et al., 2020).

'*Weighing... wanting*', in the sub-title above, is a direct reference to the 1997 artwork by William Kentridge. In his charcoal animations, paper does not only function as a ground for what is depicted. Paper bandages wounds. Sheets of paper cover the bodies of slain victims at sites of atrocities. That gesture of dignity, in *Felix in Exile* (1994), becomes a papering over of injustices as murdered protesters disappear into the landscape, without forensic inquiry, almost without a trace. An historically significant past is required for intellectual historiography, in addition to figures of significance. Instead of this, the artist

---

conceptualisation of the call for chapters of this book, with participants of the roundtable invited to contribute.

3   For ways in which such crisis has been re-interpreted for post-conflict education, see Keet's (2019, p. 17) argument for the validity of 'treating crisis and critique as analytically and historically central to the program of critical theory'.

utilises configurations of his own fallible body—as character and as image-maker—morphing into mutually-constitutive technologies of representation, power structures and human relations. However, what act as silent witnesses of mistakes, loves lost, violence, atrocity, banality are the traces of the image-maker's marking, hesitation, erasure and staining. On such pages, the borderlands between record, memory and amnesia are blurred.

Fig. I.1 Unnamed artistic intervention marks the absence of the long shadow once cast by the monument to Cecil John Rhodes at the University of Cape Town. Photo taken by Dina Zoe Belluigi (Cape Town, 2018).

Beginning with this subtitle reflects my acknowledgement, as the editor, that the creation of a book requires a particular kind of collective illogicality. Edited academic books are too expensive, inaccessible and increasingly devalued by national research assessment regimes. Book projects become suspended forever, failed receptacles in drawers and computer folders of efforts that threaten to never come to fruition. In the years it took for this collection to come together, it began to seem a meagre contribution and maybe even a vanity against the many contemporary shadows of conflict from which this book has come to light. Yet 'the book' has long been a metaphysical repository of international storytelling of the losses of diaspora, oppression and ethical injunction.

(The word beyond the word [...] outlasts the object it names, outlasts its actual reason in an intimate unreason of being. A pale nude across the bars of logic. A word that takes wing from the unspoken word as breath does from the inert body. Soul-word with memories of day and blood.

The light comes at the end of our weak nights.)

And yet the book is made of the sun's silence. (Jabès, 1977, p. 153)

Somewhere between these fragmentary references to a text, encounters, promises and imagery are evocations of *the sense and the perception* of being an academic, emerging and fading at various points across this book.[4] The ambiguities of our positioning—writing as academics from within, beyond and about institutions—become apparent. We weigh injunctions to that which is *more* than the self, family, community, discipline, country and the contemporary. The threats and humiliation of falling from position, grace or stature are felt, while wanting truth, justice, forgiveness, openings.

This book brings together the writing of twenty-one academics, memory activists and artists into ten chapters about different contexts, and from varied vantage points and periods of time. In this introductory chapter, I interweave the ways in which the authors engage with the central questions of 'being', 'conflict', and 'the academic' within the content and form of their chapters. In this process of introductory interweaving, I have created a discontinuous fabric of jarring shapes, bleeding colours and exposed loose dead-ends, because as much as there are commonalities in aspects of what is evoked in these chapters, there are contestations and contrasts which eschew conclusiveness and coherence about these central questions. This is of course colourised by my own reading and interests, and is in no way a representative whole of the separate parts of the book, nor commensurate with the power of any chapter. I have also utilised this introduction as an opportunity to share insights into book-making processes, and the thinking behind my curatorial choices for the chapters' juxtapositions alongside each other and their grouping into two 'parts', with five chapters exploring past conflicts and five exploring conflicts in the present.

---

4   See more on endeavours akin to aesthetic education in post-Apartheid South African art, in the recent book *Undoing Apartheid* by Premesh Lalu (2022).

On Being

In the periphery of one's vision, while reading across this book, are affective flickers *other than* conflict. Peace, however, is not the subject, object nor direction of travel of these chapters. This was not the product of *intervention* on my part as the editor. Rather, as evoked by the book's title—*Being in Shadow and Light: Academics in Post/Conflict Higher Education*—the call for chapters was an invitation to contribute towards discussions about liminal states of 'being' from the particularity of 'the academic' in the gradations between relational sites ('shadow' and 'light') and temporalities ('post/conflict'). Set alongside and against the words in this title, a range of questions and prompts were offered[5] to open and extend the subject to the authors' acts of narration. Whether the authors' eventual final chapters were produced through processes of play, expression, witnessing or refusal of call-and-response, or bound to the fidelity of other grounds (be that memory, experience, disciplinary frames, imagined audience), is a question for meta-critique. Rather—as if cognisant of dangers—the chapters do not offer a g-d's-eye gaze of ontological, idealised or normative notions of states and sites of peace in the past nor future. Linear progress leading from conflict to peace cannot be found here either, nor are tidy solutions and recommendations offered for consumption. Similarly, the figures which emerge are not constructed within the enabling fictions of the conventions of (auto) biography.[6] Rather, as the authors 'hold' the uncertainties of ethico-historical states and sites before us in their chapters, what emerges is heterologous, and sometimes ambiguous.

'The people who have been interested in these issues and in thinking about university communities as subjects in the conflict have been those who identify with or have been involved as victims or groups in resistance to the conflict', Juan Sebastián Flórez Herrera reminds us in

---

5   A four-page concept note was circulated via networks and on social media, with the open call for chapters. A shortened reproduction of the questions is reproduced at the end of this introduction.

6   Life history—the matter of a number of these chapters—is ambiguously positioned in the academy, as literary rather than scientific, due to concerns about intimacy and sentimentality (in addition to subjectivity). For more on the treatment of the individual as an object of study within academic disciplines, and the construction of 'linear masculine lines as authentic selves', see Rassool (2004).

the discussion recorded in Chapter 1. Indeed, all who have contributed to this book have lived or are living in states and sites affected by various types and levels of conflict, which they have been impelled to represent. The richness of finding ways through dilemmas—of omission (Chapters 1, 2, 3), trauma (Chapter 5), displacement (Chapters 4, 7), injustice (Chapters 7, 8) and distortion (Chapters 6, 9, 10)—are brought forth through the emic-etic positioning of the authors. As such, the modes of enquiry and representation are often discontinuous: conversations (Chapter 1, 4), critical ethnography (Chapter 2), scholarly review (Chapter 3), vignettes and case studies (Chapter 5), interview (Chapters 6), oral life history (Chapter 7), ethnographic poetry (Chapter 8), critical discourse analysis (Chapter 9) and speculative inter-textual collage (Chapter 10).

In a number of the chapters, the authors explicitly broach the question of *how to represent* such being. Decades after Theodor Adorno's ethical cautions about the aesthetics of remembrance and recollection after historical trauma, in Chapter 8 Fadel Jobran-Alsawayfa's ethnographic poetry features as a source of expression and sense-making under current conditions of oppression. He utilises this poetry with emancipatory intent when practising his academic functions and constrained freedoms in Palestine. In other chapters, the toll of representing memories is made apparent. Across the transcribed audio recordings that fragment Rida Anis's account in Chapter 7, of her life as a woman academic before and after the 2011 Syrian crisis, reflections are peppered with the fortitude required to continue that retelling. Anis ends the chapter with the care to *withhold* that which should not be exposed to the light of day. In both of these chapters, the temptation to offer an 'authentic' voice for consumption by dysconscious audiences is resisted. The seamlessness of academic craft of presentation is undone through changes in tone, hesitations, jumps in time and place, and interruptions of flows of surety. In ways such as these, the chapters consciously disrupt the reception of life history as communication. Similarly, critical approaches (Kratz, 2001) are adopted by representing *living* as method in the academic life history of Hebe Vessuri, the cultural anthropologist interviewed by Guillermo López Franco, Nissa Yaing Torres Soto, Alejandra Aray Roa and Paulette Joseph in Chapter 4.

For authors a shade removed in the generation *after*, the struggles of representation differ slightly. Scholars inevitably reckon with the dearth of ancestral scholarship, which Hemalatha Pradeepkumar runs up against in her searches for published insider insights into the lives of academics during the ethnic-based armed conflict in her country of Sri Lanka (Chapter 3). The destruction of archives by the state to expunge collective memories, leaves Brent Meistre with the task of deliberating traces of inherited artefacts which once belonged to, or were confiscated from, dissident or banned South African academics (Chapter 2). What dis/engagement *after* representation in official accounts may mean for future enclosure features in the conversation between Natalia Maya Llano, Juan Camilo Domínguez Cardona, Juan Sebastián Flórez Herrera, Catalina Puerta Henao and Adriana Rudling in Chapter 1, following their contributions to a published report about universities' roles in extra-judicial truth-seeking mechanisms in Columbia. These concerns about probing archives and about their potential use-value for transformative collective commemoration and remembrance, are shared by intellectual communities countering dominant narratives, canons, accounts and collections, and pushing for reclamation (see for instance Brusius and Rico, 2023; Netshakhuma, 2023; Ngoepe, 2019).

These are not the expected pursuits of academic citizens socialised for professional success as the 'next generation' after conflict.[7] Rather, an ethical injunction shapes such intention, as Henao articulates towards the end of Chapter 1.

> the value of education as the ultimate goal—'just keep educating'— especially as we have been understanding this work is not finished and a lot more narratives are going to emerge. Our aim in participating in this work is not to necessarily publish articles and get salary points, but to understand ourselves and for those generations that are coming up to understand and know what happened and why the decisions we made as a society led to certain things.

---

7   For instance, for more on the professional socialisation of academic citizens selected to be the 'next generation' after racial oppression, see Sule (2014) on the USA and Booi et al. (2017) on South Africa. Mis-shaping of academics' critical consciousness was shared when discussing similar academic development programmes in Bosnia-Herzegovina and Serbia with participants of the roundtable in Istanbul in 2019.

There is ample occasion on these pages where authors diligently point readers to established sources, whether through citation or when utilising publications as 'data'. Included are reports (Chapters 1, 3, 6), state dossiers (Chapter 2), journalist reporting (Chapters 3, 9) and the research publications of the subjects of the studies (for instance, Chapters 4, 6). The chapters are not operating to replace nor cover-over those perhaps more dominant or seemingly 'official' sources, but rather to complement, complicate or problematise the surety of their conclusiveness, the will to power of enclosure, and to keep truth-seeking alive in remembrance.

More integrated, agonistic openings are made through troubling the compositional order of the landscapes of conflict. This is done by foregrounding the processes, politics and conditions of production of those representations, and their makers. These may be confidential, covert insights, deemed inconsequential messy minutiae in 'conflict transformation' or peace-making, that over time become erased from institutional and academic memories locally, and inaccessible to scholars and practitioners of other conflicts or contexts. The rich terrain of academic subjectivity involves trade-offs, denials and regrets of allegiances and acts committed during conflict, and processes of transition and sometimes even transformation. This is not to denigrate nor accuse actors of reneging on the practice of their academic responsibilities, as if academic autonomy could only be read through idealised frames (Belluigi, 2023). It is rather to 'understand ourselves and the generations to come' (Henao, Chapter 1) who will continue to be situated—though not fixed—within interplays of haunting conditions and fraught intellectual ancestral agency.

The chapters' differences reveal that temporal changes, distance and circumstances affect the proximity of academics to visceral experiences (pain, fear, denigration, temptation, hope). They also impact the opacity/lucidity of our sight to ascertain the direction of travel from the risks and costs to be endured, escaped or recollected. Entangled in the nature of conflict—whether moral, social, epistemic, cultural, political, armed, etc.—is the internal-external nature of oppression and division. While the lines between civil war, domestic conflict and external oppression are not neatly drawn, what should be borne in mind is how these affect the nature of academic relations, networks, and conditions. This is particularly of concern for the critical functions of academia during and after periods of intense conflict (Russell, 2023).

On Conflict

Characterisation of violence, oppression and conflict are themselves bound up in narratives about the past, present and future which may be flattened, ossified or emptied out by those dominantly-placed in nation-building, development and universities. It is possible that 'conflict' has again been opened to re-interpretation and re-signification in the pages of this book, because the question, the illusion and the spectre of peace were not placed within the terms of engagement, as I discussed in the section above. Either/or binaries of conflict/peace carry with them associations of war. That is not to say that many of the chapters do not engage with states and sites of being in relation to violent or armed conflict; on the contrary, all of the chapters in Part I—which engage with the past and its legacies—are set explicitly within contexts affected by armed conflict, as are two chapters in Part II about contemporary conflicts. However, in this book the dominant grounds for such conflict are entangled in subordinate and often intimate conflicts, divisions, harms, fears and struggles.

Some of these began long before the notion of the contemporary nation-state was implemented; others have mutated anew in the present. All but one of the countries discussed herein were colonised. The outlier—England (Chapter 10)—continues to enjoy the coloniality of matrices of power of imperial and racial capitalism (Quijano, 2000). Conflicts in these chapters include countries which gained independence as sovereign nations from the Spanish Empire, including Colombia (Chapter 1), Argentina, Brazil, México and Venezuela (Chapter 4); from the Ottoman Empire, Syria (Chapter 7); from the British Empire, Nigeria (Chapter 9), Sri Lanka (Chapter 3) and South Africa (Chapter 2). While the Republic of Ireland gained independence over a century ago, Northern Ireland (Chapters 5, 6) continues to be unsettled by partition, a feature of British solutionism to 'the problem' of Cyprus, India, Israel/Palestine (Chapter 8) and others. The Cold War explicitly frames Meistre's attempts to comprehend the investigative practices of 'enquiry' of the South African state security apparatus (Chapter 2). It also underpins the mid-to-late twentieth-century dynamics of the Latin American countries which Vessuri traversed (Chapter 4), and the backdrop of the internal instability of many of the contexts discussed herein, including Syria and Palestine. The reach of global capitalism and its current iteration as neoliberalism appears in the two chapters on industrial conflict (in Nigeria, Chapter 9; and in England, Chapter 10).

The chapters have, however, been (dis)ordered to disrupt the semblance of unilinear chronology across periods of geopolitical conflict. Part I comes not to an end but a pause, bookended between two chapters about the same geographic context: Northern Ireland. Intrusions of 'post'-conflict habitus and traumatised bodies into contemporary formal medical education is the subject of Chapter 5 by Jenny Johnston, Mairead Corrigan and Helen Reid. It is the past in the present which makes apparent the coloniality of denials of the hidden curriculum (Lawrence et al., 2018) in that chapter. In Chapter 6, it is the present where threats of physical violence and threats of political interference in institutional autonomy are current realities faced by the author, Colin Harvey, when engaging in public intellectualism. He discusses the chilling effect on collective agency when an academic figure is singled out as a scapegoat of change. The primary question posed in that chapter, is the state of social sanction on public discourse *after* the cessation of violent, armed conflict. What looms in the shadows is institutional ir/responsibility. The contrast between that chapter which begins Part II and the first chapter of Part I was a deliberate curatorial decision. Part I begins this book with a conversation about the *proactive* engagements of universities in public deliberation and pedagogy, about their role in harms and injustices in post-conflict Columbia and their praxis as a public truth-seeking mechanism. The contrast with the chapter beginning Part II raises questions about the temporal relation between conflict and university legitimacy, and the markers of risk and responsibility for mobilising public discussions about, and by, post-conflict institutions. Common to both chapters are cautions sounded about the conditions of possibility for institutions and academics to enact their critical functions while affirming such practices.

Wrestling for power is common when rapid changes are imposed through social regulation. The legal and policy dimensions of conflict-affected universities are weakly framed in international law, enabling belligerent states to break commitments to rights and protections time and time again (Kangas et al., 2023). At the time of writing in November 2024—despite international attention brought to the signatories of such commitments—the vast destruction of academic infrastructure, and the targeting, criminalisation and loss of academic citizens' lives in Gaza is ongoing without reprieve (South Africa, 2023, p. 55); as is the continuation of the 'forgotten higher education crisis' (Hassan, 2024) of Sudan. The centring of 'being' herein brings social regulation—including the legal and policy frames of countries and universities—into proximity with social formation. This is the case even within chapters one might assume would be more legalistic in orientation. For instance, when discussing retaliations endured for publicly deliberating constitutional change as an expert in human rights law (Chapter 6), Harvey discusses academic freedom alongside solidarities and counter-networks which sustained his commitment to continue his Third Mission engagements. Set against a backdrop of the surveillance and censorship of academics in Apartheid South Africa, Meistre brings to the foreground the minutiae of the ways in which academic citizens' resisted constraints to their academic autonomy and creatively enacted their academic freedom otherwise (Chapter 2). In differing ways these chapters point to the lack of reckoning with the conditions for academic freedom following regulatory changes after the cessation of the Cold War, which has been described as a both a conceptual and epistemological 'crisis' in higher education studies generally (Dang et al., 2023), and in South Africa particularly (Belluigi, 2023). What could have been a legalistic discussion of harms and complicity is rather a deliberation of the mobilisation of the various functions of the university and the sociocultural projects of public pedagogy which surrounded truth-seeking endeavours in Columbia (Chapter 1).

Social formation *in transition* is a feature of many of the chapters. This is explored in terms of questions about academic practices of the functions of (higher) education, research and social responsibility in a number of the chapters. Authors raise concerns about the effects of the hidden curriculum on medical practitioners' formation (Chapter 5), and on peace education (Chapter 3). The science of science (a subset of what is currently dubbed 'higher education studies') emerges as the *raison d'être* of Hebe Vessuri's practice (the source and subject of Chapter 4). Richard Hudson-Miles collages his way across various inter-textual fragments of the past and present Euro-American university in Chapter 10. These figurative renditions in eight 'scenes' ('excellence', 'rebellion', 'revolt', 'strike' and so on) of the conditions of collective academic formation in contemporary England are set against and alongside reverberations of the university's internal conflict in Europe's pasts. And it is the very question of the erosions of conditions for quality academic functions that sees Nigerian academic unions pitted in conflict against institutions and public neoliberal authorities within Chapter 9, by Gregory Obinna Ugbo and Herny Chigozie Duru. Ethical dimensions—underpinning the integrity of academic subjectivity and of critique within academia—emerge as such authors consider 'how academics relate to themselves, others and knowledge and the possibilities of thinking and behaving otherwise' (Durán del Fierro, 2023, p. 4) when academic communities and institutions are recognised as states and sites (ab)normal.

Situated and practising within such mundane petty and grand conflicts, are (re)formulations of *being* a thinker, intellectual and academic. Herein is awareness of historiography of the present[8]— with self-consciousness about what is excluded or othered, in writing about our being in conflict, and the being of those before us. Each chapters' account may function as 'little narratives' (Lyotard, 1984) and complicating counter-stories of the academic and academia in transition. These are neither dispassionate nor contained, perfect nor whole. They are in parts uncertain and affected, and in such ways are reflective of the human condition of being an academic.

---

8   See Fuller (2015, p. 98) for accounts by authors of the science of science and scientists, where the concern is for 'what it means to conduct a decent scientific life' within 'normal conditions', or what is perhaps better seen as operating with hopes uncrushed by having never been an academic in conflict, if that is even possible.

On the Academic

Meandering across the book are currents that cannot quench the thirst for comprehending subjectivities of the academic. These authors' acts of narration—as speaking subjects and as narrators of representations—are assertions of agonistic enquiry into our formation. Conflict is the palimpsest of identities formed in the frictions between words, spaces, sentences, paragraphs, references, tables and images; and the worldmaking these elements, when combined, create in our imaginations.

This struggle of authoring, authenticity, authority and authorship is not surprising. Academic development focuses on mastery of representation for two of the three core functions of the university—education and research. Gatekeeping processes of educational summative assessment and professional evaluation school academics' mastery of representation, when their arguments are about academic knowledge of subjects in the 'real world' beyond the university. The capacity of the 'worker bees' of academic service to write powerfully about experiences or arguments *within* the academy is un-developed, despite the importance of academic freedom for academic autonomy and institutional governance. This is all the more obviously stunted when allegiances, loyalties, complicities and vulnerabilities threaten the legitimacy of the academics' critical function. Ubgo and Duru's analysis exposes such incapacitation, and in turn inefficacy, of contemporary Nigerian academics' discourses of academic freedom (Chapter 9). What academic development rarely acknowledges is that academic citizens accept concessions to continue academic practice, even when conditions are highly monitored or constrained by powerful actors and structures. Candid insights about academic mobility to Russia during the Cold War reveal that such concessions have ranged from the 'safety' of permitted and vetted topics for research and teaching, to academics' engaging in dissimulation, to permit 'internationalisation' (Pallot in Kangas et al., 2023). Such negotiations colour the gaps between what little is exposed in published sources (a concern of Pradeepkumar in Sri Lanka, Chapter 3), and remind us of the 'creativity' required to continue critical functions of academic resistance (visualised by Meistre, about South Africa, Chapter 2, and in the scenes of Hudson-Miles in Chapter 10) and public pedagogy (in the contemporary practice of Harvey, Chapter 6). Such 'insider' representations of agency and of resilience may face multiple levels of scrutiny at the time of production, through internal sanction, institutional and state surveillance, and international pressure.

Of concern is how such scrutiny is exercised by fellow academics safely at a distance, when analysing the agency and resilience of 'local' researchers of conflict-affected states and sites. Operative criticism of normative scholarly frames have shown that those outside, firstly, serve to judge such acts and interventions as insufficient and impure, and, secondly, to undermine and silence the authorial theses of 'local' academics studying and living with such dynamics (Hajir et al., 2021). Writing from Northern Ireland—a context where social scientists had conspicuously deferred engagement with social divisions until the safety of the cessation of armed conflict (Taylor, 1988)—Livingstone (2003, p. 2) exposed the wilful ignorance of constructions of science without geography:

> Of all the human projects devoted to getting at the truth of how things are, that venture we call science has surely been among the most assiduous in its efforts to transcend the parochial. It has been extraordinary diligent in deploying mechanisms to lay aside prejudices and presuppositions and to guarantee objectivity by leaving the local behind. Credible knowledge, we assume, does not bear the marks of the provincial, and science that is local has something wrong with it.

Against the force of such taken-for-granted stratifications and othering, authors of this book negotiate 'local' experiences produced by fellow 'insiders' as sources lighting ways into interpretation. In Part I, Pradeepkumar (Chapter 3) scratches her way through fragments of published documentation and reports, in search of revelations of conditions from the period of violent conflict to post-conflict 'recovery', which produced contemporary Sri Lankan academics' consciousness of the critical functions of the university. Adversarial local discourses in the media between factions within Nigerian universities are analysed by Ugbo and Duru, in order to comprehend such conditions (Chapter 9). Hudson-Miles draws upon and against scholarly and creative arts representations, and his own photographs of strike action, to construct dialectics of the states of being in conflict in England's universities (Chapter 10). Authors of the chapters in this book have drawn widely from situated sources—including their selves—to explore how academics' subjectivities, experiences, relations and practices are impacted by universities' social histories, the political climate within institutions and environments in which they are situated, and the dynamics and memberships of networks (Russell, 2023). Dominant narratives of national histories of belligerent countries and universities under sanction or boycott are complicated, as are those espousing democracy and equality, with insights across the book of academics' resistance, compliance, inadequacies and collusion. These authors narrate the self to colourise the figure of the academic. This resonates with Stuart Hall's (2000, p. 5) reminders of how identities are constituted within and through representation, where

> we need to understand them as produced in specific historical and institutional sites within specific discursive formations and practices, by specific enunciative strategies. Moreover, they emerge within the play of specific modalities of power, and thus are more the product of the marking of difference and exclusion, than they are the sign of an identical, naturally-constituted unity—an 'identity' in its traditional meaning (that is, an all-inclusive sameness, seamless, without internal differentiation).

The terms 'states' and 'sites' carry associations of locatedness, permanence and stability. These chapters create fissures within such received notions. In particular, there is a disjointedness between im/mobility and dis/placement. At times within the chapters, we are presented with cruel inversions of refuge and home which impact academic formation and status. Jobran-Alsawayfa specifically weaves such threads across poetry and stories within Chapter 8. He allegorically links his academic flourishing to the ease of movement and interaction he enjoyed while learning on a student visa in England, in contrast to the heavy-handed bordering and surveillance of permissions necessary to travel legitimately as a Palestinian academic within and beyond Israel. Threats and suspicions intervene into the spaces of nurture of one's country of birth, in the accounts of Harvey (Chapter 6), Meistre (Chapter 2) and Vessuri (Chapter 4) too. Binaries of dis/place/ment are reconfigured, myths of academic mobility problematised.[9]

---

9   For recent complications of academic im/mobility, see the edited collection by
    Burlyuk and Rahbari (2023) on the resilience, solidarity, care and precarity
    experienced by migrant Majority World academics based in Minority World

In/accessibility marks the entry and exits to parts of academia in the life histories of Vessuri across the American continents and England (Chapter 4), and of Anis across the Middle East and the USA (Chapter 7). Because they managed to retain their status as 'academics', unlike many refugees, neither were assumed to be beyond the 'right to research' (Reed and Schenck, 2023). Yet historical narration of such dynamics by displaced women academics from the Majority World remains under-written. Their stories create reverberations between Part I and Part II, across time and continents. Both narrate the struggles for agency, self-determination and academic voice in relation to contexts where their gender as women is constructed with different affordances, constraints and burdens to which they adapted and, where possible, resisted. In the chapters by many of the women authors intersecting conflicts of institutions of marriage, family, religion, university are brought to the fore in active voice: of Vessuri, through the selected excerpts of a conversation (Chapter 4); by Anis, in her oral storytelling (Chapter 5); and in the vignettes of Johnston, Corrigan and Reid (Chapter 5) that connect and compare care-fully their social locations and experiences to the context, the discipline and their students. Role conflicts—between their responsibilities to their intellectual work and to their students, family, self and country—are brought into relation with embodied transitions including pregnancy and childcare.

Contextualised within a time of 'stark social and intellectual hierarchies' in eighteenth-century Britain and Ireland, historian Leonie Hannan (2023, p. 185) has interpreted the lives of 'curious individuals' through an inclusive construction of 'knowledge-makers'. Such non-institutional negotiations of the social and the intellectual allow for the comprehension of subjectivities at times when the favour, status and protections of the club goods for the 'high intellectual' agent prove threadbare. Within this book, authors expose the fear of being similarly threatened by the precarious and peripheral, despite their 'high intellectual' status, when displaced, in diaspora, or exile, or expressing dissent.

---

universities. See also the articles reflecting 'stuck and sticky' experiences which characterise the Critical Academic Mobilities Approach in a recent special issue of *Higher Education* edited by Tzanakou and Henderson (2021).

From the vantage points of being a son, artist and prior academic from the social institutions of family, university and culture, Meistre negotiates the awkward multi-generational implicatedness of boundary-crossings between secrets, oppression and the 'known'. Artefacts and visual elements assist with the 'look' of the past in his chapter, just as they operate in the book by Millei and colleagues (2004), as a way around the dominating narratives of the past, when evoking childhood memories of living during the Cold War. The generations on the cusp of *after* in Part I de-mythologise past relations of the university and its academics as benignly good within conflict-affected societies. While the authors have very different positions, perspectives, histories and memories, commonly shared is the commitment to resist hegemonic representations, for the common good of plural historical and collective narratives of harm, hope, responsibility, truth and justice. The penultimate two chapters, firmly centre the struggles as *within* universities, and for the purposes of the universities' reasons for being (see Derrida, 1983 on the *raison d'être* of the university). Romanticised discourses surrounding the university of the past are not extolled (an accusation levied at the founders of Critical University Studies)— neither of the western European university nor the African university. The collectivity of academics is not naively offered as panacea. Rather, what is problematised are the politics which undermine the conditions of academic functions which continue to hold virtue.

Against the sanitisation of the complexity and particularity of *being* an academic figure, authors herein look to the states and sites of conflict as spaces which shape living. Conflict *within academia* troubles its enclosure as the realm of interest for state actors in politics at the grand level, grounding it within the many social, cultural, economic and indeed epistemic politics that shape everyday being as academics. These are not the (auto)biographies of hero-, martyr- or master-narratives of renowned academic figures in conflict. Some of the authors herein may be accomplished; however, none of us are in/famous enough to be protected by coalitions, nation-building frames or international acclaim. There are variations too in how 'established' we are within our disciplines, institutions and current/host contexts. Most of the authors are not primarily scholars of the university, of higher education, or even of conflict. I raise this as each of these facets matter as referential frames when the intellectual authority of 'the academic' is constructed. None are safe 'enough' from harm, ridicule, social sanction or professional risk. Accusations of self-aggrandisement and perpetuating of melodramatic political discourses (Anker, 2014) are to be expected when writing about 'academic freedom' and 'conflict'. Sources of fear and of accusation come from outside the institution: the state, militant and criminal rings, institutions of religion, family/clan, far right or left groups. They also come from within, from policing by groups and cabals of staff and students, threats of costs to promotion and career stature, and from self-censorship. There is also exposure of funding levers. The proportionate difference in the types, levels and intensity of threat, violence, censure and punishment is readily acknowledged by Harvey in Chapter 6. However, acculturation to censorship, chilly climates and discrimination exerted over time and even over generations lessens collective awareness of the boundaries of such transgressions, particularly when the possible terrain of thinking has been shrunk.

Mubashar Hassan (in *Free to Think*, 2024, 30:00) recently spoke about the effects of soft authoritarianism on the collective cultures of academic practice in Bangladesh. Reflecting on his own decisions to escape the confines which has made him a 'psychic refugee' in his own country, he continues seven years later to 'live in the mental prison in some way, in that I still have to negotiate with myself "what should I write?", "what should I not write?" [...] but this is what I do, this is part of what I am'. As the editor, I was made aware of most of the authors' cognisance that they were operating at the cusp of transgressing the safe zones of the usual habitus. Cautious hesitancy in back-and-forth emails, delays and silences of voice messages, written annotations, cut out and reinserted tracts and revisions, attest to such negotiations. These representations were crafted—to varying degrees—in conversation with the present and future, not only through my engagement but also with those who provided blind and later unblinded reviews. It is a reality of this subject that that which poses the most risk has been expunged: omissions necessarily haunt this collection by the living. Perhaps an editorial decision would have been to mark those erasures with blackened redactions in reference to the representational practices of editors of my own country, in the ways Meistre visualises and discusses in Chapter 2. Instead, the mantle of questioning and challenge for commemoration is extended to you the reader, as I repeat the questions to which these authors have responded with courage, integrity and humility:

> What are the conditions and trajectories that constitute academic identities and practices when academic and state authority is displaced, in contestation and transition?
>
> What is left unsaid, off the record, outside the room, in whispers about being an academic while negotiating such conditions?
>
> What are the traces, legacies and intergenerational impacts of such differences in influence and orientation for academic cultures?

Authorial decision-making—weighing integrity and exposure in the present against evocation and comprehension of readers in the future—ultimately sat on the shoulders of the twenty people who have penned this work. Having bitten the bullets of silence, mistruths and humiliations while waiting, these acts of crafting the word in place of the bullet, for some, or in place of the wound, for others, have in themselves, become practices of opening.

> All beginnings are invisible: we learn to see little by little. In this way the book is made. (Jabès, 1977, p. 16)

Bibliography

Abdulateef, S., Ajaj, N., Anis, R., Shaban, F., Belluigi, D. Z., and Parkinson, T. (2020). Sharing the Burdens of Responsibility for a Better Future in Transnational Academia: Reflections of Displaced Syrian Academics on an Atypical Academic Development Event. *ETL Learning and Teaching Journal*, 2(2), 393–396. https://doi.org/10.16906/lt-eth.v2i2

Anker, E. R. (2014). *Orgies of Feeling: Melodrama and the Politics of Freedom*. Duke University Press Books. https://doi.org/10.2307/j.ctv1134d8x

Belluigi, D., and Parkinson, T. (2020). Building Solidarity through Comparative Lived Experiences of Post/Conflict: Reflections on Two Days of Dialogue. *Education and Conflict Review*, 16–23. https://discovery.ucl.ac.uk/id/eprint/10109100

Belluigi, D. Z. (2023). De-idealising the Problem of Academic Freedom and Academic Autonomy: Exploring Alternative Readings for Scholarship of South African Higher Education. *Southern African Review of Education*, 28(1), 10–31. https://pure.qub.ac.uk/files/553663734/Deidealising_academic_freedom_FPV.pdf

Brusius, M., and Rico, T. (2023). Counter-archives as Heritage Justice: Photography, Invisible Labor and Peopled Ruins. *Journal of Visual Culture*, 22(1), 64–92. https://doi.org/10.1177/14704129221146494

Burlyuk, O., and Rahbari, L. (2023). *Migrant Academics' Narratives of Precarity and Resilience in Europe*. Open Book Publishers. https://doi.org/10.11647/obp.0331

Dang, Q. A., Matei, L., and Popovic, M. (2023). Reimagining Academic Freedom: An Introduction. *Philosophy and Theory in Higher Education*, 5(2), 209–222. https://doi.org/10.3726/PTIHE.022023.0209

Debele, S. (2020). Waiting as a Site of Subject Formation: Examining Collective Prayers by Ethiopian Asylum Seekers in Germany. *Critical African Studies*, 12(1), 52–64. https://doi.org/10.1080/21681392.2019.1697311

Derrida, J. (1983). The Principle of Reason: The University in the Eyes of Its Pupils (C. Porter and E. P. Morris, Trans.). *Diacritics*, 13(3), 3–20. https://doi.org/10.2307/464997

Durán del Fierro, F. (2023). The Ethical Dimension of Academic Critique: Subjectivity and Knowledge within the Chilean Academic Community [Doctoral thesis, University College London]. https://discovery.ucl.ac.uk/id/eprint/10179187/

Free to Think (2024, May 16). *Navigating the 'Mental Prison' – Mubashar Hasan on Higher Education in Bangladesh* (Vol. 38). https://open.spotify.com/episode/76rnleyeGXDpyT4sDQXUpf

Fuller, S. (2015). Never Pure: Historical Studies of Science as if It Was Produced by People with Bodies, Situated in Time, Space, Culture, and Society, and Struggling for Credibility and Authority. *Aestimatio*, 8, 97–100. https://doi.org/10.33137/aestimatio.v8i0.25948

Hajir, B., Clarke-Habibi, S., and Kurian, N. (2021). The 'South' Speaks Back: Exposing the Ethical Stakes of Dismissing Resilience in Conflict-Affected Contexts. *Journal of Intervention and Statebuilding*, 1–17. https://doi.org/10.1080/17502977.2020.1860608

Hall, S. (2000). Who Needs 'Identity'? In P. Du Gay, P. Evans, and P. Redman (Eds), *Identity: A Reader* (pp. 1–17). Sage.

Hannan, L. (2023). *A Culture of Curiosity*. Manchester University Press.

Hassan, M.-A. (2024, February 20). *The Forgotten Higher Education Crisis of Sudan*. Academic Freedom under Threat: Global and Local Perspectives. Scholars at Risk Ireland Conference, Belfast, Northern Ireland.

Inayatullah, N. (2017, February 25). Hope: Uncrushed and Crushed. *Out of Crushed Hope: Third World, National Liberation and the Weight of Structures*. 58th Annual Convention of the International Studies Association, Baltimore, Maryland. https://www.academia.edu/36370368/Out_of_Crushed_and_Uncrushed_Hope_panel_talk_docx

Jabès, E. (1977). *The Book of Questions: Book of Yukel, and Return to the Book* (R. Waldrop, Trans.). Wesleyan University Press.

Kangas, A., Mäkinen, S., Dubrovskiy, D., Pallot, J., Shenderova, S., Yarovoy, G., and Zabolotna, O. (2023). Debating Academic Boycotts and Cooperation in the Context of Russia's War against Ukraine. *New Perspectives, 31*(3), 250–264. https://doi.org/10.1177/2336825X231187331

Keet, A. (2019). Crisis and Critique: Critical Theories and the Renewal of Citizenship, Democracy and Human Rights Education. In M. Zembylas and A. Keet (Eds), *Critical Human Rights, Citizenship, and Democracy Education: Entanglements and Regenerations* (pp. 17–34). Bloomsbury Publishing. https://library.oapen.org/handle/20.500.12657/61927

Kratz, C. (2001). Conversations and Lives. In L. White, S. Miescher, and D. W. Cohen (Eds), *African Words, African Voices: Critical Practices in Oral History* (pp. 127–161). Indiana University Press.

Lalu, P. (2022). *Undoing Apartheid*. Wiley.

Lawrence, C., Mhlaba, T., Stewart, K. A., Moletsane, R., Gaede, B., and Moshabela, M. (2018). The Hidden Curricula of Medical Education: A Scoping Review. *Academic Medicine, 93*(4), 648–656. https://doi.org/10.1097/ACM.0000000000002004

Livingstone, D. N. (2003). *Putting Science in Its Place: Geographies of Scientific Knowledge*. University of Chicago Press.

Lyotard, J. F. (1984). *The Postmodern Condition: A Report on Knowledge*. Manchester. University Press.

Millei, Z., Piattoeva, N., Silova, I., and Zin, M. (2024). *(An)Archive: Childhood, Memory, and the Cold War*. Open Book Publishers. https://doi.org/10.11647/obp.0383

Netshakhuma, N. S. (2023). Exploration of the South African Student Activism Archives as a New History Education Resource on Teaching First-Years at University. In *Handbook of Research on Coping Mechanisms for First-Year Students Transitioning to Higher Education* (pp. 348–362). IGI Global. https://doi.org/10.4018/978-1-6684-6961-3.ch021

Ngoepe, M. (2019). Archives without Archives: A Window of Opportunity to Build Inclusive Archive in South Africa. *Journal of the South African Society of Archivists, 52*, 149–166.

Quijano, A. (2000). Coloniality of Power and Eurocentrism in Latin America. *International Sociology, 15*(2), 215–232. https://doi.org/10.1177/0268580900015002005

Rassool, C. (2004). *The Individual, Auto/biography and History in South Africa* [Doctoral thesis, University of the Western Cape]. https://www.sahistory.org.za/archive/individual-autobiography-and-history-south-africa-ciraj-shahid-rassool

Reed, K., and Schenck, M. C. (Eds). (2023). *The Right to Research*. McGill-Queen's University Press. https://www.mqup.ca/right-to-research--the-products-9780228014553.php

Russell, I. (2023). The Limits on Critical Voice in Conflict-affected Universities: Evidence from Sierra Leone and Sri Lanka. *International Journal of Educational Development*, *96*, 1–8. https://doi.org/10.1016/j.ijedudev.2022.102685

South Africa. (2023). *Application of the Convention on the Prevention and Punishment of the Crime of Genocide in the Gaza Strip (South Africa v. Israel)* (pp. 1–84). International Court of Justice. https://www.icj-cij.org/sites/default/files/case-related/192/192-20231228-app-01-00-en.pdf

Taylor, R. (1988). Social Scientific Research on the 'Troubles' in Northern Ireland: The Problem of Objectivity. *The Economic and Social Review*, *19*(2), 123–145.

Tzanakou, C., and Henderson, E. F. (2021). Stuck and Sticky in Mobile Academia: Reconfiguring the Im/mobility Binary. *Higher Education*, *82*(4), 685–693. https://doi.org/10.1007/s10734-021-00710-x

PART I

PAST CONFLICTS AND THEIR LEGACIES

1. Truth and Reparations: A Conversation on the Participation of the Higher Education Sector in the Colombian Commission for the Clarification of Truth, Coexistence and Non-repetition[1]

Natalia Maya Llano, Juan Camilo Domínguez Cardona, Juan Sebastián Flórez Herrera, Catalina Puerta Henao and Adriana Rudling

Introduction

Despite the much-acclaimed signing of the 2016 Final Peace Agreement (henceforth, Final Agreement) between the Government of Colombia and the *Fuerzas Armadas Revolucionarias de Colombia—Ejército del Pueblo* [FARC-EP, Revolutionary Armed Forces of Colombia—People's Army], the country remains the setting of several complex internal armed conflicts (CICR-C, 2023, p. 5). Different types of conflict-related harms are still being registered in most legally recognised categories of victimhood. Current administrative reparation frameworks cover present and past individual and collective victims going back to 1985[2] arising from the ongoing hostilities between the state and dissident groups from this as well as previous waves of non-state armed group demobilisation, cartels involved in the illegal substances industry,

---

1   This chapter is available in Spanish (https://doi.org/10.11647/OBP.0427.11), on the additional resources tab on the website listing for this volume, at https://www.openbookpublishers.com/product/0427#resources

2   Those who suffered harm before this date are only considered victims for the purposes of symbolic reparations.

    https://doi.org/10.11647/OBP.0427.01

criminal gangs, and the insurgent group *Ejército de Liberación Nacional* [ELN, National Liberation Army].[3] Thus, for instance, displacement is on the rise again for the first time since 2018 after an almost continuous fall since the 2012 public phase of negotiations with the FARC-EP (CODHES, 2021).

Colombia is also the home of one of the most complex and ambitious transitional justice projects to date (Bakiner, 2019). The administrative reparations programme established by Law 1448/2011, which absorbed the previous reparation initiatives of Law 975/2005, is welded together with the *Sistema Integral de Verdad, Justicia, Reparación y No Repetición* [SIVJRNR, Comprehensive System of Truth, Justice, Reparations and Non-Repetition; henceforth, the Comprehensive System] of the Final Agreement. This new four-pronged transitional justice model added a truth commission, a special court for war crimes and crimes against humanity, a search unit for the disappeared with different periods of operations to the existing apparatus of reparations. Victims, who took part in the peace talks through five delegations of twelve selected representatives (Verdad Abierta, 2015), are arguably at the centre of all these mechanisms. Their harms and strategies for resistance, both of which have recognised territorial, temporal and personal distinctive features, have been incorporated into the work of the truth commission known as Commission for the Clarification of Truth, Coexistence and Non-repetition (henceforth, the Commission). According to Decree 588/2017, which regulated the Commission's operations, it had the following objectives:

> i) contribute to the clarification of truth about the internal armed conflict and offer an explanation of its complexity that facilitates a broad understanding of what occurred; ii) promote the acknowledgement of the dignity of victims, the impacts and violations of their rights; the voluntary recognition of responsibilities

---

3   This Guevarista-aligned armed group, inspired by the Cuban Revolution, was established in 1964. Together with the FARC-EP, a group of agrarian extraction and Communist orientation, and the *Ejército Popular de Liberación* [EPL, Popular Liberation Army] these three groups make up what is now known as the first wave of insurgencies of the current internal armed conflict. While (most of) the EPL demobilised together with other second wave guerrillas in 1991 (see Sánchez and Rudling, 2019, p. 13), the ELN entered into a new process of negotiations with the Petro administration starting from November 2022.

(individual and collective), and the acknowledgement by [Colombian] society of what happened; iii) contribute to coexistence in the territories; and iv) identify and promote the necessary conditions for non-repetition.

The Commission formally and publicly released its main volume titled *Findings and Recommendations*[4] in an event attended by the then incumbent President Gustavo Petro and Vice-President Francia Márquez on June 28, 2022. In his brief intervention, Petro promised to take charge of the implementation of the recommendations for non-repetition included in the report. Until the end of its mandate, two months later,[5] the Commission also released ten other volumes, one of which contains fourteen chapters dedicated to different territorial aspects, and almost ninety illustrative cases (CEV, 2022a, pp. 13–14). The victimisation and harms suffered by the higher education sector, its coping strategy and response to the violence are outlined in a territorial chapter titled *Urban Dynamics of the War*[6] and *Case 52 / Universities and Armed Conflict*[7] (henceforth, *Case 52 / Universities*). While the former is a written document in the style of a report, the latter is a complex collection of materials submitted by the higher education sector to the Commission. Now part of the Commission's Transmedia, the five chapter analysis put forward in *Case 52 / Universities* embeds evidence from nineteen reports, two databases, timelines, and maps, as well as videos, and written testimonies produced throughout the armed conflict.[8] Both will be discussed in greater detail below.

The conversation this chapter is based on took place online in March 2023, more than six months after the mandate of the Commission was

---

4 The Spanish-language original title is *Hallazgos y recomendaciones*. See: https://www.comisiondelaverdad.co/hallazgos-y-recomendaciones-1

5 The original three-year mandate of the Commission was extended to August 2023 by the Colombian Constitutional Court (six months for the Final Report and two months for the social appropriation and dissemination of its findings), in response to the legal challenge brought by representatives of various victims' groups, who argued that the unforeseen and unprecedented challenge of the COVID-19 pandemic affected the capacity of the Commission to carry out its duties and affected the development of its tasks.

6 The Spanish-language original title of this chapter is *Dinámicas urbanas de la guerra*. See: https://www.comisiondelaverdad.co/colombia-adentro-1

7 The Spanish-language original name of this case is *Caso 52 / Universidades y conflicto armado*.

8 For details, see: https://www.comisiondelaverdad.co/etiquetas/transmedia-digital-de-la-comision

over, at the initiative of Adriana Rudling. Two years prior, Adriana participated in the performance evaluation of the Commission (see USAID, 2021) and took a particular interest in how specific groups transitional justice projects usually overlook, such as the business sector, members of academic communities, and even the security forces, engaged with it. The recording of the conversation Adriana facilitated was transcribed and adjusted for length and content by all its participants.

The focus of this chapter-conversation is on providing a descriptive multi-situated account of the involvement of the higher education sector in the work of the Commission from the perspectives of four protagonists of that task. Juan Sebastián Flórez Herrera, who worked as a researcher in the Commission, was the rapporteur for *Case 52 / Universities*. Natalia Maya Llano was an analyst with the Commission, working primarily with its first objective stated above—that is, truth clarification. Natalia was part of the team behind the territorial chapter titled *Urban Dynamics of the War*. Catalina Puerta Henao and Juan Camilo Domínguez Cardona led the two sections on victimisations and insurgent groups, respectively, of the report titled *The Political Violence and the Armed Conflict in the Universidad de Antioquia 1958–2016: Contributions to Memory and Truth Clarification Regarding Impacts and Relationships*[9] submitted by the *Universidad de Antioquia* (henceforth, UdeA) to the Commission in 2021.

Starting from a decolonial commitment, we decided together that this chapter should be presented as a conversation in a Spanish and English version, respectively. This serves two functions: on the one hand, the voice of the collaborators of the Commission is preserved; and, on the other hand, it supports knowledge dissemination on this subject beyond Spanish-speaking audiences. Given her facilitator role, Adriana, a UK-trained foreign researcher based in Colombia for several years, chose to be the final author. This bilingual conversational format should also remind the readers of the unique and layered position of those engaged in the conversation. Adriana advocated for this format as an apt means for her to serve as a conduit between Spanish- and English-speaking only spaces. Natalia, Catalina, Juan Sebastián and Juan

---

9   The Spanish-language original title of this report is *La violencia política y el conflicto armado en la Universidad de Antioquia 1958–2016: Aportes a la memoria y esclarecimiento de sus impactos y relaciones*.

Camilo are all researchers who contributed to a national-level truth-seeking process, itself a part of larger transitional justice project, as we will explain further below. They did so from the vantage point of their respective academic communities while continuing to be committed and active members in them. Their simultaneous work for and within these academic communities as staff and activists meant they had to grapple with the contradictions and continuities arising from their participation in the Commission, their own and others' fears about what it might mean now and in the (more distant) future, and work towards finding a narrative to do justice to the involvement of the higher education sector in the armed conflict. One of the points we close this conversation with that we believe is worth considering in greater detail in the future is where our protagonists fit into the generations of academics engaged in such work and what responsibility, if any, might they have to those coming after them.

The next two sections contextualise this conversation by providing brief introductions into the harms suffered by the higher education sector and the reparations regimes that seek to redress them. The conversation, as will be shown below, is a descriptive but situated account centring the acknowledgement and truth clarification functions of the Commission regarding this sector, emphasising three aspects: (1) the roots of the participation of the higher education sector in the Commission; (2) the diversity of motivations, capacities and expectations of this sector from these interactions; (3) the outcomes of these interactions and future directions of work on acknowledgement and truth clarification for the higher education sector.

The Colombian Internal Armed Conflict and the Higher Education Sector

Although scholarly debate about the starting point of the armed conflict continues (see CHCyV, 2015), the Commission chose 1958 as the point of departure for its analysis. It is also noteworthy that the Commission operated with a more complex notion of responsibility that went beyond the four broad categories of armed actors, namely state security forces, the leftist insurgent groups, the pro-state paramilitaries and the cartels involved in the illegal substances industry. As an extrajudicial mechanism that did not seek to assign criminal responsibility for conflict-related harms, the Commission also indicated that the boundaries between these categories and civilians, including those operating different state institutions and branches of government, have not always been clear. One such example are the self-defence groups established by civilians and authorised by the state to fight the first-wave guerrillas founded in the 1960s. The Commission grounds its choice to begin its analysis in 1958 in the 'legalisation' of the exclusion of the political Left promoted by the National Front (see Mazzei, 2009; Sánchez, 2001). This agreement to alternate political power was signed by the Conservative and Liberal parties, the two traditional parties that initiated a period of political violence known as *La Violencia* or The Violence in 1948. Although the Conservative and Liberal parties arguably sought to end this bloodshed, which left around a quarter of a million people dead and countless displaced, banning Leftist political parties past this point also meant that some of the armed groups founded during *La Violencia* gained new members as a result. The FARC-EP, for instance, was a mix of members from older armed groups and people who saw this pact as a restriction of their political rights. Despite some differences relating to strategy and ideology, especially regarding international questions such as the Cuban Revolution and the Maoist and Communist currents, all the first-wave guerrillas can draw a straight line to 1958 on matters internal to Colombia.

Contact with the illegal substances industry affected all social groups, including state and non-state armed groups, regardless of their origin and orientation; and by the end of the 1980s, illegal substances sustained the persistence of political violence in the country (see CEV, 2022, p. 384). From this point on, victimisation reached shocking levels, especially amongst the civilian population since none of the armed actors took any precautions to protect them, violating their duties under International Law. According to numbers provided by the Commission itself, 450,664 people were killed between 1985 and 2018, with the period between 1995 and 2004 being the deadliest, as it registered nearly 45% of the total victims. Additionally, for the period between 1985 and 2018, the Commission puts the numbers of people forcefully displaced at 7,752,964 (CEV, 2022, p. 195). At least 81% of the fatal victims were civilians (CNMH, 2013). Established in 2011, the Single Registry for

Victims (RUV, *Registro Único de Víctimas*) reports a total number of 9,572,044 conflict victims,[10] where nearly 90% were victims of forced displacement. This total number corresponds to almost 19% of the population of Colombia (Sánchez and Rudling 2019, p. 46).

The higher education sector has been involved in the armed conflict in different ways, depending on the region and the stage of the armed conflict. Reports going back to the late 1970s have shown staff and students' resistance strategies such as protests, trade union organisation, and participation in activities such as literacy campaigns that, without having any association with insurgent groups, could be characterised as left-aligned. Starting in the late 1960s, and particularly after the adoption of the *Estatuto de Seguridad* or Security Statute in 1978, these activities were perceived with suspicion, and their persecution—which employed an increasingly violent combination of legal and illegal means and actors—intensified towards the end of the 1990s. This entailed a series of unconstitutional restrictions of freedoms and liberties as well as serious violations of human rights, including the right to life. It is important to note that the first organisation of relatives of detained-disappeared people, initially known as *Colectivo 82* or Collective 82, was established in the early 1980s and more than half of the direct victims it represented then were university students illegally detained and disappeared by state security forces (Rudling, 2019).

In the 2000s, some universities, particularly in the Caribbean, were heavily restructured under the influence of state-aligned paramilitaries (see Jiménez Ortega et al., 2020). Their victimisation took on a collective character as well, where academic life itself suffered as a consequence of the conflict in two ways. On the one hand, individual victimisation was escalated through violations to the right to life, threats, illegal dismissals or other forms of coercion ending in resignations or even exile. On the other hand, the cumulative and systemic effects of individual victimisation were exacerbated through the collective victimisation of certain activities or particular educational tracks or specific educational institutions. Only in a few universities did the infiltration by armed actors reach their management level, as was the case of the *Universidad de Córdoba*, located in the northern city of Monteria (Verdad Abierta,

---

10   For the updated numbers of victims, see: https://www.unidadvictimas.gov.co/es/
registro-unico-de-victimas-ruv/

2013; Maya, 2018). Nevertheless, it has been documented that in other higher education centres—and especially public universities such as the UdeA in Medellín, and the *Universidad Nacional de Colombia* (UNAL), with campuses all over the country and the capital city of Bogotá (see also, Archila Neira and Roncancio, 2021)—the violence intensified since the 1980s. Conversely, these universities were infiltrated by state and non-state armed groups for recruitment or intelligence gathering purposes (see UdeA, 2021). The numbers that demonstrate the impacts of the armed conflict on the higher education sector are alarming. Based on *Case 52 / Universities*, cases of forced disappearance and extra-judicial killings were recorded each year between 1962 and 2011, with only one exception—1968. This is how we reach a total of 588 students killed and averages of 12.2 each year and one student a month (CEV, 2022b).

The Right to Truth for the Higher Education Sector

The victims' right to truth begins to take on a social and collective character in Colombia with the demobilisation of the pro-state paramilitaries in the early 2000s. Prior to this, victims had access to individual legal truth based on criminal or administrative law (Sánchez and Rudling, 2019, 25–26). The *Grupo de Memoria Histórica* or the Historical Memory Group—now *Centro Nacional de Memoria Histórica* or the National Centre for Historical Memory—that emerged from Law 975/2005, began to produce national- and regional-level reports about the paramilitary phenomenon. That is where these armed groups' involvement in higher education, particularly their capture and reorganisation of certain regional higher education centres, was highlighted for the first time (see CNMH, 2018). Nevertheless, to date, none of those reports focuses particularly on this sector and its experiences during the armed conflict.

With the expansion of victims' rights under Law 1448/2011, higher education centres are covered by a distinct right to collective reparation as they are understood as social organisations whose individual and collective rights were violated in the conflict. Thus, several public universities, such as the *Universidad del Atlántico*, the *Universidad de Magdalena*, and the *Universidad Popular del Cesar*, initiated the corresponding process to be recognised as subjects of collective reparations. Furthermore, given the emphasis on victim participation, the appropriate reparation measures had to be agreed between the *Unidad para la Atención y Reparación Integral a las Víctimas* or the Unit for the Assistance and Reparations of Victims (henceforth, the Victims' Unit), the state agency in charge of the reparation, and the representatives of the higher education centres. A measure that cut across all these institutions was related to the right to truth. All their representatives sought to restore the good name of individual victims affiliated to their institutions and safeguard the reputation of their universities by reconstructing memory on the conflict-related harms suffered.

The Final Agreement, and especially the establishment of the Commission, allowed higher education institutions to continue with their truth-seeking processes, now with the expectation that their findings will be included in this new state-sanctioned narrative of the armed conflict. The Commission gathered data not only from reports it solicited, but also from public and private events at national and regional levels. Additionally, its staffers and volunteers carried out individual and group interviews through the twenty-eight Commission territorial offices around the country and abroad. Several volumes of the Final Report, focused on the patterns of harms and motivations, make sporadic references to the higher education sector, the geographical and temporal patterns of resistance and violence perpetrated both from within and against the universities. Nevertheless, the chapter titled *Urban Dynamics*, which, as we outlined above, is part of the territorial approach of the Commission, and *Case 52 / Universities*, which is of the Transmedia, capture the experiences and perspectives on the armed conflict of several universities. The Transmedia is a modern communication strategy that sought to make the Commission's work more accessible to a more diverse audience beyond the written documents that make up the report. Finally, the higher education sector appears in the Commission's recommendation number fifty-seven, where the national government and local authorities are tasked with, amongst other things, guaranteeing coverage, access and permanence for students (CEV, 2022, p. 878).

Initial Introductions

Adriana: Let's start by talking about how you came to this subject of work and research—the higher education sector in the armed conflict.

Natalia: In 2016, as a journalist, I joined a project called *Hacemos Memoria* or Making Memory, which was funded at that time by the DW Akademie of Germany and the Faculty of Communications of the UdeA and aimed to carry out research as well as promote a public dialogue on the armed conflict and the serious human rights violations that had taken place in the country. In 2018, we came across the issue of collective reparations, and we realised that there were three universities in the Caribbean that had been recognised as subjects of collective reparations: the *Universidad de Córdoba* in 2012, *Universidad del Atlántico* in 2015, and the *Universidad Popular del Cesar* in 2017. We wanted to report on these three cases at *Hacemos Memoria* and put this subject on the table given the upcoming creation of the Commission. The question was whether the UdeA should seek to be recognised as a subject of collective reparation, continue with the processes of memory that were already taking place in some collectives internally, or start working with the Commission on this path of truth and clarification. In 2020, when I joined the Commission as a researcher in the Urban Dynamics of the Armed Conflict team, I found that, to understand what happened in the cities, it was key to account for these effects and these resistances in and from the universities. Finally, in September 2021, I was part of the national recognition event organised by the Commission on universities.

Catalina: I came to the report that the UdeA submitted to the Commission as one of the two people responsible for the component on victims. Previously, I had designed the first line of attention and reparation in Medellín in 2018 in relation to disappearances and worked as the main researcher for the *Casa de la Memoria* Museum or House of Memory Museum[11] here, in Medellín. I also held a position as expert in the Justice and Peace Jurisdiction of Law 975/2005, where I contributed to the conceptualisation of several sentences related to the actions of the *Autodefensas Campesinas de Córdoba and Urabá* [ACCU, Peasant Self-Defence Groups of Córdoba and Uraba]. At that time, I reconstructed the actions of the Córdoba Bloc in the case of the *Universidad de Córdoba,*

---

11   See https://www.museocasadelamemoria.gov.co/

gathering all the information from the newspaper *El Meridiano de Córdoba*, and I designed the reparation measures for their victims. My focus has always been on understanding the dynamics of violence, the genealogy of the concept of victim, the internal enemy, and what truth and clarification are. When the Commission arrived at the UdeA, of course I wanted to be part of this national project.

Juan Camilo: Unlike Catalina or Natalia, I did not come to this issue through an academic research route, but through the administrative route. I was the Postgraduate Coordinator of the Institute for Regional Studies of the UdeA and in 2017 there was a discussion at the managerial level about how our university, which has nine regional branches, could help with its regional work to implement the Final Agreement. Bringing together more or less fifteen academic units with very different views on this proposal, the Special Peace Unit emerged as a unique figure in Colombian universities to articulate peace initiatives simultaneously based outside and inside the UdeA. As we were committed to making the Final Agreement a territorially relevant issue, when we signed a framework agreement with the Commission, its Commissioner Saúl Franco[12] explicitly asked us to prepare a report from the perspective of clarification to explain the reasons why what happened, happened in this university. The Commission believed we had all the internal capacity to do so, and the current Rector agreed, but, over time, we realised that it was more difficult to talk about clarifying responsibilities than about the harms.

Juan Sebastián: Since I enrolled in the UNAL in 2009, I quickly became involved in student activism related to memory, perhaps because of its place in Colombian society as a tool and as an exercise in resistance in different settings. One of our first activist activities was to paint a mural to commemorate the confrontation of enormous proportions that took place on May 16, 1984 which involved sectors of the insurgency, four forces of the security forces and dozens, if not hundreds, of students without any

---

12 Saúl Franco is a medical doctor by trade, with a PhD in Public Health. He has some forty years of experience as a university educator and researcher on violence and armed conflict and their impact on life, especially on the health of individuals and communities. For his full profile, see: https://web.comisiondelaverdad.co/la-comision/los-y-las-comisionadas/saul-franco

affiliation to the armed groups who participated in university protest scenarios. There were no truth clarification exercises in the institutions nor in the Victims' Unit about this event, but the memory of it was very strong and year in and year out it was ritualised in different activities (see Flórez Herrera, 2019). Together with the people with whom we shared this activism during university, we established a work collective called *Colectivo Archivos del Búho*[13] or the Owl's Archives Collective. Our objective was to catalogue, provide basic preservation conditions under this idea of self-managed work, and promote the social appropriation of archives related to the student movement, activism and processes related to the armed conflict in universities for research purposes. In 2019, I joined the Commission's Bogotá-Soacha-Sumapaz marco-territorial team at an initial stage of the research and, a year later, its Urban Dynamics team as part of the Territories Directorate. For this very small team of three cities, with very different realities, aiming to have a national reach, the issue of universities became increasingly relevant. When the decision was made to write the *Case 52 / Universities* for the Transmedia, it was up to me to write it between 2021 and June 2022 with the inputs provided by other territorial teams, but trying to give the higher education sector its specificity. Like Natalia, I participated in the work around the national recognition event for universities in September 2021 and in the Bogotá-Soacha-Sumapaz team we did a local recognition event[14] of the universities in November 2021.

The Universities and their Pathway to Acknowledgement

---

13   See https://trenzarmemorias.org/index.php/2022/10/23/archivos-del-buho-2021-reventando-silencios-memorias-del-16-de-mayo-de-1984-en-la-universidad-nacional-de-colombia-Bogotá-enjambre-libros-colectivos/

14   A variety of methodologies were adopted within the Commission to fulfil its different objectives. The recognition or acknowledgement of the dignity of victims, the impacts and violations of their rights; the voluntary recognition of collective and individual responsibilities, and the acknowledgement by the Colombian society of what happened was the second objective of the Commission, as explained above. The main methodology associated with recognition was titled 'encounters for truth'. For more details, see: https://web.comisiondelaverdad.co/en-los-territorios/objetivos/reconocimiento

Adriana: How did you decide to go down the path of clarification and truth at UdeA?

Natalia: *Hacemos Memoria* brought together interested sectors of the UdeA, academic units, associations of professors, retirees and graduates, to ask ourselves whether we should aim for truth clarification or take the more institutional path of seeking recognition as a subject of collective reparation. We then turned to the wisdom of a distinguished UdeA researcher on conflict issues, María Teresa Uribe de Hincapié, who, in a very clear and beautiful manner, said that first we had to look ourselves in the eyes as a university community and talk to each other about what happened to us and why this happened, and then, if we wanted to, we could take the path of reparation. She did not even think that, if the UdeA were to be recognised as a collective victim, the reparation should be economic. Instead, she thought it should be more political and social so that the institution could rebuild its relationship with society and play a more active role in crucial issues for the Department of Antioquia, the region, and the country, particularly in the implementation of the Final Agreement. This was the starting point for this decision, although it also generated some disagreements, which Juan Camilo will expand on.

Juan Camilo: As I said, in September 2018, the Commission put forward a request to the UdeA. In 2019, between February and March, the *Unidad Especial de Paz*[15] or the Special Peace Unit was created, and in September of that same year, the Rector of the UdeA asked us to prepare a draft of the report to submit to the Commission. As Natalia said, we went to Professor María Teresa Uribe to settle the matter about which path to take between clarification and reparation, and as she proposed that we first consider truth, the Rector took on that political position and said: this is how we will do it.

So, that is when me and Professor Juan Guillermo Gómez—a very important person in the UdeA, with a high degree of credibility and influence on the Left—were asked to write this report: I took the first stab and then we wrote the draft together. Juan Guillermo Gómez then called Orlando Arroyave, who, together with Catalina, wrote the

---

15 For more details, see https://www.udea.edu.co/wps/portal/udea/web/inicio/institucional/unidad-especial-paz

chapter on victims. In February 2020, responding to the Rector's request, we presented a relatively short joint document to the group of academic units interested in the issue of peace for discussion. This document was met with great opposition, as some felt that it put the UdeA and its researchers at risk, that its approach was revictimising, that they feared that the idea of the UdeA as a victimiser would stick. On February 10, 2020, the Commission endorsed the document as it stood, with its disruptive approach. My component of the document, which I had to draft myself almost by default because nobody wanted to do it, was very problematic because it was about insurgent presence and action in the UdeA. Soon after, the UdeA was closed due to the pandemic, so we did the report under the most extreme conditions imaginable, because it had to be delivered by December 2020 at the latest, according to the agreement with the Commission.

Adriana: At the same time, I was involved in a performance evaluation of the Commission. Shortly after starting that work, we realised that they did not have a vision of when they were going to stop receiving reports and, as we feared that the people and organisations that interacted with the Commission would feel disillusioned, we asked them to be clearer about their processes, including the timeline for the reports received. That date of December 2020, which then became April 2021, also came about because of our recommendation. Now I would like to ask Juan Sebastián about his memories from this period of work with the Commission and its relationship with the universities.

Juan Sebastián: The Commission's relationship with the universities had perhaps two moments, not necessarily linear. Progress was made from the beginning of the Commission on this issue until now, but this was a momentary impulse really and for decades there was neither generalised reflection nor extensive work by the universities on their own past. For my own research work on the events of May 16, 1984, I started by looking at what kind of academic works dealt with the relationship between universities and armed conflict, and there were one or two books on this by 2017. By the time the Commission ended, more or less thirty-five contributions had been received between reports and databases, so you could say that progress was made as never before in the development of the field of study that is the field of universities and the armed conflict looking inwards, towards their own affairs and role in the conflict.

From Law 975/2005 onwards, more and more versions of the armed conflict began to appear from the side of the state, but before that it was the universities that were the leaders in the production of knowledge in this area. The Commission opened up to the country with a noble intention, shared by many sectors, to bring together efforts based on reports, cases, testimonies, the different instances of participation and events organised to build a collective account of what happened to us as a country during the armed conflict. This brought together the universities as spaces/institutions responsible for research and the production of knowledge in two ways: one, which is the easiest to deal with, is that the university contributes with its academic production to the construction of truth about the armed conflict from the outside insofar as it was about other actors or conflict mechanisms it was not directly involved in; the other, which has a higher cost, is more difficult because it implies recognising oneself as we have already discussed here—looking inwards, looking into one's own eyes, as professor María Teresa Uribe de Hincapié said. The latter implied dealing with a fragmented community, one in which the voices that make the most noise are those that carry out collective activism around issues of memory and can distort other types of stories, which perhaps do not want to be made known. I say this because, alongside victimisation, in universities there are also cases or sectors that endorsed these harms, not only participated in them, but also played a central role in shaping them. This happened when their directors made decisions that meant that the institution was the agent of violence or turned its back on its students and teachers and left them to their fate. Approaching the armed conflict as an outsider who analyses it, as was the case in the first phase, was easier because looking inwards also implies thinking about all of these responsibilities.

I could say very little about how the Commission approached universities in general because, as the Commission was a large entity with different types of territorial and national teams, and a projection of a score of institutional alliances that was not always fluid or clear, agendas could well be advanced in different sectors by different commissioners without us, who were part of the different teams, being aware of them. However, I can say that in the working group in charge of the national recognition of universities, priority was given to those with which research work had already been done and the importance of truth clarification was already recognised. This was the case of the UdeA, the *Universidad del Valle*, the *Universidad Industrial de Santander*, the UNAL in Bogotá, the universities of the Caribbean Coast, all recognised as collective subjects of reparation, and the *Universidad de Nariño*. This recognition exercise I took part in raised a lot of expectations and entailed the very active participation of rectors, teaching staff, trade union sectors and teachers interested in contributing. This journey, in which the universities first approached the Commission as consultants, then began to recognise themselves as communities involved in the armed conflict, and later on were recognised by the Commission in different local spaces and national space, set things in motion. Here, in Bogotá, it was during the last period of the Commission that most activities were carried out with the UNAL. Thus, there was an acknowledgement of the *Colectivo 82* case by the Vice Rector's Office—something that had never happened before—with the participation of Commissioner Franco. This act was paradigmatic of the activation I was talking about because it allowed the universities to begin to look at their own past.

The Commission-university relationship was not the same in all cases: in some cases, as in the UdeA, the universities had larger teams; in others, as in the case of the UNAL, it was one professor and three student assistants; and on the Caribbean Cost, the universities structured several teams with the help of international aid funding. It was uneven and even today this is still uneven across the higher education sector.

The Higher Education Sector and the Commission

Adriana: I like this conversation because I feel that we are answering the questions that I had in mind for this conversation without me having to ask them explicitly. My next question was precisely about this diversity of capacities, expectations and motivations for universities interacting with the Commission.

Juan Camilo: In the first meetings with Commissioners Saúl Franco and Alejandro Valencia,[16] it was very clear, as Sebastián said, that the Commission was also looking to the universities—particularly the UdeA—to be a platform for territorial access in its first year. We have nine regional headquarters, three huge headquarters in Urabá, so the first place the Commission operated at a territorial level was in Urabá, the Bajo Cauca Antioqueño, and Oriente, where the UdeA had headquarters. The UdeA helped the Commission a lot logistically, even providing a room for meetings in our Extension Building before it established its territorial office in Medellín. Another key role was played by our professors, who, at the end of the Commission, helped to review documents and participated in readings and commented on the drafts of the Final Report.

Catalina: The UdeA, although it had not done so in terms of clarification before, has been researching what happened with armed groups here internally for decades. In the Political Science Programme, we have several studies of what the *tropel*[17] represented; in the Institute of Political Studies, about groups that operated internally; and in the Faculty of Law and Political Studies, to which I belong, on the issue of rebellion, sedition and states of exception, and what political repression represented. This is in addition to all the experience they have at the Institute of Regional Studies, specifically with the research group on Culture, Violence and Territory.

For the UdeA report, we met in large plenary sessions where we proposed minimum standards to be taken into account in each research team because, although everybody was free to write their report according to the guidelines we received, we had to have methodological and epistemological clarity and explain why the chapter was written the way it was. When I arrived at this research, made up of an interdisciplinary group of twenty-six researchers, there was already a

---

16 Alejandro Valencia is a lawyer by trade. He has nearly thirty years of experience in the promotion and defence of human rights and vast experience in historical truth issues as he has been an advisor to multiple truth commissions around the world. For his full profile, see: https://web.comisiondelaverdad.co/la-comision/los-y-las-comisionadas/alejandro-valencia

17 The term relates to student protests that may turn violent, especially when inadequately handled by the crowd control of the state or university security forces.

division of labour in relation to the frameworks of how to understand this phenomenon. Professor Leyder Perdomo worked on what they call the Counterinsurgent Power Bloc, using a concept by Vilma Liliana Franco (see Franco Restrepo, 2009), to explain theoretically what the influence of paramilitarism had been, seeking to understand both its effects and the political force that the extreme right represented within the UdeA. Camilo's group and a great researcher specialising on guerrillas, Mayra Alejandra Burbano, took on the task of unravelling the knot of some of the guerrillas active inside the UdeA about which information was available. I, together with Orlando Arroyave, a psychologist and researcher specialising in moral damage, was commissioned to write the chapter titled 'Victims, resistance and survival'. I proposed an analysis that would dismantle the notion of truth because, if it was a clarification report, it was necessary to understand the patterns, the historical periods, the causes, the multiple actors and how they were interlinked in order to understand how the effects on the university community as a whole were produced under a broad concept of harm that included, for instance, even the environmental impacts.

After several discussions that made it clear that the aim was to show the plural truths of the different actors, we created a database based on the concept of underreporting, as it was neither possible nor our intention to define the absolute universe of victims. My proposal for a methodology to document the 329 cases of human rights violations between 1965 and 2016 in a historical perspective was very well received. Our approach to recent history implied, given my understanding of the clarification and collective gaze of the harms, understanding those historical periods, defining the variables behind the specific forms of violence, the actors who had participated in them—including the institution itself—the political places we occupy as a university community, and identifying, as far as possible, the specific harms to specific individuals. Epistemologically, it could be said that we set out to shed light on the conditions that, on the one hand, made these massive harms possible under these characteristics and, on the other hand, mean that the stigmatisation and militarisation of university protest continues today. As UdeA, we understood that there is a gigantic impact, we know that we were victims of many things, but we also feel we are politically active subjects, and we have made clear decisions among which are to combat fear and to resist. In the end, there were five sections to the report, as can be seen online; and *Hacemos Memoria*, which worked under a logic of memory, was an important source for us.

Adriana: I would like to give the floor to Camilo to tell us more about this diversity of expectations and capacities within the UdeA and the results of the work with the Commission.

Juan Camilo: The Commission wanted to take advantage of the UdeA's proven capacity to document the armed conflict in the case of Antioquia, since we have documentation on violence since the 1930s and 1940s, which means we can even say that it predates the current armed conflict. The Commission knew that there were different kinds of support available to it here. While we are mostly talking about the UdeA report here, the UdeA also sent experts on ethnic and gender issues to support the work of the Commission. There was constant and very useful feedback in the Commission from different backgrounds, such as sociology, history, anthropology and law.

Adriana: My question was rather similar to what Juan Sebastián was saying when he was explaining that within the same universities there were different ways, capacities, visions and even knowledge when it came to interacting with the Commission.

Catalina: In the three components that make up the bulk of the UdeA report—guerrilla, counterinsurgency and victims—we implemented qualitative and quantitative methodologies from the social sciences, but nobody told us how to do it, nor did they give us a pre-set form. The UdeA had a much larger group of researchers compared to the other universities. The documentary work, interviews and databases involved multi- and interdisciplinary work in the teams, according to their own design, where previous skills were called upon for the purpose of clarification. I believe that this was done in similar ways throughout the country. The case of UNAL is different because there, Professor Mauricio Archila—a specialist in social movements, trade unionism, protest—worked only with three students and the level of harm had been enormous. At UdeA, we set out to read ourselves in the most critical way and say, 'we also caused harm to ourselves in this way'.

Adriana: Maybe Natalia can help us close this question.

Natalia: I wanted to go back to the motivations and expectations of the higher education sector in the country when interacting with the Commission. As a result of the process with *Hacemos Memoria* in 2018, I became aware of a different way of approaching the Commission by the universities in the Caribbean. The case of the UdeA is particular because here it was the commissioners who came and sought us out, also because Commissioner Franco is an exiled UdeA graduate. The Caribbean universities, which had been recognised as victims subject of collective reparation, sent an official letter to the Commission in its first months of work in January 2019 asking it to take on their cases as a macro element for their analysis. The path taken by these universities with the Victims' Unit was different: to be initially recognised as victims, to build a plan for collective reparations, to establish a timeline, some reparation measures, which we now know have not been very successful unfortunately. A few months later, they managed to get Commissioners Marta Ruiz[18] and Carlos Ospina[19] to visit the region and meet with the committees in charge of organising for collective reparations within the *Universidad de Córdoba*, *Atlántico* and *Popular del Cesar*, as well as with members from the other universities in the Caribbean and some guests from the UNAL. Their demand was to exchange experiences in order to build a report that recognised all of the universities of the Caribbean, including those of Magdalena, Sucre, Guajira and Cartagena, which were missing. This approach, different from that of the UdeA, had a very particular motivation that was part of the Commission's mandate

---

18   Marta Ruiz is a journalist with more than fifteen years of experience covering different aspects of the armed conflict. Her work has focused on the analysis of rural development issues, the dynamics of war, the defence of freedom of expression and the right to information. For her full profile, see: https://web. comisiondelaverdad.co/la-comision/los-y-las-comisionadas/marta-ruiz

19   Carlos Ospina is a retired Colombian Army Major. His appointment was celebrated at the time as an attempt by the Selection Committee to balance the narrative and acknowledge potential opposition to the Commission, given the rejection of the first version of the Peace Agreement in the October 2016 plebiscite. Ospina resigned from the Commission two months before the delivery of the Final Report. For details related to this case, see: https://www.elespectador. com/colombia-20/informe-final-comision-de-la-verdad/perfil-del-mayor-carlos-guillermo-ospina-galvis-el-comisionado-que-renuncio-a-la-comision-de-la-verdad/

to acknowledge and dignify victims. This became clear with the publication of a statement titled 'The Universities of the Caribbean at the Commission', which spoke of a demand for acknowledgment of all public universities by the Commission, as one of the most important institutions of the transition.

Adriana: Speaking to the outcomes, where do you see this work going and what do you think has been achieved in this whole process? On the one hand, I am referring to the relevance and impact you see in relation to the universities themselves and, on the other hand, to the relevance it may have for the Comprehensive System.

Juan Sebastián: To a large extent, as Catalina has also pointed out, the people who have been interested in these issues and in thinking about university communities as subjects in the conflict have been those who identify with or have been involved as victims or groups in resistance to the conflict. In the case of UNAL, the people who have written theses on its relationship with the armed conflict almost always have a background in activism, being victims or relatives of victims, or are simply people who identify politically with specific political sectors or with the victims' struggles and hence their interest. This has been the case of the four of us, who, being part of university communities, from different walks of life and for different reasons, ended up getting involved in the issue of the memory of the armed conflict in the universities. Those of us who are part of these kinds of initiatives are not going to stop doing them. For us, in the *Colectivo Archivos del Búho*, for example, this last year was very important because we were able to contribute to the work on the fortieth commemorative event of the *Colectivo 82* case and the different activities to make it visible. We are going to work on a hidden memory, with many burdens, which is known as the case of the Tenjo Massacre, a military operation of EPL militants who were, in turn, mostly students or graduates of the UNAL who ended up being surrounded, extrajudicially assassinated, and their bodies exposed by the security forces. I keep doing this, not because I am linked to a university, but because I am linked to the *Archivos del Búho* and this is what we do. I am also in contact with Wilson Gómez (see Gómez-Agudelo, 2018), who handed over, in my view, the most comprehensive database in existence on school and university students killed between 1929 and 2011, and continues to work with people from the *Universidad Uniminuto* on these issues. That will keep happening.

At the institutional level, I am a little more pessimistic because one thing, symptomatic of the universities in Bogotá, is that the interest in these issues seems to have ended with the change in university management and the end of the Commission. From *Archivos del Búho*, we were hoping for a meeting with the Vice Rector's Office at the UNAL to tell them that the *Universities Case*, in which they participated, is the largest piece of the Commission's Transmedia. We are especially interested in this because the universities are the 'heirs' to the Commission's Legacy. I imagine that this has been difficult because we lack a particular connection with management and our main ally, Mauricio Archila—who led this research from within the UNAL—has retired. This shows what kind of priority this has now.

This Commission left this baseline, showing—particularly in cities with an older university tradition such as Medellín, Popayan, Cali, and Bucaramanga—that the armed conflict cannot be understood without the universities, since several commanders of all kinds of armed groups were their graduates. It was also shown that there were clear connections between paramilitarism and university sectors, in some cases from within the institution itself, as they were places of intervention and even counter-insurgency laboratories. It was very telling how, a week after the National Security Statute was approved on September 6, 1978, the arrests of university students from various universities, but mainly from the UNAL, began and lasted until mid-October of that year. A total of 150 students were captured, detained and tortured by state agents. As universities have a central place in the armed conflict, one would hope that this issue would not just be part of the temporary initiatives of institutions such as the Commission, but that the universities themselves would permanently focus on the problem of their relationship with their past. From my experience as a student at the UNAL in Bogotá, I can say that this recent past is being forgotten and the dimension of the harms is the size of a two-story building that they are trying to cover up with a rug. Today, universities continue to be one of the territorial spaces from which links are established with armed structures of all kinds and cities. There must be a reflection on our past in order to transform these things that continue to take place and are very serious.

Final Reflections on Truth Clarification and Acknowledgement by and in the Higher Education Sector

Adriana: Who wants to continue with their reflections on the future of this work inside or outside the universities?

Catalina: In the UdeA report we found that in 98% of the cases there is a combination of impunity, no clarity about who is responsible and no real reparation of redress. I totally agree with Sebastián: the work continues for everyone.

There are several things in relation to the UdeA report that I would like to point out. The process of stigmatisation of public universities and that terrible tendency to appeal to justifying discourses such as 'they must have done something' or 'it had to be those people from the UdeA' that are reproduced by the traditional media started with the National Security Statute. We are still missing a great deal of intergenerational work so we can openly speak about fundamental rights, a mission that has been lost since the 1970s among universities. Many of the students enrolling now have no idea who all of these professors and students commemorated in the murals of the university were. This does not imply that we should dwell in our pain, in an idea of being a victim, but we should understand how this past calls into question what it means to be educated in a public university, what it means to be a member of a public university in this society and why we have a commitment to social justice, fundamental rights and the obligatory transformation of this society. A constant in the report was to understand that violence against university communities, no matter which group it came from, affected the possibilities of change in the projects of knowledge and finding a modicum of justice. Today, it must be understood that public universities have always worked for the most vulnerable in the community and what happened in the universities is one of the maximum representations of violence and structural failure of society.

The work continues at the UdeA to understand the dimension of the damage; we want to implement a process of attention and interdisciplinary accompaniment that documents each of the cases in the database we delivered in depth and seeks reparations not from the state, but starting with ourselves, from our understanding of what happened, and then take this knowledge beyond the classroom and the academic space we inhabit. Is the legal system going to do anything? I do not think that is our aim, especially if we understand that the Commission was not judicial in nature, although its work contributes context to the cases of the judicial body of the Final Agreement, the Special Jurisdiction for Peace.[20] I think our quest has always been to some extent libertarian grounded in 'we are going to narrate and continue to narrate this atrocity and oppose it by trying to change the conditions through education'. As all of this vindicates the value of education as the ultimate goal—'just keep educating'—especially as we have been understanding this work is not finished and a lot more narratives are going to emerge. Our aim in participating in this work is not to necessarily publish articles and get salary points, but to understand ourselves and for those generations that are coming up to understand and know what happened and why the decisions we made as a society led to certain things.

Juan Camilo: A key way forward for the UdeA project is to differentiate between armed conflict and political violence in order to untangle what we understand by armed conflict. Why? Because political violence in the UdeA can be traced back almost fifty years before the armed conflict as such began. Twenty days ago, a twenty-five-year-old man lost his hands, and another man of the same age ended up with burns over 30% of his body. Last June 8, an eighteen-year-old-girl practically died immolated in her house while she and her friends were assembling potato bombs. Is that part of the armed conflict or not? This is not a minor question. If we broaden the spectrum to talk about political violence, the university becomes a much larger field of research and, on the one hand, new victimisations appear and, on the other, new groups are responsible for these harms. The first explosive device detonated at the UdeA was a stick of dynamite thrown in 1944 by Liberals against the Conservative Rector because he refused to remove the Virgins from the study halls.

---

20   *La Jurisdicción Especial para la Paz* or the Special Jurisdiction for Peace began
     operating in 2018 as did the Commission, but it has a nearly twenty-year-long
     mandate. For more details, see: https://www.jep.gov.co/JEP/Paginas/Jurisdiccion-
     Especial-para-la-Paz.aspx

For Miguel Ángel Beltrán,[21] the Commission's account of the 1958–2018 period falsified the history of university violence because, he said, the first person killed by violence against the university was a student murdered at the UNAL in a student protest in 1904. Moving beyond the armed conflict and extending it to political violence would be a possible way to enrich the research.

Almost two long years after writing our report for the Commission, it has been difficult to publish it and hold a public event with our students. My dream since 2018 is that we will have those responsible for the actions we documented—mainly members from the urban structures of the FARC-EP, the ELN and the security forces—come to the event and explain what the harms they participated in were and discuss the report so that this does not happen again. I agree with Sebastián that part of not speaking clearly to the students about the effects that this has had on the academic community is that things are repeated because they are still convinced that a youth in an armed group is possible. In this generation they were radicalised by the repression deployed by the Duque administration since 2018, especially in the strikes of 2019, 2020 and 2021. The UdeA experience could help open a debate in this new framework. On the other hand, there is no debate at the UdeA on the role of internal democracy and whether and when conditions to return to student representation would be ripe. Many other issues like that have yet to be debated, to look ourselves in the eyes and say 'we disagree, this is inaccurate, this is not true'. I believe that this is what will come soon after this report is made public in the UdeA.

Catalina: We did not think that the report for the Commission would be public because there were so many of us and it had to be delivered by a certain date, as refined as possible. In editing it now for publication and dissemination, we have made a rigorous revision of many things and added an analysis of how we understood truth clarification to give it a more cohesive and integrating narrative. The report is titled *Political*

---

21 Miguel Ángel Beltrán, a university professor, was imprisoned under false charges of being a FARC-EP collaborator. Despite being freed after three years, it would take nearly five years for the Supreme Court to clear him of all charges (Beltrán Villegas, 2018). Together with María Ruiz Aranguren and Jorge Enrique Freytter, Beltrán also submitted a report to the Commission on universities in the armed conflict (see Tavera, 2020).

Violence and Armed Conflict, and the chapter on victims shows those complex characterisations I talked about and what that has implied in terms of the dialogues we have had after that experience. It is special that the report is being published for mass distribution because making people aware of it is also one of our tasks. We aim to have it published by the second half of 2023 and we want to take it to the regions to broaden the possibility for other voices to join in.

Juan Camilo: I am fully convinced that if the ELN signs a peace agreement during the Petro administration there will be a new small truth commission, which would be very important for universities given that the ELN's presence and actions in this setting are absolutely key to its emergence and current operations. This issue does not end here because the conflict is not over, and this could be a new line of research for us.

Natalia: Like Sebastián, I would like to refer to how crucial it is to clarify what happened in the armed conflict in the universities in order to understand what happened in the cities. I agree with Carlos Mario Perea, a scholar of urban violence in Colombia, who says that cities have been very absent in our peace negotiations. This is understandable in some measure because the conflict is mainly situated in the rural areas, where most of the victims come from. The Commission, with its chapter on Urban Dynamics, wanted to focus on these other cases instead, showing that this urban violence had links with the conflict, and that is why it has been so difficult to elucidate and clarify them.

I fear that this will not have sufficient echo in the institutional framework for peace that remains from the Final Agreement, and particularly in the Comprehensive System. Ultimately, the nature of the Commission was different, in its interaction with the territories, and in its emphasis on listening. There was a voluntary willingness of the institutions and social organisations and trade unions to come to the Commission and say, 'this is what happened to us, this is our story, we want it to be acknowledged'. Its work is different from that of other institutions in the System and I fear that *Case 52 / Universities* will not have the continuity we would like. However, I feel that, as Catalina, Camilo and Sebastián pointed out, the universities that actively participated in the Commission are still doing things, expanding on these questions, they still want to publish the UdeA report, which hopefully will have much more echo, we still want to explore other cases, as Sebastián said, because there are people who are very involved and interested in student activism in university communities. I think that this is also the continuity that we can see and hope for. What we learned from this exercise of remembering is that this questioning of the past is done in the present in order to interrogate the present and challenge it. I think that the great value of this work of memory and clarification lies in being able to interrogate the violence that we still experience in three directions: violence against the university campuses, violence perpetrated from the university campuses, and intra-mural violence or violence that takes place within the university campuses.

Tentative Conclusions

More than a year after the end of the mandate of the Commission, we can say that it provided an unprecedented space for the higher education sector to initiate an institutional path of reflection on its participation in the armed conflict. The different university communities that participated in the spaces provided by the Commission built on their previous processes of (self-)recognition to evaluate both the effects and impacts of the armed conflict and their coping strategies and resistance to it. This chapter-conversation shows that the direction this work will now take depends on the universities themselves and their members and whether they decide to follow and commit to this path. The seeming lack of interest on the part of the institutions in this topic, even those that are part of the transitional justice system of the Final Agreement, and the persistence of violent conflicts in the country call into question the scope and future of the work of truth clarification. However, as Natalia Maya Llano, Juan Camilo Domínguez Cardona, Juan Sebastián Flórez Herrera and Catalina Puerta Henao outlined, it is precisely the uninterrupted cycle of violence that hinders this work that also makes it more urgent and necessary at the same time. While none of them intend to give up this work in the short or medium term personally, the only prospect for renewed institutional interest in this issue comes from the Petro

Government's proposal of *Paz Total* or Total Peace.[22] These simultaneous peace talks with several armed groups, among which the ELN stands out as the oldest insurgent group, may give new impetus to the truth clarification and reparation initiatives that involve the Colombian higher education sector. But it remains to be seen when or indeed if any peace agreements will be signed with these groups in the next few years.

Acknowledgements

We would like to thank the editor, Open Book Publishers, and the reviewers for their generosity and commitment in providing us with insightful feedback and especially for allowing us to develop this chapter in a dual-language format. All mistakes in both versions of this chapter remain our own.

Bibliography

Archila Neira, M., and Roncancio, E. (2021). Violencia en la Universidad Nacional de Colombia, 1958–2018 [Violence in the Universidad Nacional de Colombia, 1958–2018]. *Revista Controversia*, 217, 383–430. https://revistacontroversia.com/index.php/controversia/article/view/1243/1005

Bakiner, O. (2019). The Comprehensive System of Truth, Justice, Reparation, and Non-Repetition: Precedents and Prospects. In J. H. R. DeMeritt, J. Meernik, and M. Uribe-López (Eds), *As War Ends: What Colombia Can Tell Us About the Sustainability of Peace and Transitional Justice* (pp. 230–248). Cambridge University Press. https://doi.org/10.1017/9781108614856.011

Beltrán Villegas, M. Á. (2018). *La vorágine del conflicto colombiano: una mirada desde las cárceles* [The Vortex of the Colombian Conflict: A View from the Prisons]. CLASCO and IEC-CONADU.

CODHES [Consultoría para los derechos humanos y el desplazamiento]. (2021, February 16). *Desplazamiento Forzado en Colombia ¿Qué pasó en 2020?* [Forced Displacement in Colombia. What Happened in 2020?]. CODHES. https://codhes.wordpress.com/2021/02/16/desplazamiento-forzado-en-colombia-que-paso-en-2020/

CHCyV [Comisión Histórica del Conflicto y sus Víctimas]. (2015). *Contribución al Entendimiento Del Conflicto Armado En Colombia* [Contribution to the Understanding of the armed conflict in Colombia]. CHCyC.

---

22   See Janetsky (2023, September 19).

https://indepaz.org.co/wp-content/uploads/2015/02/Version-final-informes-CHCV.pdf

CEV [Comisión para el Esclarecimiento de la Verdad, la Convivencia y la No Repetición]. (2019). *Lineamientos metodológicos* [Methodological Guidelines]. [Unpublished document produced by the Commission].

—(2022a). *Informe final. Hallazgos y Recomendaciones* [Final report. Findings and Recommendations]. CEV. https://www.comisiondelaverdad.co/hallazgos-y-recomendaciones-1

—(2022b). *Metodología para el Esclarecimiento de la Verdad* [Methodology for Truth Clarification]. CEV. https://www.comisiondelaverdad.co/metodologia-para-el-esclarecimiento-de-la-verdad.

—(2022c). *Caso 'Universidades y conflicto armado en Colombia'* [Case study 'Universities and Armed Conflict in Colombia']. CEV. https://www.comisiondelaverdad.co/caso-universidades

CICR-C [Comité Internacional de la Cruz Roja – Colombia]. (2023, March 22). *Retos Humanitarios* [Humanitarian Challenges]. CICR-C. https://www.icrc.org/es/document/colombia-retos-humanitarios-2023

CNMH [Centro Nacional de Memoria Histórica]. (2013). *Basta Ya! Colombia: Memorias de guerra y dignidad. Informe General de Grupo de Memoria Histórica* [Enough Already! Colombia: Memories of War and Dignity. General Report of the Historical Memory Group]. CNMH. https://centrodememoriahistorica.gov.co/wp-content/uploads/2021/12/1.-Basta-ya-2021-baja.pdf

—(2018). *Paramilitarismo. Balance de la contribución del CNMH al esclarecimiento histórico* [Paramilitarism. An Assessment of the Contribution of the CNMH to Historical Clarification]. CNMH. https://centrodememoriahistorica.gov.co/wp-content/uploads/2020/01/PARAMILITARISMO.pdf

Franco Restrepo, V. L. (2009). *Orden contrainsurgente y dominación* [Counterinsurgent order and domination]. Siglo del Hombre/Instituto Popular de Capacitación.

Flórez Herrera, J. S. (2019). 16 de mayo de 1984: pasado y presente en disputa. Algunas reflexiones a propósito del aniversario 35 de los acontecimientos [16 May 1984: Past and Present Under Dispute. Some Reflections Concerning the 35th Anniversary of this Date]. *Revista Controversia*, 213, 269–295. https://revistacontroversia.com/index.php/controversia/article/view/1182/955

Gómez-Agudelo, J. W. (2018). Acontecimiento y escucha: revisión de estudios sobre 'el estudiante caído' y los movimientos estudiantiles en Colombia [Event and Listening: A Review of Studies about 'the Fallen Student' and Student Movements in Colombia]. *Revista Latinoamericana de Ciencias Sociales, Niñez y Juventud, 16*(1), 71–87. https://revistaumanizales.cinde.org.co/rlcsnj/index.php/Revista-Latinoamericana/article/view/2872/895

Janetsky, M. (2023, September 19). *Colombia's President Has a Plan for 'Total Peace.' But Militias Aren't Putting Down their Guns yet.* World News. https://apnews.com/article/colombia-total-peace-gustavo-petro-armed-conflict-d213efd008f73004da8269740b592a70

Jiménez Ortega, M., Corena Puentes, E., and Maldonado Badrán, C. (2020). *Las fracturas del alma mater: memorias de la violencia en la Universidad del Atlántico. 1998–2010* [The Cracks of the Alma Mater: Memories of Violence in the Universidad del Altántico. 1998–2010]. Universidad del Atlántico. https://investigaciones.uniatlantico.edu.co/omp/index.php/catalog/catalog/view/70/85/285

Maya, N. (2018, May 24). *La reparación colectiva de la Universidad de Córdoba: un caso emblemático pero poco satisfactorio* [Collective Reparations in the Universidad de Córdoba: An Emblematic, but Unsatisfactory Case]. Hacemos Memoria. https://hacemosmemoria.org/2018/05/24/unicordoba/

Mazzei, J. (2009). *Death Squads or Self-Defense Forces? How Paramilitary Groups Emerge and Challenge Democracy in Latin America.* The University of North Carolina Press.

Rudling, A. (2019). What's Inside the Box? Mapping Agency and Conflict within Victims' Organizations. *International Journal of Transitional Justice, 13*(3), 458–477. https://doi.org/10.1093/ijtj/ijz025

Sánchez, N. C., and Rudling, A. (2019). *Reparations in Colombia: Where to? Mapping the Colombian Landscape of Reparations for Victims of the Internal Armed Conflict.* Queen's University Belfast. https://reparations.qub.ac.uk/assets/uploads/ColombiaReparationsPolicyReportFORAPPROVAL-SP-HR-NoCrops.pdf

Sánchez, G. (2001). Introduction: Problems of Violence, Prospects for Peace. In C. Bergquist, R. Peñarada, and G. Gonzalo Sánchez (Eds) *Violence in Colombia, 1990–2000: Waging War and Negotiating Peace* (pp. 1–38). Scholarly Resources Inc. Imprint.

Tavera, E. (2020, July 9). *Universidades públicas, bajo sospecha* [Public Universities, under Suspicion]. Hacemos Memoria. https://hacemosmemoria.org/2020/07/09/universidades-publicas-bajo-sospecha/

USAID [United States Agency for International Development]. (2021). *Truth, Coexistence, and Non-Recurrence Commission Performance Evaluation. Final Report,* US Department of State. https://pdf.usaid.gov/pdf_docs/PA00XM1T.pdf

UdeA [Universidad de Antioquia]. (2021). *La violencia política y el conflicto armado en la Universidad de Antioquia 1958–2016: Aportes a la memoria y esclarecimiento de sus impactos y relaciones. Informe general* [Political Violence and the Armed Conflict in the Universidad de Antioquia 1958–2016: Contributions to Memory and Clarification of its Impacts and Relationships. General Report]. Universidad de Antioquia.

https://www.udea.edu.co/wps/portal/udea/web/inicio/institucional/
unidad-especial-paz/programas-proyectos/contenido/asmenulateral/
violencia-conflicto

Verdad Abierta. (2013, March 7). *La toma de la Universidad de Córdoba* [The
Takeover of the Universidad de Córdoba]. VerdadAbierta.com. https://
verdadabierta.com/la-toma-de-la-universidad-de-cordoba/

—. (2015, January 5). *¿Hasta dónde han llegado los aportes de las víctimas al
proceso de paz?* [How Far Have the Contributions of Victims to the Peace
Process Come?]. VerdadAbierta.com. https://verdadabierta.com/
lo-avances-que-las-victimas-aportaron-al-proceso-de-paz/

2. The Whiteboard:
Reflections on a Personal Archive of Apartheid-era Items from the Security Police of a University Town

Brent Arthur Meistre

Introduction

This text engages with detritus from the mid-1980s of Apartheid South Africa, although aspects of it stretch to before and after that intensive period of repression and violence. The Apartheid regime exerted control over its people by waging a war against all ideological and political positions other than its own, in part through the suppression of the activities of civic organisations, the liberal press and public universities. The government harnessed the backing and skills of the Western intelligence services mobilised for the Cold War, including the Central Intelligence Agency (CIA), to combat the spread of Communism through its Security Police. This fervour about the 'rooi gevaar' [translated from Afrikaans as 'red danger'] intersected with the longer held propaganda about the *'swart gevaar'* ['black danger' or 'fear']—the threat posed by the majority population to the stability of political and economic domination by the minority government and those citizens racialised as 'white'. The ensuing oppression manifested in violence on those categorised as 'non-white', and in targeted actions against political groups and their leadership within the country and those in exile within neighbouring countries, as the resistance against oppression grew. This included coordinated action against the banned

 https://doi.org/10.11647/OBP.0427.02

African National Congress (ANC) and its military wing, '*Mkhonto we Sizwe*' [translated from isiXhosa as 'Spear of the Nation'].

One small city of the country—a place at the time called Grahamstown (now Makhanda)—is the backdrop of this chapter. Situated on the once colonial frontier of the British Empire, the settlement is home to the national monument commemorating the arrival of the 1820 Settlers; one of the country's oldest newspapers; a high court; and one of the country's oldest public higher education institutions. Through such mechanisms, the city came to act as a centre of Anglo-Saxon education and culture within a mostly rural context from late colonialism and throughout Apartheid. Taking a god's-eye view of the city from the hill of the Settler's Monument, a straight line of sight runs centrally across the city from the entrance of the Rhodes University library, across the main administration building with its imposing clock tower, down the wide High Street to the large spire of the Anglican cathedral. The city design unravels in different directions from that line, with white-to-black gradient swatches for the areas demarcated for 'whites' and 'coloureds'. Further on, the 'Black' townships sprawl up and over the hill of Makana's Kop into the haze of peripheral vision, where the many extensions of the township continue out of sight. These signifiers of the Apartheid policy of racialised 'separate development' reflect the segregated design of the country's higher education sector: along racial lines, and by supposed ethnic groupings, including divisions of 'Europeans' between those English and Afrikaans socio-linguistic institutions.

Black intellectual life was rooted largely outside of university contexts, such as through the church and resistance movements; however, a few Black students were admitted to English-speaking universities, and in later years universities were established for 'coloured', 'Indian' and certain ethnicities of 'Black' student groups in their immediate vicinity. In the city of Grahamstown, there was Rhodes University alone. By the time the state declared the first State of Emergency in 1985 in that region of the country, the University was already suspected of operating as a breeding group for political resistance. The local Security Branch (SB) focused much of their attention on these two divided worlds, between the activist groups within the township and the university. While aspects of the two are deeply interwoven, this chapter concerns itself largely with the political activities of the university staff and students. Because the white supremacist delusions of the Apartheid government could not conceive of sophisticated Black intellectual leadership nor its capacity to inform the resistance, much attention and resources were focused on what was believed to be the sole locus of control: the white left.

Born in 1975, I grew up on the 'white side of town', where the 'white liberals', 'subversives' or 'lefties' were monitored and often controlled by the numerous spies placed strategically in the town and its universities. This was undertaken by the agents of the Security Police, of which my father was the 'Head' from 1984 to 1993.

It is now common knowledge that spies and informants were recruited from, and planted within, the staff and student population. Reported to the SB (in Keniston, 2013, p. 55) by a 'source' in Rick Turner's academic circle at Rhodes University was the following report about his activities:

GEHEIM/SECRET
On 2.9.1969, he accepts service at Rhodes University at Grahamstown as lecturer in Political Science. On the same date, he attends the 'Free Universities' first lecture and gives a lecture about 'Jean-Paul Sarte' a philosopher who propagates change through violence.

Rick Turner, who held an academic position at Rhodes for six months during this period, was assassinated in 1978. Some spies disguised themselves as prominent members of the student anti-Apartheid leadership, thereby manipulating campus and localised politics through their 'handlers' at the local branch of the Security Police. Over the 1980s, student spies on the campuses were increasingly exposed during their studies. Others broke cover later. Recently published texts and memoirs of such student actors have revealed the extent of such manipulations and betrayal at that time (Ancer, 2019), and the lack of capacity of such agents to reflect self-critically, and truthfully, in the present (Forsyth, 2015).

Less publicly acknowledged was the University's routine participation in the sharing of information with the state. There were 'several sources amongst the secretaries and general bureaucratic lifeblood of the place', writes Olivia Forsyth (2015, p. 123), the prominent undercover Security Police Officer who posed as a Student Representative Council (SRC) leader. The extract below demonstrates an alumni's surprise at revelations within a file kept on him by the Department of Justice:

> [what] alarmed me, was an item marked 'GEHEIM' [Secret] Item 49, dated 19 November 1970, stated: 'His name appears on a list sent by the authorities of "Rhodes University" of students who have yet undertaken military training'. (Streek, 2005, p. 161)

The Security Branch exploited student data held by the University administrative system. This was used in a range of ways, including sending unnamed letters to parents of student activists (often signed 'concerned academic') pressuring them to dissuade their children from political activities.

There was more knowledge in the public domain of the state's use of academics as expert witnesses in cases against student activists. Because of Afrikaans-speaking universities' close relations to the state, most were from such institutions. One such case was brought against Rhodes student Guy Berger, who later became an academic at that same institution in the early post-Apartheid period.

> The police regarded the study groups as cells recruiting students into more serious activity, but I wasn't in that league at all. But in order to make it seem more sinister than it was, they brought in a professor of politics from the then Rand Afrikaans University. (Guy Berger in Warman, 2014, p. 63)

In addition to direct interference and infiltration, the Security Police monitored those staff and students they suspected of activism through telephone 'tapping', the planting of 'tomatoes' [listening devices] in various objects in university and domestic environments, mail interception and the confiscation of materials, which is the subject of this chapter.

Academic citizens could be interrogated, arrested and detained without trial for ninety days. This excerpt, from the student newspaper at the time, names my father's interaction on the matter with the then Vice-Chancellor.

> Dr Henderson met with Colonel Meistre of the Grahamstown Security Branch last Friday and described the meeting as a 'full and frank exchange of views'. The Colonel told Henderson he would grant study rights only if the university provided him with details of the student's academic history [...] So far, only one Rhodes detainee, Karen Thorne, has actually received study materials, through the efforts of her lawyer. ('Missing', 1986, p. 3)

More severe treatment of dissidents included incarceration without trial, house arrest, torture and banning. Amnesty International (1978, p. 90) documented that 'Banning orders have also been widely used against university students and teachers, who have as a result been prevented from continuing with their studies or teaching duties [...] They were all prohibited from entering any university, school or other educational institution under the provision which apply to most banning orders'. The implications for knowledge dissemination and reproduction were dire. A banned person could not gather with more than three people, be quoted or cited or be published unless the text was blocked out, usually in large, bold, multiple formations of crosses. Specific words which were banned had to be redacted in solid, bold black or, as was the practice of some publishers who intentionally visualised the censorship, printed as blank, as I show in this chapter. The poet, author and artist Breyten Breytenbach, who served seven years for terrorism charges, used this as a creative and subversive device on page 50 of his novel *The True Confessions of an Albino Terrorist* (1984), detailing his arrest and prison sentence.

A Silent Witness/A 'Mute' Artist

The creative work I do as a South African visual artist emerges from this recognition of absence, the muteness and invisibility of texts, in the erasure of voices and of silences, and in the minute traces of gaps in 'other' information.

> The art of trauma, because it aims to represent in some fragmentary way something that eludes our grasp, often verges on the indecipherable. This is one reason why, as we have seen, so many artists have recourse to the subsymbolic index. (Iverson, 2017, p. 83)

A schism developed early on between my creative work as a visual artist and my inarticulateness as an academic citizen at Rhodes University. I completed my undergraduate and postgraduate studies there, later moving from junior lecturer through to senior lecturer, and leading the Photography Section at the School of Fine Art. During that time, I avoided describing my artistic work to the viewer. In part this was because the absence and negation of the word itself was (and still is) a key subject of my and, in turn, their exploration. However, I have come to recognise that underlying this was the shame of the adolescent 'mute' witness I was during Apartheid, and a sense of being an implicated subject.

My first year as an academic citizen at Rhodes University was in 1995, a year after the country's first democratic elections, when public discourse was geared towards the establishment of the Truth and Reconciliation Commission (TRC).[1] When it became known to my father's colleagues that I had enrolled at the university, shock and an implied betrayal was communicated about the choice of that English-speaking, liberal university. It was an institution they had been monitoring and surveying for decades. A senior administrator of the University asked my father: 'what trouble can we expect this year?' Because of my proximity to my father's work, and having directly encountered Olivia Forsyth, I knew that there were student spies on campus and that I may be presumed one. Recently, I read an account of a Security Branch officer which revealed that 'young people were identified early on and became SB [Security Branch] agents at educational institutions where they could study with all fees and costs paid for by the SB [...] the system was open to abuse [...] usually senior cops had their kids educated "free of charge"' (Erasmus, 2021, p. 259). Although I was not approached, there was understandably suspicion about me. 'The police are here!' was a common call when I arrived at parties. Throughout my studies, staff and students asked about my father, leading me early on to define and to state my political position, and to retreat into the shadows of the photography dark room, with public engagement framed by the viewfinder.

> Shame is both an interruption and a further impediment to communication, which is itself communicated [...] This ambivalence [in the shame response] is nowhere clearer than in a child who covers his face in the presence of the stranger, but who also peeks through his fingers so that he may look without being seen. (Sedgwick and Frank, 1995, p. 137)

---

1   As part of the transitional process from Apartheid to democracy, the TRC was established in 1995 and chaired by Desmond Tutu. This restorative justice provided a structure for victims of human rights violations to give statements and for perpetrators to give testimony of the truth and apply for amnesty. Many of these concerned political killings of academics and students.

As much as it enabled the hiding of my face, the camera also functioned as a way to arrest and shape the world around me. As a child I was ocularcentric, taking in the world through acts of looking, watching and turning away. My memories are frozen in time through my attempts to frame and contain through looking devices. As a passenger of my father's vehicles during his responses to unrest, scenes of death and violence and meetings with informants, I learnt to reflect, deflect and manage my witnessing. I would duck down between the seats, stealing side views out of windows and catching fleeting glimpses of the rearview mirror. The car—as the dark chamber of the inside of a camera body with refracted light muting the world by shatterproof glass—later became the narrating subject of my first solo exhibition *Rode*. This looking extended to experiencing those around me, as a silent observer. Schwab (2020, p. 14) describes how 'children of a traumatised parental generation [...] become avid readers of silences and memory traces hidden [...] Like photography, traumatised bodies reveal their own optical unconscious. It is this unconscious that second-generation children absorb. Without being fully aware of it, they become skilled readers of the optical unconscious revealed in their parent's body language'.

In the twenty-five years I have practiced as a visual artist I have explored, and attempted to undermine, the control exerted by the camera, through the framing of the viewfinder and, by extension, the photographer. My work has circled around the problematics of representation in all its failures, but also its possibilities, in suggesting the 'unsaid', the unsayable and notions of truth. Through this struggle I developed a performance persona—'the stranger'—who appears in my stop-motion animated films[2] as a mute figure being moved and shaped by exterior forces without agency. As the performed self, he functions as both a perpetrator and victim embodying an understanding of trauma that moves beyond 'the literal invasion of the unfiltered outside into the psyche' (Baer, 2000, p. 9), or as a gap in memory which cannot be reconciled towards making whole.

The muteness, masking and opaqueness in my work, however, is also an opening that asks the viewer to set towards it more closely, to lean into it as an experiential act to bear witness to the phantom which

---

2   See https://vimeo.com/221867227 for an example of this work.

inhabits the work. This strategy has evolved through years of processing, uncovering and negotiating this subject.

> What may need to be scrutinized in narrative is less its 'message', less its ostensible affirmations, and much more its interstices, its gaps, its moments of passage, the moment when something falls silent to indicate a transference, the moment when one begins to hear other possible voices in response. (Brooks, 1994, p. 86)

The chapter draws from the research process for my creative art practice which is typified by ethereal and unstated manifestation. As part of that research, I have been cataloguing how specific artefacts, objects and traces act as memory vessels or as triggers of specific events which are rooted in the political, social and cultural events which manifested the Cold War, southern Africa, in the domestic life of my childhood. My memories are triangulated with historical texts, primary interviews and the cultural detritus of VHS films, music cassettes and other artefacts common during that stage of the dying throws of Apartheid. Some of these refer to general events broadly situated across South Africa during that timeframe. Others refer to relations and events particular to the university town of Grahamstown, and items brought home from my father's office for me, which I have retained in my personal archive. I have curated a few of these poignant items herein. In part, these describe the layers of complexities which circulate below the surface of my art-making. More importantly perhaps for this chapter, they bring to the fore the tension between being an implicated subject and the social and historical responsibility of being an artist-academic. That tension underscores this chapter in a manner that seeks resolution but also recognises the irreconcilable within the logic of the text. It is within the filmic artworks I am currently constructing, however, that I hope this traumatising tension might cohere and coagulate. I am unsure of whether this exploration—of the deployment of power and control, of the manipulation of (mis)information, and its effect on legacies of knowing in the present—will be reparative, problematically psychologising history or holding value for academic knowing.

> How can we represent what is, by its own definition, by its very nature unrepresentable, (without denying the traumatic experience and the cause of this experience, the evil, the terror), without banalizing it, trivializing it, spectacularizing it, finally repressing it for a second time. (Weibel, 2009, p. 256)

The Photograph

Fig. 2.1 Black-and-white hand-printed photograph (97 x 157mm), circa 1986.
Identities obscured by the author. Author's collection.

This appears to be a small celebration—an important event, hence the photographic document.

It is a small, hand-printed, black-and-white photograph depicting four white men in an office. One of the men is pouring J. C. Le Roux champagne into a glass. A man on the left turns towards the camera, his eyes focused on a figure whose directional hand-gesture enters the left margin of the frame. Another man, on the right, has his hand in his pocket and appears off in thought. On the desk, to the left alongside files and books, is a binoculars case; and on the opposite desk, a silver metal briefcase sits near an assortment of rubber stamps.

On the back of a closed wooden door is a dartboard. Above it is a political poster of South African Communist Party (SACP) leader Joe Slovo.[3] He peers down from above, watching their small 'success'

---

3   The poster was part of Joe Slovo's campaign at the National Executive Committee of the ANC at its National Consultative Conference held in Kabwe, Zambia in 1985 to become a non-African member of the NEC. It may also be related to his 1986 appointment as general secretary of the SACP. For further reading, see: https://www.saha.org.za/nonracialism/the_movement_is_very_big_now.htm and https://ourconstitution.constitutionhill.org.za/joe-slovo/

celebration below. Almost a target for a rogue dart, is the voter's X on the bottom right of the poster.

To the far right, clipped by the camera's viewfinder, is a whiteboard. It displays an array of differently sized photographs of individual headshots and group images. You might recognise some if you knew them. Many are of students, lecturers, researchers, activists and informers.

> For years, Security Branch agents had operated on the campuses of the liberal Left, English-language universities. Such infiltration was aimed primarily at the short-term goals of spotting and quelling any semblance of anti-apartheid or anti-government activity. Agents who passed through the universities were sometimes unmasked or left prematurely to continue with more regular police work. (Bell et al., 2003, p. 84)

The identikit photographs on display are of people being watched and monitored, who have been previously arrested or detained. One End Conscription Campaign (ECC) member reported on this: 'six security policemen walked in on a general body meeting. They told everyone to remain seated and not to talk. They then photographed everyone in the room and took down our names' (End Conscription Campaign, n.d.b, p. 2). Those pictured on the board could have belonged to or simply been associated with a range of organisations and groups, including The National Union of South African Students (NUSAS), the Conscription Review Action Committee (CRAC), Delta, the End Conscription Campaign (ECC), the United Democratic Front (UDF), Black Sash, The Congress of South African Students (COSAS), the Black Student Movement (BSM). Some of the photographs were of parents of my school friends. Less than 400 meters from the office pictured in this image, the university had become:

> a prime focus for infiltration. But the aim was much grander than to monitor the several staff and students tagged as subversives; it was to place agents on the campuses who would become part of liberal, even radical, university life. They would rise through the ranks of student politics to positions of power and influence both within and outside academia and South Africa. (Bell et al., 2003, pp. 84–85)

I know this office, I know this room, I know these men. This is the Security Police Branch Office in Grahamstown and these are Security Policemen. One of them is my father.

The room pictured is the White Desk, where political matters concerning the white left wing were investigated and monitored. A Johannesburg Security Policeman, Paul Erasmus, testified during the TRC hearing that 'every Security Branch in the country was divided up along those lines, albeit making provision for the population or the specific populations within the defined area. Effectively it was a division along the line of desks, you would have an Anti-Terrorism Desk, a Church Desk, a so-called Indian Affairs Desk, a White Affairs Desk and so on'.[4]

The photograph was probably taken in 1986 a few years after Joe Slovo's wife, Ruth First, was killed by a letter bomb sent to her university office in Maputo, Mozambique. She was a prominent political SACP leader, activist and one of the founding members of the ANC. The bomb was concealed inside a package of books whose delivery was overseen by Johannesburg Security Police Officer and spy, Craig Williamson, who later infiltrated and manipulated the International University Exchange Fund (IUEF) in Sweden (Ancer, 2017). This was one of a number of such letter bomb killings of academics and activists during Apartheid.

I was around ten years old when this photograph was taken. Later, I ended up studying Fine Art Photography. When I began working at Rhodes University as an early career academic in the early 2000s, there was an unspoken recognition intimated by some of the senior staff whom my father had previously monitored and detained during Apartheid. Some I had encountered when a child, during times when my father transported them between various spaces while questioning them. It was a small town. The slippages between my father's work and our domestic life where such that I became complicit in state processes. First, as a child witnessing the unknown; later, as an increasing conscious and knowing adolescent, entwined in a business of the ilk Hannah Arendt (1963) described as the 'banality of evil'.

One such slippage involves what was within the silver case pictured in the photograph. It was a 35mm film camera, probably the one used to take the photograph. I knew it well and how to use it. It was brought to our home at some point, because our family did not own a camera. I had an interest in photography. Later, I needed a camera to photograph my

---

4   Testimony on October 16, 2000 in Johannesburg. See: https://sabctrc.saha.org.za/
     originals/amntrans/2000/201016jh.htm

art portfolio when applying to the university. I eventually became the Head of Fine Art Photography at the same university, several years later.

The Stamps

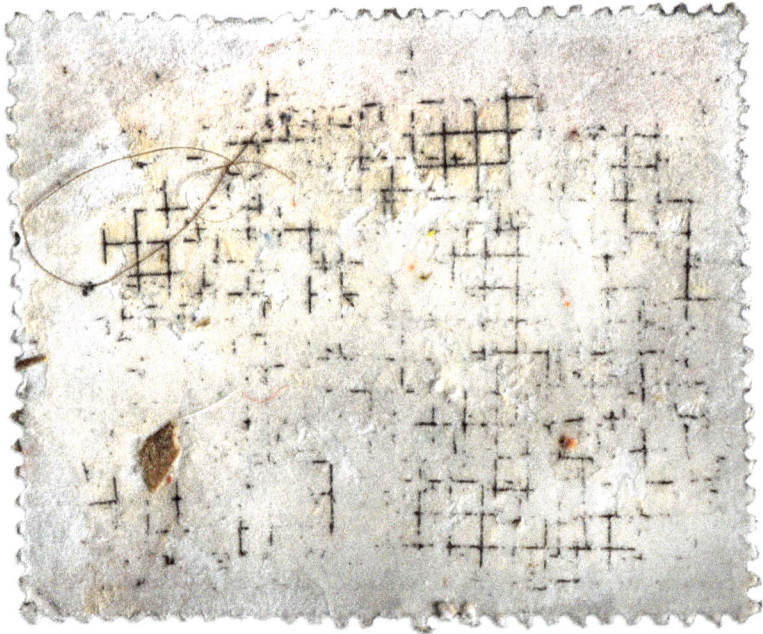

Fig. 2.2 The back of a large format Mozambican stamp (1980) on which a matrix of adhesive gauze, paper fibres and a human hair are attached. Photo: Brent Meistre (Belfast, 2022).

My father had a habit of bringing stamps home for me from the office. Two to three times a year he would arrive with a bundle of stamps in his briefcase. Later, I was to read that this was common practice. When Security Branch units intercepted mail under the Post Office Act (1958, Act No. 44) and destroyed letters 'each morning in a furnace [...] SB members asked the officer responsible to save the stamps for their collections' (Erasmus 2021, image caption, n.p.).

Some of the stamps I have were carefully clipped out from the envelope's body; others torn from the postcard or parcel packaging, carrying with them the small traces of the vessel with which they had been couriered. A creative and artistic child, I would pore over the exotic images, designs and colours of the various stamps from all over the world. As I became more aware of my father's work, and of the workings of his tightly knit group of colleagues, I eventually figured out that they had come from mail that had been intercepted. Hundreds of letters, postcards and parcels never reached their intended destination. The closer I looked, the more I became intrigued. There was another story to these stamps: the small traces of their origins, destination and content were hinted at, but the promise of a safe passage would now never materialise. As with many instances in our upbringing, what appeared as something inane and banal like a stamp collection, harboured other, cynical layers.

I was told at some point that secret, coded messages and microfilm were hidden under stamps. Of this, I am uncertain. However, after hearing that, the stamps took on another level of intrigue. I imagined the sender in a far-off country: the 'terrorist' licking the stamp, the trace of their saliva, even small hairs visible, such as in Fig. 2.2. How bodily and personal it was, their DNA preserved in situ. I imagined what might have been in the parcel or the message conveyed in the letter. How it smelt, the bleed of the ink on the thin crisp airmail paper. The pressure exerted by a drying-out Bic pen. They seemed imbued with a certain melancholic residue. The intended receivers were photographed and on display, on the office whiteboard. These stamps, and the intimate knowledge they carried, which I had handled as a child with interest as tiny artefacts from the small, exceptional world of my upbringing, later became a burden as I realised they were some of the last remaining pieces.

The Security Police destroyed almost all its confiscated items and official records in the early 1990s. This was reportedly the result of a verbal order to carry out such a 'massive and systematic destruction of records' that it necessitated subcontracting large paper recycling companies, such as Nampak and Sappi (Dlamini, 2020, pp. 14–15). Prior agents intimate that such destruction was a norm:

> letters to Botha calling for the release of Mandela or displaying any other anti-South African sentiment had always been summarily destroyed. I once saw a consignment of thousands of Christmas cards, written by Norwegian children to Nelson Mandela, being destroyed. It was one

of the rare times when I was saddened—each one had a hand-drawn picture and a Christian message from a child who sincerely believed that Mandela would receive and get to read their message. (Erasmus, 2021, p. 162)

During Apartheid, stamps and letters functioned as a central means of covert communication, dissemination and distribution of knowledge and information. An underground activist in the country shared how 'I longed for communications from my contacts in exile. Their brief coded messages, written in "invisible ink", were a lifeline, filling me with new resolve' (Suttner, 2011, pp. 14–15). The use of code and encryption was common in communicating between activists within South Africa and those in exile. There were many variations on these coded messages, which were pre-determined by those communicating. Often terms and phrases in letters referenced a parent or family member (see Fig. 2.3). When they were described as being ill, for example, it may have been to indicate issues within the organisation or the leadership. A former activist described how 'messages started to come through which caused us great concern; "mother is unwell", "mother is very ill" all of which suggested we had a serious problem. We had no idea what it was. Had we been betrayed? Had we been discovered?' (Newland, 2012, p. 162).

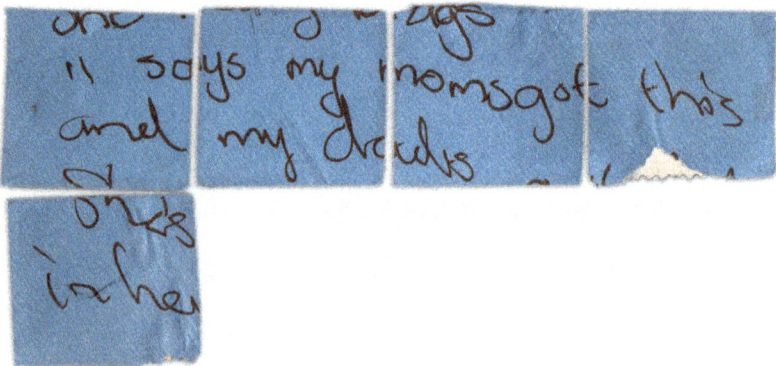

Fig. 2.3 The back of five small Finnish stamps from 1986 that were cut out. Rearranged by the author. Note the reference to 'mom' and 'dad'. Photo: Brent Meistre (Belfast, 2022).

The postal system was used extensively by anti-Apartheid activists to distribute information such as pamphlets, newsletters and small publications locally and internationally. Excerpts of Suttner's (2011) autobiography describe this.

> *I had been preparing a special edition of 10, 000 copies of the underground pamphlet Vukani!/ Awake!, including a translation of the Freedom Charter into Zulu. Each copy of the newspaper had to be painstakingly produced then inserted into an envelope. And each of these had to be stamped and secretly posted.* (Suttner, 2011, p. 1)
>
> I gradually came to know the whereabouts of just about every postbox [...] I used a variety of envelopes, varied the typing of addresses and staggered the times that I posted the envelopes, to make it harder for the pamphlets to be discovered [by the SB]. (Suttner, 2011, p. 17)

A large amount of the intercepted mail would have come from the movement in the United Kingdom, and faith and community pressure groups in the United States of America (see Fig. 2.4), especially during such drives as the letter writing campaigns of Amnesty International. Much of these targeted the release of political activists, some of whom were students and academics detained without trial. These letters were sometimes mailed directly to local police stations.

Some stamps would have concealed information. The larger sized stamps would have drawn the Security Police's attention, where double-sided adhesive gauze attached flat items such as microfilm or a small message. The stamp (Fig. 2.2) from Mozambique is either such an example or may have been manufactured for police training purposes to illustrate this covert technique. The positioning of the stamp on the envelope—askew, slightly rotated, placed on the left-hand side or even upside down—may have been a means of conveying a particular message. Schechter (2012, p. 55) is one activist who wrote about how 'if anything happened, I was told to send a postcard to a mail drop in London with the stamp upside down'.

In my small stamp collection, a large proportion of the stamps from the United States appear to be of intentionally chosen imagery. Some seem subversive gestures and others pointed protests. Cognisant that the mail would likely be viewed or intercepted by those in the state system, much of the imagery celebrates democracy, freedom, liberty, justice and Black heritage as in Fig. 2.4.

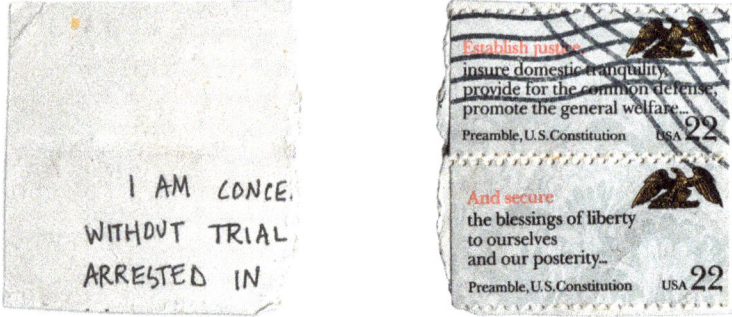

Fig. 2.4 The back of a postcard stamp with the hand-written words 'arrested' and 'without trial', and the front of a 1987 stamp celebrating 'welfare' and 'dignity' in the democratic constitution of the USA. Photo: Brent Meistre (Belfast, 2022).

A stamp from the UK (Fig. 2.5) illustrates a St John's Ambulance worker treating an injured woman lying in the road. Alongside the ambulance and above her head on the pavement lie protest banners. She is dressed in a bold black and white dress with matching earrings—pointed iconography of the Anti-Apartheid Movement (AAM) in the UK. Although this stamp might directly refer to the AAM call to boycott the South African Cricket tour, it also references the UK-based anti-Vietnam War protests of 1965. There seems an intentionally implied intersectionality in the stamp choice, its visual representation and the cropped words and sentences appearing on the underside: 'organisation' and 'detention'.

Fig. 2.5 The front and back of a UK 1987 stamp with reference to Anti-Apartheid Movement (AAM) protests. Photo: Brent Meistre (Belfast, 2022).

Most of the stamps are almost mute. They do not or cannot say anything. I cannot be certain whether all the stamps in my collection were from intercepted mail. Some, more than likely, were also from official mail between my father's counterparts in other countries. The Netherlands, Sweden, Spain, Austria, Poland, France, Canada, Belgium, Norway, Finland, Denmark, Romania, Japan, Australia, Germany, Israel, Lesotho, Namibia, Botswana, Zimbabwe, Kenya, Rwanda, Madagascar, Cyprus. They hint at the vastness of this global analogue network of tactile knowledge interchange, monitoring, and surveillance. In a world before email, messaging apps and other digital technologies, it was through such tangible, hand-held traces that the machinations of power were made present.

In the public domain, it was on the book and the published word that the colonial and later Apartheid government focused much of its power, surveillance and control. Through the Suppression of Communism Act (1950) and the later Internal Security Act (1982), thousands of publications, newspapers, journals, books and individuals were banned. It is to these artefacts in my collection that I now turn my focus.

The Books

Returning to the photograph in Fig. 2.1, opposite the room depicted was my father's office. It was sparse and austere, typical of the aesthetic of the Apartheid government administration at the time. In the middle of the hand-polished floor were two blue vinyl-covered chairs facing a large desk with two telephones and a photograph of my mother, my sister and me. Against the wall, on a separate small desk, was a fax machine with a large encoder to scramble messages. Near the heavily barred window that overlooked a shopping arcade was a locked glass-door cabinet that housed books. This was always the focus of my attention.

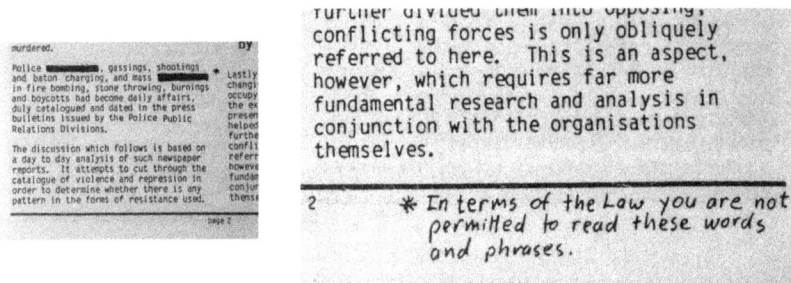

murdered.   by

Police ███████, gassings, shootings
and baton charging, and mass ███████ ★ Lastly
in fire bombing, stone throwing, burnings   change
and boycotts had become daily affairs,   occupy
duly catalogued and dated in the press   the ex
bulletins issued by the Police Public   presen
Relations Divisions.   helped
                                             furthe
The discussion which follows is based on   confli
a day to day analysis of such newspaper   referr
reports. It attempts to cut through the   howeve
catalogue of violence and repression in   fundan
order to determine whether there is any   conjun
pattern in the forms of resistance used.   thense

                                    page 2

rurther urviueu them into opposing,
conflicting forces is only obliquely
referred to here. This is an aspect,
however, which requires far more
fundamental research and analysis in
conjunction with the organisations
themselves.

2   ✳ In terms of the Law you are not
             permitted to read these words
             and phrases.

Fig. 2.6 Some publications explicitly indicated censorship by the state. These two images of the same page show redacted words from *The Democrat* (1986) with the editor's handwritten explanation on the right. Photos: Brent Meistre (Belfast, 2022).

As a child, I would wait for my father in his office and stare at the books. Many of them had blank, cracked or cellotaped spines. I could not make out what the titles were, slowly panning to get a glimpse of a word, a letter, a small clue. It was fruitless, but I was fascinated. We did not have many books, or even a bookshelf, at home.

After waiting for my father for some time in his office one day, I asked about the books and specifically pointed at one of the small books. Its top half had been slightly nudged forward and askew, revealing what looked like a mechanical object. This time he went to his desk drawer, unlocking it to get another set of keys to unlock the cabinet. He told me the books were taken from 'the terrorists'. He pulled out the small book I was interested in. It had an image of three cameras on the front. He said it was a camera manual, but then slowly turned the cover to reveal that its contents were a disguised communist publication smuggled into South Africa.[5] As a young boy interested in photography and books, this real world of secrets, spies and cameras was thrilling. But I had to keep this to myself.

Over thirty-five years later, I encountered this book cover in July 2022. I knew exactly what it was and purchased it via a website in South Africa. What was titled *The Camera Book: Everything You Need to Know about Choosing and Using Photographic Equipment to Create Better Pictures*

---

5   This was very much like a version of the Russian Somizdat, where a clandestine handmade version of the original was circulated underground whilst the Tamizdat was the foreign or publication from abroad (see Meret, 1966, p. 5).

was in fact *The African Communist: Journal of the South Africa Communist Party* (Fig. 2.7), published in London and printed in East Germany. The cover of the European version is completely different. However, for distribution in South Africa, it was cleverly changed to a very popular camera book that would draw no particular attention in the mid-1980s. Other journal issues of *The African Communist* were similarly changed, with covers such as *Landscape Gardening: Flowers and Fruits of Fields and Hedgerow*. Suttner (2011, p. 11) describes how:

> A limited number of people received *The African Communist*, the official organ of the SACP; and *Sechaba*, the official organ of the ANC, which were both produced outside of the country and posted into South Africa. Sometimes illicit publications had fake covers, or fake titles [...] many of these publications were intercepted by the police.

This was another instance of where my interest in photography and books became entangled with the strange parallel and contrary relationship between the image and text as displaced signifiers, similar to the relationship between the images of the stamp and the texts they concealed on their back.

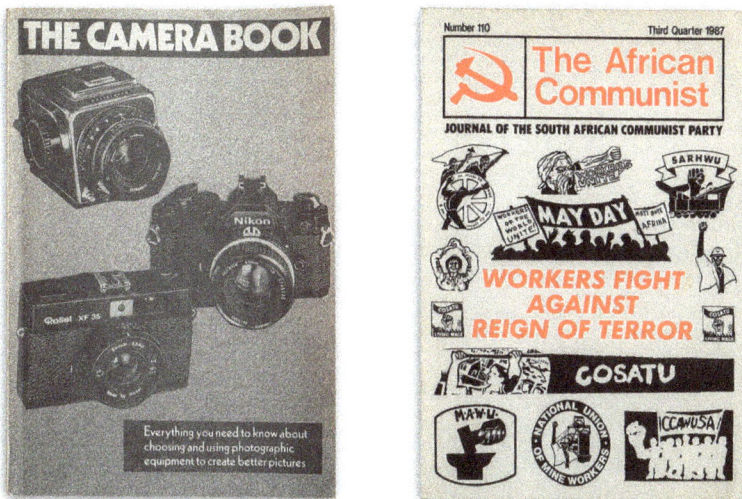

Fig. 2.7 Two versions of the same edition of *The African Communist* (1987). The left version with disguised cover for distribution in South Africa and the other for distribution elsewhere. Photo: Brent Meistre (Belfast, 2022).

The book cabinet also contained political material that had been seized from academics and political activists either during house searches, arrests or by intercepting their post. Warman (2014, p. 53) described what this involved for one such academic citizen at Rhodes University, 'After Guy [Berger] admitted to the police the location of a trunk containing his banned books, he was made to spend a night inventorying the contents and explaining the origins of each item'. The books in the cabinet were kept for court proceedings and some had related numbers inscribed on their front. Some were read or studied for training purposes by members of the Security Police. After becoming an officer, my father told me that his political training included having to study various political ideologies and concepts. What struck me at the time was that he was also trained on how to use paper from a book or newspaper as a lethal weapon.

There were VHS cassettes in the cabinet of banned films, documentaries and foreign TV programs, and also recordings seized from journalists. There were also videos the Security Police had made themselves when recording protests and political funerals filmed with a JVC video camera. It was the same video camera I experimented with as a young boy learning to make my first stop-motion animations. Once when I gripped it and put it on my shoulder and leaned towards the eyepiece, I could smell smoke and gun powder residue. I also discovered a large brown spent rubber bullet cartridge in the bag. The camera and a gun had been aiming at the same targets.

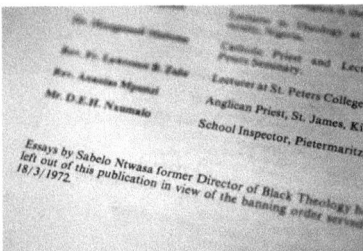

Fig. 2.8 Notes on contributors in Black Theology (1972) indicating banned authors. Photo: Brent Meistre (Belfast, 2022).

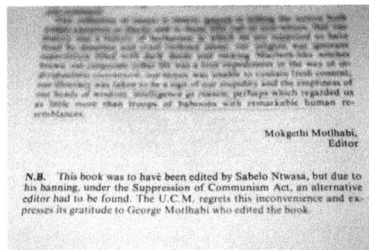

Fig. 2.9 Editor's note on the Foreword to Black Theology. Photo: Brent Meistre (Belfast, 2022).

Over the months and years that proceeded that first encounter with the small book, I would ask my father when I visited his office if I could look at more of the books. At some point he began bringing them home, mostly concerning theology and education. A book on Rev Trevor Huddleston, one by author Alan Paton, a small book of poetry by B. D. Lalla, an isiXhosa phrasebook and Henry Miller's *Tropic of Cancer*. Like the stamps, I carefully handled and studied the books. Their dust jackets and bindings had been removed, yet they had unique traces, markings, under-linings, annotations and even names inscribed in them. They were well handled, well read, in various stages of undoing,[6] crudely taped together and their pages tanned. The traces in the folds, the creases, the deep crooks and page edges evoked the bodily absence of their readers. I had a growing sense of an empathic loss associated with these book objects and those who handled them. You could feel the reader in and on the books—the traces were as tangible as the urgency of the texts, of the injustices described and suffering endured.

In some of the books, the authors, editors and publishers are not named, and those who are use pseudonyms. Banned persons could not be published or quoted. There were also certain pre-determined words that could not be published, which would be censored by being blacked-out or struck through in bold (see Fig. 2.6). As discussed, these came to function as a subversive tool to highlight the draconian Apartheid regulations to the general public. One such strategy was used by the banned editor of *The Daily Dispatch*, Donald Woods, who later fled South Africa. In that publication, large sections—and at times the entire page of letters to the editor—were published blocked out in black ink. A song from 1986 by singer and ANC political activist, Jennifer Ferguson, reveals the impact of these bans and sums up the sentiment during this time:

---

6   It is likely some of the books would have been unbound and deconstructed by
     the SB searching for concealed items. The head of the Dutch Anti-Apartheid
     Movement, Connie Braam, explained that during the ANC's Operation Vula
     infiltrating weapons and banned persons back into South Africa, 'computers
     would be chosen as the communications system, so floppy disks with the new
     codes would have to be taken in [to South Africa] [...] The cardboard of the back
     cover [of the book] was split and partly hollowed out. A sort of envelope was the
     result, just big enough to hold a passport' (Braam, 2004, pp. 98–99).

And you don't know any answers
to any questions anymore
The TV news is lying
And the newspaper's got big white gaps
And fat black lines
And walking in the streets of Jo'burg
No-one looks eye to eye anymore...
... anymore... ('Ashley's Song')

Counter-intelligence was a key function of the state sections of the earlier Bureau of State Security (BOSS) and later National Intelligence, the Security Police and later Stratcom (Strategic Communications). Through the placement and recruitment of editors, journalists and informers in press rooms and publishing houses, the state controlled and monitored publishing in South Africa. In some cases, it was openly known who was checking and reporting in-house. This applied locally:

> Grocotts' Mail, the Grahamstown printers, have been told by [Security] branch not to print ECC material. They refused to print our WJP poster at the last moment, which indicates that they are complying. (End Conscription Campaign, n.d.b, p. 2)

Through the government's Department of Information and other front organisations, the Apartheid state also produced many counter-intelligence publications and other forms of propaganda such as films and television documentaries, posters, pamphlet and sticker campaigns to counter critique of the South African government. Notorious Security Policeman and member of Stratcom, Paul Erasmus (2021, p. 87), described that:

> Senior figures in the John Major government were apparently startled to read a Stratcom gem: an 'ANC' booklet entitled Negotiations and the Way Forward. Having helped compile it, I faxed a copy to Ward [Harvey] in Glasgow, before mailing hundreds for him to channel to all and sundry.

Some of the publications were literally produced tit-for-tat with publishing release timeframes parallel to those of international publications and organisations they were monitoring. For instance, in early 1978 Amnesty International published a report on *Political Imprisonment in South Africa*, and by March the Bureau for Information had published a comprehensive rebuttal contesting the report, titled

Amnesty for Terrorism. Another example was the widely distributed *The Rape of Peace* published by the Veterans (for Victory) Association of South Africa, a government front organisation attacking the End Conscription Campaign (ECC) and conscientious objectors. At a local level in Grahamstown, smear campaigns were launched against individual student activists by the local Security Branch. These were part of projects aimed at 'hostile organisations', such as Babushka, 'which used campus-based front organisations to counter bodies such as the Black Students Society (BSS) and the UDF' (Erasmus, 2021, p. 191). A report by the End Conscription Campaign (n.d.a, p. 2) documented that:

> Approximately ten smear pamphlets of various descriptions have been distributed at Rhodes University and in town. These included attempts to link ECC with the Soviet Union or with 'necklacing'[7] and violent death, as well as personal attacks on individual ECC members. In one instance, a pamphlet accused an ECC member of having been convicted of shoplifting.

Many of the banned books in the collection were published in the UK, with printing done in the UK, Zambia and East Germany. Most research and publishing was undertaken by the International Defence and Aid Fund, Amnesty International, United Nations and the Anti-Apartheid Movement. While it was illegal to import, distribute, possess or quote banned books or persons, some banned books were kept for research purposes in libraries. In time, librarians within and beyond the university became agents of the state by reporting who accessed such books.

> In the case of 'possession prohibited' and internal security bannings, a library has to seek permission to hold each title. Such titles may only be used for study purposes after individual application to the Directorate of Publications or Department of Justice as appropriate, a catch 22 situation which requires the motivation to use the book which by definition has yet to be seen by the user. (Merret, 1966, p. 5)

Despite banning and censorship laws, a number of South African publishers managed to circulate books in the public domain that

---

7   Necklacing is a South African term for the practice of placing a car tyre doused with petrol around the neck of a person, like a necklace, which is then set alight. During Apartheid it was a brutal punishment usually reserved for *impimpi*, a slang word for 'traitor' or 'informer'.

were critical of the Apartheid government. The most prolific and political of these were Ravan Press and the Black-owned Skotaville Publishers, Lovedale Press, Bateleur, Ad Donker and Taurus. The editors of Taurus did the typesetting themselves for secrecy and to avoid censors, distributing books through mailing lists without prior notice of publication. The excerpt below is an instance of how academics circumvented publishing laws.

> Three lecturers in Afrikaans literature at the University of the Witwatersrand—Ampie Coetzee, Ernst Lindenberg and John Miles—decided to publish the novel, which was about a relationship between a coloured man and a white woman (a forbidden relationship in South Africa). The whole publication process was kept secret, and only 1000 copies were printed—and sold out within two weeks. It was a delicate matter of timing and secrecy. (Coetzee, 1984, p. 32)

Similar to the clandestine versions seen in examples such as *The Camera Book*/*The African Communist*, writers, artists and musicians used alternative ways of inserting texts-within-texts, songs-within-songs and films-with-films. Academic and writer Nadine Gordimer's *Burger's Daughter* (1979) contained a banned pamphlet, and Andre Brink's *Rumours of Rain* (1978) reproduced a large section of Bram Fischer's court testimony (Merret, 2008, p. 5). A similar strategy was used in the film *Shotdown* (Hannay and Worsdale, 1987) about a secret agent investigating a subversive theatre group, which was then banned. Inserted within the film were both banned theatre pieces and the banned film *De Voortrekkers* (1985) written by Matthew Krouse. Similarly, Bright Blue's song 'Weeping' (1987), about brutality during the State of Emergency, subversively includes the musical refrain of the banned ANC anthem *'Nkosi Sikelel iAfrika'* [God Save Africa].

Despite the subversive ways academics and artists resisted the Apartheid regime, the impact on the greater scholarly and academic project was all encompassing. Internally, the suppression and banning of Black intellectuals and their texts intentionally silenced the Black experience within the country, and thereby reduced possibilities of mutual solidarity and understanding between white and Black academics. The system of censorship 'seeks to bury certain ideas and even to ensure that people are forgotten, as in the case of banned persons' (Merret, 2008, p. 4). One example of the extreme repression meted out on academics was the state's treatment of Neville Alexander, which was documented in an Amnesty International (1978, p. 89) report:

> The 10-year prison sentence imposed on Alexander by a court of law was thus augmented by an additional punishment imposed administratively by the Minster of Justice. A former university lecturer with a doctorate in German Literature, Neville Alexander is prohibited from entering any educational institution in South Africa under the terms of his present banning order.

The overt reality and impact on the central functioning of education, research, publishing and critical discourse between students and academics was described by the SACP member and academic Raymond Suttner, who himself was jailed:

> I was already a very successful young academic, very ambitious, publishing like mad and obviously 'making it'. But all this was suddenly interrupted - by my presentation of a thesis that contained extracts from the writings of the eminent banned author, Jack Simons. I was told to withdraw the quotations, as including them contravened the law. (Suttner, 2011, p. 6)

Academics in South Africa were also isolated from global educational and research networks, often being denied passports to attend conferences. If they did attend, they often felt at an intellectual deficit due to isolation and sanctions. Many intellectuals fled South Africa and researched from exile.

ANC Speaks (Authorship withheld, 1977) was the first overtly political book that my father brought home (Fig. 2.10). It had been cellotaped together where it had been halved like an animal's ribcage. The tape that held it once together was peeling off, having bleached the paper in a stitch-like pattern. Coincidentally or intentionally, the book was split open on a chapter by an unnamed author identified as Umkhonto Guerrilla, 'V.M.'. The pseudonym '*Umkhonto*' is derived from the name of armed wing of the ANC '*Mkhonto We Sizwe*' [Spear of the Nation]. The chapter describes the Luthuli Detachment infiltration from Zambia into the then Rhodesia, en route to various parts of South Africa to set up armed resistance cells. This military detachment was one of the first to cross into South Africa comprised of trained guerrilla fighters, signalling the beginning of the ANC's full military engagement with the Rhodesian and South African states. I recently discovered that my father would have been on the other side of the Zambesi River patrolling the border as a young man of nineteen years old. He was sent as part of the South African Police who were secretively deployed as a counter-insurgency force. The Luthuli Detachment of the ANC had attacked and wounded a number of the South African policemen, as described in that book. This event would have been a bitter wound and embarrassment, with the book reminding my father and his colleagues of that time. The South African Communist leader Chris Hani, who led the first Luthuli Detachment campaign into Rhodesia, was later assassinated in the lead-up to the first democratic elections in South Africa.

Fig. 2.10 Pages 118–119 of the banned *ANC Speaks* (Authorship withheld, 1977), with cellotape traces where the book was torn in two halves. Photo: Brent Meistre (Belfast, 2022).

An unintended outcome of these books being brought home to me by my father was that they did not get destroyed when the Security Police erased its documents and materials in anticipation of its disbandment. These books remain today as a disparate collection in a fugitive archive. Another outcome was that I became politicised, and deeply concerned about the death penalty and the compulsory military conscription that I would soon be facing. A withdrawn and shy child, I was by no means an activist, but I joined a small group at high school who refused to engage with compulsory military cadets. Later, when I was sixteen, I signed an Amnesty International petition at an End Conscription Campaign meeting at the University. My father found out from an informer and was angry. However, as these were the dying days of Apartheid and my father had already known for almost a year prior of Mandela's inevitable release, he chose only to warn me about 'the Communists' and wrote to my school to request they respect my right to object.

Another book brought home to me was Nelson Mandela's *The Struggle is My Life* (1978), which contained all his speeches, writings and documents. The book had an aura all of its own (Fig. 2.11). Mandela had been serving a life-sentence on Robben Island with many other political prisoners. According to state legislation at the time, his picture could not be published and he could not be visually represented in the media in any form. This book included his portrait.

For banned organisations, the most vital function of the printed book was the dissemination of information, through reproduction or copying and distribution. Many of those recruited into the Anti-Apartheid Movement in the UK were involved in distributing texts to South Africa. These were hidden in various ways, such as by Communist Party dock workers in cargo ships, and by Ford and Vauxhall factory workers beneath and within the seats of vehicles being exported to South Africa from the UK (O'Hara, 2012). Two of the books my father brought home requested that the reader pass them on. One tiny booklet with news reports on censored events stated in bold on the back cover, 'when you have read *Assagai*, please pass to a friend'. The other was Mao Tse Tung's *Aspects of Guerrilla Warfare*.

A key aspect of this distribution was the dissemination of visual material, particularly photographs and imagery of political leaders who could not be published or displayed publicly. Many would not have been seen by the South African public for a number of years, or even decades, as they were either in exile or serving lengthy prison sentences. In *The Struggle is My Life*, the first image in the illustration section is of Nelson Mandela himself (see Fig. 2.11). Illuminated by a studio flash, the youthful face of the leader is full of vitality, strength and a sense of hope. The page opposite it was designed to be left blank. Yet that page in this book is not blank. Darkened print ink had also transferred onto the opposite page, a ghostly imprint of him, covered with a patina of those adoring him, before the book was confiscated, and then later those who sought to harm him. It is layered with the traces and subtle markings of hands and fingers having gripped, held, touched and braced the page— as readers pressed down to look closely at the leader. It had probably been photocopied or re-photographed many times, with the cracked book's spine a deep fissure marking those criminalised acts, almost a way of undoing the book binding to reveal its nature.

Fig. 2.11 The first page of the illustrations section of Nelson Mandela's (1978) book *The Struggle is My Life*. Photo: Brent Meistre (Belfast, 2022).

These two book pages bring me back to the whiteboard shown in the first photograph (Fig. 2.1). Beneath the photographs of the faces on the board is the whiteboard with layered traces and temporal handwritten blue, black and red ink marker gestures, some thinly drying out and others in fresh bold caps. The nature of the whiteboard and its primary function is that of inscription, over-inscription and erasure. As such, it mirrors the memory processes of learning, knowing and forgetting— much like the 'mystic writing pad' where traces of markings remain, which Freud uses as a metaphor for residues in the subconscious. In a university class, even when the whole central area of a whiteboard is wiped clean, inevitably there are always traces of those who have written before, some of which seem impossible to remove. The margins of such boards harbour half-words partially erased, faint or washed out. The readings of these textual fragments crisscross and layer each other as if they are a form of exiled narratives and incomplete stories; however, what may be read into the photographed whiteboard is its overlapping of 'training', studying and targeting, that reveals disappearing and erasure as far more ominous.

Conclusion

This chapter offers one limited perspective from a person who had a partial look into the clandestine world of spying and monitoring that played out in a university town. It offers reflections of some of the experiences of slippage between my father's work-world and my coming of age during a tumultuous, destabilised period in a microcosm of global politics. More direct accounts are accessible in the autobiographies and biographies that have recently emerged about white left-wing academics, activists, students and spies during this time period. Those specifically about Rhodes University and the town of Grahamstown [Makhanda] have included Janice Warman's *The Class of '79* (2014), Bridget Hilton-Barber's *Student, Comrade, Prisoner, Spy* (2016), Olivia Forsyth's *Agent 407* (2015), Rosemary Smith's *Swimming with Cobras* (2011) and Jonathan Ancer's *Betrayal: The Secret Lives of Apartheid Spies* (2019).

To ground my personal archive and memories, I required openness to the peripheral murky terrain of knowing and not knowing. Traces and remnants on the objects in my possession, the stamps and confiscated books, sometimes only point to certain events during this time period. As textual and visual sources, they harbour complex layers. In the past, they acted as vehicles for the exchange and dissemination of furtive information and knowledge between academic citizens and activists, at a time when the state controlled, manipulated and contained the flow of knowledge, ideas and information. Such books were also read by the Security Police and studied for political examinations at Police College (PolKol).

In a number of additional ways of doing and discourses, state intelligence is not unlike the academy. Investigating, evidence, sources, questioning and interrogating, observing, monitoring and surveilling are words used comfortably in both contexts. Similar to research practices, in the intelligence world there are established processes of 'scrubbing of identifiers' to protect sources, informants and 'assets'. In South Africa, this was regulated by the Official Secrets Act which Security Police officers signed during Apartheid, and which continues to restrict what can be made public knowledge. It is unclear what the current state security relation is with public universities about their academic citizens.

As objects, these stamps and books do not provide a whole picture or narrative. Even the words on them have been blocked out, erased, truncated. This is frustrating because they have importance as some of the few remnants of the dangerous unknown during a dark, violent time in South African history. I have attempted a close re-investigation and re-observation of the small traces of evidence of some of these histories as a form of witness. This has involved researching and revealing the small narratives to which they hint, while acknowledging what is beyond my own certainty or knowing.

The representation I have constructed within this chapter has required me to work against the methodological instinct embedded in my artistic visual practice which I have protected from logic, scrutiny and capture. The many decoys and deflections I have used in that work were in an attempt to remove myself, as neither the central protagonist/antagonist nor victim/perpetrator from which the central figure of 'the stranger' character evolved. While that phantom figure moves around seemingly without agency, the films hint that he may harbour knowledge and that there may be the potential of him 'telling'. However, in my performance, this is negated by his muteness and tongue-tied mumblings. While such creative arts research seemingly operates very differently to the narrative realism of this chapter, both recognise the impossibility of the subject in the no-persons land of only ever being able to evoke the past.

Acknowledgements

I would like to thank Dina Belluigi for her belief and guidance in the work. I am also very grateful for the grace and generosity of former students, lecturers, political activists and police officers who provided clarity for this undertaking. This chapter is dedicated to all those whose personal lives and careers were stunted, upended, and destroyed in numerous unseen ways. I am humbled by the many academics and cultural workers who resisted Apartheid and its machinations, inspiring critical thought and bringing change.

Bibliography

Amnesty International. (1978). *Political Imprisonment in South Africa: An Amnesty International Report.* Amnesty International Publications.

Ancer, J. (2019). *Betrayal: The Secret Lives of Apartheid Spies.* Tafelberg.

Arendt, H. (1963). *Eichmann in Jerusalem: A Report on the Banality of Evil.* Faber & Faber.

Authorship withheld. (1977). *ANC Speaks: Documents and Statements of the African National Congress 1955–1976.* African National Congress.

Baer, U. (2000). *Remnants of Song: Trauma and the Experience of Modernity in Charles Baudelaire and Paul Celan.* Stanford University Press, https://doi.org/10.1093/fmls/38.1.99-d

Bell, T., and Buhle Ntsebeza, D. (2003). *Unfinished Business: South Africa, Apartheid, and Truth.* Verso.

Braam, C. (2004). *Operation Vula.* Jacana.

Breytenbach, B. (1984). *The True Confessions of an Albino Terrorist.* Taurus.

Brooks, P. (1994). *Psychoanalysis and Storytelling.* Blackwell.

Coetzee, A. (1984). Tauras Publishers. *Index on Censorship, 13*(5), 32, https://doi.org/10.1080/03064228408533784

Dlamini, J. (2020). The Terrorist Album: Apartheid's Insurgents, Collaborators, and the Security Police. Harvard University Press, https://doi.org/10.4159/9780674245587

Editor withheld. (1963). *Assagai* [Magazine], no. 3. Publisher withheld.

End Conscription Campaign. (n.d.a). *Grahamstown and Rhodes University Internal Work Report (1985–1988).* University of the Witwatersrand, Historical Papers Research Archive, Collection Number: AG1977. http://historicalpapers-atom.wits.ac.za/uploads/r/historical-papers-research-archive-library-university-of-witwatersrand/0/0/d/00d386e97df9ab4efdd1 3325426b3df73d3f95dd6687b24b87ec4819c86ae10e/AG1977-A22-3-001-jpeg. pdf

—(n.d.b). *Rhodes University Internal Work Report (1985–1988)*. University of the Witwatersrand, Historical Papers Research Archive, Collection Number: AG1977. http://researcharchives.wits.ac.za/uploads/r/historical-papers-research-archive-library-university-of-witwatersrand/b/b/1/bb114a2207fa92e6a823bf485b53f3605202fe5a8acb772c29f94c9c062b5057/AG1977-B6-1-11-001-jpeg.pdf

Erasmus, P. (2021). *Confessions of a Stratcom Hitman*. Jacana.

Ferguson, J., and Simon, B. (1986). Ashley's Song [Song]. On *Hand Around My Heart* [Album]. Shifty Music.

Forsyth, O. (2015). *Agent 407: A South African Spy Breaks Her Silence*. Jonathan Ball.

Hannay, D. (Producer), and Worsdale, A. (Director). (1987). *Shotdown* [Motion picture]. David Hannay Productions.

Heyman, D. (1987). Weeping [Song]. On *The Rising Tide* [Album]. EMI Records.

Greyling, S. (2007). *Rhodes University during the Segregation and Apartheid Years, 1933 to 1990* [Unpublished Master's Thesis, Rhodes University]. http://hdl.handle.net/10962/d1002397

Inverson, M. (2017). *Photography, Trace and Trauma*. The University of Chicago Press.

Keable, K (Ed.) (2012). *London Recruits: The Secret War against Apartheid*. Merlin Press.

Keniston, B. (2013). *Choosing To Be Free: The Life Story of Rich Turner*. Jacana.

Mandela, N. (1978). *The Struggle Is My Life*. International Defence and Aid Fund for Southern Africa.

Merret, C. (1966). Political Censorship in South Africa: Aims and Consequences (pp. 3–6). https://www.sahistory.org.za/archive/political-censorship-south-africa-aims-and-consequences

Missing. (1986, August). *RHODEO*, 3.

Motlhabi, M. (Ed.) (1972). *Black Theology*. Black Theology Project of the University Christian Movement.

Nathan, J. (Producer), and Krouse, M. (Director). (1985). *De Voortrekker* [Motion picture] Matthew Krouse.

Newland, B. (2012). Bob Newland. In K. Keable (Ed.), *London Recruits: The Secret War against Apartheid* (pp. 154–166). Merlin Press.

O'Hara, R. (2012). Roger O'Hara. In K. Keable (Ed.), *London Recruits: The Secret War against Apartheid* (pp. 116–121). Merlin Press.

Sanders, J. (2006). *Apartheid's Friends: The Rise and Fall of South Africa's Secret Service*. John Murray Publishers.

Schecter, D. (2012). Danny Schechter. In K. Keable (Ed.), *London Recruits: The Secret War against Apartheid* (pp. 51–66). Merlin Press.

Schwab, G. (2010). *Haunting Legacies: Violent Histories and Transgenerational Trauma*. Columbia University Press.

Sedgwick, E., and Frank, A. (Eds). (1995). *Shame and its Sisters: A Silvan Tomkins Reader*. Duke University Press.

South African Department of Information Publications Division. (1978). *Amnesty for Terrorism*. Simondium Publishers on behalf of the Department of Information.

Streek, B. (2005). Skeletons in the Rhodes Cupboard: What Should Be Done about Them? *African Sociological Review, 9*(1), 161–166.

Suttner, R. (2011). *Inside Apartheid's Prison*. University of Natal.

The African Communist. (1987, Third Quarter, Number 110). *Journal of the South African Communist Party*. Inkululeko Publications.

The Camera Book; Everything You Need to Know about Choosing and Using Photographic Equipment to Create Better Pictures. (1987, Third Quarter, Number 110). South African Communist Party.

The Democrat. (1986, Autumn, Vol. 2, No. 1). Grahamstown Democratic Action Committee.

Tomaselli, K., and Lowe, E. (1991). *The Alternative Press in South Africa*. Anthropos Publishers.

Veterans (For Victory) Association. (1988). *The Rape of Peace*. Veterans (for Victory) Association of South Africa.

Warman, J. (2014). *The Class of '79*. Jacana.

Weibel, P. (2009). Repression and Representation: The RAF in German Postwar Art. In S. Barron and S. Eckmann (Eds), *Art of Two Germanys/Cold War Cultures* (pp. 256–259). Abrams.

3. Academics of Post-war Sri Lanka: Traces of Experiences and Impact

Hemalatha Pradeepkumar

Introduction

Elusive traces of stories of violence should be sought when attempting to comprehend conflict-affected contexts. Discrimination in educational policies and practices is frequently observed, and its persistence has negative consequences for the overall goals of education, which are to promote knowledge and learning for the benefit of society. Discrimination undermines these public goods by creating tensions and conflicts among different interest groups within the educational system. In many countries, such unrest subsequently becomes the root cause of conflict between those interest groups where ethnicity is politicised. Intrastate conflict, bounded by the social constructs of ethnicity and social institutions of religion, is one of the most common forms of war. It was central to the recent conflicts besetting Sri Lanka, to which this chapter refers.

Sri Lanka's Higher Education sector, especially institutions which were based within conflict zones, were severely impacted by ethnic-based armed conflict up until 2009. Despite this commonly known reality, there has been little exploration of this period and its post-conflict legacies. In this chapter, as a Sri Lankan in diaspora, I explore the little available grey literature and academic publications from 1960 to 2022, to seek insights into academics' experiences and their positioning within Sri Lanka universities. This is in an attempt to chart and to reflect on the struggles of hegemonic and counter-hegemonic powers post-conflict.

©2025 Hemalatha Pradeepkumar, CC BY-NC 4.0   https://doi.org/10.11647/OBP.0427.03

A central question which catalysed this chapter was: what is revealed in writings about Sri Lankan academics' ability to act as consciousness-raisers and peacebuilders despite the traumas and constraints they experienced during the conflict, and the ways in which such enactment may have been supported by interventions aimed at rebuilding and reforming HE once there was cessation of violence? A concern raised is that, when academics suffer from a multitude of adverse social, psychological, economic and ethical challenges in aspects of personal and professional life, the conditions for their enacting the university's contribution to war-torn societies remain fragile and uncertain.

Posing Questions about Academics in Post-conflict Contexts

While authoritative international bodies have asserted the role of tertiary education toward peacebuilding in conflict-inflicted nations (such as in the Bologna declaration of 1999), the capacity of higher education (HE) to build and catalyse strategies for reconstruction has been dependent on the evolution of the nation's political, cultural, demographic and international position as a knowledge society. In many post-conflict contexts embracing democracy within university campuses—which are often positioned as sites for debates on politics, reformatory strategies, education reconstruction and economic development (Buckland, 2006)—this becomes problematic. In addition, humanitarian agents, key stakeholders, and voluntary sectors have considered education as a pillar in their relief efforts in the immediate crisis and reconstruction periods (UNHCR, 2016). However, academic study of this role has indicated a myriad of complications. In this chapter, the case of Sri Lanka's academic citizens and HE institutions are considered, drawing from published academic and grey literature about the conflict and post-conflict periods.

Sri Lanka adopted a similar approach to that of many other post-conflict nations, such as Liberia (Omeje, 2009) and Uganda (Kaburu, 2014), where academics in the social sciences and humanities are helmed by civil administrations, policymakers and humanitarian agencies to approach peacebuilding using conventional peace education. The belief is in its potential to deconstruct and transform deep-rooted structures of prejudice, violence and discrimination (Omeje, 2015). Academics using this approach are expected to design curricula and build knowledge that can manifest insurgent truths, if not explicitly then as byproducts of knowledge creation about histories of genocides, warfare, enslavement and social deaths. This so-called 'knowledge creation' (Williams, 2016, p. 629) has underpinned the epistemological foundation that purports peace as being knowable, teachable and learnable. However, the ability of academics in a post-conflict context to influence students (Marcia and Alexander, 1993; Mufdi and Slaihate, 2014) and to guide HE institutions' complex transition from violence to peace (Akkad and Henderson, 2021), is subject to concern and requires critical analysis.

One of the reasons for raising uncertainty about the capacity of academics to optimise peace and learning conditions in post-conflict nations is the struggles they have faced personally and professionally, such as economic constraints, corruption, dilapidated education system, violence, insecurity, threats, subjugation, oppression and brain drain. In their study on the impact of conflict on professionals in Northern Ireland, Campbell and McCrystal (2005) and Moore (2018) found that professionals experienced emotional and psychological distress due to the post-conflict legacies of poverty, social exclusion and discrimination. Psychosocial analysis reveals that an individual exposed to a prolonged culture of violence and conflict develops a distorted worldview (Kelman, 2010; Education under Attack report, 2014), leading to an impaired ability to teach or learn, disinterestedness, distraction and mental health issues. Likewise, Belluigi and Parkinson (2020) and Campbell and Healey (1999) have provided insights into the difficulties academics experience co-existing with other academic groups from more stable communities. In addition to the dynamic tensions of post-conflict conditions on academics, peacebuilding agendas have been found to weaken the already threatened conditions for academics (Milton and Barakat, 2016). In part, this is because peacebuilding agendas often enact decontextualised, Western blueprint frameworks (Chandler, 2013), wherein local academics' intangible dimensions of trust, identity and civic participation are too easily neglected.

Even though the academic community occupies a difficult position within the conditions of conflict and post-conflict contexts, literature has overlooked academics within the discussions linking tertiary education and conflict. Rather, more focus is on peace studies education (Galtung,

2010; Harris and Lewer, 2008), the risks and opportunities for HE (Feuer et al., 2013), and its post-conflict roles (Buckland, 2006; Milton and Barakat, 2016; Tahirsyzaj, 2010; Tierney, 2011; Tomlinson et al., 2005). While there is precedent in academic autobiographies, it is rare to find current scholarship focused on the academic community and their agency explicitly framed as a concern about the effect of conflict (Akkad and Henderson, 2021; Belluigi and Parkinson, 2020; Parkinson et al., 2018).

As an academic, I continue to embrace the hope of an unhindered democratic public sphere and exercise my agency by articulating and exploring this at every opportunity through my practice. The desire to gain insights and write about Sri Lanka's ethnic conflict emerged from my personal experiences of it, as a child and adolescent, through my days of schooling. The ethnic conflict in Sri Lanka has had a direct impact on me, resulting in the loss of loved ones and of shelter. Being part of a minority ethnic group in Sri Lanka has given me insight into how the majority ethnic group used—and to some extent, continues to use—unearned privileges to oppress other groups. However, the interconnectedness and overlapping nature of ethnicity, culture and gender issues were/are often not fully recognised. It was only during my doctoral studies, much more recently in my scholarly and professional life, that I had the opportunity to delve deeper into higher education and the broader social-political aspects of Sri Lanka's conditions of subjugation and oppression. I also realised that my academic career, somewhat at a remove in India, provided me with the distance and space to develop a mature consciousness and the capacity to critique. While undertaking the literature review to inform the framing for the research project of my doctorate, I noticed a significant gap in reporting on the Sri Lankan ethnic conflict compared to conflicts in other nations such as East Timor, Iraq, Myanmar, Rwanda and Syria.

To undertake the critical scoping review, I searched online and within grey literature databases for English language publications on Sri Lankan HE published between 1960 and 2022. I was surprised to find that very few of these related to how conflict periods and the later reformation strategies impacted HE in general, and that first-hand accounts from within the academic community were particularly scarce. Given the extensive history of Sri Lanka's higher education, which has developed under the colonial rule of four different powers from 1505 to 1948, I have included a brief overview of important facts and milestones in the nation's higher education system on different sections of this chapter, thus remaining in line with the scope of the chapter.

A particularly important source was a website titled University Teachers Human Rights—Jaffna (hereafter UTHR(J)). This is managed by HE academics from the city of Jaffna which was once an epicentre of the war. This website began publishing reports on human rights violations in 1988 written by academics of the University of Jaffna (UTHR(J), 2014a). Although it started as a branch of the national organisation, it continued to function against several odds long after the violence ceased. This resource has elaborately reported several aspects of violence, oppressive circumstances, atrocities and powerlessness of the civilian community of Jaffna. Recognising the social nature of HE, I read this to comprehend how such incidents and their impacts on the broader conflict zone mentioned in these resources might correspond to the academic community residing within the same context, with some making explicit reference to schoolteachers' agency post-conflict, from which I imagine how academics may too have navigated their positions. As an academic based in India, and as a woman born to a minoritised ethnic group in Sri Lanka, my interest in this question is very much informed by my personal and professional positionality.

My analysis begins with the period of violent ethnic conflict. I then shift to consider how the case of Sri Lanka related to that of other comparable contexts, looking at the impact of conflict on HE and the position of HE reforms post-conflict. Finally, I question the psychosocial impacts on academic citizens and related systemic recognition and support.

During the Sri Lanka War

Ethnically diverse, the country endured a civil war from the year 1983 to 2009 between the two largest ethnic groups: Sinhala groups, which accounted for 74.5% of the total population and were predominantly Buddhist; and Tamil groups at 12.8%, which are predominantly Hindu. Many scholars attribute the conflict to discriminatory policies and ethnicisation of the political landscape in Sri Lanka, specifically highlighting the dominance of separatist sentiments related to ethnicity, culture and power in the pre-war context (Hettige, 1992; Moore, 1993; Tambiah, 1986). The Sri Lankan government adopted various unethical practices to sustain its political motives through inequality and oppression, which were implemented in HE, too, through political appointments to increase the proportion of professorships within HE for Sinhala academics, and the organisation of a pogrom against Tamil academics within public universities (Godwin et al., 2014).

These chaotic political realities gave rise to the Tamil militant youth movement of the Hindu community in 1970, called the Liberation Tigers of Tamil Eelam (LTTE). This emerged from the northern province's Jaffna city, which was claimed in the hopes of an independent Tamil homeland. The once vibrant city became the epicentre of war for three decades from 1981, causing mass displacement and destruction of infrastructure. The country's socioeconomic development was impacted, exacerbating endemic political, economic and educational inequalities (Lopes Cardozo and Shah, 2016). At the cessation of violence in 2009, large numbers of civilian causalities and war crime allegations were attributed to the government forces and the LTTE (United Nations, 2012), with mass graves discovered in two conflict-inflicted regions under the control of the army since 1990 TamilNet (2018). Scholars such as Balachandran (2015) quantified the exposure and impact of the war on children. The degree of impact and the living conditions during the war was reflected by the alarming rate of suicide within the refugee camps, during which Sri Lanka recorded the highest suicide rate in the world (MSF, 2002).

A striking feature of the Sri Lankan war was the efforts, by both the militants and the government, to limit and prohibit reporting on the war even after cessation of the conflict. Watchdog groups, such as Human Rights Watch (2009) and Amnesty International (2009), released accusation reports on how access was denied to the international media community since 2008. The killing of journalists was also highlighted, as were the destruction to television and newspaper offices, to instigate fear (Helbardt et al., 2010). Correspondingly, academics, most notably in the northern province, condemned the Sri Lankan government for imposing restrictions on journalists and scholars visiting the war zone (Helbardt et al., 2010). In later periods, the virtual domain provided them with some allowances for reporting, which has continued online into the present, such as about the recent brutal attacks on minority ethnic civilians in 2022 (Kumanan, 2022). A range of grey literature has indicated that academics, media reporters and even NGOs were under pressure to publish or share details of the war with outsiders. Those who did were often labelled as 'Tiger supporters' (Helbardt et al., 2010, p. 358), in that it was presumed their allegiance was to the militant group bearing that name—perhaps as a part of academic self-surveillance to avoid personal and professional risks in a conflict setting, where Helbardt and colleagues (2010) have found that conflict-affected scholars often rationalise opposing sides of the war to show neutrality. For example, one such academic in Sri Lanka, Paliawadana, showed support through a newspaper publication in the year 1988, titled 'Violence: Who is Guiltless?', which encouraged civilians to remember 'ourselves' rather than lend themselves to the creators of the problem (Brian, 1995a). Sri Lankan academics, especially those from conflict settings, were accused of being mostly compliant under the dictatorship of the ruling political party. They operated within universities—particularly those within the conflict zones, which reportedly staged services glorifying state brutality and political ideology of the time (UTHR(J) 2014b).

The thirty-year-long conflict affected HE institutions and their academic communities, with students reportedly subjected to torture and humiliation to a greater extent than academic staff, with some killed by public shootings (UTHR(J), 2014b). An important case is that of the University of Jaffna, founded in the year 1970 and located within the epicentre of the conflict, where the Tamil community is settled. Although their concentration was high in that region, the university accommodated students and staff from multi-ethnic groups since its inception (Mahendran, 2016). Russell (2022) explained that the institution was driven by notable leftist and progressive intellectuals from various communities. The author further points out the increasing violence between Tamil and Sinhala groups in parts of the island, and the 'Black July' (p. 903) anti-Tamil pogrom in 1983 which, significantly, made the Sri Lankan government refrain from sending Sinhalese students and academics to Jaffna University. In time, the institution became a mono-ethnically Tamil institution. Wickramasinghe (2014) highlighted how it became the key site for militants, who emerged from a group called the Tamil student federation, and who operated on the campus as their base camp. So-called 'heli drop' operations on Jaffna University ended disastrously, costing lives and mass devastation to the infrastructure. Persistent shelling of densely populated areas was a feature of the war generally, with the University of Jaffna targeted in particular—here, academics reported losing their limbs (Brian, 1995b) following various attacks on its premises. Jaffna University's public library, which at the time was the largest and best equipped in South Asia, was razed to the ground by political leaders and police officials in 1981 (Thamil Venthan, 2020).

One of the first high-profile attacks on the academic community was the assassination by militants of the popular academic come human rights activist, Dr Rajani Thiranagama—a founder of Jaffna's UTHR branch and Head of the Department of Anatomy at Jaffna University. She had become increasingly conscientised and then militarised from exposure to state injustice, with her intellectual and emotional passion coming in her writings such as the co-authored 'The Broken Palmyra' (Hoole et al., 1992), a documentation of the violence in the area in the 1980s. Following her assassination, the killing and kidnapping of student activists and renowned poets continued. These assassinations and disappearances induced fear, causing a subsequent decline of publishing activities within UTHR. Both freedom of expression and the exercising of academic freedom became dangerous enactments.

As a result of witnessing discriminatory education policies and political oppression, Tamil academics became increasingly dissatisfied (Godwin et al., 2014). Subsequently, academics of the Jaffna University formed the human rights group called the University Teachers Human Rights (UTHR) in 1988, as part of the National Organization University Teachers for Human Rights. This group supported and lead demonstrations across the island against discriminatory actions and policies of the government. The UTHR was said to be dissolved in 1989 after the government assassination of its leader, Dr Ranjani Thiranagama. However, its work continued by bringing to light the human rights violations of war on its virtual website titled UTHR (University Teachers for Human Rights—Jaffna, Sri Lanka) until 2015, managed by the academics of Jaffna University. Sensitive information was disclosed on the website, including details of many leading academics held captive for ransom by the militant groups during the peak times of war.

Reports by local academics and social activists have highlighted concern about the extent and effect of academic migration and displacement during and after the war (Chandra and Rasika, 2017; JUSTA, 2014; Mahendran, 2016; Sam, 2017), including the subjection of academic citizens to forced mobility (Russell, 2022). In a study by Russell (2022) which looked at the role of Sri Lankan universities in post-war recovery, Guruparan, who was the head of law at the time, reported that local government players deliberately facilitated the mass migration of academics during the war. This was an intentional effort to reduce the Tamil ethnic academic community for future generations (Russell, 2022). In addition to this, the unrest prevailing in the country during the years of conflict led many academics across the island to leave the country (Chandra and Rasika, 2017). Such displacement cost the country invaluable human capital, with a brain drain that consequently sacrificed the nation's intellectual capabilities (Magee and Pherali, 2019). Those remaining often adopted self-preservation tactics, often appearing detached and unapproachable (Matthews, 1995). The HE sector as a whole was pushed to a neglected and under-developed state. However, the lack of studies and evidence-based research on the Sri Lanka conflict has failed to bring out the subtleties of living as academics in conflict. There is very little attention paid to those academics who remained during the conflict and made efforts to motivate students and their families to improve their status quo as a part of their sense of public duty and commitment, in contrast to that which has emerged in recent research on conflict-affected contexts, such as the Syrian war (Akkad and Henderson, 2021).

Transitions to Peace

Evidence and studies situating Sri Lanka HE in post-conflict redevelopment is limited, often overshadowed by urgent humanitarian concerns. This is because post-conflict contexts are faced with tangible challenges. These include rebuilding destroyed infrastructure, dealing with displacement, de-arming and de-mobilising combatants and preventing the potential recurrence of conflict (Boyle, 2014; Steenkamp,

2009). Several steering networks have functioned to establish sustainable peace and reconstruction of post-conflict nations, such as UNHCR, UNESCO, UNICEF, International Rescue Committee, CARE USA, the World Bank, and the Norwegian Refugee Council (UNHCR 2006); UNESCO's Education in Situations of Emergency, Crisis and Reconstruction Programme (UNESCO 2003) volunteers.

HE has been positioned as a catalyst within major post-war recovery interventions, including playing a role in stabilisation, securitisation, reconstruction, state-building and peacebuilding (Milton and Barakat, 2016). These interventions align with mainstream state-building strategies and depend on the complexities of engagement within conflict zones. Although education is considered a panacea for a broad spectrum of social malaises, such as discrimination, gender issues and misogyny, and might contribute positively by training individuals towards economic or reconstruction needs, it does not often directly focus on state matters (Milton and Barakat, 2016). In such ways, research on post-conflict HE aligns with the cautions raised in Bush and Saltarelli's (2000) seminal work *The Two Faces of Education*, about how education can ameliorate and exacerbate tension.

The aftermath of the civil war experienced by the Tamil community faced both formalised state security-related measures and restrictions, including security checks, random arrests, registration with the police and a general culture of suspicion which was described by Helbardt and colleagues (2010) and Carey and colleagues (2022). Nithyani (2020), a Sri Lankan student at Harvard, argues that, even in recent times, the state has continued disenfranchising members of the Tamil community by keeping them under surveillance or suspicion of terrorism according to the Government's Prevention of Terrorism Act.

In Sri Lanka, the government and international sectors paid attention to reconstructing infrastructure. Development was swift, wiping out the signs of neglect and the ruins of the war. For instance, electricity supply resumed for about 85% of the houses in the affected region by 2012, just four years after the war ended, including rebuilding highways that connected the Northern Province to the rest of the country (Ministry of Finance and Planning, 2014). Post-war reconstruction support included reconciliation and restitution efforts, releasing lands to the displaced in the northern province, investigating missing civilians, rehabilitation, formation of reconciliation task forces and the development of roads/ railways (Kanagarthnam, 2019). While these were crucially important for rebuilding post-war Sri Lanka, the attention for reforming HE and its capacity to contribute to building peace and reconciling conflicting groups and societies was sidelined (Kathirgamar, 2017). The state's deprioritisation of HE during post-war reformation became evident early on. In the budget speech given by the Deputy Finance Minister a year after the conflict, in June 2010, the reconstruction initiative of the Northern-province epicentre of the war does not identify the university at all (Kathirgamar, 2017; Ministry of Finance and Planning, 2016). The cost incurred in rebuilding Jaffna University's infrastructure, because of its significant destruction during the war, might have been comparatively more challenging than that of primary and secondary education (Davies, 2004; Milton and Barakat, 2016), which perhaps might have laid HE in its neglected position within Sri Lanka reformation. This may also have been an approach commonly adopted internationally, where other education sectors are prioritised. International bodies, such as The UN General Assembly Declaration for Refugees and Migrants in 2016, have asserted that re-initialising early childhood education in post-conflict is of the highest priority compared to other education sectors (Milton, 2018). In addition, the age group of the majority of HE academic citizens falls outside of the most vulnerable categories (Chatty, 2014). Studies of other post-conflict contexts have pointed out that the rebuilding of university infrastructure requires high financial assistance for restoring resources, establishing a skilled workforce, technological support systems and technical provisions in maintaining the more complex management required (Rose and Greeley, 2006) during post-conflict. HE sectors are sophisticated systems requiring a high level of support and finance, without which they sit in a neglected position among other post-war reconstruction dimensions.

The World Bank review (1994–2002) (Buckland, 2002) on lending to the education sector post-conflict revealed that there was, on average, only 12% allocation for tertiary education while there was 51% allocation for the primary and secondary education sectors (Buckland, 2005). In some cases, such as in Iraq (Agresto, 2007) and East Timor (Hill, 2000), no resources for tertiary education were allocated in the post-conflict period. Such examples point to the partisan funding allocation among the reformation of various education sectors in post-conflict societies. However, this imbalance in fund allocation has appeared to endure a plausible ground, when the World Bank reported 40% fund allocation (World Bank, 2004) to tertiary education to Rwanda post-conflict (seventy-five times more than what is allocated for primary education) which benefitted just 2% of the affected population who are part of the tertiary education sector (Hilker, 2010).

The neglect of HE by donor agencies may have been informed by how HE was conceptualised and operationalised during both pre-conflict, conflict and post-conflict periods in Sri Lanka. HE for the most part functioned passively within economic development and national public dialogue, historically. Reports as old as 1901 indicate that HE in Sri Lanka was established to provide administrative services to its colonial rulers and, as such, academic matters were deliberately misdirected away from engaging with dominant social discourses (Alawattegam, 2020). And during the conflict, as discussed above, many academic citizens disengaged from socially critical education and research matters.

The neglected position of Sri Lanka's HE within post-conflict reformations had serious ramifications in terms of poor coverage and quality of HE leading to an unskilled graduate labour force, which continues to be a concern in public discourse. Within the last decade, a report by the state Finance Ministry (Ministry of Finance and Planning, 2016) reported that the government's total expenditure on the reconstruction of the northern province from 2009–2013 amounted to US $2 billion which was reportedly focused on infrastructure development. However, neoliberal logics led to a neglect of the rural economy and the relative support of livelihoods and job creation, impacting unemployment in the youth population (Kathirgamar, 2017) of the Jaffna peninsula. Only 17% of the population affected by war were employed as civil servants by the state (such as bureaucrats, teachers and health care workers), with the remaining population within informal labour in the fisheries, agriculture, and construction sectors (District Secretariat of Jaffna, 2014). Nearly 88% of the youth aged between eighteen and thirty-six had no opportunities for vocational training or HE, leaving Jaffna youths in a severe unemployment crisis which persisted until 2014 (Kathirgamar, 2017).

This reality stands in stark contrast to some of the reporting of the period. A World Bank report (World Bank, 2010) characterised the post-war transformation of Sri Lanka as a transition from stagnation to rapid economic development. This vision, according to Biller and Nabi (2013), included Sri Lanka emulating an export-led economy and public-private partnership, in building infrastructures and creating business-friendly conditions. A patriotic and socially conscious academic has reported that academics and social workers increasingly turned education into economic goals (Brian, 1995a), supporting the opening of private tutorials and private medical practices, immediately after the disruptions of the war as a means to establish private gains. These are some of the examples he cited to substantiate his claims about immorality within academics and social workers in the post-conflict period. Such shifts in HE in post-conflict societies, including the deprioritisation of the critical role, are heavily influenced by the World Bank's dynamic interpretation of human capital theory (Lebeau and Sall, 2011) and the application of neoliberal logic.

While the Sri Lankan government claims that reconstructing lives in the conflict-affected areas is their priority (Ministry of Finance and Planning, 2016), other projects aimed at post-conflict development in Sri Lanka as explained in detail by Athukorala and Jayasuriya (2013) included initiatives to boost tourism, create economic opportunities, construct a port/airport in Hambantota (Attanayake, 2018) and promote industrial growth and businesses. Since this chapter primarily focuses on higher education within the context of conflict and post-conflict situations, it does not explore the specific details of post-war recovery interventions compared to other state-building projects.

The sections above provide indications of the dramatic changes to the landscape which academics navigated while operating within the university's shifting social terrain. The complex nature of the professional, personal and political impacts the capacity of academics to contribute generatively to reformations, with their positioning as critical change agents described double-edged (Wilson, 2000). When HE institutions are aligned with dominant state norms, it is fair to assume that educators will mainly satisfy what the state wants them to do, as was reportedly the modus operandi of those who remained under the repressive political climate of the conflict period. In the post-conflict period, this would have included transmitting ideas of nationalism, patriotism, progress for modernism and international development mantras for employment within their teaching and research, for instance. Some may define themselves and their academic practice steadfastly within the confines of their disciplines and their intellectual identities; others would see their responsibility sitting with the social good of universities. As in times of peace, this may align with that which dominates nationally, or be different or even in opposition to it. Such dynamics become significantly complicated and entangled within the complex terrain of ideologies in conflict-affected contexts. The ambivalent social standing of post-conflict academics places them in a trickster position, as pointed out by Lopes Cardozo and Shah (2016). Although critical questions concerning scholar's credible and neutral reactions to opposing sides of the divide in conflict settings have been discussed much by scholars (Helbardt et al., 2010), neither position spares them from the tremendous dangers of war and the legacies of conflict after the cessation of violence. This chapter now turns to the ways in which educators, including academics, are reported to have taken on the social mandate at the time.

Education Post-conflict

Two studies have focused on school teachers' ability to act as peace agents in Sri Lankan post-conflict society while recognising their experiences of the violent insurgency during the war. Of interest is that these were published in the last decade. Lopes Cardozo and Hoeks (2015), and Duncan and Cardozo (2017), explored how schoolteachers examined, operated and interplayed their agency within reformation strategies and the challenges sustaining the long-term vision and maintaining the transformative impetus. Such studies about the schoolteacher's agency, conflictive conscientisation, values and professional role may have resonance with HE academics, as both are intellectuals working for educational institutions. They have the potential to lever pedagogical function as the hub for creative ideology, by creating space that can produce activist intellectual networks (Baud and Rutten, 2004). Also, education throughout the life course can function ideologically in ways which engender collective imagination and action of citizen's rights and the public good of society (Baud and Rutten (2004).

While education at primary and secondary levels was recognised as crucially important for attempting to recreate peace and reconciliation by introducing formal peace education in Sri Lankan schools, its implementation was losing its grounds from 2006 to 2011 (Lopes Cardozo and Hoeks, 2015). In a 2011 field study on schoolteachers' engagement with peace education in Sri Lanka, it was revealed that one-fifth of the study participants had been unaware of any peace education programmes (Lopes Cardozo and Hoeks, 2015). This deficiency in the execution of peacebuilding programmes is most likely due to communication gaps between the main actors of the reformation and local implementers such as educators and academics, as noted by Sommers and Buckland's (2004). The effect of disregarding local educators in peace education tends to create an outsider sense for educators in their own land (Tahirsyzaj, 2010).

One of the primary reasons cited is that the Ministry of Education in Sri Lanka is said to have offered limited assistance to teachers on how to facilitate the objectives of peacebuilding through teaching and learning processes (Cardozo, 2008). Even though UNICEF (2012) has asserted that teachers are the crucial building block for restoring normalcy in a conflict-affected environment (INEE, 2011), sufficient investment for the holistic development of the academic community is often lacking. Although Sri Lanka implemented reconciliation through peace education in primary and secondary schools, teachers were found to have not been provided with adequate training and assistance (Duncan and Cardozo, 2017; Harris and Lewer, 2008). The majority of teachers from secondary schools participating in Duncan and Cardozo's (2017) study raised concerns over the unreasonable assumption of the state that teachers have relevant skills to deliver peace education without formal training. The state seemingly ignored the subjective impact of war and the reproductive dangers of social engineering within education, instead prioritising economic development in its curriculum as a peace-making initiative. Subsequently, intercultural activity and counselling remained under-focused, with a general lack of financial support further aggravating such problems. Ineffective evaluation and monitoring systems contributed to the slow-paced progress in this and other sectors. Under these conditions, teachers who had tried to transform and negotiate the vision of reform were (and ostensibly still are) confronted with ambiguity regarding the characteristics, conditions, nature and outcome of such endeavours. Researchers have argued that the lack of clarity of the crucial elements of the reformation made the implementation process lose its ground (Duncan and Cardozo, 2017; Kelman, 2010; Lopes Cardozo and Hoeks, 2015).

As potentially strategic actors within reforms, teachers have been found to sometimes be critical, complex and troublesome when contesting reforms that do not resonate with their ideological position (Vongalkis-Macrow 2007). Educators from post-conflict societies may carry strong opinions on the war and are usually shaped by boundaries and conditions set by the effects of war (Lopes Cardozo and Hoeks, 2015; Lopes Cardozo and Shah, 2016; Shah, 2012; Shah and Cardozo, 2016). Facing a vacuum of intellectual leadership on the issue in Sri Lanka, teachers from the minority ethnic community actively began to pursue teaching curricula informed by their beliefs, cultures and histories, to challenge the barriers of identity and prejudice which had so far existed between the different ethnicities. This was explored by Duncan and Cardozo (2017), who discuss how such teachers began using texts that were not authorised by the Ministry of Education to teach school students, for the purpose of telling their own version of the truth about war. The author also highlighted institutional agency, citing the case of a Catholic institution which created a text based on their own belief and conviction titled 'The Art of Joyful Living' (p. 87), to create potential for religious reconciliation.

Educators from conflict-affected contexts should receive training in peace education. When teachers with conflicting opinions actively pursue interactions and shared experiences with students, debates are stimulated in classrooms which may question the state's narratives on war crimes, discrimination and torture during the conflict (Coulter et al., 2013). Although teachers were said to have been aware of what not to do, such as to not incite ethnic hatred in their students, the lack of systemic training left them mostly unaware (Harb, 2008) of the risks associated with sensitive discussions and controversial topics—which is why scholars have argued that educators expected to teach peace education should arguably be trained simultaneously, to support them in building a safe classroom for discourse at a sufficient level of discomfort to encourage students into a process of open critical inquiry (Coulter et al., 2013) and the educator's own self-criticality.

Despite research suggesting the passive benefits of investing in peace education through the tertiary education sector (Feuer et al., 2013), Sri Lanka has continued to prioritise initiatives in peace education only within primary and secondary schools. At a much later date, peace education was introduced to HE, as a post-graduate diploma on the subject for student's study in one of the urban universities in Sri Lanka (Postgraduate Diploma in Conflict and Peace Studies—PgDCPS 2022/23, n.d.). However, there is as yet neither evidence nor studies published to give an evaluation of that programme's effectiveness on student learning. Similarly, there have been no reports about development in this area for academics and HE staff generally.

The impact of conflict-affected conditions for teaching, including the institutional context, can thus be seen to play an important role in determining, limiting or enabling the agency of educators to inform and implement curricula within such circumstances. This has been recognised as including the impact of conflict on students and colleagues, resource allocation before and after the war, training for educators and politicisation (Akkad and Henderson, 2021). In that sense, the Sri Lankan HE academic context would differ from that of other educational institutions, particularly in terms of students' aspiration for peace education and resource allocation. Thus, a limitation of the section above is that the different systems may not be comparable. Indeed, even HE institutions within the same national context may differ. Given the lack of published studies on Sri Lankan HE which consider the conditions and experiences of academics, there is much scope to explore this area.

Post-conflict Research

Universities and academics also have the responsibility to generate, build on and critique knowledge that is relevant to society's everyday challenges, and the importance of access to such knowledge for the public. Almost a year after the end of the civil war, Helbardt and colleagues (2010) characterised research practice in Sri Lanka as partial, non-neutral, morally loaded or leaning to one side of a political polarity. As recently as 2017, Dundar and colleagues (2017) reported that Sri Lanka fails to maintain hard data to gauge its research activities, and regulatory bodies such as the University Grant Commission do not include indicators to monitor research statistically. The question of this function of universities is rarely within the scope of post-conflict development, despite the changes of continued segregationist knowledge (re)production and of international research interference in post-conflict contexts.

Failed states, and those transitioning from conflict, often lack the capacity to develop research abilities (Tierney, 2011) for reasons such as scholars having fled the country or having been forced to leave at the outbreak of the war (Parkinson et al., 2018), lack of resources and international collaborations and reduced funding for research. Between 1990 to 2012, approximately 251 Sri Lankan academics migrated to other countries across various disciplines, in part because of safety issues during the period of civil war and thereafter because of the limiting conditions (Chandra and Rasika, 2017). Academics and students were also unlawfully denied their opportunity to acquire doctorates and complete other courses for reasons such as lab closures, ceased fund allocations and university closures both during and after the civil war (Chandra and Rasika, 2017). In such ways, academics in general could be seen to have been deprived of professional development opportunities related to research. This problem preceded the war—Sri Lanka's education sector's scientific and social research functioned somewhat in isolation since decolonisation, without many international collaborations.

While academic migration and its brain drain impacted the capacity of the system to grow and flourish in terms of research, what is of interest is that I have noticed that most of the few published works on Sri Lanka are produced by Sri Lankan academics living in other countries. This may indicate more auspicious conditions are exploited by them there, including possibly more academic freedom within the diaspora. Nevertheless, the nation continues to suffer from a deficiency of researchers, intellectual leadership, investment and academic development, which combine to impede those within the system from keeping pace with the frontiers of knowledge.

Despite modernisation efforts, it has been argued that Sri Lankan academics are struggling to keep pace with the neoliberal benchmarks due to long years of isolation because of war (Wendy, 2011). As indicated above, there are indications that they have not been presented with opportunities for professional development or training programmes for educational and research development. Thus, Sri Lankan academics have been reported as finding coping with global academic reforms challenging (Tahirsyzaj 2010). Additionally, the poor financial stability of the country has directly impacted the pace and efficacy of reforms, with academics doing dual jobs with low salaries while attempting to move towards massification. In Sri Lanka, a senior professor's salary was reported as 30% lower than the salary of a senior manager within the corporate sector in the mid-2010s (Asian Development Bank, 2016). To balance the economic conditions, educators have been found to seek opportunities for additional income, such as offering private tuition, which often leads them to be stressed and overworked, with increased attrition from academia (Hoeks, 2012).

Psychosocial Crises, their Impact and Support for Academics

The effects of war on HE, including the destruction of infrastructures, loss of human capital and reduced resources, hollowed out university communities by death and brain drain. In addition to this, there was the effect of contextually pertinent social divisions on the university's sense of community and the interactional dynamics of those who remained. Indications were that the structurally imposed displacement of academics during the war was not systemically addressed thereafter. As this chapter has indicated, the institutional case of the University of Jaffna offers striking insights about the sector, because of what it faced at the extreme end of resistance and politicisation, and in turn violence and oppression during the conflict. Similarly, the case reveals concerning implications for the country's post-conflict academic communities. I began by discussing how legacies of the deep-rooted social divisions along ethnic and religious lines seemed to have naturalised among students and academics over the years, in the name of heritage, cultural rights and war in the University of Jaffna.

The process of replenishment of academics during the post-conflict period at Jaffna University reflects this, with the politicised nature of its academic recruitment the subject of research by Russell (2022). Of those employed in the year 2010 within that institution, only 9% were senior academics, while this proportion was higher in other established institutions at that time (University Grants Commission, 2011). A 2014 report by the Jaffna University Science Teachers Association similarly reported on witnessed unethical practices related to the recruitment of academic and non-academic staff, in addition to practices within academic departments of the university (JUSTA, 2014). The report stated that academics from the Tamil ethnic community who had left during the war and tried to return were often rejected based on discrimination. Their applications and appointments were blocked by administrative hurdles, while politically favoured candidates saw their progress uninterrupted. In 2016 it was reported in the press that younger Tamil staff members, who had either been educated or employed elsewhere in the country, also had to fight for their access to employment in the university (Mahendran, 2016). Authorities were accused of being sycophantic toward political leaders (Sam, 2017) whose agenda on recruitment appeared to be supporting existing power structures by offering recruitment to local graduates more likely to be aligned with their political ideologies.

Another area of concern is commemoration, a seemingly fraught part of institutional culture. An example reported online was when the deans of various departments from the Jaffna University added their voice to that of army officials when communicating with students via a public communique, advising that they refrain from commemorating 'Tamil Eelam Heroes Day' (TamilNet, 2019). The day is one which remembers the fall of militant group leaders from Jaffna, including student and staff activists from the university. This action presumably was an attempt to suppress students' freedom of expression on the campus, perhaps in fear of politically oriented discourse or critique of the state. However, the ban was overcome with the support of more than three hundred other students, who paid tribute to the war heroes of their ethnic origin. The stance of academics being sensitive or cautious post-conflict and acting publicly against some seemingly political issues (such as commemoration) but not others (such as recruitment), raises distrust about whether they are prejudicial. Biased recruitment and clashes with the student community over the cultural ownership of the university space have somewhat resurrected wartime practices, albeit by other means, in Jaffna University. The above ethnicised and politicised practices are believed to have aided the creation of the now mono-ethnic institution.

As indicated in the prior sections, HE experienced devastating effects, with teachers (both educators and academics) positioned at the forefront during the conflict. The role of academics in the reconstruction of conflict-affected societies may be hampered by their lived experiences of living and working in conflict-affected nations (Akkad and Henderson, 2021). It is possible to imagine some of the consequences for them, whose life is most likely affected by social, emotional and ethical aspects such as poverty, social exclusion and discrimination (Moore, 2018). A few international studies (Akkad and Henderson, 2021; Abdo, 2015; Barakat and Milton, 2015; Belluigi and Parkinson, 2020; Milton, 2018) have helped to highlight the psychosocial trauma and post-traumatic stress endured by academics within conflict-affected conditions. However, what I noticed is that less attention and studies seem to have been on academics who remain in situ, including those who have written about Sri Lanka.

War provides the conditions for severe stress, with those working in psychology pointing to how it can cause transient personality decompensation even in adults with stable personalities. Baum (2012), in his study researching professionals' experiences, stated that professionals are in a state of loss of hope and are left vulnerable with their possible defence mechanisms weakened during violent conflict. In another study by that author (Baum and Ramon 2010), which explored professional growth during turbulent times, professionals were reported to have heightened emotional arousal and to often be unprepared or under-developed professionally, sometimes struggling to balance concerns for their professional responsibilities with objectively justified worries about the safety and well-being of their person and their families. The severe stress caused by the psychodynamics of war has been described as limiting academics' capacity to act collectively, and to extend solidarity towards social justice movements in conflict societies (Belluigi and Parkinson, 2020). Based on Helbardt and colleagues

(2010), and Lopes Cardozo and Shah (2016), academics face difficulties in developing obfuscation to achieve neutrality, apolitical perspectives and coexistence with other groups of stable communities, as found by Campbell and Healy (1999).

In Sri Lanka, limited mental health resources and services combined with cultural stigmatisation of psychological problems and poor access, particularly within the Jaffna Peninsula, are also reflected in the few studies. According to Kanagarthnam (2021), rehabilitation centres in Jaffna were characterised by societal isolation, lack of transparency, security and independence. There has been some reporting on the limited services for children, such as the fact that schools in the northern province provided one counsellor for a population of over three hundred students (Lakshman et al., 2020). The post-war reconciliations with the northern province did not initially address the psychological well-being of children and teachers affected by war (Duncan and Cardozo, 2017) in their peace education programmes introduced within secondary schools. Later attempts to address this by Deutsche Gesellschaft für Internationale Zusammenarbeit (GIZ) were beset by allegations about the minimal number of students and teachers receiving counselling (Duncan and Cardozo, 2017).

There is a lack of clarity and published empirical research on the nature of such support for the academic community, in addition to addressing their material needs following displacement, and employment opportunities and equality. From the accounts of the situation, and due to the longevity of war, it might be possible that the effects of war perhaps were taken as normal for teachers and academics. It is also evident from the literature pertaining to Sri Lanka that academics from post-conflict periods may not have been considered as potential change agents by peace-building actors, other than endeavouring in peace studies as directed by agencies implementing the reform agenda.

Concluding Reflections

This chapter explored literature available on conflict-affected Sri Lanka, its academic sector and specific educational programmes related to conflict. In the process, light was shed on the deep-set devastation of the country's violent war and its legacies on its academic citizens and infrastructure, particularly those situated within the regions most targeted for resisting political oppression. As I read and wrote, I tried to find insights and raise questions about those agents' capacity for leading change through academic functions. Reading these texts in conjunction with other studies on conflict-affected societies, it became apparent to me how academics and universities are affected by conditions which cause destruction on multiple dimensions of life, including material and psychosocial.

In this chapter, I have demonstrated that a precondition for the success of the role of academics within reconstruction is the structural enablement and public perceptions of those actors. Although multiple researchers from across the world have identified and argued for the validity of HE as a catalyst within major post-war recovery interventions, I showed how in Sri Lanka it has remained deprioritised and disabled. There has been a dearth of acknowledgement and attention paid to how academics' contributions to reconstruction will be shaped by their contextual experiences and individual capacities, in addition to the conditions of institutional support from policymakers and curriculum developers, and the perceptions of various stakeholders, including the attitudes of students and administrations. The rare engagement expressed, within a narrow range of literature on Sri Lankan post-conflict HE, is that academics require significant institutional support and nationwide revision if the capacity of academics to alleviate conflicts and impact society is to be realised.

A concern is the possible risk when academic agency is downplayed and neglected by the larger political processes and reformatory agencies. Academics may consciously or unconsciously reproduce the political, ideological and sectarian struggles they have lived through during conflict. There may be interest in inciting hatred or violent action in young people they are directly in contact with. Therefore, appropriate training to raise awareness of sensitivities and risks in various peace-building strategies for academics is arguably essential. Moreover, the state's lack of governance on the observable influence of further conflict increases the chances of a relapse into sectarian divisions and violent conflict (Collier, 2008; Fransis, 2012). Sri Lanka has recently been identified as a country at risk by the International Crisis Group (ICG) (Daily Financial Times, 2020); with the Scholars at Risk network reporting the civil unrest within the HE community (SAR, 2022) when the state confronted students' peaceful protest for the resignation of the nation's president, with tear gas and water cannon.

A concern raised in this chapter is that reformation strategies within Sri Lankan HE are shaped by neoliberal orientations. These focus on building human capital to support the state's economy while neglecting conflict-related needs. In turn, these may have limited academic criticality and rewarded intellectual docility. Furthermore, when facing challenging economic conditions, they might adopt a lifestyle for economic survival rather than acting upon the notion of responsibility for social good (Heath and Burdon, 2012). This mode of survivability by academics threatens to fundamentally alter the public good mission of HE and impairs the nation's capacity to develop democracy, political agency and critical thinking.

While this chapter provides valuable insights on academic experiences within conflict and post-conflict settings, it primarily focuses on higher education within the epicentre of war. Therefore, its findings may not fully capture the impact on other universities across the island, which vary in terms of demographics, psychological impact, experience and political ideologies. It is important to recognise that HE institutions in the northwestern provinces of Sri Lanka—the epicentre of the conflict—may have faced significant disparities that are not representative of other institutions on the island. Nonetheless, this chapter's evidence sheds light on how academics address social justice under extreme conditions within the context of Sri Lankan higher education governed by a centralised state-funded university grant commission.

Given the paucity of research on HE in Sri Lanka post-war on these issues and from the perspective of academic citizens, further exploration of the context is needed, particularly from those with lived experiences who remained during and after the conflict. Addressing this knowledge gap may contribute complexity to discourses on HE teachers as change agents in post-conflict societies. The voices of such academics would contribute to breaking the silence on what has been described as the 'war without witnesses' (JDS, 2009).

Bibliography

Abeyratne, S. (2004). Economic Roots of Political Conflict: The Case of Sri Lanka. *The World Economy*, 27(8), 1295–1314, https://doi.org/10.1111/j.1467-9701.2004.00645.x

Amnesty International. (2009, August 14). *Sri Lanka: Attacks on Free Media Put Displaced Civilians at Risk*. Amnesty International. https://www.amnesty.org/en/latest/news/2009/08/sri-lanka-attacks-free-media-put-displaced-civilians-risk-20090814/

Agresto, J. (2007). *Mugged By Reality: The Liberation of Iraq and the Failure of Good Intentions*. Encounter Books.

Akkad, A., and Henderson, E. F. (2021). Exploring the Role of HE Teachers as Change Agents in the Reconstruction of Post-conflict Syria. *Teaching in Higher Education*, 1–18. https://doi.org/10.1080/13562517.2021.1965571

Alawattegam, K. K. (2020). Free Education Policy and its Emerging Challenges in Sri Lanka. *The European Journal of Educational Sciences*, 7(1). https://doi.org/10.19044/ejes.v7no1a1

Abdo, W. (2015, February 6). *To Be Syrian and a Professor: Recipe for Tragedy*. Al-Fanar Media. https://www.al-fanarmedia.org/2015/02/to-be-syrian-and-a-professor-recipe-for-tragedy/

Asian Development Bank (Eds). (2016). *Innovative Strategies in Higher Education for Accelerated Human Resource Development in South Asia: Sri Lanka*. Asian Development Bank, https://www.adb.org/sites/default/files/publication/185628/strategies-higher-education-sri.pdf

Athukorala, P.-C., and Jayasuriya, S. (2013). Economic Policy Shifts in Sri Lanka: The Post-Conflict Development Challenge. *Asian Economic Papers*, 12(2), 1–28. https://doi.org/10.1162/ASEP_a_00203

Attanayake, C. (2018). *Mattala: Attracting Business into a Lonely Airport*. National University of Singapore.

Balachandran, P. K. (2015, October 17). *War Has Had Severe Psychological Effects on Kids in Lanka's North: Psychiatrist*. The New Indian Express. https://www.newindianexpress.com/world/2015/oct/17/War-Has-Had-Severe-Psychological-Effects-on-Kids-in-Lankas-North-Psychiatrist-830787.html

Balasooriya, A. S. (2007). *What Is Peace Education?* [Unpublished report]. Pannipitiya. http://asbalasooriyaoneducation.blogspot.com/2007/09/insights-into-peace-education.html

Barakat, S., and Milton, S. (2015). *Houses of Wisdom Matter: The Responsibility to Protect and Rebuild Higher Education in the Arab World*. Brookings. https://www.brookings.edu/wp-content/uploads/2016/06/En-Higher-Ed-Web.pdf

Baud, M., and Rutten, R. (2004). *Popular Intellectuals and Social Movements: Framing Protest in Asia, Africa, and Latin America.* Cambridge University Press.

Baum, N. (2012). 'Emergency Routine': The Experience of Professionals in a Shared Traumatic Reality of War. *The British Journal of Social Work, 42*(3), 424–442. https://doi.org/10.1093/bjsw/bcr032

—, and Ramon, S. (2010). Professional Growth in Turbulent Times. *Journal of Social Work, 10*(2), 139–156. https://doi.org/10.1177/1468017310363636

Belluigi, D., and Parkinson, T. (2020). Building Solidarity through Comparative Lived Experiences of Post/conflict: Reflections on Two Days of Dialogue. *Education and Conflict Review, 2,* 16–23. https://discovery.ucl.ac.uk/id/eprint/10109100/1/Belluigi_Article02_Belluigi.pdf

Biller, D., and Nabi, I. (2013). *Investing in Infrastructure: Harnessing Its Potential for Growth in Sri Lanka.* World Bank, https://documents.worldbank.org/en/publication/documents-reports/documentdetail/956441468103456742/investing-in-infrastructure-harnessing-its-potential-for-growth-in-sri-lanka

Boyle, M. (2014). *Violence after War: Explaining Instability in Post-conflict States.* John Hopkins University Press.

Brian, S. (1995a, October). *Chapter 7: A PERSPECTIVE ON NONVIOLENCE.* UTHR(J): University Teachers for Human Rights (Jaffna). https://uthr.org/BP/volume2/Chapter7.htm

—(1995b, October). *Chapter 4: THE PSYCHOLOGICAL ASPECTS OF THE INDIAN MILITARY ACTION.* UTHR(J): University Teachers for Human Rights (Jaffna). https://uthr.org/BP/volume2/Chapter4.htm

Buckland, P. (2002). *Analysis of World Bank Loan and Grant Education Expenditure (Completed and Active) in 21 Conflict-Affected Countries, 1994–2002* [Annual Report]. World Bank. https://books.google.co.uk/books?hl=en&lr=&id=fJoKm7DjDFEC&oi=fnd&pg=PR9&dq=review+date+Education+and+Postconflict+Reconstruction.&ots=miRdyq3ufH&sig=CQyU7UGMbiSEM9vcoS2epnu8YBk#v=onepage&q&f=false

—(2005). *Reshaping the Future: Education and Postconflict Reconstruction. Washington.* World Bank, http://documents.worldbank.org/curated/en/860731468138857154/Reshaping-the-future-Education-and-post-conflict-reconstruction

—(2006). *Post-Conflict Education: Time for a Reality Check.* Forced Migration Review, 7–8. https://www.fmreview.org/education/buckland

Bush, K. D., and Saltarelli, D. (Eds). (2000). *The Two Faces of Education in Ethnic Conflict: Towards a Peacebuilding Education for Children.* UNICEF Innocenti Research Centre. https://www.unicef-irc.org/publications/pdf/insight4.pdf

Campbell, J., and Healy, A. (1999). Whatever You Say, Say Something: The Education, Training and Practice of Mental Health Social Workers in Northern Ireland. *Social Work Education, 18*(4), 389–400, https://doi.org/10.1080/02615479911220391

Campbell, J., and McCrystal, P. (2005). Mental Health Social Work and the Troubles in Northern Ireland: A Study of Practitioner Experiences. *Journal of Social Work, 5*(2), 173–190. https://doi.org/10.1177/1468017305054971

Cardozo, M. T. A. L. (2008). Sri Lanka: In Peace or in Pieces? A Critical Approach to Peace Education in Sri Lanka. *Research in Comparative and International Education, 3*(1), 19–35. https://doi.org/10.2304/rcie.2008.3.1.19

Carey, S. C., González, B., and Gläßel, C. (2022). Divergent Perceptions of Peace in Post-Conflict Societies: Insights from Sri Lanka. *Journal of Conflict Resolution, 66*(9), 1589–1618. https://doi.org/10.1177/00220027221104719

Chandler, D. (2013). International Statebuilding and the Ideology of Resilience. *Politics, 4*(33), 276–286. https://doi.org/10.1111/1467-9256.12009

Chandra, G., and Rasika, N. (2017). Brain Drain from Sri Lankan Universities. *Sri Lanka Journal of Social Sciences, 40*(2), 103–118, https://doi.org/10.4038/sljss.v40i2.7541

Chatty, D. (2014, March). *Ensuring Quality Education for Young Refugees from Syria in Turkey, Northern Iraq/Kurdistan Region of Iraq (KRI), Lebanon and Jordan—Refugee Studies Centre.* https://www.rsc.ox.ac.uk/completed-projects/ensuring-quality-education-for-young-refugees-from-syria

Collier, P. (2008). *The Bottom Billion: Why the Poor Countries are Failing and What Can Be Done About It.* Oxford University Press.

Coulter, S., Campbell, J., Duffy, J., and Reilly, I. (2013). Enabling Social Work Students to Deal with the Consequences of Political Conflict: Engaging with Victim/survivor Service Users and a Pedagogy of Discomfort. *Social Work Education: The International Journal, 32*(4), 439–452. https://doi.org/10.1080/02615479.2012.668180

Daily Financial Times. (2020). *Sri Lanka Identified as Country at Risk of Conflict in ICG's Watch List 2020.* SyndiGate Media Inc.

Davies, L. (2004). Building a Civic Culture Post-conflict. *London Review of Education, 2*(3), 229–244, https://doi.org/10.1080/ 1474846042000302852

District Secretariat of Jaffna. (2014). *Statistical Hand Book 2013 Jaffna District.* District Secretariat of Jaffna. http://jaffna.dist.gov.lk/index.php/en/downloads/statistical.html

Dobbin, J., Jones, S., Crane, K., and DeGrasse, B. C. (2007). *The Beginner's Guide to Nation-Building.* RAND.

Duncan, R., and Cardozo, M. L. (2017). Reclaiming Reconciliation through Community Education for the Muslims and Tamils of Post-war Jaffna,

Sri Lanka: Research in Comparative and International Education. *Research in Comparative and International Education, 12*(1). https://doi.org/10.1177/1745499917696425

Dundar, H., Millot, B., Riboud, M., Shojo, M., Aturupane, H., Goyal, S., and Raju, D. (2017). *Sri Lanka Education Sector Assessment*. The World Bank. https://documents1.worldbank.org/curated/en/150171497946826450/pdf/116438-PUB-PUBLIC.pdf

Feuer, H. N., Hornidge, A.-K., and Schetter, C. (2013). *Rebuilding Knowledge: Opportunities and Risks for Higher Education in Post-conflict Regions* (Working Paper No. 121). ZEF Working Paper Series. https://www.econstor.eu/handle/10419/88345

Fransis, J. D. (2012). Introduction: Understanding Policing in Transition Societies in Africa. In *Policing in Africa* (pp. 3–36). Palgrave Macmillan UK.

Galtung, J. (2010). Peace Studies and Conflict Resolution: The Need for Transdisciplinarity. *Transcultural Psychiatry, 47*(1), 20–32. https://doi.org/10.1177/1363461510362041

Godwin, C., Neloufer, de M., Nirmal Ranjith, D., Lakshman, D., Pavithra, K., Indika, K., Marie, P., Jayadeva, U., and Devaka, W. (2014). *University Governance Autonomy and Accountability: Direction for Change*. Workshop Report 54.

Harb, I. (2008). *Higher Education and the Future of Iraq*. Special Report, USIP. https://www.usip.org/publications/2008/01/higher-education-and-future-iraq

Harris, S., and Lewer, N. (2008). Peace Education in Conflict Zones—Experience from Northern Sri Lanka. *Journal of Peace Education, 5*(2), 127–140. https://doi.org/10.1080/17400200802264321

Heath, M., and Burdon, P. D. (2012). Academic Resistance to the Neoliberal University. *Legal Education Review, 23*(2). http://www5.austlii.edu.au/au/journals/LegEdRev/2013/17.html

Helbardt, S., Hellmann-Rajanayagam, D., and Korff, R. (2010). War's Dark Glamour: Ethics of Research in War and Conflict Zones. *Cambridge Review of International Affairs, 23*(2), 349–369. https://doi.org/10.1080/09557571003752688

Hettige, S. (1992). *Unrest or Revolt: Some Aspect of Youth Unrest in Sri Lanka*. Goethe-Institut. https://catalogue.nla.gov.au/catalog/2648584

Hilker, L. (2010). *The Role of Education in Driving Conflict and Building Peace— The Case of Rwanda*. UNESCO. https://unesdoc.unesco.org/ark:/48223/pf0000191301

Hill, H. (2000, December 20). *Low-Tech but with Aspirations High*. The Australian Higher Education Section.

Hoeks, C., C., M., Q. (2012). *Srilankan Teachers as Agents of Peace* [Master's thesis, Graduate School of Social Sciences, University of Amsterdam]. https://educationanddevelopment.files.wordpress.com/2008/04/master-these-ids-sri-lankan-teachers-as-agents-of-peace-cc3a9line-hoeks.pdf

Hoole, R., Somasundaram, D., Sritharan, K., and Thiranagama, R. (1992). *The Broken Palmyra: The Tamil Crisis in Sri Lanka—An Inside Account*. The Sri Lanka Studies Institute.

Human Rights Watch. (2009, March 23). *Sri Lanka: No Let-Up in Army Shelling of Civilians*. Human Rights Watch. https://www.hrw.org/news/2009/03/23/sri-lanka-no-let-army-shelling-civilians

INEE. (2011). *Understanding Education's Role in Fragility, a Synthesis of Four Situational Analyses of Education and Fragility: Afghanistan, Bosnia-Herzegovina, Cambodia and Liberia*. IIEP.

Jabbar, M. A., and Sajeetha, T. F. (2014). *Conflict Transformation in Post War Sri Lanka. South Eastern University of Sri Lanka*. University of Sri Lanka. http://ir.lib.seu.ac.lk/handle/123456789/1512

Jaffna University Helidrop. (2022). Wikipedia, https://en.wikipedia.org/w/index.php?title=Jaffna_University_Helidrop&oldid=1074439347

Jayshree, B. (2009). *The Sri Lankan Conflict*. Council on Foreign Relations. https://www.cfr.org/backgrounder/sri-lankan-conflict

JDS. (2009). *Witness of the 'War Without Witness'*. http://www.jdslanka.org/index.php/multimedia/pictures/193-witness-of-the-war-without-witness

JUSTA. (2014, December 8). The Jaffna Precedent in University Council Appointments and Militarization of Education in Sri Lanka. *Colombo Telegraph*. https://www.colombotelegraph.com/index.php/the-jaffna-precedent-in-university-council-appointments-and-militarization-of-education-in-sri-lanka-justa/

Kaburu, G. (2014). *Teaching for Social Justice in Northern Uganda: The Case of Mission Girls' School*. The Ohio State University.

Kanagarthnam, J. (2019). Sri Lankan Reconstruction and Reconciliation: A Special Reference to Northern Province. *International Journal of Academic Research*, 2(2), 53–59. https://www.iajournals.org/articles/iajsse_v2_i2_53_59.pdf

—(2021). Political, Social and Economic Issues of the Rehabilitated Ex-combatants in the Sri Lankan Northern Province. *International Journal of Teaching & Education*, 6(7). https://ijessnet.com/wp-content/uploads/2022/10/3-38.pdf

Kathirgamar, A. (2017). *The Failure of Post-War Reconstruction in Jaffna, Sri Lanka: Indebtedness, Caste Exclusion and the Search for Alternatives* [Doctoral thesis, City University of New York]. https://academicworks.cuny.edu/gc_etds/1901

Kelman, H. (2010). Conflict Resolution and Reconciliation: A Social-Psychological Perspective on Ending Violent Conflict Between Identity Groups. *Landscapes of Violence*, 1(1). https://doi.org/10.7275/R5H12ZX0

Kitchin, R. M., and Hubbard, P. J. (1999). Research, Action and 'Critical' Geographies. *Area*, 31(3), 195–198. https://doi.org/10.1111/j.1475-4762.1999.tb00083.x

Kumanan. (2022, January 25). *Sri Lanka Military's Latest Assault Weapon: Barbed Wire Wrapped Palm Frond*. Journalist for Democracy in Srilanka. http://www.jdslanka.org/index.php/news-features/human-rights/1074-sri-lanka-militarys-new-assault-weapon-barbed-wire-wrapped-palm-frond

Lakshman, I., Rajeshkannan, R., and Schubert, M. (2020). Continuing Education During Times of War: Experiences of Children in Northern Sri Lanka. *European Scientific Journal*, 16. https://doi.org/10.19044/esj.2020.v16n35p1

Lebeau, Y., and Sall, E. (2011). Global Institutions, Higher Education and Development. In R. King, S. Marginson, and R. Naidoo (Eds), *A Handbook on Globalization and Higher Education* (Vol. Ch. 8, n.p.). Edward Elgar Publishing.

Lopes Cardozo, M. T. A., and Hoeks, C. C. M. Q. (2015). Losing Ground: A Critical Analysis of Teachers' Agency for Peacebuilding Education in Sri Lanka. *Journal of Peace Education*, 12(1), 56–73. https://doi.org/10.1080/17400201.2014.940516

Lopes Cardozo, M. T. A., and Shah, R. (2016). 'The Fruit Caught between Two Stones': The Conflicted Position of Teachers within Aceh's Independence Struggle. *Globalisation, Societies and Education*, 14(3), 331–344. https://doi.org/10.1080/14767724.2016.1145572

Magee, A., and Pherali, T. (2019). Paulo Freire and Critical Consciousness in Conflict-affected Contexts. *Education and Conflict Review*, 2, 44–48. https://discovery.ucl.ac.uk/id/eprint/10081479/1/Paulo%20Freire%20and%20critical%20consciousness%20in%20conflict-affected%20contexts.pdf

Mahendran, T. (2016, July 27). Clash At Jaffna University: Conversations on Culture and History - Part II. *Colombo Telegraph*. https://www.colombotelegraph.com/index.php/clash-at-jaffna-university-conversations-on-culture-history-part-ii/

Alexander, W. A. (1993). *What Matters in College: Four Critical Years Revisited*. Jossey-Bass. https://psycnet.apa.org/record/1992-98891-000.

Matthews, B. (1995). University Education in Sri Lanka in Context: Consequences of Deteriorating Standards. *Pacific Affairs*, 68(1), 77–94.

Milton, S. (2018). *Higher Education and Post-Conflict Recovery*. Springer International Publishing. https://doi.org/10.1007/978-3-319-65349-5

—, and Barakat, S. (2016). Higher Education as the Catalyst of Recovery in Conflict-affected Societies. *Globalisation, Societies and Education, 14*(3), 403–421. https://doi.org/10.1080/14767724.2015.1127749

Ministry of Finance and Planning. (2014). *Annual Report 2013* [Annual Report]. Ministry of Finance and Planning. https://www.treasury.gov.lk/api/file/33f4533e-3106-4496-86b3-73f696652e05

—(2016). *Annual Report 2015* [Annual Report]. Ministry of Finance and Planning. https://www.treasury.gov.lk/api/file/9d7d5089-59a2-48ab-a7a9-955482cf3f62

Moore, M. (1993). Thoroughly Modern Revolutionaries: The JVP in Sri Lanka. *Modern Asian Studies, 27*(3), 593–642. https://doi.org/10.1017/S0026749X00010908

—(2018). Social Work Practitioners in Post-conflict Northern Ireland: Lessons from a Critical Ethnography. *International Social Work, 61*(3), 383–394. https://doi.org/10.1177/0020872816644664

Mufdi, M., and Slaihate, B. (2014). The University's Role in Promoting its Students' Social Awareness from the Students' Perspective at Balqa Applied University. *International Journal of Education, 6*(4). 71-92. https://www.macrothink.org/journal/index.php/ije/article/view/6744

Nithyani, A. (2020, August 31). *The Sri Lankan Civil War and Its History, Revisited in 2020.* Harvard International Review. https://hir.harvard.edu/sri-lankan-civil-war

Omeje, K. (2009). Introduction: Discourses of the Liberian Civil War and Imperatives of Peacebuilding. In *In War to Peace Transition: Conflict Intervention and Peacebuilding in Liberia* (pp. 1–16). University Press of America.

—(2015). Promoting Peace and Conflict-Sensitive Higher Education in Sub-Saharan Africa. *African Conflict and Peacebuilding Review, 5*(2), 33–56. https://doi.org/10.2979/africonfpeacrevi.5.2.33

Pacitto, J., and Fiddian-Qasmiyeh, E. (2013). *Writing the 'Other' into Humanitarian Discourse: Framing Theory and Practice in South-South Humanitarian Responses to Forced Displacement.* Refugee Studies Centre. https://www.rsc.ox.ac.uk/files/files-1/wp93-south-south-humanitarianism-contexts-forced-migration-2013.pdf

Parkinson, T., Zoubir, T., Abdullateef, S., Abedtalas, M., Alyamani, G., Al Ibrahim, Z., Al Husni, M., Omar, F. A., Hajhamoud, H., Iboor, F., Allito, H., Jenkins, M., Rashwani, A., Sennou, A., and Shaban, F. (2018). 'We Are Still Here': The Stories of Syrian Academics in Exile. *International Journal of Comparative Education and Development, 20*(3/4), 132–147. https://doi.org/10.1108/IJCED-06-2018-0013

Postgraduate Diploma in Conflict and Peace Studies – PgDCPS 2022/23. (n.d.). Faculty of Graduate Studies. https://fgs.cmb.ac.lk/course/3698/

Psychological Trauma of the Civil War in Sri Lanka. (2002, April 26). *Médecins Sans Frontières (MSF) International.* https://www.msf.org/psychological-trauma-civil-war-sri-lanka

Rajan, H. (1995, October). *Peace: Understanding our Reality!* UTHR(J): University Teachers for Human Rights (Jaffna). https://uthr.org/history.htm

Reddy, J. (2005). *5/6ths of Iraq's Higher Learning Institutions Burnt, Looted, Wrecked; 48 Profs Slain; UNU Calls for World Help to Repair System.* United Nations University. https://reliefweb.int/report/iraq/iraq-56ths-iraqs-higher-learning-institutions-burnt-looted-wrecked-48-profs-slain-unu

Rose, P., and Greeley, M. (2006). *Education in Fragile States: Capturing Lessons and Identifying Good Practice.* Prepared for the DAC Fragile States Group Service Delivery Workstream Sub-Team for Education Services. https://www.ids.ac.uk/download.php?file=files/Education_and_Fragile_States.pdf

Russell, I. (2022). Degrees of Peace: Universities and Embodied Experiences of Conflict in Post-war Sri Lanka. *Third World Quarterly, 43*(4), 898–915. https://doi.org/10.1080/01436597.2022.2038129

SAR. (2022, May 6). *Protecting Scholars and the Freedom to Think, Question, and Share Ideas.* SAR Network. https://www.scholarsatrisk.org/report/2022-05-06-various/

Sam, T. (2017, April 17). Jaffna: A University Sinking in Mediocrity and Sectarianism. *Colombo Telegraph.* https://www.colombotelegraph.com/index.php/jaffna-a-university-sinking-in-mediocrity-and-sectarianism/

Shah, R. (2012). Goodbye Conflict, Hello Development? Curriculum Reform in Timor-Leste. *International Journal of Educational Development, 32*(1), 31–38. https://doi.org/10.1016/j.ijedudev.2011.04.005

Shah, R., and Cardozo, M. T. L. (2016). Transformative Teachers or Teachers to Be Transformed? The Cases of Bolivia and Timor-Leste. *Research in Comparative and International Education, 11*(2), 208–221. https://doi.org/10.1177/1745499916633314

Shaker, G. G. (2016). The Global Common Good and the Future of Academic Professionals. *Higher Learning Research Communications, 6*(2). https://doi.org/10.18870/hlrc.v6i2.333

Simon, K. (2012). SSHR Works to Build Trust among Students in Post-conflict Sri Lanka. *RightsNews, 30*(2).

Spencer, J. (1990). *Sri Lanka: History and the Roots of the Conflict.* Routledge.

Steenkamp, C. (2009). *Violence and Post-war Reconstruction: Managing Insecurity in the Aftermath of Peace Accords.* I.B. Tauris.

Tahirsyzaj, A. (2010). Higher Education in Kosovo: Major Changes, Reforms, and Development Trends in the Post-Conflict Period at the University of Prishtina. *Interchange, 41*(2), 171–183. https://doi.org/10.1007/s10780-010-9117-0

Tambiah, S. J. (1986). *Sri Lanka—Ethnic Fratricide and the Dismantling of Democracy*. University of Chicago Press.

TamilNet. (2018, December 6). *Skeletal Remains with Shackled Legs Exhumed in Mannaar Mass Grave*. https://www.tamilnet.com/art.html?catid=13&artid=39274

—(2019, November 26). *Colombo Attempts to Officially Block Students from Marking Heroes Day at Jaffna University*. https://www.tamilnet.com/art.html?catid=13&artid=39649

Thamil Venthan, A. (2020, May 31). The Burning of Jaffna Public Library: Sri Lanka's First Step Toward Civil War. *The Diplomat*. https://thediplomat.com/2020/05/the-burning-of-jaffna-public-library-sri-lankas-first-step-toward-civil-war

Tierney, W. (2011). The Role of Tertiary Education in Fixing Failed States: Globalization and Public Goods. *Journal of Peace Education, 8*(2), 127–142. https://doi.org/10.1080/17400201.2011.589256

Tomlinson, K., and Benefield, P. (2005). *Education and Conflict: Research and Research Possibilities*. National Foundation for Educational Research. https://files.eric.ed.gov/fulltext/ED502593.pdf

UNESCO. (2017). *Higher Education in Crisis Situations: Synergizing Policies and Promising Practices to Enhance Access, Equity and Quality in the Arab Region*. UNESCO. https://www.academia.edu/98963598/THE_REGIONAL_CONFERENCE_ON_HIGHER_EDUCATION_IN_CRISIS_SITUATIONS_Higher_Education_in_Crisis_Situations_Synergizing_Policies_and_Promising_Practices_to_enhance_Access_Equity_and_Quality_in_the_Arab_Region_

University Grants Commission. (2011). *Sri Lanka University Statistics 2010*. University Grants Commission. https://www.ugc.ac.lk/index.php?option=com_content&view=article&id=102&Itemid=70&lang=en

University Teachers for Human Rights (Jaffna). UTHR(J). (2014a). *Welcome to UTHR(J), SRI LANKA*. University Teachers for Human Rights (Jaffna), Srilanka, https://www.uthr.org/

UTHR (2014b, September 14). *Rays of Hope Amidst Deepening Gloom, Report 10: Chapter 5: North-East Notes*. University Teachers for Human Rights (Jaffna), https://uthr.org/history.htm

UTHR (2014c, September 14). *The LTTE and the Emerging Society in Jaffna, Chapter 3: The Role of Institutions*. University Teachers for Human Rights (Jaffna), https://uthr.org/Reports/Report10/Report10.htm

Vongalkis-Macrow, A. (2007). Teacher: Re-territorialization of Teachers' Multi-Faceted Agency in Globalized Education. *British Journal of Sociology of Education, 28*(4), 424–439. https://doi.org/10.1080/01425690701369376

Williams, J. (2016). A Critical Exploration of Changing Definitions of Public Good in Relation to Higher Education. *Studies in Higher Education, 42,* 619–630. https://doi.org/10.1080/03075079.2014.942270

Wendy, R. (2011, May 12). *Hope for Resurgence of Sri Lanka's North Rests on Education.* The Asia Foundation. https://asiafoundation.org/2011/05/11/hope-for-resurgence-of-sri-lankas-north-rests-on-education/

Wickramasinghe, N. (2014). *Sri Lanka in the Modern Age: A History.* Oxford University Press.

Wilson, A., J. (1988). *The Break-up of Sri Lanka: The Sinhalese-Tamil Conflict.* University of Hawaii Press.

World Bank. (2004). *Education in Rwanda: Rebalancing Resources to Accelerate Post-conflict Development and Poverty Reduction.* World Bank. http://hdl.handle.net/10986/15034

—(2010). *Sri Lanka: Reshaping Economic Geograph—Connecting People to Prosperity.* World Bank. https://hdl.handle.net/10986/21549

4. Being a Woman and a Researcher between Exile and Social Reconfiguration: An Interview with Hebe Vessuri

Guillermo López Franco, Nissa Yaing Torres-Soto, Alejandra Aray-Roa and Paulette Joseph

Introduction

Dr Hebe Vessuri is one of the most important names in cultural anthropology in Latin America. With a career of four decades in academia, she has contributed to the establishment and development of various higher education institutions and diverse research networks, informing the education and training of many generations of professionals, academics and researchers. However, her outstanding career as a social researcher can be seen not just as a story of success, but also as a story of conflict.

As early career academics from México and Venezuela, we decided to engage Vessuri in 2022 so as to gain insider insights into such lived intellectual experience. In our study of Vessuri's perceptions, we were interested in the biographical account, the different contextual elements and the interpretations of our interviewee about her own experience.

Based on the guides of Creswell and Poths (2013) for qualitative research, we used the interpretative phenomenological approach (IPA), wherein we focused on Vessuri's subjective experiences as a social actor and identified the meanings behind the experience. This functioned as the basis for our deductions of the deeper meanings involved in the phenomena of conflict (Rodríguez, Gil and García, 1999). We took these meanings to be interwoven with the bodily, material and social elements

https://doi.org/10.11647/OBP.0427.04

that constituted the conditions she experienced (Álvarez-Gayou, 2009). Phenomenological approaches in migration and conflict studies have long been utilised to describe people's thoughts through such life-story methods and semi-structured interview techniques (Martínez, 2006). Our approach to IPA was influenced by the narrative research method (Mitchell and Egudo, 2003). We follow a chronological order to reconstruct the different episodes in Vessuri's life, organised by the period she spent in each country and its historical background. We also provide information on the social and political dynamics that shaped the experiences of Vessuri in each phase of her career.

The interview was conducted and recorded on August 21, 2021 in a single three-hour session via ZOOM, with the participation of Dr Vessuri and the four members of the research team who focused on different sections of the conversation.

In this chapter, we discuss how Vessuri met the many faces of political and social change in Latin America in her academic lifetime. Born in Argentina in 1942, she began her studies in the Philosophy and Literature Faculty of Universidad Autónoma de Buenos Aires in 1962 but she changed her scope completely, moving to Oxford to study Anthropology at the University of Oxford from 1965 to 1971. Returning to the American continent, she began her professional career during the 1970s, when the Argentinian dictatorship began. She was forced to leave the country and then started a life in exile in Venezuela, in Brazil and then again in Venezuela until she moved to México and retired during the rise of narco-violence. For more than forty years, she has been a witness to both democratic and dictatorial transitions in the different countries in which she has worked. During these various stages of history, Vessuri had to face the disadvantages and challenges of being an expatriate, a mother and a woman in competitive and unequal academic systems with structures closed to career development which changed over time, with positive openings in recent years.

A central theme of her life is im/mobility. Migration is a global phenomenon; migratory movements have particular features, motivations and outcomes. When we speak about migrant women, it is necessary to understand that this process is complex. In Venezuela's case, we speak about a convulsive situation, economic crisis, instability and political conflict. All these elements have been the cause of the massive departure of Venezuelan people heading to other countries in the South American region such as Colombia, Ecuador and Peru as the main destinations (Flores, 2020). However, the migrant Venezuelan population has spread around the world. Feminine migration, as mentioned above, has specific features that can be marked by the gendered condition, implying challenges and difficulties in women's subjective experience. Understanding that experience is precisely the main interest of this chapter.

It is important to mention that migration itself is a conflict because it forms personalities, thoughts and daily actions that imply a sort of mourning and detachment as a social phenomenon (Rubio, 2012). In that sense, Vessuri can be an example of the process of being a stranger adapting to different realities, as she explains:

> When you say migrant the first time, I think maybe I felt migrant when I left Argentina and moved to Venezuela. I stayed in Venezuela from 1975 to 1987, then I went to Brazil until 1991 when I came back to Venezuela. I lived there until 2010 and that year I went to Mexico, where I lived, approximately, until 2016 when I returned to Argentina.

Such testimony reveals how our interviewee saw a turning point in her biography, when she was not free to decide when to leave her country. Before that episode, which we discuss in the next section, Vessuri was free to decide where and when she wanted to move, with the freedom to return to Argentina when and if she decided to. However, the conditions were not conducive until many years later. As a consequence, the process of leaving, detachment and mourning described by Rubio (2012) had a different development, marked by social and political conflict.

In this biographical analysis, we represent Vessuri's testimony about how she lived and negotiated through these different events and historic processes. What emerges is that she was not just a witness to political, cultural and social conflict as an intellectual studying change—she was also subject and actor. This is a feature of her own framing of her account, wherein she chose to present to us her views about herself as 'academic' who was a woman, at times a citizen or immigrant, a mother and a leader, and what such roles, identities and positions meant for being a researcher within conflict-affected and conflictive conditions.

Our Intentionality within the Dialogue and Analysis

The conversation with Vessuri took place thanks to the previous experience of one of the authors, Alejandra, who was her student in Venezuela between 2000 and 2006. Vessuri was her thesis supervisor for her Master's degree and PhD in the Venezuelan Institute of Scientific Research (IVIC). When we heard news about the book project 'Being in Shadow and Light', Alejandra was aware of many of the experiences Vessuri lived and suggested we ask her for an interview about her life as a great example of what it means to be an academic immersed in a conflicted context. There have been a number of interviews with Vessuri in recent years, but we wished to explore the different roles of her life—specifically, how her gender as a woman intersected with her migrant and exiled status and the academic profession. The conversation and writing of this chapter enabled us, younger researchers, to reflect on our own careers and their contrast with Vessuri's experience.

The intention was to provide her with an open space to let her narrate her life and offer her commentaries on society, including the changes she has lived through in the conditions of women. For that, we approached her with respect, explaining to her the purpose of the interview. Our main concern was to be thoughtful about the way we were going to cover sensitive aspects of her life, and she was quite open about her ideas and feelings. We are very grateful to her and appreciative of her honesty.

This research aims to accompany the retelling of Vessuri's life with reflections on the conditions of migration and gender from a sociological perspective. The biography of Dr Vessuri is quite known, but we provide an analysis on the social and historical background of the different episodes shared by our interviewee.

This chapter's structure follows the episodes of Vessuri's life in chronological order. The chapter provides excerpts of her testimony that set and enrich the development of the different sections. We will foreground the narrative with an initial section about the political and social conditions surrounding her experiences.

Understanding Conflict and the University

People engage with society to survive. Socialisation and social institutions are means to prevail. However, the social process rarely is smooth or aseptic—most of the time, there are difficulties based on the different interests, rights and freedom of the social actors. Educational spaces, even with shared goals of learning, are spaces where those same elements can be in controversy or dispute. This is the reason to understand the conflict and its manifestation in higher education institutions. We review the conflict within higher education and its features on the Latin American background.

To understand conflict, Sayas (2015) explains that it is present when there is an opposition in interests and goals between social actors, whether on an individual, group, national or international level. Conflict is a phenomenon inherent to social relationships that has had multidisciplinary interest as a subject of study (Sayas, 2015). Social research, in particular, can address many of the dimensions or levels of conflict.

Higher education institutions are spaces of change and, hence, conflict in modern social life. Lybeck outlined how modern, Western universities experienced and have been part of the political, economic and social revolutions from the seventeenth century to the present day (Academic College, 2021). He reviewed the role of universities as sites of public debate and competition between different communities and ideologies, and as a reflex to and reproducer of social inequalities (Academic College, 2021). Moreover, Papacchini (2001) explains how universities, as organisations, can conflict within their structure and function, and with other social institutions such as the state.

Higher education in Latin America has been a long tradition in the building of social structure. It can be traced back to the times of European colonisation. However, one of the pivotal moments was the Córdoba Movement in Argentina in 1919 (Pastrana, 2008). Influenced by the works of intellectuals such as José Enriqué Rodó, students of the Córdoba University demanded college autonomy that included: freedom for teachers' classes, participation to assign professors to the courses, democratisation of processes, free research and the involvement of the university in providing social services (Pastrana, 2008).

In Latin America, higher education studies have a sizable production, although this has not impacted on the main research publications outside of the dominant databases and publishing agendas (Guzmán-Valenzuela and López, 2014). Notoriously, this is part of Vessuri's research interest (1991; 1994; 1996). Despite that, we have insights of the development of Latin American higher education under the two great ideologies: German Humboldtian focus on research and teaching, and the French Napoleonic model of public service to form citizens—two ideas that blended together to accompany the crisis of the national states in the second half of the twentieth century facing globalisation (Brunner, 2014).

In that sense, Pinheiro et al. (2015, p. 5) go in depth classifying the pressure over higher education institutions in two dimensions, global and national, in two main areas: economical and societal conditions. The autonomy of universities, a precious feature for public universities since the Córdoba Movement in 1919 (Guzmán-Valenzuela and López, 2014), allows institutions to make their own decisions to adapt to the changing conditions.

Perhaps some of the most visible examples of how academia and universities respond to and participate in the internal and external tensions are the cases of the university movements and protests during the 1960s when university students and professors gathered in massive social movements around the world. We saw the protest against the Vietnam War and the feminist and pacifist manifestations in the US colleges, the left-wing mobilisation against Charles De Gaulle politics in the French college system and the protest and bloody repression of the students' movement in México.

Vessuri lived through a time of internal and external pressures over state education and thus higher education systems. From the exterior, we can identify the Cold War and the changes in the international economy, such as the Oil Crisis in 1974 or the global recession in 1981. On the local level, we have the different conditions of Argentina, Venezuela and Brazil in their track of unsuccessful democracies, guerrillas and dictatorships, while in México there is the deterioration of the Rule of Law due to organised crime. In all of these countries, higher education institutions faced numerous challenges to keep their autonomy and adapt to different contexts.

These different political and social movements generated or adopted by university students and academics were not strange for higher education institutions. According to Papacchini (2001), higher education institutions have a calling to be active centres for social activism, human rights and peace. Universities, students and academics cannot be politically neutral or detached from the rest of society, and academics have a role as critics of the state and war.

It was within such conditions of social unrest and change during the 1960s that Vessuri started her journey as a young student. She went to the United Kingdom along with her first husband and became very interested in social studies. She went to the University of Oxford in 1962 looking for a fresh start in Anthropology, a discipline in which she pursued a research degree. The conflict pursued Vessuri for almost her entire career, as we can see from her words and from tracing her work in the fields of higher education and anthropology to troubled conditions within Latin America.

Latin America and Universities

Latin American countries—diverse in their historical development and culture, but with shared features such as their colonial past and their pursuit of democracy and development—offer an interesting setting for social research. According to Brunner and Ganga (2016), despite the international implementation of New Public Management policies in education (Tolofari, 2005), Latin American higher education systems still rely heavily on public institutions with Estate funding and with a grants scheme for private universities (Brunner and Ganga, 2006). The understanding of public-oriented higher education in Latin America helps to explain the particular features of how politics and the economy are linked to higher education institutions. In this region, Vessuri developed her career.

Government shifts and economic developments in Latin America have transitioned along common paths, as Rodríguez (1997) outlined. During the 1950s, the populist trend in Latin American governments evolved to development approaches based on corporatism and investment in the industrial sector. However, in the years that followed, those development models began to be questioned because of the unsustainable social inequalities between urban middle classes and rural populations, in addition to dependency on the exportation of raw materials such as oil. During the 1970s, the deficits of the development model provided fertile ground for new authoritarian regimes backed by popular discontent. Military forces took control over the government in countries such as Argentina and Chile, adopting corrective economic policies based on neoliberal orientations. In Venezuela and México, however, the development model which continued throughout the 1970s and 1980s concluded in severe crises.

The complex, divergent political scenario depicted by Rodríguez (1997) is enlivened in relation to the countries where Vessuri developed her career. Table 4.1 includes each of those countries, with indications of political instability informed by archival research undertaken by the authors in 2021 at the Cline Centre of the University of Illinois. The following table spans from three years after Vessuri was born until a short period before her retirement. Looking at Table 4.1, it is possible to infer the condition of democracy and rule of law from the documented conspiracies to overthrow the legal authorities, the attempted coup d'états and those that were successful.

Table 4.1 Quantity of coups d'état and conspiracies (1945–2019).

Country[1]	Conspiracies	Attempts	Successes	Total coups
Argentina	4	11	9	23
United Kingdom	0	0	0	0
Canada	0	0	0	0
Venezuela	3	14	4	21
Brazil	0	2	5	7
México	1	0	0	1

This tabulation quantifies how the two countries where Vessuri worked the most—Argentina and Venezuela—have had a history of great political instability during the second half of the twentieth century and the beginning of the twenty-first century. Argentinians lived under a military regime with a notorious anti-communist orientation in the 1970s. Meanwhile, the effect of an oil exportation model that once boomed and

---

1   The countries where Dr Vessuri lived and worked, ordered chronologically.

then collapsed led Venezuela from an incipient civil democracy to an authoritarian regime at the beginning of the twenty-first century.

In such conditions, Latin American universities experienced a lapse of expansion (Rodríguez, 1997). Higher education institutions accompanied the development model with increases in educational offerings for the new workers and professionals needed for the economy. The traditional model of public investment in higher education and the state as a major actor in providing funding is a common feature in Latin America (Brunner and Ganga, 2016). There was much effort within the public sector to raise funding, decentralise, diversify education offered and renew the curriculum, during the 1960s and 1970s (Rodríguez, 1997). However, along with political instability and economic stagnation, universities faced troubles assuring the quality and coverage of their educational and research services.

In this growth-set-back scenario, Vessuri developed her academic career. She was a witness to the bonanza years of the economic model of the 1970s and its later collapse. Coups d'état, economic crises, and exile marked her path—a path, however, which has been successful and full of achievements as a social researcher making a positive impact in the Argentinian, Venezuelan, Brazilian and Mexican higher education institutions in which she worked.

Hebe Vessuri and the Social Sciences in Latin American Institutions

Vessuri contributed to the emergence and consolidation of the field of social studies of science and technology in Latin America. Her work serves as a respected reference for several generations who have been interested in science studies, including anthropology and the sociology of science. This includes the intellectual formation of the authors of this article.

Initially, during her first marriage and while living in Argentina, she moved to the University of Tucumán, where she worked on aspects of popular Catholicism as well as the family farm. She began her line of research on the social organisation of the agricultural population, with a specific interest in the role of the sugar industry. After the dictatorship of her exile to Venezuela, she won a contest to become a teacher at the

School of Sociology and Anthropology of the Central University of
Venezuela, later becoming a member of *Centro de Estudios del Desarrollo*
(CENDES).[2] Here, she began to work on technology issues in agriculture
in a science and technology network. It was during this period as a
member of CENDES that Vessuri's interests gradually started to evolve
into science studies, including the institutionalisation of scientific
disciplines, and research agendas. Her interest was in the interface
between higher education and scientific research, and hybridisation
processes of knowledge in Latin America. Vessuri has been a pioneer in
contributing to institutionalisation with the foundation of Postgraduate
Studies in Science, Technology and Society in Venezuela [CENDES,
1978 and IVIC in 1993], Brazil [UNICAMP in 1987] (Freites, 2006).

Due to the volume and nature of the work of Vessuri, it is perhaps
an injustice to disaggregate it. However, three main categories can be
discerned since 1980. Firstly, the sociology of science and the scientific
profession, with a special focus on Latin America as a 'peripheral
region' in the global knowledge system (Vessuri, 2019, 2014, 2013,
1994, 1993, 1987; Kreimer and Vessuri, 2018). Secondly, the science
of society relations in Venezuela, exploring its different institutions
and development of professions, disciplines and knowledge, and
the conditions of science production in that country (Laya and
Vessuri, 2019; Rodríguez, Vessuri and Bilbao, 2009; Vessuri, Canino
and Sánchez-Rose, 2005; Vessuri, 2001; Vessuri and Canino, 2001).
Thirdly, gender studies and the position of women in professional
and academic institutions. For instance, Vessuri studied the impact of
gender on women's participation in Venezuelan science production
(Vessuri and Canino, 2001), the conditions of exclusion and poverty
among Venezuelan women (Castellanos, Canino and Vessuri, 2007),
feminine participation in higher education (Canino and Vessuri, 2008)
and women in industry (Aray, Vessuri, and Canino, 2011).

In addition to her scholarship, her efforts to strengthen international
ties by promoting and coordinating regional research projects were also
significant. This was recognised formally in 2017, when she was the first

2   CENDES is a research and postgraduate institute inaugurated in 1961 by a
     visionary group of Latin Americans, who set out to create an interdisciplinary
     research and postgraduate centre dedicated to planning and development
     problems.

Latin American woman to receive the John Desmond Bernal award, in recognition of her contribution to the field of *Estudios Sociales de la Ciencia y la Tecnología* (ESCT) [Social Studies of Science and Technology]. In her career, she had been a member of the *Consejo Latinoamericano de Ciencias Sociales* (CLACSO) [Latin American Council of Social Science], the International Council of Science (ICS), the United Nations' Education, Science and Culture Organization (UNESCO), and many other college and research organisations specialising in social sciences (Society for Social Studies of Science, 2017).

The academic career and achievements of Vessuri in the consolidation of social sciences in Latin America have a significant value. Moreover, she is regarded as one of the main personalities in the study of the sociology of science in the continent.

Argentina: 'A Never-ending Dictatorship'

Look, I do not even remember how that dictatorship was because it seems like a never-ending dictatorship. It was the dictatorship of this one and the dictatorship of this other one. They were changing with the times.

This excerpt is illustrative of how Vessuri recalls the history of Argentina from 1960 to 1980, with the slippages across time of Argentinian political dynamics. She articulated that she felt the country had never been a true democracy, neither at the point in 1965 when she had temporarily left the country for her studies, nor in the early 1970s when she returned.

The Argentine military regime had already begun (Baranger, 2013) by the time Vessuri concluded her studies in Oxford; and so, when she and her family decided to leave the United Kingdom, they did not return to Argentina as originally intended but moved to Canada instead. President Arturo Illia had been overthrown by a coup d'état conducted by the Argentine Armed Forces in 1966, establishing General Juan Carlos Onganía as the new president. He implemented a new national security law that originated a guerrilla movement (Pontoriero, 2015). The national unrest grew, until General Onganía was removed and succeeded by General Roberto Levingston in 1970. After him, General Alejandro Lanusse started a democratic transition process between 1971 and 1973 (Pontoriero, 2015).

During these periods, Vessuri worked in Canada as a lecturer and researcher. She had been awarded a scholarship from the Canadian Council to conduct research in Santiago del Estero, Argentina, focused on the peasants' life. She only returned with her family in 1971, at a point when the military regime was in its final years. Fragile democracy characterised the short-lived governments led by presidents Cámpora and Lastiri, before Perón's last term in 1973 (de Pablo, 2021). President Perón died in June 1974, and his widow, the then Vice-President María Estela Martínez de Perón, assumed the presidency from July 1974 to March 1976.

Democracy in Argentina struggled within the negative international economic conditions of oil commerce, and the local political crisis (de Pablo, 2021). Another coup d'état was placed by the general Jorge Rafael Videla in the presidency in 1976, commencing yet another period of dictatorship. Vessuri was conducting her research with peasant communities of Santiago del Estero when, on March 24, 1976, General Jorge Rafael Videla took power and established a military junta. This was to become one of the worst authoritarian regimes of the twentieth century on account of its massive human rights violations (Crespo, 2017). In the interview, Vessuri described how she viewed herself as a true migrant for the first time during this period in the 1970s because of her forced displacement.

'They Kicked Me Out of my Own Country'

Videla's regime was part of a continental authoritarian movement caught up in the Cold War. It was thus primarily focused against Communism and its supporters (Novaro and Palermo, 2003). In Argentina, the pursuit of left-like movements caused thirty thousand cases of disappearances (Crespo, 2017) and significant migration. The magnitude of the Argentine diaspora during this time is hard to quantify, with estimates of over five hundred thousand expatriates, including those who left the country to escape oppression and hardship and those who were exiled by the military junta's decision (Jensen and Yankelevich, 2007). Vessuri recalled those times, when she was working in Tucumán for *Centro de Investigaciones en Ciencias Sociales* (CICSO) [Social Sciences Research Centre], and her husband Santiago—a local anthropologist and social worker—was part of *Instituto Nacional de Tecnología Agropecuaria* (INTA) [National Institute of Agricultural Sciences], being part of a program for sugarcane production (Baranger, 2013). President Perón died in 1974 and the presidency of his wife, Martínez de Perón, resulted in an escalating instability in the political and economic conditions of the country. The situation of Vessuri and her husband became more complicated until his kidnapping in 1975.

> Argentina lived through an extended period of decomposition of its democratic life, of its civil society. I lived in that moment when Perón died, I think. Immediately, repression began. Two days after they started, my husband was in prison, he was taken as a hostage, as were many others, for, I do not know, absolutely because of political and personal reasons.

Vessuri remembers with clarity the night when Santiago was kidnapped. She was left alone with her little children. She remembered the panic of trying to communicate with her family, and of their looking for information regarding his whereabouts. As with many other women of the time, she recalled, 'you did not know if your partner was killed or not, going towards different prisons looking for your husband'.

The violence against political and academic figures, such as Vessuri's husband, can be understood as part of a broader campaign of fear. She explained the phenomenon as 'intimidation by fear. You can generate fear as a collective feeling to dominate and appease the other, and keep her or him under control'. In that situation, the aim of Argentina's junta was 'to paralyse the action and reaction of the family that is supposedly involved with the people they wanted to take out'. According to Vessuri, the junta's strategy was to attack, and thereby undermine, the whole family of the individuals considered to be against the government.

Her husband was kept in a Buenos Aires prison for eleven months before being sentenced to exile. The whole family was affected, deciding to leave with him. The choice of Venezuela as a destination was coherent with the Latin American political conditions. Among many countries characterised for their authoritarian and repressive politics, Venezuela, México and Costa Rica were perceived to be open to migrants, offering legal protection for foreign refugees (Ayala and Jensen, 2017). Venezuela has been receiving Argentinian refugees for some time, including during Isabel Peron's regime before the coup. However, in response to the junta's criteria, the Venezuelan government restricted the number of approved asylum applications (Ayala and Jensen, 2017). Vessuri's family was accepted, and established themselves in Caracas during 1975, starting a new life.

Venezuela: The Paradise

After her *academic* experience in Great Britain and North America, Vessuri experienced Venezuela as a 'paradise' in opposition to the conditions which had engendered her exile from Argentina. That initial reprieve would be short-lived. However, after the 1966 insurrection of the guerrilla movement, the *Fuerzas Armadas de Liberación Nacional*, the social structure was somewhat stabilised during the 1970s.

Migration ties between Argentina and Venezuela have a longer story. During its economic development in 1970, boosted by the oil industry, Venezuela attracted a great quantity of professional and highly skilled immigrant workers to live within its border (De la Vega, 2003). The decision to migrate to Venezuela made sense for many families in South America escaping authoritarian regimes and the systematic violation of human rights, who saw Venezuela as a safe and prosperous country (Ayala, 2017; Ayala, 2014). Vessuri arrived with her family in 1975, supported by Argentinian friends already domiciled in Caracas, such as Manuel Sadosky[3] (Rivero et al., 2018). She was immediately intrigued by post-guerrilla Venezuelan society, 'it took my attention, that thrust, the independence of women, the strength they had'. During the interview, she highlighted the ways in which she remembers how this strength infused popular media.

> One thing that was very interesting to me was TV shows. I had friends in the media, where you saw that the pretty face in publicity was a young man, he was the protagonist, the host, the star, the actor that faced the crowd. And, behind the camera, the producer was a woman, the

---

3   A mathematician and calculus researcher from Universidad de Buenos Aires, Dr Sadosky was exiled from Argentina between 1974 and 1979 due to threats from anti-communist movements. During that period, he was part of the research staff of Universidad Central de Venezuela and had an important social role in helping Argentinian exiled nationals relocate to Caracas.

technicians were women, and the heavy work and designs of the show were made by women. Then I said, 'it's the world upside down'. Even in literature, in the media, women were very important. The comments of people, the regular guy saying 'my mom this, my mom that' [...]. The mom, the grandmother, that matriarchal kind of thing that worked there, it was very striking in opposition to the father figure that often was absent. Women always took care of the house and the children, right? So, this trait gave Venezuela a very particular flavour. It seemed fantastic to me, I was impressed by the strength of Venezuelan women.

That thrust of the Venezuelan woman is perhaps caused by the mother-focused society present historically in the region. A number of studies (Vessuri and Canino, 2017; Schnell-Anzola, Rowe and LeVine, 2005; Friedman, 1998; Flores, 1998; Vethencourt, 1974) have explored the importance of women in the Venezuelan family and society. The mother is the only adult with authority before her children, because the woman-mother figure handles family and social relations at her will, taking possession of the children. Men stand as a gesture or façade of formal representation and carry no weight; there is a lack of 'father culture' in the sense of sociological absence (Hurtado, 1998, pp. 161–169). This family condition in Venezuela provides an enabling 'sociocultural scenario' for women's participation in the different social spheres, including the labour market.

This particularity of Venezuelan society of the time may have been helpful to Vessuri as she made her way into social networks, enabling her to display her talent and potential, to stand out and create a space of her own from which she developed her academic life. Venezuela was experiencing a time of economic growth and consolidation of its higher education system, including research centres, for human resource formation. The Venezuelan government nationalised the oil and mining industries along with significant public investment in hydroelectric power plants (Rincón et al., 2016). In addition, guerrilla activities left a deep mark in society, where most of the casualties were men. When such violent conflict occurs, women usually take the role of maintaining families and reconstructing micro-level social structures.

Argentina and Venezuela: Contrasting Experiences for a Woman of Science

One of the most interesting experiences for Vessuri was the opposite realities of Argentina and Venezuela regarding the role of women in society. Moreover, the restrictions of Argentina in politics seemed to be reflected in the restrictions Vessuri experienced in Argentinian institutions on account of being a divorced mother, while in Venezuela she found an unsuspected openness.

In Argentina, the wider social inequities were nonetheless reproduced. Vessuri was used to the expectation that women inhabited traditional gendered roles, even when they worked in academic institutions where their rights and practices would have required legitimation by their male peers—in other words, the patriarchal model was present in the formal and informal dynamics of institutions. Women faced difficulties in accessing and developing their careers, having to defy the usual practices to succeed. Vessuri did not just challenge what was considered appropriate behaviour. She mixed two spaces that were supposed to be separated—the public work life and private domestic life intended for the care of children. As an academic mother, she brought her little children to her work, a practice all the more controversial as a divorced woman. That was a practice of resistance which made it evident that maternity was an excluding condition in the job market, as was the dissolution of matrimony.

> I was discriminated against because I wanted to teach in the Faculty of Universidad Pública Nacional, a male faculty. It was the Agronomy and Animal Husbandry Faculty [...] Then an argument with one of the members of the selection committee concluded, and I can tell because the other members said so, that I was a bad example for the kids, and the students. After all, I was a divorced woman. A divorced woman could not be a good example of a teacher in a male faculty [...] So, what happened? I won the opposition exam; I had a better academic and scientific background than any of the other young boys that contested. And, after a while, I went to the faculty with my baby in a stroller and left her to take the sun out of my office, in the hallway, in the corridor, in public, where everybody could see her—was it a challenge? Yes, it was a challenge against all that moralistic, that way of being. I mean, I married, I had a child, it was the most normal thing.

These experiences contrast markedly with her experience of Venezuela. She found that women in Venezuelan culture and society emerged stronger and more resilient than men in public spheres and in the workplace. However, their presence was strongest in private familial domains, where women were positioned at the axis, enabling them to take decisions and actions in domestic life. Vessuri's perspective on this was that the sociocultural features of Venezuela propitiated the development of a 'distinctive force' for women.

> Then that tremendous strength of women that came out with the guerrilla failure, with the failure of that world that they wanted to build back then, but that was also a backlash from the Cuban revolution, etc. I had not lived that directly, but in Universidad Central, in the student dorms, it was very intensely lived, because they found weapons. Men and women were involved in that process.

The anthropological perspective of Vessuri found an interesting case study in that moment of Venezuelan history:

> And I said, 'Well, why is this happening?'. One of the explanations I gave myself at that time was that some of the dominant traits of society regarded the fact that the country came out from a hard guerrilla fight, and there were many casualties, men and women. Of course, not only men died, but there were a lot of men that, if they did not suffer death, they suffered prison, exile, they suffered the destruction of the person, their life project, their illusion, failure, whatever. So, there were a lot of kids that were hanged for drinking, and the same thing on the football teams. Always the *'criollitos'*[4] teams in Venezuela were fantastic, the children's teams, teenage teams, but around fifteen or sixteen years old everything collapsed because they got into drinking, drugs, whatever and everything stopped, there wasn't any football team anymore, there was not anything good at all with men.

In contrast with the gradual decay in men's life and socialisation, Vessuri pointed out the importance of women to sustain the recovery of Venezuelan society after the guerrilla conflict.

> And women yes, if you saw those women that went out with their hair rollers in their heads at 6 am, coming down from the hill, leaving their

---

4   The *Organización para el Deporte Criollitos de Venezuela* [Criollitos Organisation for Sport in Venezuela] was an important sports corporation established in 1962 devoted to promoting sports among children.

kids in the subway, in the buses, whatever, taking them to the school, going to work after they prepared the meal, food for their colleagues, for the kids. And fantastic, in high spirits, joyful, joking, I don't know. Then that tremendous strength from women stood in front of the guerrilla failure, with the failure of that world that was intended to be built at that moment but received the lash from the Cuban revolution.

Vessuri found in Venezuela a young, dynamic and promising civil society led by women, but with a rather rigid structure in its institutions. The vibrant society was impacted by the influx of skilled migrants from other South American countries.

The insertion of women in Venezuela into universities is relatively recent, beginning around seventy-five years ago. However, female enrolment has come to equal and exceed that of men, even in areas traditionally dominated by men. In areas such as biomedicine and STEM (Science Technology, Engineering and Mathematics), women surpass men not only in quantity but also in efficiency (Albornoz, 1989; Aray, Vessuri and Canino, 2006; Caputo et al., 2016; Vessuri and Canino, 2017).

This increase in student enrolment was spatially increasing in the 1950s, 1960s and 1970s following the creation of new public and private higher education institutions, coupled with the expansion of the economy and institutional policy of industrialisation and technification of the country. This situation allowed large sectors of the population to be able to access university education, regardless of their social origin, sex or nationality, due to the prevailing need for human resources to be able to develop a national productive apparatus. In the case of Venezuela, Latin America and the Caribbean, the proportion of women in scientific, technological and research fields has been greater than in other regions of the globe—51% in Uruguay, 51.9% in Argentina, 51.8% in Paraguay, 52.9% in Trinidad and Tobago and 54% in Venezuela, as opposed to 26% in France and 8% in Ethiopia (Vessuri, 2017). According to the figures, more than half of the research personnel in South American countries are made up of women.

However, according to Vessuri, deeply rooted prejudices about sex differences still persist in current scientific activity, which hinder the equal participation of women in the generation of scientific knowledge and therefore its impact on the broader society. Despite all the progress in Venezuelan universities, research professors represented only 34% of the teaching staff in 2017.

Another important element to highlight is that, whilst other nations design specific public policies aimed at reducing the gaps between men and women and creating conditions for female entry and participation, it can occur under conditions of equity, in the case of Venezuela. Although the differences in access to university between men and women have been blurring over time, this has not been the result of specific actions by the state. Initially, it corresponded to the demographic change and the demand for specialised professionals in various areas to develop the nation (Caputo et al., 2016).

On the other hand, sociocultural and historical conditions also play an important role when it comes to women's positions in society. As far as the countries of Latin America and the Caribbean are concerned, there is a trait that is frequently present within society which some authors have called 'matrifocality' (Hurtado, 1998; Vetencourt, 1974) which, in the absence of the father figure, positions the mother as the centre of the family, who makes important decisions regarding maintenance, emotional needs and the organisation of the domestic space. This trait probably has implications for broader society and engenders a more receptive environment for women's access to spaces which, in other types of societies with other sociocultural characteristics, are less permeable to women.

Vessuri and her family stayed in this vibrant society until 1987. From 1976–1987, she was part of the Sociology and Anthropology College at Universidad Central (the Central University) and was involved in major academic projects including the *Centro de Estudios del Desarrollo* (CENDES) [the Development Studies Centre], a pioneering centre of postgraduate studies on social development in Latin America, focused on public policies, sociology and anthropology. Vessuri had been invited by the then-incumbent research coordinator of CENDES, Dr José Agustín Silva Michelena,[5] to participate in what was at the time a new venture focused on designing the postgraduate program. From that point on, Vessuri gradually turned from an anthropological approach to a more sociological and interdisciplinary perspective in social science studies.

---

5   Dr Michelena was a Venezuelan sociologist who was awarded the National Prize in Sciences of Venezuela. He was the founding member of CENDES.

Brazil: Mirror of Transitions

Vessuri went on to spend five years of her life in Brazil (1987–1991). She was invited there by Amílcar Herrera and Renato Dagnino, who worked at Campinas University (UNICAMP). Vessuri was appointed as the first director of the postgraduate program on Science and Technique of UNICAMP (Rivero, Echeverry-Mejía and Vessuri, H., 2018, p. 132). From that period of time, Vessuri recalls:

> It was nice to be in different contexts, and Brazil in that sense is enormous—it is practically a continent. But, look, we had very pleasant, very nice talks at the house of Amílcar Herrera, a geologist, political scientist and researcher of science from Argentina who lived in Campinas. He was the one who invited me to go to Campinas.

Despite the joyful memories she shares, Brazil was just leaving a period of dictatorship that Professor Herrera and his wife had experienced. They told Vessuri about 'people being lynched in the neighbourhoods, in the favelas, in the popular neighbourhoods of Rio de Janeiro, that they were hanging there from a post, which was the horror of how that came to be in a society'.

The history of the Brazilian dictatorship has many parallels with the authoritarian regimes of Latin America raised between 1960 and 1975 (Berdugo, 2023). On the one hand, we have the movement against socialism in which political parties, businesses, agricultural elites, the Catholic church and armed forces joined, and on the other hand, the strong opposition of these sectors against the intended Agricultural Reform of the then president João Goulart (Ramírez, 2012).

The military regime of Brazil installed a military junta government, with control over the Congress and Supreme Court of Justice. Unlike other Latin American dictatorships of the time, the Brazilian junta did not dissolve the democratic institutions, but colonised them (Berdugo, 2023) and executed a large campaign of persecution, incarceration and torture against opposition and dissidents (Torres, 2014).

By the time Vessuri moved to Brazil, the dictatorship had ended, but the scars were evident in the country trying to reconstruct its society.

> They had to deliver the power to the civilians because they had too much corruption and they did not know how to get out of the quagmire, as always happens in these cases. And there you start to see how these

societies were a mix of different things, because on the one hand, in Brazil, a university such as Campinas was created by a physician affiliated with the armed forces in the middle of the authoritarian period, and this guy funded the best research university of the country, University of Campinas. That guy was Zeferino [Zeferino Vaz], who said to the military, 'leave the scientist to me, I will take care of the boys'.

UNICAMP can be taken as an example of the complexity of the Brazilian regime, which conducted an intense process of repression but also managed projects that, in the long term, were beneficial for the country. When Vessuri arrived in Brazil, the country was in a stage of liberalisation, and UNICAMP—despite starting operations in 1966 (founded in 1962), in the first years of dictatorship—was one of the leading institutions of science and technology in the new Brazilian democracy.

Venezuela: Return and Disappointment

Even when the stage in Brazil was positive and productive, Vessuri decided to return to Venezuela, motivated by a leadership position to direct the Science Study department of the Venezuelan Institute of Scientific Research and to create Master's and doctoral programs. However, she found that the situation in the country had changed: 'I went back to experience the most disappointing stage of my life in collective terms, of society'.

The country had already begun a period of crisis in the later years of Vessuri's first period of living in Venezuela. During the 1970s, Venezuelan economic development depended on petroleum exportations and external debt (Martínez, 2008), with a lack of investment and development of other productive sectors (Taguaruco, 2018). The oil revenues allowed the administrations of Presidents Rafael Caldera and Carlos Andrés Pérez to finance public investment and services, such as education (Martínez, 2008). Vessuri had experienced the benefits of this model when working at the Universidad Central de Venezuela. However, this changed when the continuous fall of oil prices in the international market impacted the administrations of Luis Herrera Campins and Jaime Lusinchi. A series of issues arose, including the devaluation of national currency, bolivar, economic stagnation and a moratorium on its international debt payment (Looney, 1986).

Along with the economic instability, the governments in Venezuela implemented hard measures which violated the human rights of both rebel groups and civilian protesters (Taguaruco, 2018).

During the period Vessuri was in Brazil, the crisis in Venezuela had escalated. The discontent and protests against taxes and the policies implemented by President Carlos Andrés Pérez reached a climax in 1989 when gasoline and public transportation prices rose. A great number of inhabitants of the metropolitan area of Caracas began massive social unrest, including riots and pillage on February 27 and 28. The army mobilised to contain and repress the protesters. According to Taguaruco (2018), there is no certainty about the actual number of casualties during the political repression, including those from Caracas and other cities. This episode, known as 'El Caracazo' or 'El Sacudón', was a milestone of that period of decay.

There were two coup attempts in 1992; first, the dismissal of President Carlos Andrés Pérez for a trial of embezzlement, and later the provisional presidency of Ramón J. Velázquez. Bipartisan dynamics broke down. The disappointment of the population translated into a high abstention rate around the 1993 elections (Kornblith, 1996). Rafael Caldera assumed the presidency of the republic for a second time, beginning his government when a financial crisis broke out, with successive bank failures between 1994 and 1995. Because of this, the government made the decision to close the exchange market and establish an exchange control regime and price control. For these reasons, a new economic program and engagement with the International Monetary Fund commenced. Constitutional guarantees were also suspended by the regime, generating a strong confrontation with Congress when it tried to restore them (Kornblith, 1996). The severe crisis of the Venezuelan state resulted in the weakening of the health of the Venezuelan political system. It negatively affected the credibility of political leaders and leadership of the country.

Vessuri moved back to Venezuela at the beginning of the 1990s. At that time, Venezuelan society began to move to the rent-seeking logic. The national production system became dependent on government subsidies. This dependency on the government generated elites and conditions conducive to corruption, malaise and inequality in society, making social coexistence more and more difficult. With the entry of the Bolivarian Project,[6] it promised a new democratic and egalitarian government based on socialism and social economy, in spite of its neoliberal principles (Buxton, 2021). However, the fissures that were already present in Venezuelan society deepened. The country entered a debacle with processes of economic recession, stagflation and hyperinflation. Political and social violence, as well as organised crime, increased.

Disappointment and apathy were present in Venezuelan society. This was reflected in the different spaces of social life, as indicated by the testimony of our interviewee.

> The second round in the 90s was horrible and very depressing, nothing happened [...] it was a country that was falling apart, it was a system, at a time when everything was collapsing, of total immobility— everything was stagnant, absolutely nothing happened. So that was very discouraging; so many things that had to be done, so many urges when you saw that things could be done. We spent all that time proposing things for the Institute of Science and Technology, and—what do I know—and nothing happened. [...] The decade of the 90s was horrible because of the waste of time, a very valuable waste of time of Venezuela that Chávez capitalised on. It could have been anyone, but he capitalised on it. And then what came was a project with some good things and many other bad things, and it went on tumbling more and more until it ended up being finished. It could have been anything else, but it wasn't.

Once a country sought out and celebrated as a destination that was thriving, flourishing and receptive to foreigners, Venezuela had become a country with high rates of migration by its citizens to other countries, an unprecedented event in its history. For these reasons, Venezuela was a country in conflict, even though an armed conflict had not taken place in its territory during that period.

Migration is a complex process, wherein migrant people seek to be accepted and to learn the customs in a new home. Vessuri's account of her experiences reveals the ways in which political and social conflict directly affects the possibility of completing such processes in satisfactory ways. It is possible that she chose to dwell on the case of Venezuela because it became a true home to her, intellectually, professionally and

---

6   For more on the Bolivarian project and its implications, we recommend reading Lugo Dávila (2021).

personally, until the political and social conflicts began to escalate and repress.

México: At the Gates of Violence

Vessuri decided to accept an invitation from the Environmental Geography Research Centre (CIGA) of Universidad Nacional Autónoma de México (UNAM) to work as a visiting professor in 2011. Once again, Vessuri would be a migrant, but she was very familiar with Mexican culture and society because of the network of friends and colleagues she had formed through the years.

Vessuri accepted the invitation because the federal agency for science in México, Consejo Nacional de Ciencia y Tecnología (Conacyt) approved her project about the internalisation of Social Sciences, but Vessuri wanted to work in universities outside of México City, so she moved to Michoacán.

However, Vessuri's stay in México would be far from a quiet research period. In 2006 the elected president of México, Felipe Calderón, stated that drug cartels—namely Tijuana Cartel, Gulf Cartel, Sinaloa Cartel and Zeta cartel (Carpenter, 2012)—were an increasing menace and started a war against drugs precisely in Michoacán, his home state. As Pereyra (2012) explains, there was an escalating imbalance in drug cartels' structure and power; they were in a period of expansion. President Calderón's decision started an ongoing conflict that, on the one hand, pitted the Mexican security forces, including military, against drug traffickers, and, on the other hand, engendered a vicious conflict between rival bands to keep the markets and their territories. As a result, the violent deaths in México rose from 9 homicides per 100 thousand inhabitants in 2007 to nearly 25 in 2017 (Instituto Nacional de Geografía, Estadística e Informática, 2019). The situation in many regions of México was marked by drug violence, as Vessuri recalls:

> You couldn't send students to do fieldwork because it was dangerous, because the area was taken by drug gangs. It was shocking. You could see how all we have seen in Colombia was now transferring to México and how a whole country could be dominated by a narcotraffic culture. It was awful.

Vessuri experienced a time of bloody struggle between Mexican security forces and a local prominent band, *'La Familia'* or *'La Familia Michoacana'* [The Family] that had conducted vicious attacks against police agents (Carpenter, 2012). La Familia Cartel lost many members in the conflict against the state, but in 2011 it relaunched itself into a new gang named *'Los Templarios'* [The Knights Templar] (Carpenter, 2012). The violence in Michoacán did not cease.

Nevertheless, much of the violence in México during the drug war appears to be between rival bands and between the bands and the security forces, although there are a significant number of non-participant civil victims of violence, including journalists and members of the Catholic Church and even casualties of crossfires (Carpenter, 2012). Vessuri worked under these conditions until shortly before the Christmas season.

> I recall one year—my daughter was still alive, I am not sure whether it was 2011 or 2012—we were going to be together on Christmas, so I invited my children and great-children in Caracas to join us in México. The date was coming closer when I saw this full-size manifesto displayed in the newspaper, La Jornada, signed by some narco gang giving an ultimatum to the government, threatening to close the roads and set buses, cars and whatever on fire, establishing a curfew and other things. And I asked myself, 'what am I doing here? Should I warn my children and their families? Should they come or not come?' It was dangerous, but I wanted to see them. So, at that moment, we decided to stay in México City, which, historically, has been the most dangerous city because of its massive size, but it appeared to be a safe hub in the country's centre.

The Vessuri family spent a time in México that Vessuri labels as 'fantastic' even with the threat of narcos surrounding the holidays. Vessuri explains that she saw this in México but it was not disconnected from the reality of other Latin American regions. As she views it, it is a 'hellish thing':

> It all blends together: narcotraffic, armament, drugs here and there—a terrifying thing that also gets to Venezuela. In the past, there were no drugs in Venezuela. In the worst-case scenario, it was a small corridor for Colombian cartels to import drugs. But nowadays in Venezuela there are gangs, and in the confusion you cannot tell if you are dealing with the military, guerrillas of this colour or this other colour, with this cartel, with this other cartel or just with regular criminals. In this world that is getting more complex, that transforms itself, we are in another order of

things. There are no more quarrels between Peronists and anti-Peronists as it happened in Argentina or even Brazil; this contemporary world is quite different. México has suffered through it and that has expanded to the whole country, not just a state or a region. Crime has taken different shapes, not just one crime family or another. The whole country is subject to this hellish thing that I don't know how to mend because it is not just México, it is larger than that. Everything is a great business articulated around certain goals.

In fact, drug trafficking is considered a global enterprise (Keh and Farrell, 1997) and we can see how it has been shaping the history of America and the rest of the world in the last decades. It is interesting to note how Vessuri identifies a change in the nature of the conflicts: in the past, she experienced the ideological conflict, the political repression, the dictatorships and the insurgence; twenty years later, when Latin America started a slow transition to democracy, she observed that the conflict goes now between the different states and their struggle to preserve law and order against a billionaire criminal industry—the political fight has been displaced for a state of violence and uncertainty. As an anthropologist, Vessuri observed the different progressions of social conflict whilst trying to find her place, because, as she said, 'my strategy was to be like a bulldozer'. She was involved with the society she lived in and studied, opening new perspectives and new paths.

Drawing Conclusions for Our Future

This chapter has represented Vessuri's account as an academic struggling with, and overcoming, difficulties which intersected with the political conditions of her homeland and host countries, and her social positioning as a woman and as a migrant. This included living in societies with ongoing social and political crises, such as Argentina and México, and those societies trying to recover in the aftermath of colonial occupation and military autocracy, such as Venezuela. Political and economic shifts, constraints and freedoms impacted on the universities in which she worked. As a woman, the limitations she experienced intersected with discrimination based on her sex; as an academic woman, she did not receive the same advantages in academia as their male peers; as a mother and later a divorced woman, she faced discrimination and prejudice because she represented a way of living contrary to the moral standard.

Her framing of her first period of residency in Venezuela demonstrates her intellectual agency in seeking a new way of understanding the role of women in society. However, it is important to recognise the significant limits to that agency within her personal and professional life. She was forced to leave her homeland because of the political conflict that exploded in Argentina and directly impacted her husband as a political target and later an exile. From then on, her position as a woman intersected with her condition as a forced migrant. Migrant women have been found to subordinate their decisions to the will and professional interests of their male partners (Robaina, 2020). This occurred twice for Vessuri: when her first husband travelled to study in England, she followed him, finding the career she wanted to pursue as an anthropologist; and later, when her second husband was imprisoned and forced to leave the country, she accepted exile herself.

Migration process analysis illuminates the underlying reasons for migration that have enabled transnational development through the interaction of different peoples from different national backgrounds (Moreno, 2012), along with issues of acceptance, identity, adaptation and openness to new beliefs, experiences and costumes. Vessuri accomplished much because she became a prestigious scholar and a rewarded researcher, despite the limitations of the conflicts and the challenges she was able to overcome. In part, this was because she pushed against such limits by drawing on her positioning within intellectual systems and, where possible, within societies wherein women's participation was enabled. Support networks played an important role, especially those of family and friends of prisoners of conscience and exiled nationals who assisted in times of extreme need, including during the imprisonment of her husband in Argentina and her arrival in Venezuela as a refugee. In more sustained, mundane ways, she was also supported by women's networks to support families and the social structure of Venezuelan society after the guerrilla conflict.

The different social processes represented within this chapter are not reflections of a distant past. Social discontent and political unrest have not ended in Latin America. The promise of democracy and justice can be very fragile, as Vessuri's life story reminds us. Despite this, she observed how rights can be achieved and defended by societies and within universities. She lived under conditions of sociocultural and political conflict; yet to this day she remains steadfast in her conviction that solidarity, and that the effort to communicate with 'the other', is key to understanding alterity. As early career scholars, it is important for us to recognise how Vessuri developed this approach through her scholarship with marginalised people, and through her experiences of *being* a woman, a migrant and a social scientist during and after conditions of conflict.

We hope this narrative of the experiences of Vessuri over time has been as fulfilling, enriching and informative for our readers as it was for us as the interviewers. The discussion with Vessuri brought out insights about the overlap between academic professions and social action, the historic roles of the government and institutions in shaping the context in which scientific careers are developed, the nuances of gender and family that configure the possibilities of women within scientific careers and the decisive role of social networks for support and access to opportunities against the social structure. Moreover, it casts light on the tapestry of political, economic and cultural features that have shaped academic careers beyond the walls of university.

Acknowledgements

Our gratitude to Dr Hebe Vessuri for her time and to Dr Inocencia Orellana Hidalgo for her support and advice on the preparation of the interview.

Bibliography

Academic College (June 16, 2021). *The Unitopia Process. Live Discussion with Eric Lybeck [TAKE TWO]* [Video]. Youtube. https://youtu.be/7sUzpJ76a0Q

Álvarez-Gayou, J. L. (2009). *Cómo hacer investigación cualitativa. Fundamentos y metodología* [How to Do Qualitative Research. Basis and Method]. Paidós Educador.

Albornoz, O. (2013). *La universidad. Reforma o Experimento. El discurso académico contemporáneo según las perspectivas* [Reform or Experiment. Contemporary academic discourse according to perspectives].

UNESCO. https://biblioteca.isfodosu.edu.do/opac-tmpl/files/tc/24403-LaUniversidadReformaoExperimento.pdf

Aray, M. A. (2006). *La Dimensión femenina de la ciencia y la tecnología: La mujer entre la vocación académica y el trabajo industrial* [The Feminine Dimension of Science and Technology: Women between Academic Calling and Industrial Work] [Master's Degree Thesis, Instituto Venezolano de Investigaciones Científicas].

Aray, M. A., Vessuri, H., & Canino, M. V. (2011). La realidad femenina en las industrias del agua [Feminine Reality in Water Industry]. *Revista Venezolana de Estudios de la Mujer, 37,* 85–104.

Ayala, M. (2014). La formación de comités y redes de solidaridad y denuncia de los exiliados argentinos en Venezuela en su lucha contra la dictadura militar. Interacciones locales, regionales y trasnacionales (1976–1981) [The Committee and Solidarity Networks Formation and the Complaint of Argentinian Exiled Nationals in Venezuela in their Fight against Military Dictatorship: Local, Regional and Transnational Interactions (1976–1981)]. *E-l@tina, 12*(46), 2–23.

Ayala, M. (2017). La experiencia del Comité Venezolano de Solidaridad con el pueblo argentino (Cacas-Mérida, 1976–1983) [The Experience of Venezuelan Solidarity Committee with Argentinian People (Cacas-Mérida, 1976–1983)]. *Opción, 33*(83), 12–136.

Ayala, M., and Jensen, S. (2017). *Exiliados argentinos en Venezuela (1974–1983)* [Argentinian Exiles in Venezuela (1974–1983)] [Doctoral Thesis, Universidad de Buenos Aires]. https://repositorio.filo.uba.ar/jspui/bitstream/filodigital/10010/1/uba_flyl_1_2017_se_ayala.pdf

Baranger, D. (2013). 'LE TENGO MIEDO A LA ARGENTINA' Entrevista a Hebe Vessuri. ['I Am Scared of Argentina' Interview with Hebe Vessuri]. *Avá. Revista de Antropología, 23,* 11–43.

Berdugo, I. (2023). Las dictaduras militares de Argentina, Brasil, Chile y Uruguay y la justicia transicional [The Military Dictatorships in Argentina, Brazil, Chile and Uruguay]. *Revista Sistema Penal Crítico, 4,* e31437. https://doi.org/10.14201/rspc.31437

Bidegain, G. (1987). Democracia, migración y retorno: los argentinos, chilenos y uruguayos en Venezuela [Democracy, Migration and Return: Argentinian, Chilenenan and Uruguayan]. *International Migration, 25*(3), 299–323.

Bonilla Valencia, S., and Hernández Vásquez, S. (2021). Habitar en tierra ajena: estudio sobre las condiciones de vida de mujeres migrantes venezolanas en Colombia [Living in a Foreign Land: Study on the Life Conditions of Immigrant Venezuelan Women in Colombia]. *Revista Latinoamericana Estudios De La Paz Y El Conflicto, 3*(5), 160–182. https://doi.org/10.5377/rlpc.v3i5.12808

Brunner, José Joaquín (2014). The Latin-American Idea of the Public University: Narratives in Divergent Scenarios. *Educación XX1, 17*(2), 17–34. 10.5944/educxx1.17.2.11477

Brunner, J., J., and Ganga, F. (2016). Reflexiones en torno a economía política y gobernanza de los sistemas nacionales e instituciones de educación superior en América Latina [Reflections on Political Economy and Governance of Higher Education National Systems and Institutions in Latin America]. *Inerciencia, 41*(8), 573–579.

Buxton, J. (2021). Continuity and Change in Venezuela's Bolivarian Revolution. In R. Desai and H. Heller (Eds), *Revolutions* (pp. 11–128). Routledge.

Canino, M. V., and Vessuri, H. (2008). La Universidad en Femenino. Un cuadro de luces y sombras en la UCV [University in Feminine. A Portrait of Shadow and Light in UCV]. *Arbor, 184*(733), 845–861. https://doi.org/10.3989/arbor.2008.i733.229

Caputo, C., Vargas, D., and Requena, J. (2016). Desvanecimiento de la brecha de género en la universidad venezolana [Vanishing of Gender Gap in Venezuelan University]. *Interciencia, 41*, 154–161.

Carpenter, T. G. (2012). *The Fire Next Door: Mexico's Drug Violence and the Danger to America*. Cato Institute.

Castellanos, A., Canino, M., Vessuri, H. (2007). Mujeres pobres en el torbellino del cambio social: Un estudio de caso de la dinámica privado/público [Impoverished Women in the Vortex of Societal Change: Case Study on the Public/private Dynamics]. *Revista Venezolana de Economía y Ciencias Sociales, 13*(1), 209–231.

Cline Center for Advanced Social Research. (2021). *Coup d'Etat Project*. University of Illinois. https://clinecenter.illinois.edu/project/research-themes/democracy-and-development/coup-detat-project-cdp

Crespo, M. V. (2017) Legalidad y Estado de excepción en el Estado Burocrático Autoritario. El caso de la dictadura argentina de 1976 [Rule of Law and Emergency State in the Authoritarian Bureaucratic Regime: Case of Argentinian Dictatorship]. *Dictadura en América Latina. Nuevas Aproximaciones Teóricas y Conceptuales*, 97–127. Universidad Autónoma del Estado de Morelos, México.

Creswell, J. W., and Poth, C. N. (2016). *Qualitative Inquiry and Research Design: Choosing among Five Approaches*. Sage Publications.

Dávila, M. L. (2021). Bolivarian Project and Bolivarian Socialism: Promote Community Organisation 'from above' as the Construction of People's Power Construction of a Subject. Espacio Abierto, 30(4), 184–212. https://www.redalyc.org/journal/122/12269416010/html/

De la Vega, I. (2003). Emigración intelectual en Venezuela: el caso de la ciencia y la tecnología [Intellectual Immigration in Venezuela: Science and Technology Case]. *Interciencia, 26*(8), 259–267.

De Pablo, J., C. (2021). ¿Qué tiene de década el período 1964–1974? [What Is a Decade Regarding the 1964–1974 Period?]. *Serie Documentos de Trabajo.* https://doi.org/10.7440/res50.2014.16

Flores, M. (2020). Mujeres migrantes venezolanas: Entre políticas audiovisuales y cadenas de cuidados [Immigrant Venezuelan Women: Between Audiovisual Policies and Care Networks]. *Encuentros: Revista de Ciencias Humanas, Teoría Social y Pensamiento Crítico, 12,* 75–87. https://doi.org/10.5281/zenodo.3951224

Freites, Y. (2017). El Premio John Desmond Bernal 2017 para Hebe Vessuri [John Desmond Bernal Prize 2017 for Hebe Vessuri]. *Bitácora-e Revista Electrónica Latinoamericana de Estudios Sociales, Históricos y Culturales de la Ciencia y la Tecnología, 1,* 57–61.

Friedman, E. J. (1998). Paradoxes of Gendered Political Opportunity in the Venezuelan Transition to Democracy. *Latin American Research Review, 33*(3), 87–135. doi:10.1017/S0023879100038437

González Ordosgoitti, E. (1991). En Venezuela todos somos minoría [In Venezuela We All Are Minority]. *Nueva Sociedad, 111,* 128–140.

Guber, R. (2015). *La etnografía. Método, campo, reflexividad* [Ethnography: Method, Field and Reflexivity]. Siglo Veintiuno Editores.

Hurtado, S. (1998). *Matrisocialidad* [Mother-Sociality]. Edición EBUC-FACES/UCV.

Instituto Nacional de Estadística, Geografía e Informática. (2019). Patrones y tendencias de los homicidios en México [Patterns and Trends of Homicide in Mexico]. *En Números, Documentos de Análisis y Estadísticas, 15.*

Jensen, S., and Yankelevich, P. (2007) Una aproximación cuantitativa para el estudio del exilio político argentino en México y Cataluña (1974–1983) [A Qualitative Approximation to the Study of Argentinian Political Exile in Mexico and Catalonia (1974–1983)]. *Estudios Demográficos y Urbanos, 25*(2), 399–442. https://doi.org/10.24201/edu.v2212.1284

Keh, D., and Farrell, G. (1997). Trafficking Drugs in the Global Village. *Transnational Organized Crime, 3*(2), 90–110.

Koechlin, J., and Eguren, J. (2019). *El éxodo venezolano: entre el exilio y la emigración* [Venezuelan Exodus: Between Exile and Immigration]. Colección OBIMID, Vol. 4. Hecho el depósito legal en la Biblioteca Nacional del Perú N.o 2018-18681.

Kornblit, M. (1996). Crisis y transformación del sistema político venezolano: nuevas y viejas reglas de juego [Crisis and Transformation of Venezuelan Political System: New and Old Game Rules]. In A. Álvarez (Ed.), *El sistema político venezolano: Crisis y transformaciones* [Venezuelan Political System: Crisis and Transformation] (pp. 1–31). IEP-UCV.

Kreimer, P., and Vessuri, H. (2018) Latin American Science, Technology, and Society: A Historical and Reflexive Approach. *Tapuya: Latin American Science, Technology and Society, 1*(1), 17–37. https://doi.org/10.1080/2572986 1.2017.1368622

Laya, D., and Vessuri, D. (2019). The Scientists of the IVIC in the Evolution of Science and Technology Policy during the Chávez Administration in Venezuela. *Tapuya: Latin American Science, Technology and Society, 2*(1), 176–198. https://doi.org/10.1080/25729861.2019.1616953

Looney, R., E. (1986). Venezuela's Economic Crisis: Origins and Successes in Stabilization. *The Journal of Social, Political and Economic Studies, 11*(3), 327–337.

Martínez, J., H. (2008). Causas e interpretaciones del Caracazo. [Causes and Interpretations of 'Caracazo']. *Historia Actual Online, 16*, 85–92.

Martínez, M. (2006). Práctica de la metodología cualitativa. Introducción [Qualitative Methodology Praxis. Introduction]. In *Ciencia y arte en la metodología cualitativa* [Science and Art in Qualitative Methodology] (pp. 65–71). Editorial Trillas.

Mitchell, M. C., and Egudo, M. (2003). *A Review of Narrative Methodology.* Defense Science and Technology Organization.

Moreno Maestro, S. (2012). Mujeres migrantes en la era de la globalización. Ecuatorianas y senegalesas en Sevilla [Immigrant Women in Globalization Area. Ecuadorian and Senegalese Women in Sevilla]. *Revista Andaluza de Antropología, 3*, 94–124.

Novaro, M., and Palermo, V. (2003). *La dictadura militar (1976–1983), Del golpe de Estado a la restauración de la democracia* [Military Dictatorship (1976–1983), from Coup d'etat to Democracy restoration]. Paidós.

Kreimer, P., and Vessuri, H. (2018). Latin American Science, Technology, and Society: A Historical and Reflexive Approach. *Tapuya: Latin American Science, Technology and Society, 1*(1), 17–37. https://doi.org/10.1080/2572986 1.2017.1368622

Papacchini, A. (2001). Universidad, Conflicto, Guerra y Paz [University, Conflict and Peace]. *Nómadas, 14*, 225–243.

Pastrana, E. (2008). La reforma universitaria, el movimiento de Córdoba y sus repercusiones en Colombia [University Reform, Cordoba Movement and its Sequels in Colombia]. *Educere, 12*(41), 313–318.

Pereyra, G. (2012). México: violencia criminal y 'guerra contra el narcotráfico' [Mexico: Criminal Violence and 'War on Drugs']. *Revista mexicana de sociología, 74*(3), 429–460.

Pontoniero, E. (2014). Guerra revolucionaria y contrainsurgencia: el Ejército argentino y la seguridad interna bajo la presidencia de facto del general Juan Carlos Onganía, 1966–1970 [Revolutionary War and

Counterinsurgency: Argentinian Army and the Internal Security under the De Facto Presidency of General Juan Carlos Onganía]. *VII Jornada de Sociología de la Universidad Nacional de La Plata.*

Ramírez, H. (2012). El golpe de Estado de 1964 en Brasil desde una perspectiva socio-política [1964 Coup d'état in Brazil from a Sociopolitical Perspective]. *Revista PolHis, 9,* 255–266.

Rivero, P. J., Echeverry-Mejía, J. A., and Vessuri, H. (2018). Más allá de las ciencias, los científicos y la gestión de la ciencia y la tecnología: Conversación con Hebe Vessuri [Beyond Sciences, the Scientist and the Management of Science and Technology: Conversation with Hebe Vessuri]. *Cuadernos de antropología social, 48,* 129–144.

Robaina, S. (2020). Mujer, investigadora y migrante [Women, Researcher and Immigrant]. *Controversias Y Concurrencias Latinoamericanas, 12*(21), 31–51. http://ojs.sociologia-alas.org/index.php/CyC/article/view/206

Rodríguez, G., Gil, J., and García, E. (1999). *Metodología de la Investigación Cualitativa* [Qualitative Research Method]. Ediciones Aljibe.

Rodríguez, I., Vessuri, H., and Bilbao, A. L. B. (2009). Facing Up to the Challenge of Interdisciplinary Research in Gran Sabana (Venezuela). *Human Ecology, 37,* 787–789.

Rodríguez, R. (1997). Política y universidad en América Latina [Politics and University in Latin America]. *Política y Sociedad, 24,* 5–22.

Rubio, P. (2012). *La inmigración y sus duelos* [Immigration and its Mournings]. Poise. Universidad católica Luisamigo. https://doi.org/10.21501/issn.1692-0945

Sayas, R. (2015). Conflicto [Conflict]. *EUNOMÍA. Revista En Cultura de la Legalidad, 8,* 212–221.

Schnell-Anzola, B., Rowe, M. L., and LeVine, R. A. (2005). Literacy as a Pathway between Schooling and Health-related Communication Skills: A Study of Venezuelan mothers. *International Journal of Educational Development, 25*(1), 19–37.

Society for Social Studies of Science. (2017). *Bernal Prize 2017: Hebe Vessuri.* https://www.4sonline.org/prize/bernal-prize-2017-hebe-vessuri/

Taguaruco, J. (2018). Violencia institucional y protesta social en Venezuela: la interpretación del caracazo (1989) desde los movimientos de derechos humanos [Institutional Violence and Social Protest in Venezuela: An Interpretation of Caracazo (1989) from Human Rights Perspective]. *Revista Caribeña de Ciencias Sociales, (junio).* https://www.eumed.net/rev/caribe/2018/06/violencia-institucional-venezuela.html

Tolofari, S. (2005). New Public Management and Education. *Policy Futures in Education, 3*(1), 75–89. https://doi.org/10.2304/pfie.2005.3.1.11

Torres, A. (2014). Dictadura en Brasil (1964–1985). La militancia política, el encarcelamiento y la tortura [Dictatorship in Brazil (1964–1985). Political Activism, Imprisonment and Torture]. *Confluenze. Rivista Di Studi Iberoamericani, 6*(2), 167–200. https://doi.org/10.6092/issn.2036-0967/4762

Vargas, D., Requena, J., and Caputo, C. (2016). Género en la ciencia venezolana: desvanecimiento de la brecha. *Interciencia, 41*(3), 162–170.

Vasilachis, I. (2006). La investigación cualitativa [Qualitative Research]. In I. Vasilachis de Gialdino (Ed.), *Estrategias de investigación cualitativa.* [*Qualitative Research. In: Qualitative Research Strategies*] (pp. 23–60). Gedisa.

Vessuri, H. (1987). The Social Study of Science in Latin America. *Social Studies of Science, 17*(3), 519–554. https://doi.org/10.1016/S0160-791X(03)00020-4.

—(1993). Perspectivas recientes en el estudio social de la ciencia [Recent Perspectives on Social Studies of Science]. *Interciencia, 16*(2), 60–68.

—(1996). Pertinencia de la educación superior latinoamericana a finales del siglo XX [Relevance of Latin American Higher Education during the 20th Century]. *Nueva Sociedad, 146*(6), 102–107.

—, and Canino, M., V. (2001). El género en la ciencia venezolana (1990–1999). [Gender in Venezuelan science]. *Interciencia, 26*(7), 272–281.

—(2001). Enfermería de salud pública, modernización y cooperación internacional: El proyecto de la Escuela Nacional de Enfermeras de Venezuela, 1936–1950 [Public Health Nursery, Modernization and International Cooperation. National School of Venezuelan Nurses Project]. *História, ciências, saúde-Manguinhos, 8,* 507–539.

—(2005). Ciencia, política e historia de la ciencia contemporánea en Venezuela [Science, politics and history of Contemporary Venezuelan Science]. *Revista Venezolana de Economía y Ciencias Sociales, 11*(1), 65–87.

—, Canino, M. V., and Sanchez-Rose, I. (2005). La base de conocimiento de la industria petrolera en Venezuela y la dinámica de lo público-privado [Knowledge Basis in the Oil Industry of Venezuela and the Public/private Dynamics]. *REDES: Revista de Estudios Sociales de la Ciencia, 11*(22), 17–49.

—(2007). Training of researchers in Latin America and the Caribbean. In M. Mollis and M. Nussbaum (Eds), *Research and Higher Education Policies for Transforming Societies: Perspectives from Latin America and the Caribbean* (pp. 141–152). UNESCO.

—(2013). ¿Quién es el científico social en el siglo XXI? Comentarios desde los contextos académicos y aplicados y desde la corriente principal y la periferia [Who is the Social Scientist in the 21st Century? Comments from Academic and Applied Context and from the Main Current and the Peripherals]. *Sociológica* (México), *28*(79), 201–231.

—(2014). Cambios en las ciencias ante el impacto de la globalización [Changes in Science Facing Globalization Impact]. *Revista de estudios sociales*, 50, 167–173.

—, and Canino, M. V. (2017) Equidad de Género en Venezuela: Situación Actual y Estrategias a Futuro [Gender Equity in Venezuela: Current Situation and Strategies for the Future]. In H. Vessuri and M. V. Canino (Eds) *La otra: El mismo. Mujeres en la ciencia y la tecnología en Venezuela* [The She-other: Himself. Women in Venezuelan Science and Technology] (pp. 107–144). Fundación Editorial El perro y la rana.

—(2019) Crises that Mismatch Canons in Science: Provincialization, Transnationality, Conviviality? *Tapuya: Latin American Science, Technology and Society*, 2(1), 26–31, https://doi.org/10.1080/25729861.2019.1586193

—(2019). Las culturas de la ciencia. Una aproximación a su estudio desde América Latina [Cultures and Science. An Approximation to their Study from Latin America]. *Ciencia e Investigación, Reseñas, 7*(1), 89–103.

—(2021, August 25). Online Interview by ZOOM.

Vessuri, M. C. (1994). La ciencia académica en América Latina en el siglo XX [Academic Science in Latin America during the 20th Century]. *Redes: Revista de estudios sociales de la ciencia, 1*(2), 41–76.

Vethencourt, J. L. (1974). La estructura familiar atípica y el fracaso histórico cultural en Venezuela [Atypical Family Structure and the Historic and Cultural Failure in Venezuela]. *Revista Sic, 37*(326), 67–69. http://64.227.108.231/PDF/SIC1974362_67-69.pdf

5. Hidden Legacies of the Troubles: Post-conflict Pedagogy as Resistance in Northern Irish Medical Education

Jenny Johnston, Mairead Corrigan and Helen Reid

Introduction

Northern Ireland (NI) is part of the United Kingdom (UK) and, as a context for medical education, appears unremarkable at first glance. Affordances for the training of doctors appear indistinguishable from either Great Britain (GB) or the neighbouring Republic of Ireland (RoI). Yet what marks this region as different is its complex history of terrorism, civil unrest and subsequent cultural trauma, known euphemistically as 'the Troubles'. This tumultuous historical period, stretching from 1969–1998, has a long tail in terms of population health and the experiences of both healthcare professionals and users. As such, NI provides a febrile and rapidly changing sociocultural backdrop for educating future generations of healthcare professionals.

As clinicians and academics teaching undergraduate medical learners at Queen's University Belfast (QUB), we experience a powerful dialectic: that is, the clash between centralised formal curricula and assessments, and situated on-the-ground complexities encountered by doctors, patients, learners and teachers; the former are reified through regulatory discourses and their implementation, while the latter remain largely unspoken, yet are fundamental to lived experience and to practising medicine within this region. Indeed, the realist ontology and positivist epistemology of medicine often exist in tension with the

    https://doi.org/10.11647/OBP.0427.05

relativism and multiple truths of lived experiences of conflict. Thus, the post-conflict context creates a situated form of the hidden curriculum. This is a concept which critical theorist Giroux has described as a covert pattern of socialisation which prepares learners to function in the existing workplace and in other social/political spheres (Giroux and Penna, 1979). In other words, social, cultural and historical awareness must be learned alongside formal curricula. In NI, that means engagement with unique post-conflict legacies.

In this chapter, we argue that NI's post-conflict status, healthcare legacies of the Troubles and ongoing contested identities are routinely elided in medical education. We explore the ontological and epistemic tensions routinely encountered, consider how prominent medical discourses of standardisation and efficiency promote centralised curricula which may not fully cater to situated patient needs, and discuss the influence of residual colonialism. We explore these dialectics using a critical sociocultural lens, drawing on theorists including Freire (1970), Zembylas (2019) and Holland and Lave (2001). Each theoretical contribution is briefly described where it appears; we are cognisant that readers may interpret theorists differently or may not be familiar with those particular lenses.

Finally, we draw on our own identities as educationalists embedded within this context to suggest an authentic, critically conscious and trauma-informed pedagogy. We see this as embodying a form of resistance against homogenising, colonising and neoliberal influences, instead advocating for practices which acknowledge our complex situated identities as educators and better serve the needs of our population.

Our Positionality as Authors

Given the topic under discussion, our positionality is essential to understanding our arguments throughout this chapter, particularly for readers from other locations who may be new to the nuances of NI's circumstances. Additionally, the field of medical education itself is a contested space, drawing on the strength of multiple disciplines but also replete with ontological struggles; hence, a positional statement is an essential element of all our work. All three of us are longstanding medical educators in NI, giving us an emic perspective. Jenny and Helen are clinical academics and practising general practitioners (GPs, or family doctors) working in Belfast, NI. Mairead is an educationalist with a background in sociology. All three of us share a critical social constructionist orientation, and a dual axiological aim: to operationalise education as a means of improving on-the-ground healthcare, and to recognise, respect and learn from the diversity of stakeholders within medical education communities.

While this is our shared common ground, our reflective insights are also informed by our contrasting experiences. We each contribute a case study to illustrate an aspect of our arguments. Of the three of us, Helen is the only one not from NI as she comes from the Isle of Man, a small island in the Irish Sea which is a British Protectorate and which has a very different history of social and political relations. She moved to live in NI much later in her life. While Mairead and Jenny are both from NI, Mairead comes from a Catholic/Nationalist and rural background close to the border with the RoI. Jenny, on the other hand, comes from a Protestant/Unionist and urban background in Belfast. Hence, at least theoretically, our histories in person (Holland and Lave, 2001) position us at the exact interface of the enduring NI conflict. As will become apparent throughout the chapter, our identities are of enormous significance within NI, which retains social, cultural and educational polarisation, even segregation, to a large degree. Being 'othered' is an inherent aspect of living in this part of the world where name, geographical location and school commonly lead to assumptions about one's ethno-political background. We will return to the significance of this later.

We recognise that our privilege as academics affords us the option of critical perspectives; we are white, middle class and living in an affluent country where, despite prevailing neoliberal agendas, we are afforded space to reflect and write. Yet we are also all female and hence marginalised within traditional patriarchal institutions. Within academia, we occupy a space at interdisciplinary boundaries between medicine and various social sciences, a sometimes uncomfortable position which invites criticality but also carries some risk in questioning the status quo. Throughout the chapter, we do our best to make implicit assumptions explicit for readers in other contexts; to the extent to which it is possible, we invite continuing dialogue and requests for clarification.

A Short History of Northern Ireland

For the benefit of readers who are unfamiliar with NI and its ethno-political conflict, we present here historical points which we feel are important to understanding both our academic experiences and our arguments throughout this chapter. We are not historians, and we direct readers elsewhere for comprehensive political analysis (Bardon, 1992; Irish Boundary Commission, 1925; Milliken et al., 2021). The impact of the conflict on normal life here is explored later in the chapter, including through vignettes which detail our own experiences.

The entirety of our complex history cannot be concisely covered and is well beyond our current scope. We use the term 'Northern Ireland' pragmatically and without political intent, acknowledging that even the name of this geographical area is contested: other terms include the North, the North of Ireland, the Six Counties, Ulster, and the Province.

NI comprises much of the northern portion of the island of Ireland and neighbours the RoI, with which it shares a currently unmarked land border. The island of Ireland is steeped in long, traumatic and contested histories. After Ireland was colonised by Britain in the sixteenth century, Catholic Gaelic-speaking peoples in the northern part asserted the greatest resistance to British rule. Aiming to quash the dominance of Northern clans culturally, linguistically and militarily, the seventeenth-century political project known as the Plantation of Ulster incentivised mainly Protestant people from England and Scotland to take land from the previous owners. Centuries of institutionalised ethno-sectarian tensions between these groups followed, as the British Empire operationalised settler colonisation to 'civilise' and anglicise Ireland.

Ireland remained part of the British Empire until the early twentieth century, when the Easter Rising (1916) and the bloody Irish Civil War (1921) paved the way for an Ireland independent of Britain. Partition of the island occurred when the six counties of modern NI chose to remain part of the United Kingdom. The other twenty-six formed the independent Irish Free State, eventually becoming the RoI. Post-partition, NI remained mired in state-sanctioned sectarianism; having been designed as a 'Protestant state for a Protestant people'. Social structures were designed to favour those who were loyal to the Union with England, Scotland and Wales. Inequalities and injustices abounded in the early days of the state; for example, many Catholic Nationalist people, without the benefit of land ownership, were ineligible to vote and electoral boundaries were said to have been gerrymandered to the benefit of the Protestant Unionist state. Catholics were discriminated against in housing and jobs. Eventually, the cracks in society devolved into the catastrophic years of violent conflict known as the Troubles.

A political settlement was reached in 1998 that ended the Troubles with the signing of the Belfast Agreement, also known as the Good Friday Agreement (NIO, 1998). More than twenty-five years after its signing, the work of reconciliation and transformation is still to be completed. Sporadic violence and community tensions flare throughout the year, and sectarianism is still omnipresent, particularly in communities of high socioeconomic need. Everyday life here is punctuated by social and cultural reminders that its recent history is very different from other parts of the UK. Most social structures—the family, places of religious ritual, cultural centres and even medical practices—remain distinctly influenced by the ethno-political groups they serve. Holland and Lave term this 'local contentious practice', contributing directly to the fault lines of enduring struggle (Holland and Lave, 2001).

Contemporary realities are thus highly complex; polarised sensibilities and endemic trauma persist along with the ideological chasms which often characterise life here. In 2023, NI marked a century of existence and twenty-five years of sometimes tenuous peace. The cessation of violent conflict brought funding for regeneration, growth and the removal of visible signs of the NI/RoI border, such as military checkpoints and watchtowers. The Good Friday Agreement enabled mechanisms for residents to self-identify as Irish, British and Northern Irish, including dual citizenship; in other words, it embraced multiple truths and identities.

Despite much progress, however, significant division remains. Flags and murals demarcate the edges of neighbourhoods on a street-by-street basis, and civil unrest flares intermittently. Most recently, concerns by the Democratic Unionist Party (DUP) about post-Brexit trade agreements led to the collapse of NI's government (2022–2024). The absence of a regional government for long periods of time since 1998 has worsened NI's healthcare crisis. For primary and secondary schools, traditional religious divides still determine to a significant degree the cultural infrastructure, curricular content and attitudes passed on to students. Within tertiary education, the study of the precedent, content and consequences of conflict in Ireland form entire academic departments and subjects of enquiry. Yet the impact of NI's political divisions for health and healthcare and the significant contributions of healthcare workers and surgeons who developed cutting-edge surgical techniques for patients with horrific injuries (Coon, 2019) are rarely acknowledged in medical curricula.

Prevailing Discourses of Medicine as Freirean Banking

In the UK, and thus in NI, the development of medicine and medical education have followed that of other countries in the West; that is, medicine has been organised around positivist Enlightenment principles of rational thought and the scientific method, and impacted heavily by discourses of industrialisation. Positivism in medicine occupies the status of a God term (Lingard, 2009). Medicine is often considered apolitical, driven by discoverable and reproducible 'facts' (Park et al., 2020). Prevailing Cartesian assumptions about the separation of mind and body have evolved into the clinical gaze; this is a mechanistic approach to medicine and a pervasive discourse in which emotions, embodied experience and narrative are discarded in favour of more objectively reliable clinical signs and laboratory tests (Foucault, 1963/2017).

All of this reinforces a culture of Freirean banking education (Freire, 1970), i.e. the depositing of untroubled facts into the empty bank accounts of medical learners' minds. Indeed, this is often considered virtuous and necessary to produce safe doctors and is a central tenet of the competency-based medical education movement (ten Cate and Billett, 2014). The large amount of content knowledge that medical learners must study leaves little room to develop critical thinking. However, it makes it more difficult for learners to develop into critically conscious doctors who are self-reflective, who understand discourses of power and privilege and who are aware of the contexts which affect others' lives (Kumagai and Lypson, 2009).

We argue that a combination of the clinical gaze, banking education and residual colonial influences elides the complexity and multi-voicedness of NI's history of conflict. Medicine, and by association medical education, are often constructed as apolitical, driven by discoverable and reproducible 'facts' (Park et al., 2015). Hegemonic educational practice and widespread manufactured consent suggest to learners that their knowledge is directly transferrable to any context. This epistemic assumption is underpinned by naïve realism but does not always stand up to real world messiness. For undergraduates and many specialty trainees based in NI, a steep learning curve of situated learning must be traversed in the workplace. We work in and with traumatised communities, where learning goes far beyond formal centralised curricula. Our work exists in dialogue (and sometimes in dialectic) with other humans, each person nested within their own multiple layers of context (Holland and Lave, 2001; Billett, 2014). The impact of historical trauma on the island of Ireland is widespread in healthcare, manifesting as a sociopolitical determinant of health. We give some examples of how this is encountered in on-the-ground practice in Table 5.1 below.

To move beyond banking models requires a fundamental epistemic shift towards *'conscientização'* [critical consciousness] and the development of radical problem-posing education (Freire, 1970). We see this as an important step in developing an authentic, trauma-informed pedagogy, growing from the parent concept of trauma-informed practice. This has gained traction in recent years and refers to efforts to effect systemic change throughout organisations centred around understanding the global impact of trauma on the individual, including on health and education outcomes. From this basis, we argue for a trauma-informed pedagogy of medical education which reflects the ubiquity of trauma in modern society along with its impacts, which teaches learners skills necessary for working with traumatised patients and populations, and which helps them to develop self-awareness and self-care practices necessary to prevent burnout and attrition.

We have previously outlined the value of problem-posing education to medicine at large, particularly in recognising market forces at work in healthcare and in addressing structural inequalities impacting health and healthcare (Johnston et al., 2022). While Freire's critical pedagogy is familiar to medical educationalists in parts of South America and is prevalent within adult and higher education across the globe, it is not often mainstream within medical educational practice in the Global North (Manca et al., 2019). NI's complex contexts for medical education and practice offer an exceptional case which powerfully underlines this call to move towards embodied and situated critical consciousness. Despite centralised and standardised curricula, medical education cannot exist within a social vacuum, since the core work of doctors takes place within communities and is socially constructed within the consultation.

In Table 5.1 below, we draw on our own observed experiences and those of our colleagues to tabulate some of the layered conditions of current medical practice in NI. These are frequent circumstances which both doctors and medical learners must negotiate as a basic element of practice. They range from the dangerous to the traumatic and simply confusing. We have found that often, for example, we encounter queries from international postgraduate students wondering why virtually the entire machinery of NI shuts down for two weeks in July. Many similar temporal or even existential nuances are indicative of a sociocultural infrastructure which cannot be considered truly post-conflict; but rather is reflective of a liminal space of division, where violence is easily re-sparked. This illustrates the ways in which current forms of 'one size fits all' banking education exist in dialectic tension with on-the-ground practice.

Table 5.1 Illustrative examples of contexts for contemporary medical practice in Northern Ireland.

Perceived segregation of healthcare

- In the past the organisation of healthcare reflected the segregated communities that they served, with staff in GP surgeries, for example, all being from the same 'community'. Hospitals and GP surgeries continue to be associated with one or other community, based on their location in a nationalist or unionist area. During the COVID-19 pandemic, for example, some patients from Protestant 'Loyalist' areas of South Belfast declined to attend the primary care Covid Centre because it was situated in a predominantly Catholic 'Republican' area.

- The segregated nature of healthcare has led to perceived inequities in the allocation of healthcare funding for nationalist communities west of the River Bann from governments aligned to unionism.

Challenges of negotiating different community traditions

- The positioning of local healthcare staff within one of the two communities, can lead to doctors 'othering' and being 'othered' as a nationalist or unionist, based on name, schooling, residence and place of work. Despite this, doctors have always been able to make home visits to patients in all communities regardless of their perceived affiliation. During these visits, to prevent their cars from being stolen, damaged or hijacked for paramilitary during the Troubles, 'Doctor on call' signs would be left in cars.

- Tacit assumptions, used to label people as belonging to either community or as an 'other' to both communities, are often necessary to be 'culturally competent' in navigating the social dynamics and potential dangers of working across the divide.

- This local knowledge is not afforded to doctors not from NI or even to younger generations who were born after the Troubles. Similarly, they may not be aware of the significance and symbolism of flags and coloured road-markings and graffiti linked to histories and national allegiances to the United Kingdom or to the Republic of Ireland.

Psychological

- Health professionals risk secondary trauma, burnout and attrition from witnessing the impact of violence on patients' physical and psychological health.

Temporal rhythms

- July 12 is a bank holiday unique to NI that is celebrated by Ulster Protestants to commemorate the victory of the Protestant King William of Orange over the Catholic King James II at the Battle of the Boyne (1690). It marks the start of the 'Twelfth Fortnight' when many people in NI take annual leave, making it difficult to recruit GP locum cover.

- The 'marching season' which occurs from April to September with most of the marches by groupings linked to unionism and Republican marches at Easter, often lead to tensions between the two communities and to civil unrest, resulting in people restricting their movements and to road closures, hampering access to healthcare services and to GP home visits.

- Civil unrest and, in the past, bomb threats would mean GP practices closing early.

Access issues for GPs making home visits

- 'Peace walls', used to separate Catholic/Republican and Protestant/ Loyalist communities from each other to avoid conflict, are high walls located mainly in Belfast with gates for pedestrians and/or vehicles that are opened and closed at set times daily. Civil unrest can lead to the gates being closed with little warning, blocking key routes for GPs making home visits.

- During the Troubles, some streets and houses in these areas would have no names or numbers to confuse security forces, which posed challenges for GP home visits and emergency services.

For those not situated within post-conflict societies, or for those who have moved to NI more recently and work outside of healthcare, these aspects of practice may seem shocking. A 2023 BBC police drama, *Blue Lights*, has been highly popular (BBC, 2023). It has been lauded for its accuracy in demonstrating post-conflict legacies for working within policing in NI. It introduces viewers to aspects of NI which are not always obvious to those who did not grow up here, just as we are attempting to do for our readers. Similarly, it follows the on-the-ground learning experiences of new police trainees. We argue that medical education should follow the police in offering not only generic training but also support in dealing with post-conflict legacies, traumas and tensions. Engendering critical consciousness requires much greater transparency in formal and informal curricula around the situated needs of both patients and learners. This is particularly relevant for medical learners who have come to NI expecting it to be similar to other parts of the UK, which we discuss in more detail below.

Enduring Struggles: Post-Conflict Identity Formation

We have seen how in the case of NI, the complexities of a still-contested post-conflict zone are routinely elided in formal medical curricula, existing mainly within a hidden curriculum (Lempp and Seale, 2004). In medical education terms, this is well understood as a form of workplace learning which is separate to formal curricula (what is published) and informal learning (corridor conversations, informal learning opportunities, such as over lunch). Hidden curricula are unacknowledged and unspoken, creating socialisation through sets of implicit rules, and so are influential in terms of professional identity formation (Hafferty, 1998).

We refer to identities in this context as dynamic parts of ourselves which develop within sociocultural contexts and which drive human activities (Holland, 2001). Identities are both a main cause of conflict in NI and a central concern for medical learners, who must establish clear professional identities to be effective in their work. The analytic lens of Holland and Lave's social practice theory allows us to consider how individuals form their identities against their social, cultural and historical backdrop. Both positional (on-the-ground, given by others) and figured (imagined, aspirational) identities are possible (Holland, 2001). Crucially, this theory also posits that the influence is bidirectional: individuals can, through identity and agency, also influence their various contexts. Thus, an opening is created for potential societal transformation—in this case, through the development of critical consciousness (Holland and Lave, 2001).

The Troubles and their post-conflict legacies can be seen as examples of Holland and Lave's enduring struggle—a large-scale ideological conflict with social, cultural and historical aspects, against which identities are formed at both individual and societal levels. Such conflicts generate dialectics which play out through local contentious practice (LCP) (Holland and Lave, 2001). In Northern Ireland, this has traditionally been viewed in interactions between the two majority-placed ethno-political groupings—often defined broadly as Protestant/Unionist and Catholic/Nationalist, although these labels elide much complexity. Less visible is how the core enduring struggle of the Troubles has created further conflicts for medical learners (as well as police, as we discussed above, and presumably many other on-the-ground public services).

Many medical learners brought up within NI will have experienced an indigent form of social engineering, and thus will identify with (or be positioned by others) within one or other of the main two ethno-political communities which remain engaged in contentious practice. Those who migrate to learn or work in NI are also positioned within this ingrained conflict, and thus confronted with their own dialectic struggles in making sense of themselves. In both cases, tension may exist between positional and figured identities, a polarisation which leaves learners 'stuck' and unable to undertake the kind of resolution work needed for personal or societal transformation.

Additionally, learners in workplaces (hospitals and clinics, where more than half of undergraduate and all postgraduate medical education takes place) are frequently drawn into forms of local contentious practice, impacting on their agency and intentionality (Johnston, 2022). For each individual learning to practise medicine at the site of an enduring struggle, their life experiences and existing identities (their history in person) are brought into dialogue with the contexts of the ideological struggle in which they are placed (Holland and Lave, 2001). Some will have direct familial experience of the Troubles, while others will have been relatively protected from consciousness or trauma about it. These existing identities intersect with the sociocultural contexts of formal and hidden curricula.

Inevitably, whether willingly or not, learners are drawn into local contentious practice through exposure to the healthcare legacies of the Troubles. Bringing such forms of contentious practice into dialogue with their own histories in person, against a background of enduring struggle, creates a further important dialectic. The possibility exists that in its resolution a space for change can be created, on an individual or societal level, or both. A key principle of our call for post-conflict pedagogy is that learners should be mentored and supported in recognising and resolving this dialectic. In doing so, they may benefit from a stronger sense of their professional selves within these circumstances, and a greater understanding of the situated needs of their patients. Table 5.2 illustrates some common examples of how these healthcare needs are encountered within medical practice.

Table 5.2 Illustrations of healthcare legacies of the Troubles.

Paramilitary and criminal activities

- The Good Friday agreement in 1998 promised a cessation of paramilitary activities and the release from prison of paramilitary prisoners. However, all the main paramilitary groups continue to exist, the most serious threats from dissident Republican groups who rejected the 1998 Agreement. Paramilitaries are now involved in criminality and violent activities and forced internal displacement of individuals from areas.

- Sectarianism intersects with racism in areas controlled by paramilitaries.
- Healthcare professionals continue to deal with physical injuries and mental trauma of patients living in these areas.

Physical health

- Trauma-related behaviours such as smoking, excess alcohol and drug use are prevalent in areas impacted by the Troubles. Life expectancy is lower with high levels of multimorbidity and polypharmacy.
- Emergency consultations may include gunshot wounds, rioting injuries and burns from homemade bombs.
- Routine consultations can include arthritis flares from marching with bands, or tinnitus following historic bomb blasts.
- Kneecapping is a form of 'punishment' derived from 'the Troubles' that led to surgeons in NI becoming highly skilled trauma specialists to whom surgeons from across the world turned to for training.

Mental health

- Areas impacted by the Troubles have high levels of deprivation, suicide, anxiety, depression, and post-traumatic stress disorder. NI has the highest levels of suicide in the UK (NISRA, 2022b) which is linked to deprivation.

High levels of prescribed psychotropic drugs

- NI has the highest level of prescribed psychotropic drugs, antidepressants and pain killers in the UK. These drugs are often sold on the black market, of which doctors must be mindful when prescribing.

Medical evidence for Troubles victims pension scheme

- In 2021 a Troubles victims pension scheme and a Troubles Permanent Disablement Payment Scheme (also referred to as the Victims' Payments Scheme) were introduced for people who suffered physical or psychological injuries in the Troubles for which doctors can be asked to provide medical evidence.

To summarise so far, we have presented two important dialectics. One is created by the tension between homogenous, centralised medical curricula and the needs of on-the-ground patients, doctors and learners. A second, related dialectic exists between learners' prior identities and experiences, and the local contentious practice which maintains NI's enduring struggles. Both of these are cogent in the development of ideas of self and the process of professional socialisation. Supporting students in positively resolving these dialectics has important implications for the recruitment and retention of qualified doctors, for job satisfaction, and for developing critical consciousness in the service of patients.

In the next section, we focus on the experience of the increasing numbers of migrant medical learners, who may experience these dialectics differently from those brought up in NI. We discuss how decolonisation is a relevant project to developing post-conflict pedagogy and explore residual colonial influences on NI medical education.

Challenges Faced by Migrant Medical Learners

Since it came into being in 1921, NI has traditionally been seen as a homogeneous society which is overwhelmingly white and Christian (NISRA, 1991). It is unsurprising that NI was not a popular destination for inward migration during the Troubles. This was accompanied by waves of outward migration, including an exodus of qualified professionals (the brain drain) which remains a concern to this day (Trew, 2010). Since the normalisation of everyday life with the cessation of violent conflict, and as it has settled into a sometimes uneasy post-conflict state, the demographics of NI have moved towards a somewhat more cosmopolitan and multi-ethnic society. These diverse new entrants to NI society include people from EU states, asylum seekers, refugees and economic migrants, who still comprise a small percentage of the overall population (NISRA, 2022a) and are often concentrated in large urban centres.

Within NI healthcare, there has traditionally been a higher proportion of migrants than is reflective of broader NI society (DfE, 2018). This complexity is highly visible in the experiences of international healthcare staff and learners coming to work and study in NI. Examples include nurses from the Philippines and doctors from British Commonwealth countries, as well as former British colonies such as India. At present, around 12% of medical students at our own institution are from a country of residence other than the UK, Ireland, Isle of Man or Guernsey. A majority of these are from Southeast Asia, the UAE and Canada. For many of these learners, NI represents the UK at large, and therefore is positioned within the global prestige economy as a high-status location for training and clinical practice. Even professionals coming from the rest of the UK or RoI may be relatively ignorant of the unique affordances of medical practice in NI, and indeed of what it is like living and working within its society. In identity terms, their figured identities may be out of step with how they are positioned once here; they may have little understanding of the conflict or its present-day legacies through local contentious practice.

In the first of three autoethnographic case studies as medical educators in NI, Helen describes her experiences as a migrant doctor and clinical academic below. Engaging with a rapid acquisition of sociocultural knowledge is essential for these learners, who each also bring their own histories-in-person to the table. This might include intersectionalities of race, gender and culture from beyond the British and Irish Isles; these are explored later in the chapter in our discussion of decolonising curricula. When revising the chapter, we also received a comment that all three case studies perhaps tended to minimise our experiences; this caused us some self-reflection, as a result of which we must acknowledge that this may well be the case and indeed is a commonly encountered coping mechanism within NI society.

Case Study 1: Prof. Helen Reid on Being a Migrant Academic Doctor

I am an outsider-insider. I share my unique journey up to this point to contextualise this assertion. At the time of writing, I am in my fifteenth year living and working in NI. I was born and spent my first eighteen years living and learning outside the UK, on a small island nation physically situated in the middle of the Irish Sea. Aged eighteen, I moved to England to study medicine. While looking and sounding typically 'English', I was (as my tuition fee bills attested) an 'overseas' student, being neither from a UK nor an EU country. With this chapter's focus on the perspective of educators rather than that of students, I fast-forward through my student phase and initial years working as a junior doctor in England. Migrants all have their unique stories as to what brought them to where they are. It is a question I am not infrequently asked by colleagues, students, friends and patients; 'what brought you to NI?' My response rarely falters. 'Love', I say.

The person who has been my partner, since early student days, hails from NI. Our shared decision to move here was driven by practical considerations. When I considered NI as a place to live and work as a doctor, I regarded it as another part of the UK, offering convenient geographical proximity to family. Certainly, the Belfast of my childhood in the 1980s and 1990s, viewed only through the lens of mainstream media, was a scary grey place of guns and tanks. But that was all in the past. I understood that post the Good Friday Agreement, all was peaceful and well in NI. I certainly do not recall any consideration that I was relocating to a post-conflict society.

I completed all my postgraduate training in General Practice in hospitals and GP practices in the Greater Belfast area, alongside developing myself as a clinician educator. I now work as a full-time clinical academic, spending half my working week as a practising GP and half within the University engaged in educating and developing the next generation of doctors. I consider myself a critical scholar and educationalist. While my research (primarily into assessment and workplace learning) is all about questioning the status quo, it is a rare luxury to take the time to reflect on what being an educator in a post-conflict society really means. My formal curricular planning and delivery is strongly influenced by that of an external regulatory body. Perhaps in writing that, I am complicit in educating for stability rather than change. Now there's a dialectic from someone who espouses a commitment to social justice and raising the critical consciousness of learners I am involved with! Maybe I have become an insider. Yet, as an outsider, I recognise my unique positionality and ability to notice things. And what I notice about NI, as a post-conflict society, comes predominantly from my clinical practice.

One of my first jobs as a doctor in NI was in a hospital geographically positioned close to interface areas that had witnessed an excess of violence during the Troubles. It wasn't long before I was bristling whenever a patient referred to me as 'that English doctor' (with or without an uncouth/derogatory adjective). While something of the valency of my discomfort at this descriptor could be explained by my proudly non-English national identity, there was more to it. What I was reacting to was the implicit assumption that I was English and, by association, affiliated with the Unionist/Loyalist community. Perhaps I generalise horribly, but people from NI like to 'place' others. Loyalist or Republican? Nationalist or Unionist? Protestant or Catholic? Green or orange? It's there in black and white on every job application form: 'which community do you identify with?' Yes, there's always a 'neither/ none' box available, but NI society is largely structured around such binary distinctions. Names, accents, addresses, schools. Even the way someone pronounced the name of the hospital where I first worked. In my professional and relatively privileged circles, these are rarely explicitly named, yet constantly implicitly ascertained. I attach some shame to the realisation that, within about a year of living in NI, I was honing my ability to similarly 'pigeonhole' colleagues, patients and friends. This pigeonholing was not something I was aware of, nor desired, before I moved to NI. As a student I'd met several people from NI, including my future partner. At that stage, I knew nothing of putting them into boxes determined along lines forged through past conflict.

An early job working in psychiatry was particularly challenging. I struggled with the language patients used in reference to themselves and others, stories of persecution and horrendous traumas. I struggled to tease apart their actual lived experiences from potentially delusional perceptions. Patients' accounts, which I initially naively assumed were creations of disordered minds, could well (viewed through the lens of more years of clinical and life experience in this strange corner of Ireland) have been descriptive accounts of past and present events. The hospital clinicians and GP mentors who had supervised me were silent on this. Not a subject for discussion.

Past conflict lives on in individuals who may have had no direct lived experience of the Troubles. This generational trauma is seldom named in medical education, either at undergraduate or postgraduate level. I recall no explicit discussion of past conflict in my NI postgraduate training to become a fully qualified and independently practising GP. Yet, in the messy world of general practice, where we as family doctors are so close to the communities we serve, Troubles-related trauma is writ large— very obviously in terms of individuals living with the physical and psychological consequences of paramilitary activity; less obviously, but every bit as destructively, in the astonishingly high rates of prescribed pain medications and sedatives, far higher here than in any other area of the UK. We witness the destruction to individuals and their families that so often accompanies involvement in proscribed/ paramilitary organisations, now controlling street drug supplies.

I see this every day—we work in the face of it. Yet do I name it? Do I raise it with those who are now my trainees and students? Seldom. I try, occasionally, half-heartedly, skirting round the core issues. I do mention 'conflict legacy' in discussions with students about the astonishingly high rates of prescription of many medications with the potential for misuse in NI, in comparison with other areas of the UK. But I don't push it. I skirt around the peripheries, perhaps fearful of causing offence, trying as hard as I can to resist being pigeonholed myself. Reflecting on my positionality as an outsider insider in this strange place, I fear I have become complicit in perpetuating the 'great unspoken' of Troubles legacy in my educational practices.

Helen's reflections on being an outsider in NI (as a white, heterosexual, cisgender medical migrant from a Crown Protectorate outside of the UK or RoI) offer potential clues to the experiences of learners from other marginalised backgrounds (on the basis of race, ethnicity, sexual or gender orientation, etc.) who traditionally were not represented in either the UK's formal medical curricula or NI's dualistic society. Portrayals of 'outgroup' people often represented them in a way that othered them as being fundamentally different and in some cases of lesser value. Broader criticisms of medical curricula as 'male, pale and stale', the Black Lives Matter movement and the increasing diversity of the medical profession have led to calls for medical curricula in the UK and the US not only to diversify content but to critically examine the role of racism and colonialism in the history of medicine (Yancy, 2020; Wong et al., 2021). Medical educationalists in the UK are beginning the process of decolonising curricula (Mbaki et al., 2021), a process that is more contentious in NI because of its colonial roots, enduring struggle and ongoing local contentious practice.

Decolonising Medical Curricula in Post-conflict Northern Ireland

Graduate UK doctors are expected to serve a population of approximately sixty-seven million people across the four constituent nations, as well as a diverse array of global postings. Despite this, critical post-colonial frames have only recently become prominent in medical education. Formal UK medical curricula for undergraduate and postgraduate training are guided by central frameworks which are subject to regional review. Although carefully considered in terms of diversity, ultimately they emanate from a centralised base in London, England. This location of major professional institutions, such as the headquarters of the General Medical Council (GMC), the regulatory body for medicine and the medical Royal Colleges, has inevitable colonial undertones. Situated local needs are decentred, resulting in the standardised delivery of formal medical education decontextualised from local conditions.

The decolonisation movement has regained considerable traction in critical higher education in the UK in recent years (Wong et al., 2021). However, it requires a particularly complex and nuanced approach in the setting of NI. Decolonisation requires careful reflexivity in three aspects: power, relationship and place. It has been defined as 'involving a critical analysis of how colonial forms of knowledge, pedagogical strategies and research methodologies ... have shaped what we know, what we recognise and how we reward such knowledge accordingly' (Arshad, 2020). Drawing on critical post-colonial frameworks, intellectual decolonisation is a form of activism which considers how taken-for-granted knowledge is shaped through culture and pedagogy (Tamimi et al., 2023).

We argue that the turbulent colonial history of the island of Ireland, culminating in partition and eventually the Troubles, is an essential consideration in attempts to effectively decolonise curricula in NI. No other part of the UK exists as a highly contested colonial statelet. We acknowledge independence movements in Scotland and Wales but argue that neither country has had such a longstanding ethnopolitical conflict in the modern age. The population shifts, polarised positions and traumas associated with the civil war and partition of the island of Ireland are still (just) in living memory in the early twenty-first century. We are therefore in the unusual position of being both colonised and colonising.

This adds multiple voices and complexity to the task of decolonisation. Treating NI as being 'as British as Finchley', London—to paraphrase Margaret Thatcher's famous formulation (Murua, 2019)—not only replicates the coloniality of Anglo-centric curricula; it also risks missing the embedded power dynamics and cultural nuances encountered daily by clinicians and patients on the ground. The familiar micro-level conflict is then reinforced between the formal and hidden curricula—that is, between the established macro-structures and processes of academic medicine, and the situated knowledge needed to practise medicine in a uniquely challenging environment.

A well-recognised core element of decolonising curricula in any context is reflecting on the social construction of medicine and science through discourses of discrimination and colonialism; for example, educating on the abuse of enslaved people by individuals and institutions and considering how this power dynamic has translated into modern medicine. This can be easily seen, for instance, in the dominance of pictures of white skin in dermatology texts (Mota et al., 2024), leading contemporary learners and practitioners to have difficulty differentiating rashes in other skin tones. Additionally, Black women in the West continue to have higher perinatal mortality rates than white women (Adegoke et al., 2021), along with many other examples of unconscious bias across many protected characteristics.

So far, this chapter has described the task of decolonising as it might be approached across many Western contexts. However, decolonising within a still-contested post-conflict society requires giving extra consideration to diversifying voices and challenging discrimination. In superimposing the complexities of a radical problem-posing process on the context of NI's own complexities, extreme care is needed in managing nuance, multi-voicedness and new dialectics which will inevitably be thrown up. Epistemicide, at the heart of colonial and post-colonial discourses, is directed not only to perceived 'outsiders' but also to others within the community itself.

Alongside the most fundamental aspects of decolonisation, we need to reflexively consider how we deal with the colonial roots of civil conflict and acknowledge that any kind of knowledge production is not neutral. We cannot deny the specific constraints and affordances of NI's post-conflict society, as this would erase hard-won medical identities forged in clinical practice and destroy professional witness to patients' trauma. Dr Mairead Corrigan reflects on this aspect of post-conflict pedagogy in her case study below.

Case Study 2: Dr Mairead Corrigan on Decolonising Curricula in NI

The year 1998 was a seminal year for me. It was the year of my marriage and the Good Friday Agreement, which was preceded a month before by the tragic killing of a young Catholic neighbour of mine who was gunned down in a village pub with his friend who was a Protestant. Up until that dreadful tragic event, I was relatively untouched by the Troubles, being from a quiet rural part of NI in a community where Catholics and Protestants worked and lived side-by-side.

Having attended a Catholic grammar school, I did not have much contact with people from across the divide until I studied at Queen's

University, where I became friends with students who were Protestant who challenged my worldviews. These conversations motivated me to want to understand society more and the influence of identities like religion, ethnicity and social class for people's experiences in the world, which led me to study sociology. My interest in ethnic identities formed the basis of my PhD, and my later role as the Academic Lead for Equality, Diversity and Inclusion (EDI) in the Centre for Medical Education. Through this role, I have been party to discussions when concerns have been expressed about the 'orange/Protestant' and 'green/Catholic' sensitivities associated with the term 'decolonising' the curriculum— because of NI's history of colonisation—and to a lack of appetite for decolonising the curriculum given these sensitivities. This demonstrates how decolonising the curriculum can mean different things to different people, and how NI's unique history adds an extra layer of complexity. The different understandings of what it means to decolonise the curriculum have resulted in medical schools throughout the UK working together, facilitated by the Medical Schools EDI Alliance, to provide guidance, at which Queen's has a seat so that the unique context of NI is represented. As universities and medical schools are microcosms of society, it is no surprise then that NI's colonial history continues to cast a shadow over the curriculum.

At the heart of post-conflict pedagogy is the idea of introducing these struggles as ongoing, rather than as events of the past, and as relevant concerns to acknowledge within everyday healthcare. We advocate for a pedagogy which is intersectional and open to criticism, with critical consciousness at its centre. Yet this is only one of two pillars: what distinguishes post-conflict pedagogy from any other form of critical practice is an equal commitment to trauma-informed practice (Szczygiel, 2018), which we introduce in the next section. Thus, we see a trauma-informed approach to decolonisation as a key task of post-conflict pedagogy. As we noted above, in mentoring learners to resolve multiple dialectics, we can create a space for transformation.

Towards Trauma-informed Critical Consciousness

Freire acknowledged the deeply phenomenological and existential nature of critical consciousness, referring to it as an ontological vocation towards embracing our humanity (Hong Chen, 2016). Building on Freire, critical scholar Zembylas argues that those of us working in post-traumatic contexts must engage with all resulting complexities, including its affective aspects, to construct a reparative pedagogy (Zembylas, 2019). This sits close to the concepts we have discussed above, in using education as a means of repairing historical injustices. Reparations consider how historical discourses impact the present day, and so can be seen as a key part of post-conflict pedagogy. In social practice theory terms, individual identities evolve, and then evoke fundamental change in the system. There is an opportunity for contentious practices to shift, and perhaps even to change the deadlock of enduring struggles (Holland and Lave, 2001). In the NI context, consciousness-raising activities offer the catalyst for such expansive shifts. In this section, we expand the concept of critical pedagogy to include reparative trauma-informed practice.

The pervasive clinical gaze constructs illness as mechanical dysfunction (Foucault, 1963/2017). Typically, doctors are more comfortable accepting this dualist paradigm which separates mind and body. Yet an explosion of literature since the 1990s explores how traumatic experiences are stored in the body as well as the mind, a specific form of social health determinant which, as we noted in Table 5.2, has wide-ranging effects on morbidity and mortality (Felitti et al., 2019; Sun et al., 2021; van der Kolk, 2014). The everyday tacit, cumulative symptoms of collective trauma and social malaise which typify post-conflict medicine are rarely addressed in centralised curricula. As a result, few clinicians are equipped with explicit training in dealing with their own and other people's trauma. That learning is acquired on the job, exposing learners and practitioners to vicarious trauma and burnout.

For practising clinicians such as Helen and Jenny, traumatic legacies tied to colonialism are embedded deeply within practice and in our subjectivities as doctors. These are forms of learning and knowing we must learn to share with those coming behind us. Trauma comes in many forms, for example 'Big T', such as war, natural disasters or enslavement, or 'small t', such as divorce, alcoholism or mental health problems (Straussner and Calnan, 2014). Trauma can be collective or individual, historical, cultural or intergenerational. Troubles trauma is embodied in our patients (Porges, 2024); for the most affected, it is expressed through poorer quality and shorter lives, addictions and broken relationships. For others, it sits quietly in the background but is present nonetheless. Communities most affected by the Troubles are associated with lower socioeconomic status and greater health need. This is known as the inverse care law (Tudor Hart, 1971)—healthcare is least accessible to those most in need of it.

We suggest, therefore, that trauma-informed practice is the other pillar of post-conflict pedagogy. In practical terms, this means a commitment to recognising trauma as ubiquitous and embodied; developing an educational approach which emphasises psychological safety, trustworthiness of institutions and empowerment of traumatised people, including those who are marginalised or othered; and embedding trauma-informed approaches within attempts towards reparation and decolonising. In addition to adopting a trauma-informed approach towards our patients, we must commit to doing the same for ourselves and our learners. In case study 3 below, Jenny reflects on her experience with collective trauma.

Case Study 3: Prof. Jenny Johnston on Collective Trauma

Growing up on the northern outskirts of Belfast in the 1980s and 1990s, despite some of the worst of the Troubles happening just a few miles away, I think I was shielded from much of the worst of it. My grandparents moved to the suburbs from working-class areas of Belfast in the 1950s, accessing new housing and greater metaphorical space to live. I went to schools which included a mix of races and religions, and had many of the privileges of being second-generation middle class.

Even from within this bubble, some things stand out. On flights abroad from Belfast, security was unusually high, particularly if travelling to England. I remember being urgently evacuated from my grammar school, and hearing bombs explode in the city centre (about a mile away) while in class. Age eighteen, I used to walk to the city centre with friends after school; sometimes army Land Rovers full of English soldiers would pass us with their guns trained towards the pavement, and therefore us. I also have many stories of being 'othered', which is a common experience for Northern Irish people. For example, my Northern Irish bank notes being rudely refused in London; and being asked while working as a student in the USA if there was much 'war' where I was, and would I argue with my fellow student from the Republic?

Nowadays, I understand that the imprint of these experiences is part of NI's collective trauma, and comes with long lasting trauma responses. In 2019, on holiday in Canada, I was in the Eaton Centre mall in Toronto when the fire alarm sounded. Together with my Northern Irish husband, our first instinct was to push our baby daughter away; we pushed her buggy at speed, not just out of the mall but several blocks away to perceived safety. To our astonishment, many other shoppers and staff simply ignored the persistent sound of the alarm and continued about their business. Experience had triggered our flight response immediately. Nobody brought up in Belfast would ever dare ignore an alarm.

Our reactions were born of a childhood and adolescence during the Troubles, where frequent 'bomb scares' disrupted not only leisure activity but also school and work. Then, a 'scare' could easily be a euphemism for the real thing: evacuations, bomb squads, controlled explosions, if lucky, perhaps fire-damage sales in shops such as Marks and Spencer's which represent a comfortable and safe middle-class existence in other UK locations.

It is only in later years that those of us brought up against this background have come to consider how different a 'normal' this was, and how our reactions and reflexes in the present are set to the triggers of the past.

These are just a few of the ways in which people carrying trauma react to everyday circumstances with abnormally sensitive survival responses (fight, flight, freeze, fawn or collapse). While it is not easy to reflect upon such circumstances, it is important to interrogate our own experiences and subjectivities for what may be learnt, shared and anticipated in our engagements with each other and our patients.

Such an approach to education recognises that in the triad of doctor, patient and learner, each may be carrying a level of trauma which must be respected and treated with care. Increasingly, as the demographics of NI change and become less insular, patients bring Big T traumas of their own into this context: Jenny and Helen, both based in South Belfast, have many patients from Syria, Iran and sub-Saharan Africa. A majority of these people have arrived in NI as asylum seekers fleeing war or persecution. Other marginalised communities, such as the Roma, have long histories of intergenerational trauma resulting from genocide (Kapralski, 2015). Each of these communities requires a clinical approach to healthcare which understands cultural nuance and the impact of trauma on health behaviours and beliefs, the ability to access healthcare and clinical outcomes. In embedding post-conflict pedagogy, we empower our learners to understand themselves and their work at a level much more profound than simple mechanics. In this sense of developing new and different identities, this approach to medical education is existential.

Relevance Beyond this Context

While we have argued for the specific embedded needs of a post-conflict society located within the UK itself, we believe the principles of post-conflict pedagogy we have outlined transfer to other contexts, or in the very least, are common ground for building responsive reparative curricula that do not omit the persisted woundedness and social divisions of historical realities.

Transferrable concerns include, firstly, the manner in which colonial structural biases translate into health inequalities amongst Indigenous peoples in many post-colonial contexts. These include: the historical trauma, epistemicide and genocide experienced by First Nations peoples in North America and Australia (Browne et al., 2005); oppressed people such as Scheduled Tribes in India (Maity, 2017); the persistently higher risk faced by Black women of undertaking pregnancy and childbirth in the UK and the USA (Adegoke et al., 2021); the mortality, morbidity and health inequalities of violent conflict in prior Western European colonies such as Yemen, Sudan, the Democratic Republic of Congo (El Bcheraoui et al., 2018); and other countries recovering from the Cold War, such as those in the former Soviet Bloc and parts of Africa, Asia and South America (Haerpfer et al., 2013). Additionally, post-conflict pedagogy may have wider resonance in working with highly traumatised communities which do not meet the definition of post-conflict societies. For example, medical learners must still develop relevant skills and knowledge to work within areas of peaceful states largely defined by poverty, gang violence and structural oppression. The principles we have outlined here are likely to be of use in beginning the task of teaching inclusion medicine.

Whatever the context, we believe that the joint principles of consciousness raising and trauma-informed practice can be usefully adapted to engage and empower learners. By becoming part of their identities as doctors, an opening to greater social change is created.

Conclusion

In this chapter, we have used our own context, experiences and identities, together with critical social theories (two of whose authors, Freire and

Zembylas, wrote within divided societies), to outline a new post-conflict pedagogy drawing together the two pillars of critical consciousness and trauma-informed practice. We have considered the influence of pervasive positivism, industrialised discourses and systemic colonial oppression in creating the systems of medical education which prevail in the UK and the West at large. We explored how individual identity, formed against a complex sociocultural-historical background, can in turn influence these large-scale contexts and thereby bring about systemic change. We considered our own ethnographic histories-in-person, reflecting on what we bring to NI's enduring struggles as clinicians and critical educators. We introduced extra complexity into situated forms of decolonising curricula within post-conflict zones, and we advocated for trauma-informed attitudes and practice.

In concluding this chapter, we would like to offer our suggestions for getting started with embedding these concepts in real-life educational and clinical practice. As three educators negotiating a formal curriculum-of-omission, we feel it is incumbent on us not to leave critical reflection to medical students to navigate unsupported within clinical practice. We acknowledge the magnitude of the task, and suggest that the first step may be simply to make the unsaid explicit, as we have attempted to do throughout this chapter. Hidden curricula can be elevated into formal (and informal) ways of learning which we share with learners, through frank discussion of our clinical experiences. This is particularly cogent for medical workplace learning. Helping learners to develop critical consciousness, along with self-awareness, starts with role modelling and patient interactions. Additionally, we argue strongly for the need to acknowledge the secondary trauma that healthcare providers themselves may experience in working with fraught healthcare legacies.

Medicine's inherent positivism does not sit comfortably with the multiple voices and truths of critical post-colonial post-conflict studies. These are epistemic practices which challenge the hegemony of positivist biomedicine, replacing it with the possibilities of compassion and trauma-informed care. While on-the-ground educators work to embed change, our challenge as academics is to maintain our critical stance, to share our ideas and work, and to develop it further. In achieving the latter, we feel there is much to learn from our colleagues in medical education in other conflict and post-conflict zones, and also from other disciplines. Our work has always been situated at interdisciplinary boundaries, and this is a natural place for us to position ourselves as we embrace multiple voices and move the work of post-conflict pedagogy forward.

Bibliography

Adegoke, T. M., Pinder, L. F., Ndiwane, N., Parker, S. E., Vragovic, O., and Yarrington, C. D. (2021). Inequities in Adverse Maternal and Perinatal Outcomes: The Effect of Maternal Race and Nativity. *Maternal and Child Health Journal, 26*, 823–833, https://doi.org/10.1007/s10995-021-03225-0

Arshad, R. (2020, September). Decolonising and Initial Teacher Education. *CERES.* https://www.ceres.education.ed.ac.uk/2020/08/19/decolonising-and-initial-teacher-education/

Bardon, J. (1992). *A History of Ulster.* The Blackstaff Press.

Billett, S. (2014). Interdependence on the Boundaries Between Working and Learning. *Professional and Practice-Based Learning, 9*, 369–385. https://doi.org/10.1007/978-94-007-7012-6_18

Browne, A. J., Smye, V. L., and Varcoe, C. (2005). The Relevance of Postcolonial Theoretical Perspectives to Research in Aboriginal Health. *PubMed, 37*(4), 16–37.

Coon, R. E. (2019). 'It Was the Best of Times, it Was the Worst of Times': Healthcare during the Northern Ireland Troubles. *Journal of the University of Limerick History Society, 20*, 40–52.

El Bcheraoui, C., Jumaan, A. O., Collison, M. L., Daoud, F., and Mokdad, A. H. (2018). Health in Yemen: Losing Ground in War Time. *Globalization and Health, 14*(1). https://doi.org/10.1186/s12992-018-0354-9

Felitti, V. J., Anda, R. F., Nordenberg, D., Williamson, D. F., Spitz, A. M., Edwards, V., Koss, M. P., and Marks, J. S. (2019). Relationship of Childhood Abuse and Household Dysfunction to Many of the Leading Causes of Death in Adults: The Adverse Childhood Experiences (ACE) Study. *American Journal of Preventive Medicine, 56*(6), 774–786. https://doi.org/10.1016/j.amepre.2019.04.001

Foucault, M. (2017). *Birth of the Clinic.* Presses Universitaires de France. [Original work published 1963]

Freire, P. (1970). *Pedagogy of the Oppressed.* Bloomsbury Academic.

Haerpfer, C., Wallace, C., and Abbott, P. (2013). Health Problems and the Transition from Communism in the Former Soviet Union: Towards an Explanation. *Perspectives on European Politics and Society, 14*(4), 460–479. https://doi.org/10.1080/15705854.2013.772751

Hafferty, F. W. (1998). Beyond Curriculum Reform: Confronting Medicine's Hidden Curriculum. *Academic Medicine, 73*(4), 403–407. https://doi.org/10.1097/00001888-199804000-00013

Holland, D. C. (2001). *Identity and Agency in Cultural Worlds.* Harvard University Press.

Holland, D. C., and Lave, J. (2001). *History in Person.* James Currey.

Hong Chen, R. (2016). *Freire and a Pedagogy of Suffering: A Moral Ontology.* Springer EBooks. https://doi.org/10.1007/978-981-287-532-7_105-1

Irish Boundary Commission. (1969). *Report of the Irish Boundary Commission 1925.* Irish University Press.

Johnston, J. L. (2022). *Conflict, Culture and Identity in GP Training.* Springer Nature.

Johnston, J. L., Hart, N., and Manca, A. (2022). The Philosophy of Education: Freire's Critical Pedagogy. In M. E. L. Brown, M. Veen and G. M. Finn (Eds), *Applied Philosophy for Health Professions Education* (pp. 103–118). Springer. https://doi.org/10.1007/978-981-19-1512-3_8

Kapralski, S. (2015). The Genocide of Roma and Sinti - Their Political Movement from the Perspective of Social Trauma Theory. *S:I.M.O.N. Shoah: Intervention. Methods. Documentation, 2*(1), 39–47. https://www.ceeol.com/search/article-detail?id=836350

Kumagai, A. K., and Lypson, M. L. (2009). Beyond Cultural Competence: Critical Consciousness, Social Justice, and Multicultural Education. *Academic Medicine, 84*(6), 782–787. https://doi.org/10.1097/acm.0b013e3181a42398

Lawn, D., and Patterson, A. (2023). *Blue Lights series 1* [TV series]. Two Cities Television; BBC.

Lempp, H., and Seale, C. (2004). The Hidden Curriculum in Undergraduate Medical Education: Qualitative Study of Medical Students' Perceptions of Teaching. *BMJ, 329*(7469), 770–773. https://doi.org/10.1136/bmj.329.7469.770

Lingard, L. (2009). What We See and Don't See When We Look at 'Competence': Notes on a God Term. *Advances in Health Sciences Education, 14*(5), 625–628. https://doi.org/10.1007/s10459-009-9206-y

Maity, B. (2017). Comparing Health Outcomes Across Scheduled Tribes and Castes in India. *World Development, 96*, 163–181. https://doi.org/10.1016/j.worlddev.2017.03.005

Manca, A., Gormley, G. J., Johnston, J. L., and Hart, N. D. (2019). Honoring Medicine's Social Contract. *Academic Medicine, 1.* https://doi.org/10.1097/acm.0000000000003059

Mbaki, Y., Todorova, E., and Hagan, P. (2021). Diversifying the medical curriculum as part of the wider decolonising effort: A proposed framework and self-assessment resource toolbox. *The Clinical Teacher, 18*(5), 459–466. https://doi.org/10.1111/tct.13408

Milliken, M., Bates, J., and Smith, A. (2021). Teaching on the Other Side: How Identity Affects the Capacity for Agency of Teachers Who Have Crossed the Community Divide in the Northern Ireland Educational System. *Oxford Review of Education, 47*, 1–18. https://doi.org/10.1080/03054985.2020.1867525

Mota, M., Conceição, C., Leonardo Lora Barraza, and Milanez, A. (2024). Dermatology in Black Skin. *Anais Brasileiros de Dermatologia, 99*(3), 327–341. https://doi.org/10.1016/j.abd.2023.10.001

Murua, I. (2019). As British as Finchley? The Evolution of the Positions of the British Government and Irish Republicanism Regarding Sovereignty over Northern Ireland. *Estudios Irlandeses, 14*, 121–134. https://doi.org/10.24162/ei2019-8834

Northern Ireland Department for the Economy. (2018). *An Analysis of Migrant Workers from the Northern Ireland Census 2011*. DfE.

Northern Ireland Office. (1998). *The Belfast Agreement*. Stationary Office.

Northern Ireland Statistics and Research Agency (1991). *1991 Census Reports*. NISRA.

—(2022a). *Census 2021 Main Statistics for Northern Ireland (Phase 1)*. NISRA.

—(2022b) *Finalised Suicide Statistics in Northern Ireland, 2015–2021*. NISRA.

Park, Y. S., Konge, L., and Artino, A. R. (2020). The Positivism Paradigm of Research. *Academic Medicine, 95*(5), 690–694. https://doi.org/10.1097/ACM.0000000000003093

Porges, S. W. (2024). Polyvagal Theory: The Neuroscience of Safety in Trauma-Informed Practice. In E. C. Tronick et al. (Eds), *The Handbook of Trauma-Transformative Practice: Emerging Therapeutic Frameworks for Supporting Individuals, Families or Communities Impacted by Abuse and Violence* (p. 51). Jessica Kingsley Publishers.

Straussner, S. L. A., and Calnan, A. J. (2014). Trauma through the Life Cycle: A Review of Current Literature. *Clinical Social Work Journal, 42*(4), 323–335. https://doi.org/10.1007/s10615-014-0496-z

Sun, Y., Qu, Y., and Zhu, J. (2021). The Relationship between Inflammation and Post-traumatic Stress Disorder. *Frontiers in Psychiatry, 12*. https://doi.org/10.3389/fpsyt.2021.707543

Szczygiel, P. (2018). On the Value and Meaning of Trauma-Informed Practice: Honoring Safety, Complexity, and Relationship. *Smith College Studies in Social Work, 88*(2), 115–134. https://doi.org/10.1080/00377317.2018.1438006

Tamimi, N., Hala Khalawi, Jallow, M. A., Gabriel, O., and Jumbo, E. (2023). Towards Decolonising Higher Education: A Case Study from a UK University. *Higher Education, 88*, 815–837. https://doi.org/10.1007/s10734-023-01144-3

ten Cate, O., and Billett, S. (2014). Competency-based Medical Education: Origins, Perspectives and Potentialities. *Medical Education, 48*(3), 325–332. https://doi.org/10.1111/medu.12355

Trew, J. D. (2010). Reluctant Diasporas of Northern Ireland: Migrant Narratives of Home, Conflict, Difference. *Journal of Ethnic and Migration Studies, 36*(4), 541–560. https://doi.org/10.1080/13691830903520424

Tudor Hart, J. (1971). The Inverse Care Law. *The Lancet, 297*(7696), 405–412. https://doi.org/10.1016/s0140-6736(71)92410-x

van der Kolk, B. (2014). *The Body Keeps the Score: Brain, Mind, and Body in the Healing of Trauma*. Penguin Books.

Wong, S. H. M., Gishen, F., and Lokugamage, A. U. (2021). 'Decolonising the Medical Curriculum': Humanising Medicine through Epistemic Pluralism, Cultural Safety and Critical Consciousness. *London Review of Education, 19*(1). https://doi.org/10.14324/lre.19.1.16

Yancy, C. W. (2020). Academic Medicine and Black Lives Matter. *JAMA, 324*(5), 435. https://doi.org/10.1001/jama.2020.12532

Zembylas, M. (2019). Emotions, Affects, and Trauma in Classrooms: Moving beyond the Representational Genre. *Research in Education, 106*(1). https://doi.org/10.1177/0034523719890367

PART II

CONFLICTS IN THE PRESENT

6. 'A Virtual Target Painted on my Back…': Contested Constitutionalism in a Post-conflict Society

Colin Harvey

Contextualising 'Free to Think'

How did I end up, in 2022, making the statement contained in the title of this chapter? This is a question that you, the reader, may be asking, and one I still ask myself. I am a Professor in the School of Law at Queen's University Belfast (QUB), with an academic career of over thirty years, spanning these islands (Britain and Ireland) and beyond. Although public engagement and civic activism were always intrinsic to my work, I never really anticipated being in this position, writing a 'lived experience' narrative of my own personal/professional situation, despite my deep admiration for those who do. A sense of vulnerability and unease remains. Law Schools are changing, with critical voices and new perspectives well-established, but much heavily doctrinal work discourages such approaches, with acknowledgement of subjectivity sternly erased. Nevertheless, here I am. A small act of defiance, a signal of allyship with others under threat and at risk anywhere.

To understand this contested constitutionalism better, context is required (Harvey, 2002). Think about it for a moment. The island of Ireland is a partitioned place, home to two distinctive jurisdictions. Northern Ireland, a region of the UK (the United Kingdom of Great Britain and Northern Ireland, to give it the full title), and what I will call here the Republic of Ireland (an independent sovereign state). Common membership of the European Union (EU) covered over the

 https://doi.org/10.11647/OBP.0427.06

harsher aspects of existing fracture lines (Harvey, 2020; Harvey and Kramer, 2019). A sophisticated form of governance had managed a sustained period of relative stability from 2007, with the difficulties of this form of power-sharing plain. An agreed way of resolving the constitutional question stood behind it all, a decision for 'the people' to make (Harvey, 2021a). Popular sovereignty thus rested alongside established democratic and institutional processes (Harvey, 2021b).

Then along came a referendum in June 2016 to disrupt all of that. Afterwards, the border assumed even greater significance. The destabilising impact of Brexit for Northern Ireland is well documented, and people are living with the unfolding realities. I, like many others, spent the years since examining the consequences and suggesting evidence-based solutions to manage associated tensions and difficulties (Harvey et al., 2018a–f).

The UK-wide referendum had varying implications across the increasingly strained Union. The region where I live and work wanted to remain in the EU, but these votes were not decisive. The many pious political references to consent counted for little. The border on the island of Ireland is now an external border of the EU. A stark statement capturing the magnitude of Brexit and the risks of deepening separation. I recall recording an online video, for a series with other School of Law colleagues, alerting people to the further division that would follow: Northern Ireland rests on several fault lines (Harvey, 2016). Many of the predictions played out over the fraught years of negotiation, in a post-conflict society attempting to recover from the complex legacies of political violence. The region was a seeming afterthought in an ideologically driven project fuelled by narrow versions of English nationalism that were never going to deliver on the extravagant promises made. We wondered then what would happen when reality dawned but were often too weighed down by the urgency of emergency responses and desperate attempts to mitigate the damage.

What was going to happen next? The initial reaction on this island was a protective one, anchored in a deep commitment to locating plausible policy responses. People worked hard to preserve the gains made during the peace process. There was well-founded worry about the return of a 'hard border' on this island, and an evolving awareness of multiple Brexit-related impacts. Difficult questions emerged around conceptions of the border and its meaning, particularly for minority ethnic and migrant communities who knew and experienced the solidity of existing demarcation lines (Pivotal, 2022). This connected to ongoing and wider problems, including on the responsiveness of universities in Northern Ireland (Belluigi and Moynihan, 2023).

For many there was an obvious starting point: Northern Ireland needed a carefully crafted special arrangement to address its particular circumstances, one that respected the fundamentals of the Good Friday Agreement (the Agreement) (Harvey and Skoutaris, 2018). Continuing membership of the EU was taken for granted for so long that there was a real risk that the significance of this dramatic rupture might be downplayed. It was exhaustively debated in Ireland, for good reason (Harvey, 2020). There were genuine fears about the short and long-term impacts, and it was not apparent that those who had promoted Brexit grasped what it would mean for the island of Ireland, particularly if they opted for harsh forms of abrupt and lasting divergence from the EU.

The Agreement is a peace/political/legal agreement that acknowledges the pluralist nature of complex relationships across these islands (Harvey, 2022). It is multi-stranded for a reason, the legal and political expression of a grounded reality that most accept: the region is not like other places in the UK or Ireland. It may sound odd to recollect now, but there was always a credible argument—one that transcends the existential constitutional question—for doing something legally different for Northern Ireland. This seems like such a self-evident point. How odd it then was to watch 'muscular' forms of unionism promote and seek to impose a uniform approach. A mockery was made of prior assumptions about the UK as a pluralist constitutional arrangement. What was the entire peace process about if not to demonstrate the distinctiveness of the region and its post-conflict challenges? Did people not know the many ways that Northern Ireland was already different? It was lost and forgotten by those mired in simplistic talk of the revival of sovereignty and long-departed ideas of Britishness—a dangerous cocktail when consumed in the volatile circumstances of ethno-national conflict.

As an academic who has never viewed universities as sealed off from society, I engaged in direct public activism, including vocal support for work to ensure that no hard border returned to the island of Ireland and that rights be respected. That meant travelling far beyond lecture halls and seminar rooms. Like others, I was personally and professionally worried about the implications, including for vital human rights and equality guarantees. I remain convinced that the disturbing toxicity of the language around Brexit was about much more than leaving the EU. The whole debate was unleashing sinister forces, and in the interview below I quite consciously frame the discussion in those terms. Subsequent events have vindicated this perspective and these arguments. When the Brexit project displayed signs of unravelling, it became apparent who would be blamed (Harvey et al., 2018c).

My public response mapped comfortably onto my scholarly reflections and ongoing academic work about the impact of Brexit. Why would I not pursue these matters in the open? Public engagement was something I had always done, and it seemed like a logical response. With colleagues at QUB, Ulster University and a local NGO (the Committee on the Administration of Justice), I secured research funding to take this work further in the BrexitLawNI project (ESRC ES/R001499/1; Harvey et al., 2018a–f). Our aim was to consider the human rights, equality and conflict transformation consequences of Brexit for Northern Ireland, and we sought to be innovative in exploring the questions raised. The outputs helped to shape wider deliberations and the answers that eventually emerged. It was notable, for example, how deeply the link to safeguarding the broader peace process resonated with others.

Damage limitation only gets you so far. It was becoming clear to me that there needed to be much more focus on the constitutional future of the island of Ireland, especially in the new circumstances of Brexit. My proactive involvement in civic initiatives on this matter through, for example, the Constitutional Conversations Group and Ireland's Future, reflected well-established patterns of participation in societal debates. To put this simply: it is what I tend to do. I was pleased to be part of these social movements for change.

In April 2017, the European Council confirmed that Northern Ireland had a way back to the EU via the self-determination/principle of consent provisions of the Agreement. A vote for constitutional change would mean automatic re-entry to the EU (Bassett and Harvey, 2022). Stop and ponder the power of that intervention: opting for a united Ireland would deliver return to the EU for the region. The right not only to have a view about that outcome, but to pursue it, was supposed to be legally guaranteed in the Agreement. How could you avoid highlighting it? Surely this new dimension to an old debate had to be examined?

The significance was profound, and added to a personal and professional sense of responsibility to embark on further preparatory work on precisely this question. It also connected to something I was used to from the human rights world: testing legal promises. I was in the habit of writing more impact-relevant pieces, primarily with the aim of influencing public policy discussions, as an academic at Queen's willing to take a position and speak out on the merits of a united Ireland—something I did regularly on human rights and equality. Without in any way overstating it, I became a public figure, with all that means in the age we are in. I avoid the term 'public intellectual' because I struggle with the pretensions that surround it, even if that is what I was doing in advancing arguments about achieving a united Ireland. Two independent research reports on the EU and Irish unity attracted attention (Harvey and Bassett, 2019; Bassett and Harvey, 2022). Very little of the feedback addressed our substantive arguments. Much of the criticism circled around the company I was keeping, and the use of the university logo on the reports, even though that was and remains standard practice. What else was inspiring the reaction? I will leave others to answer that.

From 2019 to the end of 2022 matters became intense, and at times distressing, in what had the appearance of a highly personalised and directed campaign against my position at Queen's. The focus on my workplace included interventions by high-profile members of political parties, well-known public commentators, and an anonymous 'concerned QUB student' group. Collating the mountain of materials for this chapter, and for a recent conference presentation, offered a grim reminder, but also a further opportunity to consider the patterns and meaning. The whole episode continues to have the look and feel of orchestration, conveniently timed for a political moment when an 'instability narrative' was required. Future historians will hopefully have the archival records needed to make a rounded assessment of that period. My efforts to gather evidence are necessarily limited and I speak here of how it was subjectively experienced; the feeling of being made a public example of. More than one person since has noted how my treatment was being observed by others.

What happened on social media is a well-worn and familiar tale. Much of it remains publicly available; the lack of accountability is part of the picture—eerie echoes of the conflict years, fought with different techniques and new tools, contestation evolving into vicious new forms. The endless online trolling involved direct and implied threats, with some of that tied to conspiratorial allegations of the existence of a shadowy elite group seeking to take control of the professions in Northern Ireland. A definite playbook was being utilised; reactionary movements in civil society engaging in transnational dialogue, learning from each other. The relentlessness of the activity creates a disturbing sense of menace, and many of the online anonymous actors are skilled at intimidating opponents. They know what they are doing. Looking back now there were delegitimising components, with an explicit political objective: a message was being sent about participation in these constitutional conversations and how they should be conducted. A life spent teaching law did not prepare me for what followed: security advice from the Police Service of Northern Ireland (PSNI) about my arrangements—at home and at work—and much more, an exhausting insider guide to the justice system that left me concerned. If someone in my privileged position could not secure accountability, what hope was there for others? Odd moments included an interview in a BBCNI studio in Belfast where I was asked repeatedly to condemn the Provisional Irish Republican Army (PIRA), following on from a related question raised during seminars at the university (and circulated by an anonymous online account). Other experiences with BBCNI were not good, leaving me to wonder about the role of our local public service broadcaster.

I noticed more often than usual the defaults in this segregated region, how perception works, and how community background informs interactions within institutions. To a dispiriting extent the targeted campaign achieved its intended purpose, my professional life reduced to toxic caricatures. I began to understand, from an internal perspective, what accounts of epistemic injustice meant (Fricker, 2013; Fricker, 2007; Harvey, 2021c).

A public statement that I released in November 2022, underlining my lifelong rejection of violence, indicates how far things had gone.

Lines had been decisively blurred, with no sense anymore—for myself or others—of any real separation between who was in public life and who was not. Matters became even more surreal in 2022, with prominent political figures becoming involved. In this world, everyone is a potential target and the attempted silencing of progressive voices is present everywhere. Those associated with hostility to 'cancel culture' were often at the forefront—a contradiction they did not appear to appreciate.

During the 2019–2022 period, I continued my work on a Bill of Rights for Northern Ireland and had to deal with reports from the Northern Ireland Assembly, and in local media, that my appointment to an Expert Advisory Panel had been blocked. Much of this was discussed in public and is readily available via an online search. I heard many stories—often privately expressed—of what can happen to people in these situations and, in my view, there is a troubling level of quiet toleration in Northern Ireland of the entirely unacceptable. More than once the suggestion was made that having a view about the constitutional question was a form of self-exclusion, the implication being that I deserved everything that was coming my way, that I brought this on myself. Frequently though, the impact is less obvious and the risk in academic life is of isolation, which then makes you more vulnerable. There is a temptation to blame yourself, to self-censor, and to withdraw. I acknowledge that in a region like this, entire careers are constructed in this way—a pragmatic response to a conflicted space, a way of coping and surviving. It remains perplexing to me; would you really tell a human rights scholar, for example, never to engage in rights activism, or a lawyer never to have an activist view of the rule of law?

Perhaps academics are too prone to see patterns where none exist. I know not everyone will agree, but my view is that there was an element of co-ordination, linked to a broader campaign of staged instability in opposition to the Protocol (now the 'Windsor Framework'). There were twin objectives in my specific case: stifle the debate and question my employment status at Queen's. Those are strong statements, but I believe they can be evidenced. In 2022, the singling out grew louder, the security implications intensified, and in the context of increasingly angry protests about the then-Protocol, I started using the language of this podcast interview. I gave it much anxious thought before doing so. In a society where armed groups remain active and present, the repetitive targeting of people can have devastating consequences. Years of experience working with human rights activists, locally and globally, meant I was familiar with what was required, and I received wise advice about the need to escalate what was happening and place it in the public arena. I did not initially perceive myself as a 'scholar at risk', but good activist friends persuaded me otherwise. It made me wonder—and still does—about other academic colleagues facing similar challenges who do not have these networks of support. I am acutely aware this is a perilous time for courageous scholars who are prepared to carry the implications of their research into the public sphere.

I am writing this chapter in 2024, while reading back over a transcript of my interview with Rob Quinn from 2022. What strikes me is how incoherent I sound in the unedited version, and the differences between the written word and my own rambling speech patterns. At times embarrassing, in editing this, a lot is consciously left in. My inability to speak in straight lines is obvious. The use of 'I think' illustrating my self-doubting mindset, the impact of what was happening, and the difficulty of expressing personalised forms of impact. My hesitation in explicitly naming things is obvious, then and now—evidence of the lived experience of conflict, where ambiguity can be your friend. A fear lurking there too, the knowledge that many of my vocal opponents are not shy about the deployment of 'lawfare'. I was becoming worn down and you can tell that from this interview. By the end of 2022, matters had deteriorated even further.

There is much more to be said, including on any lessons that might be learned. I am conscious of how fortunate and privileged I am, and will be forever grateful for the solidarity and support received. I was not suspended, did not lose my academic job, the violent threats are still only that, and we have not been forced to move home. I have tried to contextualise my own experience and am acutely conscious of the university as a site of various culture wars. I am aware of how some of my choices are perceived. I suspect aspects of my professional standing are damaged beyond repair. Like many who engage in such work, I include an appeal here to the understanding of future generations—the hope of a measure of vindication one day, even if it may not be visible now. My strong suspicion is that more will emerge in the public domain to help us understand that post-Brexit period. It is heartening to watch as the volume of literature on a united Ireland expands (Humphreys, 2018; Collins, 2022; Connolly, 2022; Meagher, 2022; O'Leary, 2022). The work of detailed preparation is in a new and different place and my hope is that this will develop further.

I am self-aware enough to understand that appeals to 'freedom' within academic institutions do not always carry the same meaning. I do not have an absolutist view; university campuses must be safe places, free from hatred. The heightened vigilance acquired then has never left me. The overriding sense of worry, of being under a form of societal surveillance, all stays with you. Some of the most unnerving messages received (from self-identified 'veterans') were those telling me I was a 'dangerous person' and was being 'watched'. That may sound trivial, but it leaves you wondering about the human beings hidden behind those anonymised worlds. What happens if you encounter them on the street or at your place of work? Your confidence is eroded, levels of anxiety increase, knowing that powerful internal and external actors are waiting for the slightest perceived mistake. This is often compounded by forms of denialism grounded in ignorance, an attitude that dismisses your experiences. A great danger is turning in on yourself, withdrawing and becoming detached from your professional life.

What advice might be given and what could I share that would help? I have learned to be much more critical of, and reflective about, higher education. Yes, expertise matters, but there is a politics of expertise in universities that can be about control, domination and exclusion. Forms of gatekeeping that do not resemble legitimate peer-review. Scholars must be permitted to be open and honest about their views of the constitutional future of Ireland, for example.

The problems are exacerbated by the hyper-competitive and artificial performance cultures that permeate UK higher education. The risk is that sites of critical challenge, such as universities, become subservient to powerful interests and thus lose core functions. We should question more than we currently do the imposed boundaries that aim to separate universities and academics from their societal contexts and the promotion of change. Universities are too often locations for the perpetuation of oppressive hierarchies, wrapped in the deceptively inclusive and soothing language of neoliberal corporate cultures.

Words of solidarity are significant, particularly if publicly expressed. External allies letting your institution know that they are observing does help. Deeds often send a more powerful signal. The scholarly community has a role everywhere: do not allow a vulnerable colleague to become unfairly isolated and marginalised through these aggressive, externally driven campaigns of intimidation. If this is accompanied by internal exclusion, then the experience of even coming onto campus can be dreadful. The noise generated around you also carries risks for others: guilt by association. My citation strategy in this chapter, for example, may appear self-indulgent but it is deliberate. You will note the references to my own contributions—a minor form of rebellion against the airbrushing dynamic that is part of this experience.

In the worst cases, malign external actors exploit the tensions within institutions, with your plight becoming a 'debate' in which people engage—sometimes while you are physically present. This is a strange form of 'side taking', which is unnerving if you are at the core of it. Though the storm may pass, it can be difficult to reconstruct your academic involvement and credentials. The end result can be quiet forms of internal exile, a reputation harmed beyond recovery. Across a range of fields, places and institutions, we need to be vigilant for signs of this in university life and find ways to address it. As I write, I watch the horrific consequences for those who speak truthfully about Gaza.

I continue to talk about a united Ireland and how to achieve it. Not only as an available option to be studied but as an outcome that I desire, an objective that I want to see realised. I will not apologise for that. And this speaks to what is vital in any effective response. There should not be a retreat from the public sphere and critical interaction with the societies we are part of and claim to serve. Ground should not be ceded. By staying in the intellectual space, you are making the primary point. As indicated, none of this is made easier by structural factors, including those that frame life in higher education and approaches that destroy collegiality in any institution, reducing universities to insecure production lines for manufactured outputs to meet constructed games of resource allocation. The commodification of everything leads to further erosion of independent, critical civic spaces.

I hope these introductory reflections provide helpful context for what follows in this interview. As with any such personalised narrative,

I am too close to the experience to be objective. In practice, I am unsure anymore what that would even mean; I am working through the implications still.

Free to Think Podcast[1]

Colin Harvey in Conversation with Rob Quinn

Free to Think talks with Colin Harvey, a Professor of Human Rights Law and former Head of the School of Law, Queen's University Belfast about what UN experts described as a 'smear campaign' against him for his work debating the possibility of new constitutional arrangements for the island of Ireland after Brexit. An expert on human rights and constitutional law and former Commissioner of the Northern Ireland Human Rights Commission, Harvey references growing up during the 'conflict', achievements under the Good Friday Agreement, and how these are threatened by Brexit. Harvey sees the pressures on him as part of a larger struggle against human rights and democratic values going on around the world and says that academics have a responsibility to robustly defend those values, despite the risks.

RQ: Welcome to *Free to Think*. A podcast where we celebrate people who think, question and share ideas. I'm Rob Quinn [hereafter RQ], Executive Director of Scholars at Risk, and your host. With each episode we bring you conversation with interesting inspiring people whose research, teaching or expression falls at the sensitive intersection of power and ideas. We'll be speaking with those who have the courage to seek truth and to speak truth, often at great risk, as well as those who work to defend them.

Our guest today is Colin Harvey [hereafter CH]. He's a Professor of Human Rights in the School of Law at Queen's University Belfast,

---

1   This is an edited transcript of an audio file originally published online in April 2022 by Scholars At Risk's (SAR) *Free to Think* Podcast as 'Episode 22: "A Virtual Target Painted on my Back..." A Conversation with Northern Ireland's Professor Colin Harvey on the Social Responsibility of Scholars in Post-conflict Societies', conducted by SAR Executive Director Rob Quinn, https://www.scholarsatrisk. org/resources/podcast/. This transcript is published with the permission of Rob Quinn and Scholars at Risk, Inc.

a Fellow of the Senator George J. Mitchell Institute for Global Peace, Security and Justice and an Associate Fellow of the Institute of Irish Studies. He's a former commissioner of the Northern Ireland Human Rights Commission and an expert on human rights law and constitutional law. Professor Harvey is also a board member of Ireland's Future, a non-profit, non-partisan organisation which was established to promote, debate and discuss Ireland's future, including the possibility and viability of new constitutional arrangements on the island after Brexit. Colin, welcome to *Free to Think*.

CH: Thank you very much Rob, I'm delighted to be in conversation with you.

RQ: So, Colin you've been studying, writing and speaking on human rights and constitutional law for some time now. How did you get started in this field?

CH: It's a great question, I suppose to trace back my own personal history. I was born and brought up in Derry in Northern Ireland/the North of Ireland and I grew up really at the height of the conflict here. It was the words and language of the civil rights movement in Derry of the mid to late 1960s echoing in my ears and many of the people around me. That was a strong influence on me and I always have felt whatever I've done that I really wanted to stand on the side of those who are most marginalised and oppressed anywhere, the most vulnerable, and that's shaped my academic working life, whether it's in university law schools doing articles and books—footnotes and all that—but also I'd say my activism as well.

RQ: And how about on the teaching side? So, you've been in academia really for the duration of the Good Friday Agreement, how have you found students have changed over the years?

CH: I think one of the things that's remarkable about living here in Belfast is it's a relatively small community. So many of the people you teach, you eventually see when they go on to become lawyers or they're doing other things, and they go on and shape and change the world. I think that's one of the better parts of the job, to watch people go on and shape things beyond university settings. The other scary thing, Rob, I think is that—I was talking about it in class the other day—that many of the people I teach now were born post-Good Friday Agreement. And the thing that strikes me about that is there's things in my memory bank that I take for granted about Ireland, Northern Ireland, these islands or whatever, that are not part of the memory of the people I'm teaching. They thankfully grew up in a post-conflict society. We have our difficulties and challenges now but nothing like Derry in the 1970s and 1980s. So, they have experienced a new way and a new framework. Some of the things that slightly older people take for granted are really not part of their horizon. That's something to be thankful for, to be cherished at the moment. When I think in a post-Brexit landscape and environment—and things getting febrile and volatile again—that we all need to just hold on to how far Northern Ireland has actually come since the Good Friday Agreement, and make sure that this generation does not have to experience what many of us went through.

RQ: And so picking up on that, in the last six months or so your name has been brought up in the print media, on social media, even by some politicians. If I'm not mistaken, you're being compared to Nazis and paramilitaries, and I think one journalist even suggested you should be voted off the island. What's this recent notoriety all about?

CH: It's really going back a number of years now. So, I was tracing it out around work that I, and a number of others, were doing in a post-Brexit context. Maybe to explain it to your audience. In 2016 the UK voted to leave the European Union—Brexit, the 'B' word. But Northern Ireland voted to remain, so was essentially removed from the European Union against the wishes of a majority of its people, which is a big deal here, and one of the things that I, and others, said at the time was that this was going to be deeply problematic for this region. This is a post-conflict society still recovering from a serious and intense violent conflict over many decades, and that it was likely to destabilise the place. It's given nobody any satisfaction to say that turned out to be a rather accurate prediction.

I suppose then in the post-Brexit context, if you think about the island of Ireland—which is already partitioned—when the UK and Ireland were both in the European Union, that common membership of the EU was an important background assumption of the peace process. Brexit has taken one part of the island out of the EU. So, for many people here it's this practical, symbolic repartition of the island of Ireland. The issue of the border on the island has opened up again post-Brexit, and the European Union said in April 2017 (European Council) that Northern Ireland has an automatic re-entry option to the EU, if the provisions of the Good Friday Agreement on self-determination were to be exercised. And that's the issue that has attracted a lot of attention. I've done a fair bit of work in the last three or four years on urging people to face into it, to plan and prepare in a responsible and sensible way for the possibility that people here may actually vote to return to the European Union by re-unifying the island of Ireland. And I—and others—have been saying that post-Brexit it's at least plausible that people will be presented with that choice. So, getting ready, preparing, planning responsibly for the time at which the question will be asked and letting people know. That seems wise to me, and I then found myself caught up in all of that really, in terms of those bigger constitutional questions, and that's made me a target for those primarily who would like to maintain the Union with Britain, and perhaps don't want that constitutional conversation even to be happening.

RQ: So, let's bring it back to how you got called into this, at least in the media. Within that power sharing structure there was some conversation in recent months about a Bill of Rights panel that was supposed to be formed under the agreements. Is that right?

CH: Yeah, to sketch out the background and context and where I fit into this framework. I think it's important for the audience to get that background because there's really been structural destabilisation of the society as a consequence of Brexit, and there's an irony in this that many academics predicted that would happen, unfortunately living through the consequences of our own scholarly predictions playing out.

I have quite openly worked on the preparation and planning dimension of Irish reunification, and so I've written research reports and I've spoken publicly about that. And to name it for your audience, as a result of doing that I find myself attracting the attention of the main Unionist political parties. I've been the focus of comment in different forms of media and newspapers but also probably as many people will be aware, the biggest storm at the moment is social media, where I'm the target—particularly in loyalist social media circles—of some really quite extraordinary language; I've been called the most remarkable things in the last few years, nothing has been missed. But ultimately my sense of that is because I ventured into that constitutional space, quite deliberately and consciously, there's people who don't want that space to be opened up. To put it candidly, by targeting me they are attempting to send a message to people very clearly: don't go where Professor Colin Harvey has gone or this could happen to you.

I've been working for many, many years on the Bill of Rights process in Northern Ireland and was a Human Rights commissioner, I served on the Human Rights Commission for two terms, was involved in drafting the Bill of Rights proposals in 2008 to the British government, and understandably applied to be on a panel that was to be established to advise a committee of the Northern Ireland Assembly on this issue. I then find myself the subject of media speculation that the Democratic Unionist Party was allegedly blocking my appointment. Like everyone else I'm reading the media reports, so I find myself at the centre of all that—it was intense towards the end of last year (2021). My situation was debated in the Northern Ireland Assembly as well, when the committee report was eventually produced. So, it was quite an uncomfortable, difficult time, where I found myself at the centre of a whirlwind really.

RQ: So, how has that attention—the social media denigration—how has that affected you in your work?

CH: I think the first thing is I am a fairly determined person, I've been involved in public life before, when I was on the Human Rights Commission. But I never experienced anything like this. You know I grew up during the conflict, it's just a really febrile, difficult and challenging time—so I have ploughed on and I'm conscious I do not want to be derailed, but it's difficult; it's also excruciatingly embarrassing having to talk about yourself in these sorts of contexts as well. The labelling of me I find incredibly worrying. You'll know recently here a loyalist armed group, there was a bomb scare, where a van was hijacked and driven to an event that the Irish Minister for Foreign Affairs was at; I was at that event as well.

Some of these armed groups are making noises around people like me, so it's a really very unnerving time, where some of the old language of the 1980s/1990s is re-emerging here and I find myself at the centre of that. So, it is unsettling, it's concerning, you're trying to do the day job of teaching and researching.

RQ: So, we have this labelling, as you say, or 'othering', declaring you somehow outside the bounds of the profession and so forth. Just quickly, have you ever felt that your position was at risk, as a professor at the institution?

CH: Yes, I have. I'll explain what I mean by that. Certainly in 2019, when it emerged that political parties here, serious political parties and their members, were approaching the university about me and my work. It's just unnerving, it would be unnerving for anybody. Members of parties in the government going to your boss saying, this person who works in your place, do you endorse this stuff that he's doing? So, it's a nervy time. I always remain slightly on edge really, while there has been reassurance and there's enormous amounts of support and solidarity, to be candid, you just worry that sometimes your employer or the university might go: 'is this guy worth all this hassle?' You know. So that's always in your mind.

RQ: You mentioned the context, the history of violence, right? Have you ever felt physically threatened? Or that anyone that is close to you would be at risk?

CH: Again, Belfast is a small place and even if nobody has actually issued an explicit death threat against you, there is always the concern that where you've been persistently labelled, here, that people believe that. So, they don't see you as an academic, they don't see you as a civic actor, they see you as something else. In fact, some of the language recently is that I'm part of some weird conspiracy, trying to take over the place. So, it's just that, the worry is that people believe that and, in the febrile atmosphere that is here at the moment, that they act on it. I don't want to overplay that and again I really emphasise, looking at what's happening in Ukraine and other parts of the world, there are massive problems all over the world, but for me at the moment it is a concern that this non-stop labelling has consequences. Words matter and people can act on them.

RQ: So, in a recent statement, UN special rapporteurs, experts on freedom of expression, right to education, human rights defenders, and the independence of lawyers, they called what you're experiencing a 'smear campaign' and they denounced what they called baseless claims against you and warned that threats of physical attack against academics can have dire consequences not only for the academic but for the country. How do you feel about that statement? Was it helpful?

CH: I really, really appreciated the statement and the expressions of solidarity and support, Rob, that have come as a result of all this. What we've found historically—as part of the human rights movement in Northern Ireland—is sometimes this can have a real impact where local interventions don't. So, the statement was deeply appreciated by me and I'm very thankful for the intervention, also in the context of this podcast and these discussions. Sometimes when you're enmeshed in a situation, which you find excruciatingly embarrassing, you don't see it. So, what I mean by that is, you're just so used to things that you brush them aside, you don't take them seriously. Until people make you sit down, collate things, look through it, present it to other people objectively and they actually go: 'this a problem; we need to say something about this, this isn't okay'. So that's a long-winded way of saying that international support matters here. People notice, and it has an impact.

RQ: What you're describing to me sounds a lot like what we have seen experienced by scholars all over the world. You know, one of the things that I've seen in this work is that violence isn't actually the primary tool of repression, it's isolation, it's these pressures and rumours and whispers and insinuations or outright accusations that cut the ties between people and isolate the person they're trying to silence. Sometimes that's to create a space where it's easier for violence to happen, but often it's just that isolation and—I'm hearing in what you're saying—the psychological impact and dynamic on the individual in the middle of it. Is that right?

CH: Yes, Rob, so it's a very interesting way of putting it. Ultimately my view is that, I've said earlier, people are trying to send a message through me, right? So, it is character assassination, I think it's textbook stuff, because they want me to stop, and they want the conversation to stop, and they want other people not to join that discussion. And so the more impact it has on me, it sends a stronger message, but the isolation thing is interesting, just to think about my context: I'm a former Head of the Law School of Queen's, I've run this place, I've been on the governing body of Queen's, I've served in public life across the society in relatively prominent positions, including in higher education settings in the UK. My life has transformed since I stepped into this constitutional discussion. I describe it as a case of people shuffling sideways when they see you coming type thing, you know that suddenly I'm an inconvenient person to have on a project. When I stepped into this space, my life, my professional life changed. And I can only interpret that as a whirlwind that has followed, and it's intended to say something to me and others about these sorts of conversations.

RQ: So, what do you say to those who say, this is just the price of being an academic? You work on sensitive issues, you need to be prepared to take some heat for your ideas.

CH: I think that's fair, and I've never been one who's shied away from taking heat and never really been one to run out to complain about it, so in some senses I find all this embarrassing. I like engaging publicly on substantive issues, I don't like being the person who says this is a problem. But people I know and trust here—and have been involved in the human rights world for many years—they have said, 'you need to do something about this, this is not okay'. There is legitimate public debate and dialogue around ideas expressed and substantive positions. But repeated *ad hominem* slurs by individuals that are effectively playing the person and not the argument? In a post-conflict society where—for example, as we speak now—loyalist armed groups are talking about targeting the Irish Government and Irish officials around the Protocol, I would say that people like me have had a virtual target painted on my back; to say, this guy, he says he's an academic, he's not really an academic, he's something else. So, I think that there's serious democratic dialogue, there's robust democratic debate and I've been in that, in the human rights and constitutional worlds, but this is something else.

RQ: And so, what do you say to those who say it's one thing for an academic to teach your classes and write your articles for academic journals, but it's a different thing to engage with the public, to hold public events, to publish in the newspapers or speak on TV? What do you say to those who say, that's not academic work, that's politics?

CH: Well, what I say to that is there's been a major emphasis in universities here in recent times, including in various research assessment exercises, on public engagement, on the need for academics to make their work open and accessible to the wider public and also to engage in the public sphere in democratic and peaceful dialogue, in specific public debates. And I fully endorse that trend within the university context, because I receive public money and I live in a community that has all sorts of equality and rights challenges. I don't see it as my role to spend forty years sitting in a library, writing articles and books that people can't afford to pay for or access and they reside there read by a few people and not many other people. I just could not face myself—and given the background that I'm from here—to talk about human rights in a university and pack up and go home in the evening and watch what's happening, I couldn't really live with myself doing that. I've written the big books and articles around all of that but I think I'm a professor you know, we're paid to profess, and publicly funded as well. The public should expect that, and I do my work deliberately. I write books, I talk in podcasts like this, I write in newspapers because we have an obligation to explain complex things in accessible language to the public that really pays a lot of my salary. But the final point I would make, Rob, is that I'm also a person who lives here, who lives in this society; and I have rights as well, both in my professional and personal capacities—to have a view, take a position, to speak my mind, conscious that when I do that I do that like anybody else. I do think there's a responsibility on us in universities not to close ourselves off from the wider world.

RQ: You mentioned that you've gotten a lot of support. Who else has spoken up on your behalf? What's the response been of your colleagues or the university?

CH: There's been a lot of support from my colleagues in the Human Rights Centre at Queen's and in wider civil society—including the UN special rapporteurs—people who have weighed in. That's good also for the broader principles around academic freedom and the rights of not just me but my colleagues in general here at Queen's, to take positions and to engage in wider public debates.

That's been one of the great things as well. You work away during the university year—year in and year out—and you do your teaching and you go home. But you sometimes forget the impact you're having on people. Until you hit a moment of crisis and some of the most wonderful things are said, lovely things are said and emerge and that's been one of the really heartening things of the last while.

RQ: Do you ever want to say, enough's enough, you've done your part? And sort of step away and work on something else?

CH: No. And I'll tell you one of the reasons at the moment that's concerning me. We need to broaden this out around the European context. There are narratives and arguments and forces that are emergent across Europe, and the wider world, that scare me and worry me. There are voices, echoes of the past that are re-emerging around authoritarianism and around views and challenges to basic democratic rule of law, rights-based values that we perhaps sometimes take for granted. I think, for example, in the area of human rights at the moment there's a real struggle against human rights going on in parts of Europe, and around the world, and we need to robustly defend those values, against some of the vociferous platforms that we see and repetitive, aggressive anti-democratic voices that are gaining a foothold. That can prevail, you know. I'm involved in human rights and equality and constitutional law because I fundamentally believe in all the values that underpin those concepts around human dignity and human rights. And we need to be there, for those values now and speaking in a European context, at the moment. That can't just be in academic articles, that has to be engaging against disinformation and, let me be very blunt: basic lies. That has to be challenged by academics and others.

RQ: And do you think your fellow academics understand that role that you're trying to play? What would you like them to know or to do?

CH: All I would really say is it relates to the bigger point about isolation. It sounds rather pathetic to say, right, but it's around inclusion. Sometimes show and not tell, right? And what I mean by that for academics and scholars around the world, just to be included. Just to not quietly be dropped off things because you're an inconvenient colleague. Or that you may find it slightly more challenging to get funding for something if you have somebody like me involved in your project. Or for having the courage to, and I'm not talking about Colin Harvey, I'm talking about other scholars around the world, to issue the invitation when maybe some people are saying, don't, you know. I think sometimes for scholars at risk everywhere around the world there's the e-mail expressing solidarity—which is fantastic—but for scholars at risk, all around the globe, it's sometimes show, not tell. Of showing that this person, wherever they are anywhere in the world, is one of us, is a scholar and we're going to issue the invitation. He's going to be on our project, no we're not going to exclude her. I think that really matters. Not just for me but for scholars at risk anywhere.

RQ: You know, Colin, our network stretches to more than six hundred [higher] education institutions in forty countries. We work with scholars from over a hundred countries. For the academic who may be listening somewhere else and who may feel some connection to what you're describing experiencing, who may hear some similarities between their situation and your situation, and a push-back against their own work or their own ideas, what would you say to them?

CH: I would say: 'you're not alone'. There is a world of solidarity and support out there for you, that to reach out whether it's to you, Rob, or me. There are people everywhere around the world who will be in solidarity with you, to make contact, that you're not there on your own. Facing this, some of the values that are fundamental to scholarly life in universities are under attack all around the globe, and that we're all in solidarity together.

When I was Head of School I worked with your program and know that people can find a home anywhere around the world, I think that is absolutely invaluable. And just to commend the work that Scholars at Risk does and in my own context at Queen's, just give me a ring. E-mail me. If you do need to talk, if there's anything I can do, let me know as well, because we're all going through things that, when you listen to the stories and the narratives it may be different or distinct, but some of the patterns are very old and very familiar. Sometimes just hearing from other people and other experiences is enormously helpful.

RQ: Colin, any final thought you would like to share with our listeners?

CH: I just really want to express my appreciation for the invitation and the opportunity to speak as part of this podcast series. I want to commend you, Rob, for the work that you're doing. The world needs Scholars at Risk at the moment, more than ever before. I would ask anybody listening to this to support your efforts and the work that you're doing. I just want to end by saying this. Whatever happens next here, I'm not going to be derailed or distracted from the work that I'm doing. I haven't stepped into this space accidentally, what I've done I've done consciously and deliberately, because I feel I have a responsibility as an academic embedded in this society that we essentially are here to serve, to do what I've done.

Thank you again for the opportunity to talk to you today.

RQ: Well, thank you Colin very much for sharing your time and your story and for reminding us that there is a responsibility that comes with the role of being a scholar in society and that includes a responsibility to each other and to be in solidarity. So, thank you very much.

CH: Thank you, Rob.

RQ: This has been an episode of *Free to Think*, a podcast presented by Scholars at Risk, where we celebrate people who have the courage to think, question and share ideas. If you enjoyed this episode please subscribe on your favourite podcast platform like iTunes or Spotify to receive automatic updates on new episodes and while there add your five star rating review to help us reach more listeners. You can also send us your comments, reactions or suggestions for future conversations by e-mail to scholarsatrisk@nyu.edu or on social media to @scholarsatrisk. Thanks for listening and please, keep thinking.

Acknowledgments

Thank you to the anonymous reviewers for the feedback on my draft chapter.

I owe an enormous debt of gratitude to Professor Dina Belluigi. Dina's solidarity and support throughout this process remains deeply appreciated. I know I would not have spoken or written in this way without her encouragement: thank you.

Bibliography

Bassett, M., and Harvey, C. (2022). *Making the Case for Irish Unity in the EU*. GUE/NGL European Parliamentary Group. https://left.eu/new-academic-paper-on-irish-unity-in-the-eu/

Belluigi, D. Z., and Moynihan, Y. (2023). *Academic Research Responsiveness to 'Ethnic Minorities' and 'Migrants' in Northern Ireland*. Queen's University Belfast, British Academy, Leverhulme Trust, MME Thinktank.

Collins, B. (2022). *Irish Unity: Time to Prepare*. Luath Press.

Connolly, F. (2022). *United Nation: The Case for Integrating Ireland*. Gill Books.

Fricker, M. (2013). Epistemic Justice as a Condition for Political Freedom. *Synthese, 190*, 1317–1332.

—(2007). *Epistemic Injustice: Power and the Ethics and Knowing*. Oxford University Press.

Harvey, C., (2002). Contested Constitutionalism: Human Rights and Deliberative Democracy in Northern Ireland. In T. Campbell, K. D. Ewing, and A. Tomkins (Eds), *Sceptical Essays on Human Rights* (pp. 163–175). Oxford University Press.

—(2016, June 17). *EU Referendum Perspectives - Prof Colin Harvey* [Video]. YouTube. https://www.youtube.com/watch?v=_xbrx5UbhVg

—(2022). The 1998 Agreement: Context and Status. In C. McCrudden (Ed.), *The Law and Practice of the Ireland-Northern Ireland Protocol* (pp. 21–30). Cambridge University Press. https://doi.org/10.1017/9781009109840.003

—(2021a). Let 'the People' decide: Reflections on Constitutional Change and 'Concurrent Consent'. *Irish Studies in International Affairs, 32*(2), 382–405. https://doi.org/10.3318/isia.2021.32b.37

—(2021b). Popular Sovereignty, Irish Reunification and Change on the Island of Ireland. In M. Cahill, C. Ó Cinnéide, S. Ó Conaill, and C. O'Mahony (Eds), *Constitutional Change and Popular Sovereignty: Populism, Politics and the Law in Ireland* (pp. 267–284). Taylor and Francis.

—(2021c, March 30–April 1). *Epistemic Injustice, the Territorial Constitution and the End of the Union*. Socio-Legal Studies Association Annual Conference, Cardiff University.

—(2020). The Irish Border. In F. Fabbrini (Ed.), *The Law & Politics of Brexit: Volume II: The Withdrawal Agreement* (pp. 148–168). Oxford University Press.

—, and Bassett, M. (2019). *The EU and Irish Unity: Planning and Preparing for Constitutional Change in Ireland*. GUE/NGL European Parliamentary Group. http://qpol.qub.ac.uk/the-eu-and-irish-unity/

—, and Kramer, A., (2019). Brexit and Ireland/Northern Ireland. In A. Biondi, P. J. Birkinshaw and Maria Kendrick (Eds), *Brexit: The Legal Implications* (pp. 59–74). Wolters Kluwer.

Harvey, C., and Skoutaris, N. (2018). *A Special Arrangement for Northern Ireland?* QPOL. http://qpol.qub.ac.uk/special-arrangement-northern-ireland/

—, et al. (2018a). *BrexitLawNI Policy Report: Brexit, Border Controls and Free Movement.* https://brexitlawni.org/assets/uploads/Brexit-Border-Controls-and-Free-Movement.pdf

—, et al. (2018b). *BrexitLawNI Policy Report: Brexit, Human Rights and Equality.* https://brexitlawni.org/assets/uploads/Brexit-Human-Rights-and-Equality.pdf

—, et al. (2018c). *BrexitLawNI Policy Report: Brexit, Xenophobia and Racism in Northern Ireland.* https://brexitlawni.org/assets/uploads/Brexit-Xenophobia-and-Racism-in-Northern-Ireland.pdf

—, et al. (2018d). *BrexitLawNI Policy Report: Brexit and North-South Relations.* https://brexitlawni.org/assets/uploads/Brexit-and-North-South-Relations.pdf

—, et al. (2018e). *BrexitLawNI Policy Report: Brexit and Socio-economic Rights.* https://brexitlawni.org/assets/uploads/Brexit-and-Economic-and-Social-Rights.pdf

—, et al. (2018f). *BrexitLawNI Policy Report: Brexit and the Peace Process.* https://brexitlawni.org/assets/uploads/Brexit-and-the-Peace-Process.pdf

Humphreys, R. (2018). *Beyond the Border: The Good Friday Agreement and Irish Unity after Brexit.* Merrion Press.

Meagher, K. (2022). *A United Ireland: Why Unification is Inevitable and How it will Come About.* Biteback Publishing Ltd.

O'Leary, B. (2022). *Making Sense of a United Ireland: Should it Happen? How Might it Happen?* Penguin Books.

Pivotal. (2022). *Impact of Brexit on Minority Ethnic and Migrant People in Northern Ireland.* Equality Commission for Northern Ireland.

7. (Her)story
between Shadow and Light:
A Displaced Syrian Woman Academic

Rida Anis

Introduction

During a two-week period in September 2019, Rida Anis audio recorded over sixty WhatsApp messages while recounting memories of her higher education experiences in Syria, the United States of America and Turkey. In this chapter, excerpts of the transcribed messages have been selected. They serve as her account as a woman academic who has witnessed and endured various conflicts, experienced the impact of state authoritarianism and war, and who continues to practise academically while living as a marginalised, displaced academic in exile.

The tone and wording of the excerpts are familiar and intimate, without any theorising or intention of putting forward an academic 'argument'. There is, rather, occasional reflection and emotion. This is because they communicated in dialogue with collaborator and friend, Dina Zoe Belluigi, soon after the two academics had spent time together as peers at the roundtable event which catalysed the call for this book. Rida had attended with her two youngest children, and so some of the content acknowledges their shared concerns as mothers and guardians. While the messages form part of a personal testimony, they were recorded intentionally for the purposes of contributing to research.[1]

---

1   The pseudonymised, cleaned transcripts were shared as material for creative
     arts research for the *Counter // Narratives of Higher Education* (2020–ongoing)

    https://doi.org/10.11647/OBP.0427.07

The original transcript was over 19000 words long. Because it included information that might put Rida, her family and third parties at risk, it has been cleaned of such identifiers. Large tracts have been edited and some omitted, but the language and style are true to the original. The selection of excerpts and shaping of this chapter, years later, have been informed by the continued dialogue between the two intellectuals, with updates in 2024 included in the last section on Türkiye in preparation for this publication.

The dialogue has been curated into seven sections with eighteen fragmentary parts. The last section is necessarily, and intentionally, incomplete. The titles are reflective of the themes which Rida has chosen to include in this recollection of her experiences of conflicts in the different countries where she has lived and learnt, as a woman and as an academic before and since the war in her homeland.

Salutations

Good morning, dear. Actually, I'm honoured to work with you. How can we do this? I'll try my best [...] I'll be speaking about my own academic experience for the first time. It sounds strange, but exciting! I'm not sure how I'm going to start, but I will. I think I'm going step by step. Maybe it's going to look confusing because I'm not used to doing things chronologically. Sometimes, I'll be jumping to the future; another time I'll be diving into the past to have some memories refreshed [...] Let's see how this experimental task will work. I already feel it as a healing process [laughter]. I'll start speaking about the struggle we are in now. Here we go!

I'm still working as an assistant professor after more than fifteen years of academic teaching at two different universities in two different countries, Aleppo University, Syria (more than eight years) and Hasan Kalyoncu University, Türkiye (more than seven years). I've been an

---

project. They informed a three-minute video artwork by Tanzanian-born artist Eric Msumanje called *Untitled* (2019). Accessible at: https://counternarrativefilm. wixsite.com/counter/untitled. Excerpts of the original transcript also informed a visual paper about the project Belluigi and Meistre, 2021. Authoring Author-ity in Transition? The 'Counter // Narratives of Higher Education' Project. Video of paper for *Visualising Social Changes: Seen and Unseen*. https://doi.org/10.5281/ zenodo.10641677

assistant professor for quite a long time; I should be an associate professor by now. Due to the sudden movement from Syria (my country of war) to Türkiye (totally different, not only in its academic rules and procedures but also in language and culture), I've been unfortunately facing many challenges and burdens as a displaced person who does not know the language of the hosting country nor has the time to take courses to learn the new language, being overloaded with long hours of teaching and researching.

As a marginalised academic, you are expected to work harder and for longer hours to survive in exile. You literally have to start from zero and work harder than natives to survive both financially and professionally. Sometimes, you might be frustrated by new rules in the hosting country that may jeopardise your whole status as an academic, threatening you to be deported at any time, all of a sudden becoming jobless. It seems that Syrians are no longer as welcome as before. So, you always have to keep thinking about plan B or C rather than aspiring to go higher in the academic ranks.

My Mother: 'Insight for Strength'

Let me go to the earliest stage of my life. My mom has always been the source of my inspiration. She encouraged me to receive higher education as a means for women's empowerment. So, a great deal of my insight, strength and resilience comes from my mom.

She, herself, wanted to become an academic, but her circumstances didn't help. Therefore, she put all her efforts to provide for me all the suitable circumstances to fulfil her unaccomplished dream through me, later. Unlike my father who shared with my mom his efforts to provide a happy life for me and my two brothers, my mom adored education, literature and languages. She always regretted that her parents pushed her to stop her high school to marry early in the late 1960s. She always was a promising student in the French school that she used to attend in her hometown of Aleppo, Syria, learning both French and Arabic and writing some poetry. Unfortunately, her conservative community encouraged early marriages, especially for girls. So, she had to marry before finishing high school. She told me she would choose to continue her education if she could go back in time. She insists that higher education is even more crucial for girls because it provides for them a more sustainable future and better opportunities to achieve their goals.

My mom made sure that she put me and my brother in the best schools both in Baghdad, Iraq, where we were born—my father was working there—and later in Aleppo, my parents' hometown. Providing many books, stories, language courses and access to libraries was always a priority for raising her children. So, I guess I was lucky! I grew to love reading all kinds of books and literature. By gifts and travelling to visit different countries, she always encouraged us to read and learn. I have been learning English, French and parts of the holy Qur'an since I was three years old.

My mom knew French, but she didn't know English. When I was five years old, she made sure that I could go to an international school and get a British tutor to teach me English. Then, she started learning English with me. It was funny because she spoke little English with French pronunciation. She promised to take me to visit London if I successfully finished all the six levels of English before becoming fifteen years old, which I did. She fulfilled her promise to take me there on my sixteenth birthday. It was an amazing sense of joy and accomplishment! Finishing all English courses, she wanted me to continue taking all six levels of the French courses. I took five of them until I became a university student, then I preferred to focus on scoring a high GPA at college to win scholarships to continue my higher studies in Literature. In 1994, I won a Fulbright Scholarship to continue for an MA in American Literature in the USA, and soon after that I won another scholarship from Aleppo University affording my PhD studies in Literature, for scoring the highest GPA among all the graduates of that year.

Briefly speaking, my mother was my inspiration for loving reading, literature, art and languages. Years later, I conveyed loving these three areas to my three children.

My Studies: 'I Had a Dream that I Would Be an Academic Since I Was Little'

I had a dream that I would be an academic since I was a child. Yes! It's so funny! I used to read a lot and for many hours. Really, I read many magazines, books and stories, both Arabic and English. Different genres, different themes. My favourites were detective stories with the element of suspense, when I was a teenager and a pre-teenager.

When I started high school, I was thinking of majoring in a scientific field, such as Engineering, Math or Chemistry. I loved Math and Chemistry. But also, I loved Humanities and Literature. I had a hard time deciding what to major in. Finally, I decided to join the Faculty of Art and Humanities, English literature, where I excelled, scoring the highest GPA among all university students, winning two scholarships, one the American Fulbright to cover for my MA studies and another Syrian scholarship given by Aleppo University to cover for my PhD studies later. I was also given a chance to work as a lecturer at Aleppo University because I ranked number one with the highest GPA among all the graduates of English Literature that year.

As a Female Academic: 'Do I Have to Fit into my Traditional Society?'

Right after one year of my BA graduation, I started teaching English as a lecturer at Aleppo University whilst waiting for my MA scholarship to start to move to the USA to continue my higher studies. I was about twenty-three years old. I taught there for three semesters. Those were probably the hardest times of my life for decision-making as a woman. I had to decide about two crucial things: a no-late marriage and making a family—a fundamental role for women in traditional Syria of the 1990s—as well as my future academic career. Indeed, that was a turning point in my life.

My mother always emphasised the significance of higher education, especially for women, to make a difference for better future choices of careers and for families. Academically speaking, she was very proud of me for being a hardworking person, more than my two brothers. However, she was worried that my promising academic life and catching up with deadlines for my MA and PhD scholarships would delay my marriage and delay having any children. She was ahead of her time with some feminist visions, but she was worried that the new path that I decided to take might not be accepted by my still conventional Syrian society at that time. Marriage after twenty-five was too late only for women and not men for many reasons. So, she was not sure what to advise me.

I could tell that she was too stressed [...] between two fires! When I was first nominated for the Fulbright Scholarship, she was very happy. After a few months, while I was undergoing some American exams needed to win that scholarship, such as TOEFL and GRE, she changed her mind about me moving to the USA for the coming six or seven years to attain my MA and PhD there without being married, because she thought that I would be thirty years or older before I realised the importance of having a family. To add fuel to the fire, some relatives living abroad assured her that I would be gradually changing my thoughts and culture, thinking more individually and refusing my parents' future recommendations or pieces of advice while living far from them and alone with no family of mine in the US. Her worries made me very stressed, thinking that I might be on the verge of a big change in my life.

It was the first time I clashed with my mother, who was always my biggest source of support and guidance, my greatest model with all the sacrifices she had always made for us. It was true that she didn't want me to marry at an early stage because she didn't want her own story to be repeated in my case. However, she was afraid that her beloved and only daughter to whom she dedicated most of her time and efforts might be totally under-estimated by our very patriarchal society then. Most of the males used to choose their women partners only if they professed in their domestic duties, not in their academic life.

My mother and I had more arguments after I graduated from university and became twenty-two. My mom believed that after all a woman's priority was to marry, have children and establish a family. The generational gap between my mother and I was the reason behind all these arguments. I tried to convince her that she was pushing me to do something I was totally not believing in as her parents did decades earlier pushing her to a rather early marriage: ages between fourteen and eighteen were the expected times for girls to marry in Syria in the 1960s, my mother's time. Mine was only a little better—girls were expected to marry between eighteen and twenty-five, no more! I was approaching twenty-four, so she was stressed. I disagreed with her because I never thought that I had to marry at a specific age: I never believed I should marry if I wasn't completely convinced. I always told her: 'either I marry somebody who believes in what I'm doing, or I shouldn't be marrying at all'. Also, we had two different points about divorce: I believed that divorce was a great help in some cases; she never believed in divorce. So, to some extent, we disagreed on the necessity and timing of 'marriage' and 'divorce'. By the way, I successfully convinced my mother over time and made her change some of these beliefs.

I myself never believed in love at first sight. Many of these love stories that I heard about or saw turned out to be a flash and then nothing. We all had some temporary emotions. I have always thought that a good marriage is something that grows over time when two people decide to work for it together and thus it may end any time when one of the two decides not to continue. Therefore, I believe that both marriage and divorce can happen any time and for many reasons. Such thinking was not accepted in our society when I was very young, despite the fact that in our religion, Islam, it has always been approved.

Let me give our Prophet Muhammad's first-marriage story that is almost 1500-years old as an example and model. Back then, we had Arabic women asking men for marriage if they liked, we had women divorcing and women marrying for a second and third time, if they needed, no problem. Ironically enough, it is still a big problem in our society. Prophet Muhammad was with Khadijah, an honourable, smart lady who was older than him. She first considered marrying him after he did for a while a good trading business for her. She admired his honesty, hardworking nature and intelligence. So, she asked him to marry her. He was her third husband, her first and second died leaving her a fortune and a big trading business. I think Khadijah made a smart choice in choosing the right person for her. She was forty years old. She never hesitated to marry a third time when she found the right man for her.

My Marriage: 'Doing Things, Facing Problems, Trying to Solve Them and Learning Life Together'

I learned to struggle to fulfil my goals. Nothing was perfect in this life. The only way to achieve your goals is to be patient and keep struggling. Believing that anything is possible to have or lose by time and effort, I made up my mind and decided to choose someone proposing to me and start the marriage journey together before leaving to the USA so we can face all the cultural and other changes together and change safely together, if I could express myself clearly.

As a graduate from the medical school, he wanted to carry on his higher studies in the US, and I wanted to continue my MA and PhD there. We thought we would stay for just six or seven years. We stayed for twelve years. We lived and struggled there together as a young married couple and as foreign academics. We had days of love and of fighting together, good and bad moments of happiness and sadness, health and sickness. We had a deadly car accident that we both miraculously survived in our very first year in the US. We had moments of success and failure together. We had good and bad moments together. We also had a daughter and a son born there. We gradually learned what marriage was together. We learned to understand each other and still are learning now. We believe that marriage is doing things together, facing problems and trying to solve them together and learning life together.

Reflections as a Woman:
Familial, Financial and Academic struggles

Once again we come to women's issues—three things I would say that I struggle with as a woman, mother and academic. We have talked a lot about that, my dear Dina. Haven't we? We're still suffering from gender hierarchies on all levels—socially, economically and even academically. Let me start with the last one first.

Academically speaking, gender hierarchies still stand as barriers in the face of women's professional advancement even in academic institutions. Unfortunately, even among the most educated sect of people, the impact of the academic gender hierarchy is still huge; it doesn't appreciate enough or take women academics' perceptions of their own work, life, challenges, or aspirations seriously. An intellectual woman would like to be successful on all levels, marrying and raising children, sharing her responsibility in taking care of her growing parents, taking care of herself, mind and body and excelling academically. She would not accept less than all these. Yes, she has the ability to do all of these great things, maybe at different stages of her life, feeling the priorities needed each time, but she doesn't have to sacrifice any of those at the expense of only one of those ambitions.

Unfortunately, most academic institutions are still overwhelmingly hierarchical in their structure as well as in their professionals' perceptions. I mean, they still define academic success and achievement only from men's points of view without considering women's hard work of making families, having children and taking care of their elderly parents. Still, all that great work women do is not given enough consideration nor is it tolerated in competitive academic professions. On the other hand, many academic institutions don't prefer to have women academics who take breaks to raise their children or take care of their parents. If academia continues to be that hierarchical, the world will never be okay. Families are collapsing, and academic institutions are contributing to such failure. I believe all women's hard work, starting from having children to doing research and educating generations, has to be not only encouraged but also supported and organised by academic institutions before any other social or governmental institutions. Isn't raising knowledgeable generations the responsibility of such academic institutions?

Everything is hierarchical, my dear Dina, even in a family when it comes to gender. I believe that everything is hierarchical [...] relationships, work positions, the way your achievement and success are defined, even in the way you raise your children. And economically speaking, Syrians have to suffer and struggle double than others, as casualties of war and crisis on all levels since 2011. Our country was never a first-class country—it used to be third or fourth class before 2011—now it is definitely tenth class or worse, I don't know where! Anyways, speaking about myself, I have always three worries in my mind as a middle-aged woman with growing children and increasing challenges and expenses and as a full-time displaced lecturer in a hosting university. I am always struggling to secure a family settlement, an economic settlement and an academic settlement in a hosting country which is never mine. It has never been easy!

I personally believe that women have the capacity to do different things together. They have something natural about that. I mean maybe because of circumstances or whatever, things have changed. They have instinctive or spontaneous love for family relationships and family ties, making social communities and societies, bringing neighbours together.

I noticed that here in Türkiye, as I did before in Syria and the US. For example, many houses were destroyed and many buildings were demolished in Syria after 2011. Many people were killed or disappeared leaving their families. Many couldn't survive the conditions that kept deteriorating on all levels so they either died sad or were displaced, moving to other places, parting with some or all their friends and relatives. It was women, I noticed, that tried to bring things together, standing again on their feet despite their miseries, looking for their family ties, reconnecting with relatives lost or displaced inside and/ or outside Syria by all means [physical checking or searching for them through social media]. Women were emotionally stronger than men, especially in disasters and crises, such as the case of the Syrian Crisis [2011 and onwards] and, last year, the South Türkiye/North Syria Earthquake [February 2023].

Most women in tragedies act as strong survivors, I recently noticed! Amazing! In comparison, many men were easily frustrated in front of such tragedies seeing their beloved dead or injured, though they were brave enough to join battles and sacrifice their own lives for their own country and families, they rushed to rescue those buried under the rubble of the earthquake—quite amazing! The number of Syrian men having heart attacks or considering committing suicide exceeded that of women, especially if they witnessed a sudden collapse of family, status, business or work because of war or earthquakes. Women were emotionally stronger; they stood up trying to start again, to reconnect, to sew broken family ties, to bring hosting and hosted communities together, even as single parents in foreign countries. Some Syrian women, including those middle-aged and old ladies, were even able to build a new social network of friends and neighbours in their new displaced zone. Social life is very important for them; sipping coffee and chatting with friends, colleagues, or neighbours is crucial for women; it makes life and tragedies somehow bearable. I even saw some women begging for food for their children in crisis times of war and earthquakes. I didn't see men doing that! Men would prefer to die rather than doing that. For them, dignity is more important than death itself, I guess. I'm not sure! But, this is what I have recently noticed through the two tragedies of the Syrian Crisis and Turkish earthquake that my communities—Syrian and Turkish—experienced.

Back to my three concerns, I'm socially concerned as a wife and mother of three children. I'm also concerned about the financial settlement of my family amid increasing economic instability. Also, I have my academic dreams. Sometimes I'm frustrated, sometimes I'm happy. Still, I try to accomplish some of my dreams, keeping in mind to balance between these three concerns of mine. We always try, but things might be up and down. At least, I'm trying. At least, I'm struggling. I have to be strong! I have to survive! I have to dream! I have to hope! I have to be patient. After all, patience is the key for everything.

First Pregnancy in the USA: 'Again I Was between Two Fires'

All of a sudden, I got pregnant—totally unexpected! I was in the second year of my Master's. The Fulbright Scholarship wanted me to get rid of the baby because the little payment they put into my health insurance would run out by the eighth month of my pregnancy. After that, I would be left with no insurance for the ninth month; nobody would cover the costs for the delivery of my baby. My husband was also under stress—he was preparing for his American Board Exams for Physician Specialists. In fact, we were both stressed financially and academically as students preparing for exams with only part-time work to pay for our basic expenses—I was in a real dilemma. I had to take some time to decide: should I respond to my Fulbright advisors who threatened to stop my monthly living stipend? They even said that I had to go back to Syria to deliver my baby there before applying to carry on with my PhD studies in the United States. I had to choose between keeping my first baby and my dream to continue my PhD in the US.

I cry when I remember that. Sorry! Oh my God! It has been more than twenty-six years; my daughter is now twenty-seven years old, married and has already had a miscarriage herself. But it still affects me so much. That was probably one of the biggest decisions in my life. Okay! Good. I think that this process of writing your sad memories is somehow a healing process. I am already feeling good!

I was literally put between two fires. The dream that I worked hard for for years and my promise to my mother to carry on to get my PhD, were all of a sudden at stake simply because I suddenly became pregnant without planning for it. I thought I was lucky to get two scholarships for my MA and PhD from two different resources and to marry someone believing in my academic ambition, but things were going wrong after that.

'Academically I'm threatened, and so is my marriage,' I told my professor, Susan,[2] as she was the closest person to me at that time, not only as my teaching professor but also as a friend. She advised me, 'Your husband is right. You're destroying your future and his future. Look at you, you're so promising—soon finishing your MA and starting your PhD'. And she was surprised that I was the only foreigner among the MA students who were all American. I used to score A+ in her courses. I explained to her, 'Dear Susan, as a Muslim, I believe things are somehow destined. I didn't plan to have this baby. But, if it was planned for me to have it, then I shouldn't get rid of it. It's my responsibility. I'll carry on with both my MA and my pregnancy and see what God has for me'.

I remember that I worked hard to finish my MA. Also, I prepared myself for my coming baby. Because of the difficulty of pregnancy, I used to sleep in class, sleep while reading, and wake up at night. So that was the struggle as a woman, as a woman who wanted to carry on her academic ambition and her duty as a mother. I was already in love with my baby in my third month of pregnancy. Hearing the heartbeat of the baby, also my husband fell in love with the baby and was even crying on our first visit to my gynaecologist. In the fourth month, we knew it was a girl, and we started choosing a name for her: we were full of joy and excitement. We didn't care too much for our critical financial situation. We were still working for our exams, preparing and passing the exams. [...] I delivered one month earlier than expected, unbelievably after finishing my last candidacy exam for the MA and my husband finishing his Board exam, and most importantly on the last day of insurance that Fulbright was paying for; I delivered the baby at the end of the eighth month, and that was the real miracle that solved the financially critical situation. So I thought Allah was telling me, 'Okay, I'm giving you both the baby and the chance to continue your PhD—your academic dream' [...] I had my baby, and I graduated. I got my Master's degree and I was accepted to join the PhD at Indiana University, Pennsylvania, to study English and American literature and criticism.

---

2   This is a pseudonym.

I had many challenges as a mother of a newborn and as a PhD student struggling to balance between two different tasks. After a year I wanted to put my little girl in a nursery; things didn't go very well because she was emotionally too attached to me and her father. I was still taking my PhD courses, and I needed time for attendance and exams of these courses. I had a plan with my husband that each of us would study for four or five hours a day and then take care of our little girl, and we exchanged roles every day for a couple of years until I finished all my twelve courses. After that, it was easier to start preparing for my candidacy and language exams and then my dissertation at home. My husband did a very good job helping me raise the kid. Many times I took my baby with me in a toddler car seat or a stroller to libraries and even to my own school to see my academic advisors to modify or submit the dissertation proposal or discuss the themes. It took me probably eight years to finish my PhD with my first growing girl baby and the coming of a second boy baby. For a few years, I was taking care of both of them and writing my dissertation because my husband had to do his residency training in hospitals as a medical doctor. Yes, it took a longer time than expected, but I finally finished my PhD and graduated with honours with my daughter and son.

Returning to Syria: 'I Had a Commitment'

The third turning point in my life was cultural. With Fulbright, I didn't have any commitment to teach anywhere—Master's degrees were sponsored for exchange visitors, and I was one of them. For my PhD scholarship, however, things were quite different. I was sponsored by Aleppo University on one condition: I have to go back to Syria after getting my PhD to teach at Aleppo University for at least double the time of my scholarship. So, I had a commitment to teach there for at least twelve years.

After twelve years living in the US, I felt I needed to go back to Syria. Honestly, it took me more than two years to reach that decision. It was never easy! Of course, I already have reasons: I promised my parents and my university a decade before not to melt into the American mainstream, and to come back and contribute to my community both socially and academically. I owe them both. I missed home too much! I also wanted to raise my two American-born kids in Syria to be able to connect with their roots and relatives before growing older and feeling they did not belong enough to Syria nor to their bigger Syrian family and relatives. That was the deal. That was the contract. That was the plan years ago. So, my duty was to stick to my responsibilities towards my bigger family, my community and the academic institution that partially sponsored my PhD studies. I really wanted to teach generations in my home country where I was raised. I felt much debt to the university where I received my BA and excelled academically. A delayed decision because of certain circumstances, yes, but it was high time I went back home. I knew it would be hard. Never sure how hard it would be for me and for my husband after all those twelve years—with our new hybrid experience—changing us to become different from what we used to be before.

We were aware of the global statistics showing that most of the people who migrate into Western countries either for academic, financial, political or other reasons never go back home. The world has witnessed a growing movement from third-world countries to first-world countries, and not the opposite. That was probably the hottest topic discussed between me and my husband, as well as among our immigrant friends and minority groups in the US for the twelve years we had been there. We knew that only very few would leave the tempting US and go back home. Financially, culturally and politically speaking, there's no comparison between the third-world country and the first-world country. This huge difference was the greatest dilemma.

I was always orienting myself and family about the pros and cons of such a big change of moving back to Syria. It was more difficult and challenging than what my husband and I expected indeed! We had much thinking and many considerations. First, we decided differently. I made up my mind that it was time I should take my two children and go back to Syria.

It was another milestone decision I had to take in my life because my husband was not ready [...] still delaying that movement forever. I should be able to convince him. I really loved my family and didn't want us to be divided here and there, so I had to wait further for my husband to be convinced that the pros for that major shift were more than the cons against it. It wasn't easy at all. But ultimately, he agreed that we should all face the same shift at the same time to be able to stay together as one family. That was probably the most important lesson we learned together, and years later we experienced another major shift in 2015 after the Syrian Crisis. So, I was too patient to unanimously reach the second hardest decision in my life; after twelve years living in the States, it took us almost two years to decide to go back together to Syria and join our big family.

Let's stop here for a while. Tomorrow, I'll be talking about Syria. After coming back from the US, I lived in Syria for nine years teaching at Aleppo University, half of the time before the Crisis started and half of the time after. Many asked me, 'Why did you stay for four or five years during the hard times of the Crisis in Aleppo?' Making a decision to leave your country for the second time, especially after being alienated for twelve years in the US, was never easy; it was really a hard decision to be made. Tomorrow, I'll talk about that part—my experience as a human being, as a mother, and as an academic during war.

'I Belong and Don't Belong'

Going back to Syria after twelve years in the States was really hard at the beginning. Ironically enough, our experience of diaspora didn't make things easy for us in our own country. It took a while to understand the changes that we—living in the West for a while—and our relatives and friends who had remained in Syria both undertook. Time and two different places changed all of us. I felt like I didn't completely belong to the Western culture that I was in nor to the Syrian culture that I was raised in; I no more completely belonged to the Syrian culture as I used to do before going to the US twelve years ago and before. I felt both, belonging to Syria and the US. Being different from both and belonging to none. More like a global citizen belonging to more than one country, and no specific one at the same time.

I'll divide this nine-year period in Syria into two eras: before 2011 and after. I arrived in Syria in August 2006 and started to teach at Aleppo University right away. I taught for almost nine years until I left Syria in July 2015. Aleppo University was one of the best of the four state universities in the country. Aleppo itself was the second biggest and the greatest merchant and business city in Syria.

The number of students in the four Syrian state universities is too big because education there is completely free. I was shocked to know that the number of students of English literature was close to 10000 with only 13 or 14 staff of lecturers and a few teaching assistants helping. We had 48 subjects to be taught for the 4 years, 24 for each semester. Only traditional written exams were allowed for finals with a few exceptions for multiple-choice-question exams. The process of evaluation of final papers was incredible! I recall that I was given like two or three subjects to teach every semester, meaning 3000 students whose papers needed correcting. So, every semester I have about 3700 to 4200 final exam notebooks to correct. Evaluation literally took more than 2 months to be accomplished. It was indeed very time and effort consuming! So, within the four years before the Crisis, teaching was joyful but evaluating finals was disastrous and very exhausting. The number of university students dropped drastically after 2011.

'Things are Getting Better, I Am Belonging'

My third and fourth years of arriving in Syria were the best. I succeeded in convincing the dean of the faculty that multiple-choice-question exams were the only choice for evaluation without losing the teaching staff that kept decreasing in number, looking for jobs elsewhere while the number of students increased annually.

I had time for my families, my husband and children and my parents, brothers, cousins, even my old friends. It was really cool to see some of my old school and college friends. I really had the best time of my life. My American kids loved all that too. My husband and I bought a very beautiful big house. We bought land to be prepared for a farm. I had my own car, he had his own car. He established a clinic, and he became very famous with his new specialty; he made good money for the family. [3] I wasn't earning very much because academic salaries were too low in Syria, but he was earning more than enough for us. Anyway, I was enjoying my academic position, teaching, seeing my students, seeing my professors that used to teach me in my BA, and now my colleagues. I was very happy.

---

3   Rida's husband was the first physician in Syria registered on the American Board of Sleep Medicine.

'2011, an Apocalyptic Turning Point'

Since 2011, however, there has been an increasing deterioration in all aspects of life, including safety and quality of teaching and education. Things are never what they used to be before 2011. The Crisis changed and is still changing many things for the worse.

War started, devastating things were taking place, nonstop. Some people disappeared, others were killed, some were kidnapped, many displaced inside and outside the country. We saw horrible things. We witnessed horrible tragedies! Unforgettable! Month after month, year after year, safety was decreasing and violence was increasing. Fear crept everywhere. Casualties were on all levels. It became a continuous nightmare.

I taught for more than four years within war time. I never stopped going to the university despite the bad conditions and danger that was lurking everywhere, including the campus and the streets to the university. The university itself was a targeted, never safe spot, mainly because many students started protesting there against the Regime, supporting the uprising revolution that was led by the youth in most of the cities and villages of the country. The Regime, however, called them 'terrorists'. Every time the students started a protest, all the campus would be surrounded by security bodyguards and militia within less than ten minutes. And soon the chase to arrest the protesting students started. Some of these students escaped, others were never heard about. Some were kept in prisons, released or not later. Some were tortured and killed. The university became a nightmare to teachers, students, parents of students, and people working there or passing by. My nightmare as a lecturer teaching there was witnessing any violence threatening the students or other people protesting on the campus or outside in the streets.

I still remember my fear once there. I speak about the beginning of these protests when there were only tens of students going out, not even hundreds.

I recall one day I was giving a lecture. I and my students were in the classroom when we heard screaming and shouting coming from the campus; there were some students protesting outside and others trying to arrest them. Protesters were about forty or fifty people, something like that. My heart sank and started beating fast because some of my students wanted to join that protest outside, but I was trying to prevent them from doing so, trying to stop them by all means; I didn't want to lose them. I was concerned about their lives, about their safety. I was thinking as an educator and as a parent of their young people. I locked the door of the classroom from inside staying with them, begging them not to go out and join the protesters. I recall that a few didn't listen to me; they unlocked the door and left. I remember I was crying. I cried and I begged the rest of the students not to go out as a friend or as their own mother concerned about their lives. I asked them to remain indoors because only inside was relatively safe. Luckily, they responded to seeing me crying and begging. We re-locked the door and stayed there for some time until everything calmed down. Then, we all left. But these things happened several time. It was quite frightening. We saw students protesting—running away—bleeding. I was tired of fear that I wanted to leave not only university teaching but all of my country.

'University Bombings'

Teachers and parents were too concerned. Some parents forced their children to stop going to university. On the January 15, 2013, however, we witnessed the worst-case scenario. Two massive airstrikes ravaged the campus of Aleppo University. More than ninety people were killed, including students on the first day of their midterm exams and other civilians, and other hundreds were wounded.

I was seven months pregnant with my third baby. I wanted to go to the university to get my salary. While getting ready, I felt too tired. So, I changed my mind and decided to stay home to rest. Soon I heard and felt a big explosion followed by a second one. My house shook violently and windows opened wide. I thought that the explosion was a massive one. My father called me, then my husband did and also my brother. All of them asked me the same question, 'Where are you, at the university?'. I told them I was at home. 'Good', they said, 'Thanks God!'. I knew that the tremendous explosion took place at the university.

It was the gloomy day ever in life. When almost three hundred students died. We had some academics who died. Some parents who died—but only tens of them. But we had the number—they say exceeded three hundred, but we don't know for sure [...] Two missiles, on the first day of exams: on the campus of the university on the side of agricultural engineering and art, and the state dorms of students coming from outside Aleppo living there to study.

Later, we saw that on videos sent from outside there was a big, big, huge, huge hurricane of black smoke coming from that side. I would say four, five streets were destroyed. One of the biggest calamities. The Regime said this is the work of terrorists. Some of the doctors supporting the Regime were shocked, they thought that the faculties were bombed from inside, they didn't believe that the bombing was coming from the sky. So, it was a turning point in the life of many people. And there I made the decision: I'm leaving as soon as I deliver my daughter and my elder daughter passes the state exam.

'My House was Bombed by Mistake'

After delivering my baby, and two months before my daughter's exams, my house was bombed with a missile by mistake. We didn't know the source, because there was some bombing back and forth between the Regime and the opposition side. Miraculously, we weren't injured. We were inside and a big portion of the house was destroyed. It seemed that we were not meant to die yet. However, it was really creepy, messy and frightening!

Leaving our own home, city and all of the country became a necessity because of the increasing lack of safety. Starting from the incident at the university, we never went out together. One by one, either me or him. The children were not living a normal life, I know, but it was for their safety. But we were always calculating: if somebody dies, then the other one is there for the other. Because we heard stories that both of the mom and dad were killed and half of the family, leaving one or two children alone to be adopted by others or something. Many civilians were leaving their houses. Displacement became a recurrent phenomenon; some people were displaced inside Syria moving from one place to another, others sought refuge in other countries. [...]

Let me tell you that yesterday I was very emotional because of these tragic memoirs... I believe that emotionally I was up and down yesterday. Today, again, I took the day off—I'm not going to the university. Probably because of the memories coming back all together. I always look upon that period of the beginning of war, till I moved here, as the worst of my life because we saw what we saw. I thought I was going to cope better yesterday, but actually I couldn't. I was very irritated for the rest of the afternoon... It's so funny; I cleaned the house, I did laundry, I did opposite things and now my mind is clearer.

'These Were the Circumstances, and our Country's Not Okay'

Between 2011 and 2015 was the worst time of my life. With the deterioration of safety and other aspects of life in Syria, education also deteriorated; many university teachers left the country. Lack of staff forced the remaining staff to fill the gap by doubling or even tripling their efforts; they had to teach many subjects at the same time. Corruption in education increased as it did on all scales.

It was my responsibility as a teacher, with many doctors leaving the university and things deteriorating, and my students used to tell me, 'If you go then who's going to stay?'. And I used to cry, you know. It's that connection when your students, you know, you feel like they're part of the family and that you're going to turn them down. Because you're caring about your biological children and their future more.

In 2014, I started applying for university teaching jobs in the United Arab Emirates and Türkiye. Soon, I heard from the American University in Dubai. I was thinking about transferring my daughter who successfully matched for medical studies. I had a Skype interview, and I was approved to start teaching there in August 2015. However, the Head of the Department called me before New Year of 2015 and he asked me if I had any other citizenship rather than the Syrian one. I said, 'No'. He informed me, 'After New Year of 2015, Syrians will not be allowed to enter the UAE, so please come right now and leave the family because they don't have permission to come yet. We can provide some tutoring for you to be able to cover your expenses until you start teaching in our university in August, then you can bring your family'. In fact, I didn't want to go without my family because I would always be worried about my children under war. So, I apologised to the Head of the English Department at AUD. We decided to move to Türkiye and try to find jobs there. It took us more than four years to take the action of moving to another country. [...] Anyways we saw different things on the way. Horrible things. [...] We arrived in Gaziantep in July, 2015.

Türkiye: 'The Struggle to Fit in with the Hosting Country'

Tonight, I'll be moving towards speaking about my academic experience here in Türkiye. This leaves me with the last and the easiest part of my experience.

I was happy to arrive in Türkiye with my husband and children feeling safe. I was feeling very sad to leave my father, mother, two brothers, and all my relatives and friends. I was still concerned about their safety, and I didn't know when I would be able to see them again because refuge is never a normal case. Other worries were in my head: as a university doctor of English Language and Literature, I wasn't sure if I would get a position to lecture in a Turkish University. Fitting into a new hosting society, whose native language is different from yours. Fitting into that country's academic arena is even harder and sometimes impossible. As a mother, I had to put my academic career at stake for the sake of my family's safety and the future education of my children.

Within a few months, I applied to two Turkish universities in two different cities to teach. The first one was private—Hasan Kalyoncu University, here in Gaziantep where we settled. The second was Harran State University in Urfa where my eldest daughter decided to continue her medical studies. Gratefully, I was accepted into both. I chose the first; I have been teaching as an international academic at Hasan Kalyoncu University since September 2016.

Generally speaking, Turkish society is very nice. However, Turkish people are not very open to other cultures; they're still not oriented enough about other cultures, especially in the southern cities. Truly, they respect other cultures, but yet they expect all international people coming to Türkiye to adopt their own rules, norms and beliefs. Overall, I'm more pleased here as an academic than I used to be in Syria. Turkish people really respect knowledge. They respect the educated, the elderly, the family, the neighbours and the needy like nowhere else. I really love these aspects of their culture.

Being not really willing to adapt any aspect that is not Turkish. And expecting hosted people to follow precisely their norms and values,

Turkish people are not easy to deal with. So, displaced academics, like me, have sometimes to work unnecessarily harder to please authorities at work or in academia. In general, academics have to stay for longer office hours, not necessarily teaching or dealing with students. Usually, thirty to forty hours a week is expected from each academic. However, rules apply more to foreigners. This makes my family and social life much harder. Of course, being a displaced person brings more responsibilities for me in the hosting country. Another burden or negative aspect of being a foreign academic in Türkiye is the need to sign your contract every year. It doesn't matter how good you are, your contract has to be renewed annually as a foreigner; and it is a long process, an unnecessary stress, I think.

Before 2016 or 2017, the Turkish government called most of the educated Syrians to apply to get Turkish citizenship. I was one of them. I didn't complete my application; I withdrew at an early stage in the process. The deal was if I became a Turkish citizen then I had to do specific Turkish exams to be allowed by YÖK (Council of Higher Education) to teach in any academic institution, including schools, as a Turkish citizen; I didn't have to go through that as an international academic. I did not develop my modest level of Turkish; I never had time with my long hours of academic commitments. Rather than my thirty-hour weekly commitment with my university, I have another six-to-twelve-hour research commitment. I had some Syrian colleague academics who had been here three or four years earlier than me. The Turkish language of the exam was a barrier; it was not offered in English or Arabic like the driving exam. My friends' Turkish language was way better than mine, they were studying hard, yet they couldn't pass those exams easily.

'Pros and Cons'

Things are changing in Türkiye. I have been here for almost nine years. As an academic, I still think that the positives are more than the negatives. Turkish people really respect teachers and knowledge. Also, there is a tendency to develop academic research and collaborate globally with academics in different countries. Research is becoming more demanded and highly regarded. There are always national and international conferences and workshops in many cities all over the year, in Istanbul, in Ankara, even in Gaziantep where I live. Also, the expenses needed to attend such activities are mostly paid by the academic institution you belong to. Briefly speaking, I was more encouraged to conduct research in Turkey than in Syria.

Another blessing here is the number of students. Here in Türkiye, there are many state and private universities in all cities. Other new universities are still opening. Students have different options, and their number in classes is quite logical, unlike the case in Syria. Unfortunately, establishing private universities was and still is not encouraged. Unfortunately, there have only been a few state universities in all of Syria that are tuition-free compared to the many Turkish state universities that are tuition-free. These are Damascus University [1923], Aleppo University [1958], Tishreen University [1971], Al-Baath University [1979], the Higher Institute for Applied Sciences and Technology [1983] and Al-Furat University [2007]. There are very few private universities, only four or five. That's it. Every year, we have hundreds of thousands of young Syrians seeking university education. That is the main reason behind the big number of university students in classes. But a very small number of teachers and lecturers.

Another positive point is that in most Turkish academic institutions there are always plans and at least a modest budget for developing different academic facilities, such as updating curriculums, enlarging libraries, recruiting specialists, running conferences or workshops and improving research qualities every year. Also, academics and teachers are better paid in Turkey compared to those in Syria. Because of the better financial status of teachers, and more encouragement and respect for knowledge among the new generation in Turkey, it's more prestigious to be an academic here. You're even called 'Hoca'. It means 'teacher'. If you are in elementary school or you are a PhD doctor, you're so highly respected and called 'Hoca' because you're educating generations. Even uneducated people respect you when they come to know that you're a teacher. That is a very cool feeling the academics enjoy here. For example, you're going to a bank and you find that some of the employees there are not cooperative enough because you don't speak their language. As soon as you introduce yourself as a PhD lecturer or even an elementary school teacher, showing your academic ID, there will be a big change in their treatment. 'Wow! You are a "*Hoca*", you teach our students; we owe you much. We will help you, don't worry!'

'Solidarity Is Important'

As I mentioned, Türkiye is a busy place for national and international conferences and workshops where you can meet scholars and researchers coming from different cities and different parts of the world. Within years, I was able to collaborate with some distinguished ones. That added much to my experience as an academic. Late in 2018, I also joined Cara (the Council for At-Risk Academics) as you know, my dear Dina. This is how we met in Istanbul for the first time in June 2019, at Cara's Round Table. I am still with Cara enlarging my global research network. It has been almost six years. Time flies, isn't it, Dina?

Personally speaking, I believe in global interdisciplinary academic work where scholars can learn from each other and contribute together to enrich the non-hegemonic reserve of knowledge for the sake of humanity. Let's hear each other. Let's learn from each other. Let's modify each other. Let's do something together. Indeed, solidarity is important.

'Withholding, Because It Is Enough'

By the way, I didn't share all the experiences, but I thought that will probably be enough. Because I started remembering worse scenarios: when I saw some people dead or kidnapped, or some close ones who disappeared and were found.

8. Home and Abroad:
Exploring my Lived Experiences through Poetry and Narrative

Fadel Jobran-Alsawayfa

Introduction

As I write this, I am preparing for the Fall term of 2022, in my third year as Assistant Professor of Education at Bethlehem University. I am an academic who sees education as a means to liberate minds and shape the future of the students whom I teach and the people with whom I interact, despite living in an unfair, unjust world. I have learned to go beyond conversations and texts. My past shapes who I am now as an academic whose purpose is not only to deliver knowledge; one who believes in 'education for liberation' (Freire, 1972).

This chapter demonstrates how integrating narrative voices and poetic inquiry can help academics and qualitative researchers to tell their stories and communicate their findings, while preserving their authentic voice (Hordyk et al., 2014). The discussion in this chapter is structured around the validity of such a research approach in qualitative research, (re)presented in the modes of storytelling, poetry and reflective narration. I am aware of the disputes between objectivism and subjectivism in narrative research, and how revealing the latter raises questions about my positioning as a researcher and an academic writing about my own experience. Yet I cannot detach myself from the research data; it happened to me, it is about me, it is my story and experience. Andrews, Squire and Tamboukou (2013) recognise narrative researchers as 'part of the data they collect' (p. 21), who cannot isolate themselves

   https://doi.org/10.11647/OBP.0427.08

from their context. Moen (2006) affirms that 'human knowledge of the world is relative' (p. 5). In other words, narrative stories depend on the individual's experiences and values. It should be noted that narratability is not new in human and social sciences. However, there have been some basic claims about using narratives in research. One of the main claims is that narrative researchers tell their stories depending on their past and present experiences (Moen, 2008). Narrative stories are personal, we understand human experiences through the meaning individuals assign to them. Personal stories are shaped by the feelings and knowledge of the person. Moen et al. (2003) assert that several educational researchers see the notion of 'voice' in research as *the subject's* voice. The reader might decide to dismiss my authorial narrative as subjectivist. But I invite you to engage and gain a deeper understanding of my experience as an academic who not only *considers* the issues of truth and validity, but places them *at the heart* of his research, daily practices and values.

This chapter reports on my reflexive account and the challenges I faced in opening new possibilities of methodological responsibility. A particular contribution of this chapter is the discussion of how nonconventional creative methods enable researcher reflexivity and participant agency. I situate these in selected occurrences during my academic life history as a Palestinian: firstly, reflecting on my doctoral journey in a different cultural and political context, while creating the 'War on Language' project and participating in the 'Breaking the Occupation of the Mind: Arts and Culture in Palestine' event, in England. The second part of the chapter outlines my everyday realities of restriction and humiliation as an academic based in Palestine.

My Doctoral Journey: Being in a Different Cultural Context

At the academic level, I came to the Doctorate in Education (EdD) programme with many years of professional teaching experience. Both those and my life experience enabled me to engage in intellectual and personal discussions, whether that was during the formal education sessions or whilst walking home, or having lunch or coffee with fellow local and international students and with professors. The modules of the programme were a good opportunity for me to work on projects in my area of interest, giving me a space to reflect on my lived experiences and to come up with creative ideas and approaches.

It wasn't my first time in the United Kingdom, and I have travelled to several countries in Europe and across the world. What was different this time was that my family was with me. It wasn't easy, but it was a new experience. It wasn't easy for my two sons to adapt to a new culture; they went to school there, quickly learned English and made friends from around the world. They are football crazy, so they joined a football team in Chester. The coaches were impressed with their skills and performance. My wife and I also made new friends, we shared our culture and learned about other people's cultures. We participated in cultural events and we were invited to speak about the reality of our life in Palestine. We met with people who were aware of the political situation in Palestine, and we engaged in discussions and conversations with them. We received support from people many times, but at other times we were regarded as 'different others' or 'outsiders' (Anderson, 2006).

As an international student, I was fully aware of the UK's academic curriculum. I had already completed an MA in Comparative Education from the Institute of Education, University of London, in 2009. Like other UK Master's degree programmes, it was an intensive programme squeezed into one year. I made friendships but I didn't have enough time to get to know people from other cultures in-depth. Within the EdD, the module assignments and projects provided an opportunity to make long-lasting friendships, experiment and implement projects with local and international students. We engaged in discussions and shared ideas, yet stayed on the academic level. The 'War on Language' project that I devised was an opportunity to more substantially and creatively challenge cultural and mental barriers.

For that module, I wrote a poem titled 'Tell Me Why'. It was based on a visit to the Tate Gallery in Liverpool. The aim of the visit was to interact with the sculptures and instalments, to respond to them and to notice their own inner dialogue. As I discuss in this section, I was inspired by the *Tower of Babel* installation as a form of modern art. It was my first exposure to such an installation. So, I decided to translate the theme of the poem into a performance. It was first performed in the Tate Gallery, and later I interacted with eight students from eight countries to perform it at the Chester City Centre. I wanted that experience to be evocative, and I wanted participants' voices to be heard against my own subjectivities. I believe one of the purposes of qualitative research is to capture participants' experiences as told through their voices. Therefore, participants were invited to reflect and note down any inner dialogue and intuitive responses. Each participant spoke their own language: some with words, and others let their musical instruments and bodies speak instead. A video documented the interaction.

At Tate Liverpool, in the middle of the third floor stood an installation that caught my eye. I approached it, and I examined it carefully. It was the *Tower of Babel* installation by Cildo Meireles. The museum website describes it as

> a large-scale sculptural installation that takes the form of a circular tower made from hundreds of second-hand analogue radios that the artist has stacked in layers. The radios are tuned to a multitude of different stations and are adjusted to the minimum volume at which they are audible. Nevertheless, they compete with each other and create a cacophony of low, continuous sound, resulting in inaccessible information, voices of music. (Babel, 2001)

My response was visceral. I am a Palestinian who comes from a country that is exactly like the Tower of Babel: a divided place of cities, towns and villages surrounded by eight-meter-high concrete walls with electric wire fences on top. It annexes Palestinian lands, divides families and relatives from each other. We speak one language and yet we cannot communicate. We try to climb the wall, reach out and communicate. I read about Cildo Meireles and found that in all of his works, he embodies his ideas by telling his stories creatively (Menezes, 2009). Furthermore, Meireles's installations, such as 'Red Shift', are cultural and 'closer to poetry than politics' (Maroja 2016, p. 55).

In the EdD module were students from six countries, each speaking a different language. I had an idea in my head and I wanted participants' narratives, as well as mine, to emerge creatively and evocatively. The *Tower of Babel* installation was about miscommunication due to language barriers. So, what an inspiration! I decided to write a reflective poem titled 'Tell Me Why'. In that poem, I expressed my thoughts and feelings about the story of the Tower of Babel, with the theme being that people can still communicate no matter the language they speak. That theme was translated actively into performance, including my classmates and colleagues. I met with students and colleagues to plan the performance. It was helpful to have their suggestions and input shape my research project. I wanted to see how participants and myself explore and respond to the world. It is my identity as a researcher. The idea was that each student spoke their own language during the performance. Then participants switched partners so that we all communicated with each other. One of the participants suggested bringing his guitar and using it as a tool to communicate; he wanted to speak and communicate without language. The 'War on Language Project' aimed to get people physically together and communicating despite language and cultural differences. It was performed in Tate Liverpool with Master's and doctoral students from the UK, Greece, Austria, Germany, Jordan and Palestine. It was a very good experience and participants found the performance different and interesting.

I wanted to bring the project to a wider audience, so I asked the students who participated in the performance if they were willing to perform again at Chester's City Centre on a weekend. They welcomed the idea.

On the weekend, after a Saturday learning session, we gathered at the Faculty of Education's lobby and we all walked to Chester Cross, which is a three-minute walk from the university. When we arrived, it was packed with people. It was a cloudy, rainy afternoon—typical UK weather! I used multiple cameras to record the performance; I attached one to a three-legged stand and asked a colleague to use the other camera just in case. Recording started and, in pairs, participants engaged in conversations, each using their preferred language. Then participants changed partners and started new conversations. I was part of the performance, and it was so funny. I remember my first conversation was with a participant from Austria. I had no idea what she was talking about. Same for her, I guess. In that conversation, I was complaining about UK weather and saying that the weather back home must be warm, as we were having the conversation in the rain! The first conversation lasted about ninety seconds. Then I switched partners, and this time I was with the Greek participant who used his guitar to communicate with me. I started that conversation first. My first sentence was in Arabic of course: انت بتعرف تعزف على الجيتار [I see that you can play the guitar!]. He waited until I finished my sentence and played the guitar for a few seconds, and so on. We both communicated and I felt that there was mutual understanding.

As we were all communicating, locals and tourists gathered around without having a clue as to what was happening. Some took pictures, while some others just stood and tried to figure out what it was all about. The performance lasted almost half an hour. After the performance, we chatted about how it felt for everyone to perform in a public place. That project opened new doors for me to consider new opportunities to share my experiences.

Reflecting on 'Breaking the Occupation of the Mind: Arts and Culture in Palestine Event'

While studying in England, I was invited to participate in an event at Manchester Museum titled 'Breaking the Occupation of the Mind: Arts and Culture in Palestine' (2018). The organiser of the event, who came to the University of Chester, explained the theme of the event and asked for suggestions. Honestly, I was very keen and enthusiastic to do something and participate in that event. I felt that while I was in the UK I had an experience to share, so why not seize this opportunity and have my voice heard in an event that will be attended by hundreds of people? In this section, I recount the particular event that occurred in Palestine which has informed my creative output, and reflect on its performance to a non-Palestinian audience. As you will see, they are characterised by very different conditions due to my mobility as an academic.

The Story

The event I drew upon was in the summer of 2007, when I was travelling to Ramallah to participate in a workshop about drama in education. At that time, I was an English teacher exploring alternative methods to engage students. I documented an aspect of that day's experience in a poem. Usually, my reflections are written on the same day; however, this composition took longer. The event was fresh in my mind, but I couldn't find the words to express my feelings! Finding the most expressive words wasn't easy even though it was in my own language of Arabic. I struggled to put my experience on paper. Finally, I sat in silence the next day and started to write. To me, silence is the space where I can think in-depth, contemplate and reflect. It is tranquil.

I understand that meaning may be lost when translating from one language into another (Steiner, 1998). So, I have decided to present it to you in Arabic first and then in English.

'على حاجز الكونتينر،
في يومٍ من أيام تموزِ الحار
غادرتُ البيتَ وفي جَعبتي الكثيرِ من الأسرار
ركبتُ السيارة متوّجهاً نحْوَ وادِ النار
طريقٌ متعرجةً كعربيدٍ أسود
تارةً يتلوى وتارةً يتمدَّد
التحمت عجَلاتُ السيارةِ بالاسفلتِ المعبّد
مخلّفةً رائحةً قوية كالبارودِ المُبدَّد
وسائقٌ يبدو أن الطريق أكلّت من جسدِه
تمتمَ بكلماتٍ حتى وصلنا إلى أعلى التلة
حيث حاجزٌ يفصلُ بيتَ لحم عن القدس المحتلة
حاجزُ الكونتينر أو حاجزُ الموت كما يسمونه
عليهِ وقفَ جنودٌ وآخرون يراقبون من وراءِ الشَبَك
أمرَ أحدهم السائق بإطفاء المحرّك
وفتح جنديٌ آخرَ البابَ الجانبيّ وبدى مرتبك
أما أنا فكنتُ في قراءةِ روايةٍ مُنهمك
طلبَ بطاقات الهوية الشخصيّة
ناولتهُ إياها واستمريت في قراءتي القصصيّة
:رَبّتَ على كتفي قائلاً بلهجّةٍ عاميّةٍ
؟ليش ما تطلّعتَ بوجهي لمّا أعطيتني الهويّة
قلَت: لإني ما بدي أتطلّعَ بوجهك
استشاطَ غضباً وقال: إنزَل من السيارة
وقفتُ لساعاتٍ تحت أشعة الشمسِ الحارقة
ورقدَ كلبٌ بوليسيٌ يائسٌ على مَقرُبة
كقطٍ ينتظرُ نصيبَهُ على بابِ مَلحمَة
بعدَ ساعات استلمتُ هويتي ومضيت
.لكنني عدتُ من حيث أتيتُ

'At the "Container" Checkpoint'

On a hot July day
With hidden secrets I headed my way
I travelled in a taxi to Wadi En-Nar
From Bethlehem it wasn't that far.

A hill black steep road

Once shrinks, once gets broad
The rims of the taxi's tires turned bold
Because of the road they're now old.

The taxi driver looked worn out
Muttered as we reached the roundabout
There stood an Israeli checkpoint
Isolating Bethlehem from Jerusalem the Occupied.

'The Container Checkpoint', it is called
Heading to Ramallah no one can avoid
'Hey, stop the engine' a soldier ordered
As other soldiers pointed their guns and observed.

A soldier violently opened the taxi's side door
And asked for ID in Arabic, of course poor
I was reading a novel, and gave my ID, I am sure
He tapped on my shoulder: an Israeli soldier you should not ignore.

He asked: why did not you look at me when you gave your ID?
I answered: I do not want to look at your face as you see.
Get out of the taxi now he said, getting angry
The sun was burning, so I was weary

Police dog nearby laid on the floor
Like a cat waiting at butcher's door
I was given my ID after an hour
And returned to where I was before.

On the Way to Manchester

It was early in the morning in 2018 when I walked to Chester Train
Station to buy a return ticket to Manchester. It was Saturday, so the train
station was very crowded. I waited for about fifteen minutes until the
train to Manchester arrived. The journey from Chester to Manchester
usually takes an hour and a half. I boarded the train, sat next to the
window and bought some coffee. It was very cold and raining heavily
outside. I am a lover of nature, so I looked through the window and
started contemplating. The houses along the track looked large enough
for the passengers departing and small enough for those arriving; the
houses on the horizon looked very tiny, with unrevealed secrets. Trains

are not only means of transport and objects that connect places, but they are also places and spaces that bring people together and share stories. A few minutes later, storytelling began. Passengers shared snacks and stories. Two young men started talking about football, at first they argued but then the arguments died down. Opposite them, two ladies were laughing and whispering to each other. Not far off, I caught a sight of someone typing on his laptop. Just like me, he was going to a conference. In front of him sat an old man who snored, huffed and puffed. The conference guy looked annoyed, but he seemed reluctant to tell the old man to stop snoring. I felt nervous as the train approached Manchester. It was my first experience presenting at a big event. I did not know my audience and if they would understand my story.

The train arrived in Manchester on time. Allan, my EdD supervisor, was waiting outside the train station, along with another friend who was also going to the event. He waved at me, I saw him and greeted him. We walked to the museum, chatting and laughing along the way.

Opening the Event: My Poem

I stood on the stage and looked at the audience. The museum was packed full with an audience of over three hundred. My heart started to beat fast. My hands were shaking and for a moment I didn't know how to start. I wondered if those people who came to listen to me, as well as to other performers, would understand anything. I felt acutely aware of my positioning as a Palestinian academic coming to share his experiences with a non-Palestinian, non-Arab audience. That was not an easy task.

Finally, I steadied myself and started reading the poem. I felt every single word. In my head, I was imagining that day as if it was happening again. This helped me to live in the moment and express myself, my feelings and anger. The image of that dog sleeping in the middle of the road, the soldiers standing at the checkpoint, the face of the young soldier asking for my ID card.

Afterwards, some people approached me and stated that they were mesmerised by the poem! A woman who said she was from Yemen approached me with tears in her eyes and said in an accent I could barely understand: 'your poem was moving, thank you for reminding me of my home country'.

After the Event

Going public with my suffering, and the 'freedom' I felt in a new place, reminded me of the main source of oppression. For me, poetry is more than a research approach: it is a way of knowing and living, a way of resistance and resilience. Poetry helps the reader to gain a deeper understanding of my lived experiences and find resonance with their own experiences (Alsawayfa, forthcoming).

The performance of that poem became *a space* for me to share my experience and have my voice heard. Now, three and a half years later, I realise how privileged I was to have been invited to participate in that event. I have since been approached by many researchers and supporters who are willing to learn more about the daily life of Palestinians and to hear more stories narrated by Palestinians in a nontraditional way.

It enriched my scholarship. The subject of my doctoral dissertation was on the contribution of found poetry to analysing, representing and disseminating data creatively in qualitative research (Alsawayfa, 2019). I argued that poetry provides different lenses through which to understand people's lived experiences. For that study, I facilitated the composition of forty-two poems which were crafted from participants' interview transcripts and reflective journals. From these samples of their voices, a poetry book with QR codes was created and designed (Alsawayfa, forthcoming), and the poems performed and shared with different audiences.

Poetry in research is not new. For example, Chan (2003) used poetry as a means to explore her lived experience as a doctoral student. Pithouse-Morgan (2016) used found poetry to explore her professional life as a teacher in South Africa. I would humbly say that, as far as I know, I was the first doctoral student from the Arab world to use found poetry as a method of data analysis and representation in research undertaken in the UK. I am proud to have inspired other students and researchers to use poetic inquiry in their research.

I continue to use found poetry and creative approaches in my research and with my students, and at the same time, I engage in arguments with my current colleagues about the importance and significance of using such approaches in higher education.

Restrictions on Movement: Academia under the Israeli Occupation

My suffering as a Palestinian academic is ongoing. It has different forms, like a suitcase that travels with me everywhere and anywhere I go.

In my land, education has been recognised as 'an essential tool for collective emancipation' (Institute for Palestine Studies, 2021). Most universities in Palestine were established after the Israeli occupation of the West Bank and Gaza in 1967. The Israeli occupation has had a negative impact on all spheres of life. The education sector—higher education institutions and schools—has not been an exception. When the first Intifada erupted in 1987, all Palestinian universities were closed for four years. I had a cousin who studied at Birzeit University during the first Intifada. He told me that when the university was closed by the Israeli forces, instructors taught university subjects in students' dormitories and public places. This form of 'beautiful resistance' did not go without punishment. It was criminalised, with many university students and academics arrested. My cousin was administratively detained in the Negev Desert Prison Camp (Ktzi'ot). The second Intifada in 2000 was more violent. Israeli forces enforced collective punishment policies in the Occupied Palestinian Territories such as sieges, roadblocks, road gates, earth mounds, checkpoints and pop checkpoints, and curfews and prolonged curfews. Universities, such as Al-Quds University, were physically segregated from the populations they served by the construction of the Separation Wall. Physical barriers on the ground limit and prevent academic citizens from reaching institutions and moving between them. In addition to such structures, Palestinians are subject to the ad hoc whims of the Israeli soldiers at checkpoints.

According to Article 13 of the United Nations Universal Declaration of Human Rights, 'everyone has the right to freedom of movement and residence within the borders of each state. Everyone has the right to leave any country, including his own, and to return to his country'. This means that freedom of movement is a basic human right. University academics in the West Bank have to show ID cards at Israeli military checkpoints. Examination of the body, bags and personal belongings continues when travelling abroad. When permitted, Palestinians from the West Bank may only travel internationally through Jordan, while those from Gaza travel through Egypt. Below, I present narrative stories of my experiences at Al-Hamra Checkpoint and at international border crossings.

At Al-Hamra Checkpoint

In the year 2001, shortly after I graduated from Hebron University with a bachelor's degree in English Language and Literature, I applied for a job vacancy at the Arab American University of Jenin. My application was successful and in January 2001, I started working as a Teaching and Research Assistant at the university. The journey from Hebron to Jenin takes approximately two hours. I was single then, so I decided to rent a room. I went home once a month, and every time I had to walk for several kilometres in the heat, rain or mud in order to reach home or the university. This is because during the second Intifada, when the Israeli military redeployed in the West Bank, they established roadblocks and checkpoints between Palestinian villages, towns and cities. The checkpoints were set up on the roads and in the valleys to prevent people from moving. Walking did not mean that one could escape checkpoints. I walked because taxis were not permitted in many areas. Many times, I missed a class or two, or three, or even a whole teaching day. I was often harassed, humiliated and physically abused by the Israeli soldiers patrolling the checkpoints. I showed my university ID to them every time but it never worked. It was unimportant to them.

The Arabic American University was established in 2000, a few months before the outbreak of the second Intifada. I befriended John, a young English instructor from the United States of America. John and I became good friends. It was his first time in the Middle East. In November 2001, I invited John to the wedding of one of my sisters. He was so happy that he was going to see a Palestinian wedding. I warned John that our journey to Hebron would not be easy. He was aware of what was happening, and I shared many stories with him. But he had never experienced how it felt. I did not see any sign of fear or reluctance on his face. The wedding was on a Saturday, so we had to leave Jenin on

Friday to not miss the wedding because it is a never guaranteed journey and nobody can estimate how long it will take. Early in the morning, we left Zababdeh in Jenin, arriving at Al-Hamra Checkpoint at around 10:00 a.m. This checkpoint lies between Tubas and Jenin in Northern Palestine. It was installed when the Al-Aqsa Intifada broke out in the year 2000. Based on my experience, it was, and still is, one of the worst checkpoints in the West Bank; all checkpoints are terrible though. We joined a long line of cars at the checkpoint. A travelling distance of half a kilometre took two hours. As we approached the checkpoint, the taxi driver was ordered to stop and we were ordered to get out. A soldier ordered everyone to stand opposite the taxi and give our ID cards. Another soldier ordered the taxi driver to open the boot for inspection. John gave his American passport. An hour later, the soldier came back with our documents and with broken English he called John and asked where he was going. I could hear him telling John that his life will be at risk in Hebron. John argued with the soldier and insisted on going with me.

For two hours, we felt isolated from the world! If you know that checkpoint you will know what I mean. It is in the middle of nowhere. It was very cold and we were standing outside shivering. Then a soldier came holding John's passport and my ID card and said to me: 'look, you can go now but you should know his safety is your responsibility'. I nodded. We walked quickly away from the checkpoint. The air was cold and it was very quiet, but it was a kind of quietness I hated. There were not even birds in the sky to break the silence. After about an hour it was finally broken by the noise of an old van engine. I waved at the driver and asked if he could take us with him. I did not ask where he was going; the most important thing then was to leave that area. He seemed to be a good guy. He even refused to take money from us. There were three additional passengers. Not very far on, the road was blocked with massive rocks. The only way was to go around it. The van drove slowly until we reached the hill. It was a tiny steep muddy road and the wheels of the van sank in the mud. The driver asked us to get out and push the van. We tried but it barely moved centimetres. Then we decided to lift the van—yes, we literally lifted the van. I remember John was wearing off-white baggy trousers. When I looked at him, I smiled and said: 'look at your trousers, man!' He was covered in mud. He smiled back and said: 'look at yourself, man'. My face was covered in mud too.

We arrived in Hebron at around 7:00 p.m. My family and some relatives who were at our house greeted us and welcomed John. We were desperate for a hot shower. Later, we ate. My mother had cooked 'Up-Side-Down': a traditional Palestinian meal of chicken with rice and cauliflower. Some add potatoes or eggplants instead of cauliflower. It is called 'Up-Side-Down' because when it is cooking, on a stove or over fire, the chicken will be stuffed at the bottom, and when it is served the chicken will be on the top. John loved it. John plays the guitar, so after dinner he grabbed his guitar and started playing and singing. My cousins told him to feel at home.

Suffering on Border Crossings

Travelling through Jordan is a journey of suffering in itself. Whether you are a university professor, a tourist or someone going to get medical treatment, you will receive the same dismal treatment by the border police. For example, the flight from Amman to London takes about five hours; however, it might take eight to ten hours to get to Jordan from Palestine. As a Palestinian academic, every time I travel for a conference, a workshop, a summer school or a performance, I queue for hours waiting for my passport to be returned by the Israeli and Jordanian border police. I call it, as many other Palestinians do, 'Queues of Humiliation'. If you are lucky, you will not be interrogated by the border security and you will not spend hours looking for your luggage in a pile of intercepted, manhandled suitcases.

In July 2013, I travelled to Serbia for an international summer school on Peace and Conflict. Of course, I had to travel to Jordan a day earlier to be able to catch my flight on time. It was a hot summer day when I arrived in Jericho. You can imagine how hot it can be at the lowest point on earth in July! I had a big piece of luggage and a backpack. From Jericho to Jordan and vice versa, the only means of transport is by bus. In order to not lose my luggage, I wrote my name, address and mobile number on it and wrapped a red piece of cloth on the handle. First, I had to give my passport to the Palestinian Border Police, pay for the 'Leave Tax' and wait for the bus that would take us to the Israeli border to come. The waiting hall was so crowded with people, as many Palestinians travel to visit their relatives in Jordan or leave Palestine after visiting. After two hours, and before the bus had arrived, I managed to pull my luggage and put it in a trolley that takes all luggage to the Israeli Border Crossings. I say 'managed' because it is a self-service and if you do not fight to find a space for your luggage, you may either lose it or wait for many hours. The journey of suffering continued. On the Israeli border, and before getting into the passport control hall, we had to wait in the bus for two hours. Of course, nobody is allowed to get off the bus no matter the reason. I felt like I was being imprisoned in a capsule or a container. I hate waiting too. Passengers on the bus complain. One passenger shouted: 'what are we waiting for? Why are we waiting? Until when? How is this fair?' We all knew the answers to that guy's questions: simply because we are Palestinians. I desperately needed the toilet but I had to wait until we were allowed to enter the passport control hall. Instead of going to the toilet, I was greeted by long queues at passport control. Two passport control desks were functioning at that time. This meant two queues would go to one desk at a time. One member of the passport control staff shouted at us and we were subject to verbal abuse. We were very unhappy with what we heard. I said to the traveller next to me in the other queue: 'why don't they open more passport control desks?!' He replied, 'They don't treat us as humans.' When it was my turn, I was called by a female passport control officer who, instead of taking my passport, chatted with her colleague on the other desk. After a while, she demanded my passport and never looked me in the eye. She threw a glance at me while examining my passport and asked, while chewing gum, 'Where are you travelling to?' I said, 'To Serbia'. Then she asked, 'What for?' I replied, 'To join an international summer school'. She stamped my passport, and—again, without looking at me—she threw it on the desk from behind the small glass window, and with a loud voice she asked the next person to proceed.

My suffering did not end here. The journey through no-man's land takes a ten-minute bus ride; however, it took two hours. We had to wait on the bus until a border police officer came. While waiting, we had to fill information on a card and put it in our passports. In that card, I had to give the address of a relative or someone I know in Jordan! I do have relatives but I do not know their full addresses, so I left that part empty. Once inside, like on the Israeli border, I was greeted with long queues. The only thing you could hear there was shouting, passengers complaining, in the very unclean hall. After a long wait, I approached the desk, handed my passport in and waited for the officer to give it back to me. Then he shouted my name out loud and asked, 'Why didn't you put an address of someone that you know in Jordan?' I replied, 'Well, I don't know any'. He replied, 'That is none of my business, go fill that section'. I said, 'I am not staying in Jordan; I am just passing to Serbia'. He did not even reply. For a few minutes I did not know what to do. Then I decided to fill just any address. I created one, yes, I did. I gave another officer my passport and it worked. My flight was the next day, but with all the expenses for transport I did not have enough money to pay for a night in a hotel, so I went to the airport directly. I arrived exhausted at my destination, like a soldier drunk with fatigue whose only weapon is hope and willingness.

I had a similar experience when I travelled to Finland in March 2019, along with another colleague, to do a performance with university students. This poem is reflective of that experience.

'On the Way to Finland'

A month before Corona hit the world
We were preparing ourselves to go abroad
For three days we rehearsed
Scripted, planned and performed.

Cheap flights were booked
It is usual, I wasn't shocked
Early in the morning we left
And from Palestine I took a gift.

Suffering started on the waiting hall
As usual, at the Israeli passport control
There, it is impossible to have a conversation
They do not care about your education.

As I was waiting in the queue
A passport control officer shouted: 'Hey you!'
'Go back, back', he said
I murmured, and did.

They put a yellow mark on the floor
You should not go past, make sure!
I felt like in a zoo
Because of what they do.

I had some dried Za'atar in my bag
The security officer was like if he found a swag
I had to explain and my colleague confirms
It is a herb that grows on Palestinian mountains.

The suffering continued on the Jordanian side
Before entering the passport control hall, I deeply sighed
Border police officer asked everyone to stay in the queue
Humiliation, repression and bad treatment all you can see.

People in that hall were like canned sardines
Images of suffering with so many scenes
Unlabelled luggage all over the place
Like others, my luggage was not easy to trace.

Ironically, it is called Dignity Border or King Hussein!
A tiny border crossing between Jericho and Jordan
On that border we are treated like a piece of luggage
Every time I travel, in my head I have this image.

Conclusions

A dispassionate way to characterise this text would be to state that 'in this chapter, I have situated the narrative research approach and found poetry in (post)conflict academia'. However, that does not adequately represent the process of writing about my past experiences, and composing this chapter has not been easy. There was much I considered and weighed up before writing this and before sharing my experiences. I thought about the risks of documenting these immobilities or reliving memories. I thought about those who are going to read my narrative and interpret my stories.

The process involved in-depth reflective exploration, full of evocative imagination. Experimenting with creative approaches in my research projects, I was actively involved in the process and product of the research. It challenged my epistemological and ontological beliefs.

It made me realise how important it is to use 'artful inquiry' when approaching research. The issues of authenticity and 'narrative truth' are criteria for arts-based research (Chilton and Leavy, 2014; Faulkner, 2016). My authentic voice is evident in the process of inquiry and the presentation of data in the form of narrative stories and poetry (Serpa, 2022). Narrative stories and poetry have been used by arts-based researchers to allow their voice to be heard and to represent their daily life experiences (Hartnett, 2003).

The use of narrative voice and poetic inquiry is of great significance for me as an academic affected by conflict, oppression and injustice. As an academic, I use poetic inquiry and narratives in my teaching and research to communicate, explore and understand personal stories. The application of such techniques in the academic context provides a new way of thinking, expressing and meaning-making.

I encourage other academics, researchers, practitioners and students to write their self-narratives using creative, reflective arts-based methods and approaches such as poetry (Alsawayfa, 2021) and autoethnography (Furman, 2007).

Reflecting on these experiences, I feel good that such approaches worked in these ways, and that they offered me valid means to poignantly communicate my experiences. I hope that by reading this self-narrative, readers can journey, connect and reflect with me, and explore aspects of themselves. I understand this can be challenging, but I believe it might help others to better understand my life as an academic and those of fellow academic citizens in this system, as well as the conditions of the reader's own academic life.

I have decided to close my chapter with a poem. I have intentionally left it untitled to invite you to craft your own title.

> Reflecting on this chapter
> Will be an experience to remember
> Self-narrative and found poetry
> Are for me the trajectory
> They offered me the space
> To imagine, reflect and express
> To speak to my realities in my own voice.

Acknowledgments

This chapter would not have been possible without the guidance of Professor Dina Belluigi, who invited me to contribute my story to this book. Her constructive feedback and suggestions enhanced the quality of my work.

My appreciation also goes to my colleagues in the Department of Education at Bethlehem University, and to the students whose support and discussions have been invaluable. I would also like to acknowledge my students who shared their stories of oppression and injustice, which inspired me to tell my story.

I am also thankful for my wife and children, for their patience and encouragement.

Bibliography

Alsawayfa, F. (2021). Travelling to the Top of the Mountain: Research Investigation through Found Poetry as Means of Data Analysis, Presentation and Dissemination. In J. Adams and A. Owens (Eds), *Beyond Text: Learning through Arts-Based Research Practices* (pp. 69–99). Bristol Intellect. https://doi.org/10.1386/97817893835534

—(Forthcoming) *The Road to Found Poetry: Understanding People's Perceptions and Lived Experiences Creatively*. Intellect press.

Anderson, B. (2006). *Imagined Communities: Reflections on the Origin and Spread of Nationalism* (Revised Edition). Verso. https://doi.org/10.1093/fmls/cqp012

Andrews, M., Squire, C., and Tamboukou, M. (2008). *Doing Narrative Research*. Sage. https://doi.org/10.4135/9780857024992

Chan, Z. C. Y. (2003). Poetry Writing: A Therapeutic Means for a Social Work Doctoral Student in the Process of Study. *Journal of Poetry Therapy, 16,* 5–17. https://doi.org/ 10.1080/0889367031000147995

Chilton, G., and Leavy, P. (2014). Arts-based Research Practice: Merging Social Research and the Creative arts. In P. Leavy (Ed.), *The Oxford Handbook of Qualitative Research* (pp. 403–422). Oxford University Press. https://doi.org/0.1093/oxfordhb/9780199811755.001.0001

Faulkner, S. (2016). The Art of Criteria: Ars criteria as Demonstration of Vigor in Poetic Inquiry. *Qualitative Inquiry, 22,* 662–665. https://doi.org/ 10.1177/1077800416634739

Freire, P. (1972). *Pedagogy of the Oppressed*. Herder and Herder. https://doi.org/ 10.2307/30023905

Furman, R. (2007). Poetry and Narrative as Qualitative Data: Explorations into Existential Theory. *Indo-Pacific Journal of Phenomenology*, *1*, 1–9. https://doi. org/10.1080/20797222.2007.11433939

Goldman, S., and McDermott, R. (2009). Staying the Course with Video Analysis. In R. Goldman, R. Pea, B. Barron, and S. J. Derry (Eds), *Video Research in the Learning Sciences* (pp. 101–114). Routledge. https://doi. org/10.4324/9780203877258

Hartnett, S. (2003). *Incarceration Nation: Investigative Prison Poems of Hope and Terror*. Rowman Altamira. https://doi.org/10.17169/fqs-6.2.481

Hickey-Moody, A., and Page, T. (2015). *Arts, Pedagogy and Cultural Resistance*. Rowman & Littlefield International.

Hordyk, S. R., Soltane, S. B., and Hanley, J. (2014). Sometimes You Have to Go Under Water to Come Up: A Poetic, Critical Realist Approach to Documenting the Voices of Homeless Immigrant Women. *Qualitative Social Work*, *13*, 203–220. https://doi.org/ 10.1177/1473325013491448

Institute for Palestine Studies (2021). *The First Intifada (2): Radicalizing the University*. https://www.palestine-studies.org/en/node/1651342

Maroja, C. (2016). Red Shift: Cildo Meireles and the Definition of the Political Conceptual. *ARTMargins and the Massachusetts Institute of Technology*. https://doi.org/ 10.1162/ARTM_a_00131

Meireles, C. (2001). *Babel*. Tate. https://www.tate.org.uk/art/artworks/ meireles-babel-t14041

Menezes, C. (2009). *Cildo: Meireles: From Sense to Concept*. https://www. studiointernational.com/index.php/cildo meireles-fromsensetoconcept

Moen, T. (2006). Reflections on the Narrative Research Approach. *The International Journal of Qualitative Methods*, 1–12. https://doi. org/10.1177/160940690600500405

—, Gudmundsdottir, S., and Flem, A. (2003). Inclusive Practice: A Biographical Approach. *Teaching and Teacher Education*, *19*, 359–370. https://doi. org/10.1016/S0742-051X(03)00020-9

Pithouse-Morgan, K. (2016). Finding Myself in a New Place: Exploring Professional Learning through Found Poetry. *Teacher Learning and Professional Development*, *1*(1), 1–18. https://journals.sfu.ca/tlpd/index. php/tlpd/article/view/1

Saunders, E. (2018). Breaking the Occupation of the Mind: Arts & Culture in Palestine Event. Mancunion. https://mancunion.com/2018/12/07/ breaking-the-occupation-of-the-mind-art-and-culture-in-palestine/

Schön, D. A. (1983). *The Reflective Practitioner: How Professionals Think in Action.* Basic Books. https://doi.org/10.4324/9781315237473

Schubert (2006). Video Analysis as Practice and the Practice of Video Analysis. In H. Knoblauch, B. Schnettler, J. Raab, and H. Soeffner (Eds), *Video Analysis: Methodology and Methods: Qualitative Audiovisual Data Analysis in Sociology* (pp. 115–126). Peter Lang. https://doi.org/10.3726/978-3-653-02667-2

Serpa, R. C. (2022). Providing an Authentic Voice? Understanding Migrant Homelessness through Critical Poetic Inquiry. *Social Sciences, 11*(6). https://doi.org/10.3390/socsci11010006

Steiner, G. (1998). *After Babel: Aspects of Language and Translation* (3rd edn). Oxford University Press.

United Nations. (n.d.). *Universal Declaration of Human Rights,* https://www.un.org/en/about-us/universal-declaration-of-human-rights

9. The Lone Voice in the Academic Wilderness: Nigerian Academics' Experiences in Industrial Conflicts

Gregory O. Ugbo and Henry Chigozie Duru

Setting the Scene

The imperative of quality education in national development is incontrovertible in this era of education renaissance in the African context (Waswa and Katana, 2008). African educational systems have faced turbulent challenges since the emergence of formal education in the nineteenth century, with varying degrees of resilience across African countries. The Nigerian educational system has had its fair share of challenges which have ranged from poor funding, skilled workforce retention, teachers' welfare, etc. (Arowosegbe, 2023). The (mis) management of these challenges has generated conflicts that have, at times, further compounded the problems of teaching and learning within the country, which leads to unpleasant experiences for all concerned. The impasse at the time of writing between the Nigerian Federal Government (FG) and the Academic Staff Union of Universities (ASUU), which led to the suspension of all academic activities in Nigerian public universities from February 14, 2022 till October 14, 2022, exemplifies this situation. Exacerbating existing challenges, Nigeria was still in recovery mode from the impact of the COVID-19 pandemic that severely altered the global academic calendar, especially for nations lacking the digital affordances to transition to virtual learning. Nigerian universities lost two academic years during 2020–2021 and 2021–2022—and counting, since the 2022 strike was only suspended without a resolution to the issues that made

https://doi.org/10.11647/OBP.0427.09

the strike inevitable. Warning strikes and threats of strike have continued to disrupt Nigerian public universities' academic programmes at the time of writing this paper.

In this chapter, analyses of discourses were undertaken within the context of structural and economic conflicts that have arisen from unmet needs in the educational system, particularly the Nigerian higher education system, as demonstrated by the ASUU-Federal Government conflicts. The discourses were approached by analysing narratives around the issues relating to a strike, as projected in the media. In other words, the chapter discursively and reflexively explores how issues were framed in the media by reviewing how the government, media and other stakeholders represent and understand the underlying causes of the conflict espoused by the academic union. In doing so, the qualitative content analysis method was adopted to review media reports for emerging themes. This, combined with the first-hand experiences of authors as ASUU members, enabled us to make some extrapolations on the general situation of other academic staff under the umbrella of ASUU in Nigeria.

The relevance of this discourse is premised on the dynamic with which Nigerian academics, especially those based within Nigerian universities, have had to contend: perennial problems of abandonment, scapegoating, victimisation, suppression and blackmail, from the Nigerian government, parent-stakeholders and students (Arowosegbe, 2023; Bello and Isah, 2016). This is despite such academics negotiating career growth in hostile work environments and politics of control which militate against maintaining minimum global standards in personal development. This, at the same time, poses a great challenge to the academics' responsibilities to preserve the nation's knowledge base, values and cultures through teaching, research and community services.

This chapter, therefore, explores how academics negotiate their survival and development for global competitiveness in a climate where the extant political structure tends to promote priorities other than education; how they endeavour to uphold the structure of national existence through research, teaching and community services in the face of obvious alienation; and how this perceived 'outsider' in politics and policies achieves a balance under oppressive regimes that have always subsumed the academics' existence within a collectively subdued population. What are their coping mechanisms amidst unreconcilable priorities related to university education which often result in total down-tools and disruption of academic calendars and programmes, and further injustice in terms of delayed promotion, suspension of salaries and scapegoating? As authors, we expected that the outcome of this curation would add a Nigerian perspective to the lived experiences of many university academics internationally who are increasingly entrapped and victimised in vicious webs of conspiracies, yet who remain voiceless. The critical discourses from this chapter will signpost a revolution towards ending, or at least possibly ameliorating, the incessant industrial conflicts that not only disrupt teaching and learning in Nigerian universities, but erode the personae of the academics at the receiving end, who are often neglected.

Industrial Conflicts in Nigerian Universities: ASUU-Federal Government Conflict in Context

ASUU, as the name implies, is an umbrella body of all tenured academics in Nigerian public universities. ASUU membership excludes tenured academics in private and some state-owned universities in Nigeria. It is a registered union through which academics negotiate their welfare and demand the maintenance of the best standards. Conflicts between ASUU and the Federal Government have a long history worthy of recounting. As documented by Odiagbe (2012), ASUU was established in 1978 as a response to 'the need to address the deterioration of education in the country especially under the military rule but [...] [it] emerged into what was already a highly politicised environment' (p. 57). The intention behind the establishment of the ASUU had been misconstrued to be politically motivated, despite available evidence showing that the root cause of the incessant ASUU-Federal Government industrial conflict was hinged on poor remuneration and working conditions that resulted in high brain drain of academic staff (Bello and Isah, 2016; Ugar, 2018).

This history cannot be isolated from the general role the Nigerian military played in the entire evolution of the higher education system since independence from British colonialism. Odiagbe (2012) noted that military incursion into the Nigerian political sphere resulted in the decline of the premium value and respect originally accorded to Nigerian civil servants within the middle class, and within which Nigerian academics were positioned. Before the military interruption of Nigeria's democracy in 1966, the Nigerian academic enjoyed high recognition in terms of remuneration and social status (Aidelunuoghene, 2014). The Nigerian professor, for instance, was the highest paid civil servant after the Chief Justice of the Federation, and even higher than the highest-ranking Nigerian military officer (Salihu, 2019). This helps to explain the class struggle between Nigerian academics and the political class currently controlled by former military czars. The political undertone of this struggle is demonstrated by the ready perception of ASUU as a rebel or traitor group by military/political elites. For instance, the 1986 strike against Babangida's Structural Adjustment Programme led the FG to accuse ASUU of attempting to topple Bangida's government (Odiagbe, 2012, p. 53). This propaganda was peddled and propagated by the then military government even when the government—in connivance with the World Bank and other international institutions—hid under the cloak of privatisation to remove education subsidies just at the same time that other sectors were undergoing deregulation. ASUU was subsequently proscribed in 1987 for opposing the government's move to privatise the higher education sector, which impacted the commencement of high student fees to acquire higher education (Aidelunuoghene, 2014; Bello and Isah, 2016; Ugar, 2018).

Recounting the high level of communication gaps that existed between ASUU, the government, and public, Aidelunuoghene (2014) observed that since the ASUU's establishment in 1978 there has been a consistent breakdown of communication between the Federal Government and the union. The primary reason they give for this is that the breakdown is a result of government's failure to honour agreements. From the National Universities Commission's (NUC) records, ASUU has embarked on over twenty-three strikes between 1992 and 2013. The causes range from funding for the sector, such as increasing annual budgetary allocation for education and for institutions—e.g. for universities' revitalisation and the funding of state universities—and for staff—e.g. the payment of Earned Academic Allowances; to matters relating to the employment standards for academics, including the establishment of an academic staff's pension scheme (NUPEMCO) and the amendment of retirement age; and to academic freedom matters, such as the reinstatement of university councils that were prematurely dissolved, and upholding universities' autonomy among other demands (see Arowosegbe, 2023; ASUU, n.d.; NUC, n.d). Duze (2011) and Eme and Ike (2017) noted that the Nigerian government spends less than 9% of its total annual budget on education, and that allocations to Nigerian universities fall below UNESCO's 26% standard. The average ratio of teaching staff to students is 1:100 in most universities—far higher than the National Universities Commission's (NUC) prescribed 1:30 ratio and woeful when compared to the standard maintained in elite universities in the Global North, such as Harvard University's ratio of 1:4.

Odiagbe (2012, p. 16) has pointed out that 'the dispute between ASUU and the government has thus been one which has shifted from a conventional industrial relations conflict over wages and conditions of service, to one which involves a whole series of wider political questions'. Punitive measures were adopted by the Federal Government in an attempt to suppress ASUU's radical demands for the revitalisation of the Nigerian university system. According to reports by Odiagbe (2012, p. 59), six union members were sacked from the University of Lagos in 1980 at the insistence of President Shehu Shagari following Justice Belonwu's committee's reports. The academics were later reinstated in 1986, following the Supreme Court's ruling in their favour. However, the experiences they recounted indicate that they had suffered serious psychological trauma and hunger-torture due to the withholding of their salaries for six years.

Among other issues fuelling the industrial conflict is the struggle over autonomy and academic freedom (ASUU, n.d). As explained by Bubtana (2006, p. 6), academic freedom entails the 'freedom to undertake teaching and research in a free and unrestricted manner and the ability to publish research findings without fear of political and social consequences'. Academic freedom, which could be considered as a fundamental human right, is highly cherished and held as a virtue worth protecting in advanced democracies. As such, 'academic freedom is usually guaranteed even if the state was totally financing the academic system' (Bubtana, 2006, p. 6). However, the reverse has been the case where this potent right for national development has consistently been under threat in Nigeria, such that institutions, academic unions, the government, and other social actors have to negotiate its protection, which explains the Federal Government and ASUU impasse. From Odiagbe's (2012) record, the coalescing of hitherto autonomous schools after the civil war in 1970 contributed to centralising school regulation under the Federal Government, and this in part bred the unhealthy disharmony between Federal Government and ASUU over autonomy and control. Universities in particular were no longer at liberty to design curricula and research orientations that best suited their education philosophies. As such, there was a clear case of educational policy mismatch in most instances (Odiagbe, 2012). Salihu (2019) opined that the duplicity in roles and overlapping functions among the administrative and regulatory stakeholders imposed on universities continues to breed conflicts and, by extension, erode institutional autonomy.

Ya'u (2006) noted that while these were the prevalent experiences during the military regimes of 1966 to 1999, the experience of repression was not altogether different with the return of a democratic civilian government to Nigeria in 1999. According to Ya'u (2006, p. 49), 'the expectation of academics that the civil regime could respect academic freedom was shattered. One of the most telling failures of the civilian government to respect academic freedom is the case of 53 academics of the University of Ilorin who were dismissed since 1999'. There is also an instance of the five professors from the Lagos State University who were dismissed at the order of the state governor for questioning the procedure followed in the appointment of a vice chancellor (Salami, 2024).

The effect of such foregoing cases is that Nigerian universities still operate a governing and funding structure that exposes the system to political interference. The total dependence on government funding tends to undermine the efficiency and integrity of the intellectual business conducted by these institutions (Arowosegbe, 2023). Such intellectual independence is indeed fundamental, and has been a concern of academics globally, particularly as neoliberal economic logics proliferate. An example is the United Kingdom, where the intellectual community attempted to strengthen the 'Haldane Principles' which prescribe that decisions regarding the funding of research should be made by researchers and not politicians (Ghosh, 2017).

Bubtana's (2006, p. 6) assertion that academic institutions in most Arab and African countries have been in fierce battle against repressive regimes to safeguard 'academic freedom and institutional autonomy which they consider important not only for playing their role as a watchdog for society but also for nations to construct knowledge societies in which knowledge generation, dissemination, and application are the decisive factors' rightly captures the experience of Nigerian academics. Countries like Nigeria can be categorised as Bubtana's 'consumers of knowledge' (2006, p. 7) rather than knowledge creators, due to the brain drain, poorly funded and established systems of research that, when combined, create the deficit in terms of knowledge contributions to the global community. The Nigerian case is even complex in an environment where religious fundamentalists are opposed to the Western systems of education. This is most visible in the emergence of Boko Haram, an Islamic extremist terrorist group in northern Nigeria that are opposed to Western education (see Afzal, 2020; Atoi, 2022; Iyekekpolo, 2016; Peters, 2014).

The series of industrial actions that have occurred in Nigeria leave a rather sour taste in the mouths of students and parents. Scholars (see Eneji et al., 2019; Odey et al., 2020; Wojuade, 2019) have consistently observed a positive correlation between the disruption of the academic calendar and students' poor performance and, in turn, insufficient skills to cope with the demands of the labour market.

The Nigerian University System: The Ideal and the Reality

Western education in Nigeria has a colonial history. Nigeria adopted the British colonial Master's system of formal education. The country's first university was the University College, Ibadan, which predated Nigeria's independence. It was established in 1948 as an affiliate of University of London with the name changed to University of Ibadan after it severed ties with the British university. Indicating the existential significance of academia, the first indigenous university, the University of Nigeria in Nsukka, was formally opened on October 7, 1960, just seven days after Nigeria's independence. It was founded by the government of the Eastern Region of the country.

Interestingly, the original ideology that guided the premier universities in Nigeria informed their formulation in the ideal of 'the ivory tower', and as destination institutions for both Nigerian and foreign students. In other words, high standards were maintained in line with the stratified vision of the colonial regime. To put this into perspective, the best academic buildings in the first-generation universities were those erected at the inception of the universities over sixty years ago (Bello and Isah, 2016). The current downturn is within the post-colonial period, rooted in the interruption of the nation's democracy by the military in 1966 (ASUU, n.d). Ever since then, Nigerian universities have contended with the continual 'teething problems' of poor funding, brain drain/staff attrition due to some structural problems such as infrastructural decay and hostile work environments (Salau, Worlu and Osibanjo et al., 2020), poor remuneration and unhealthy disparities in comparison to other civil servants (Waswa and Katana, 2008). The average Nigerian academic practices within pitiable conditions, especially in the face of incessant hyper-inflation in the Nigerian economy. It has become a common refrain to hear from among the academic staff that the take-home salaries can hardly take one to the university's gate, indicating how paltry the average academic's salary is. A tenured professor who progressed to their career peak, as of January 2022, would receive a salary of less than $1,500 per month.

As glaring as these asphyxiating problems of higher education were, the Federal Government has continued to play the ostrich and rather heap blame on the academics that have advocated for reforms in the higher education sector. There is abounding evidence that the historisation of the struggles for the restoration of quality of higher education in Nigeria has watered down the relevance of the demands in the judgement of most Nigerian politicians. It has become a case of 'business as usual'. In other words, there is a seeming reluctance on the part of the critical stakeholders to respond to the demands which challenge their collective priorities which are mostly incongruous with the funding of public education. These are indications of the disjunct between the ideal and reality, providing insights into the discourses of such tensions and their targets, which the next section will turn to.

Conflicts in Nigerian Universities: Deconstructing the Narratives that Explain Nigerian Academics' Experiences

Conflicts are inevitable and an intrinsic part of human interaction (Ugbo, 2020). However, forestalling conflicts requires the clear strategy of cooperative relationships and integrative solutions (Valente, Lourenço and Németh, 2020). Conflicts naturally arise over incompatible needs within the frame of human interactions. How these needs are communicated and addressed is at the centre of every conflict. The education sector is not immune to this inevitability; as a social institution, it is a hub of human convergence and interaction. Hence, one would assume that effective communication would remain an essential component of conflict resolution in educational systems. Scholars have contributed by articulating conflict resolution strategies that might be deployed productively to address conflicts in higher education systems. These include arbitration, conciliation, dialogue and mediation (Mojalefa, 2021; Valente, Lourenço and Németh, 2020). As effective as these strategies have been as alternative dispute resolution strategies, the sincerity of stakeholders saddled with the responsibility of deploying this mechanism to resolve conflicts within the Nigerian context remains in question.

Importantly, theorising the typologies of conflicts is essential to our understanding of the dynamics of the ASUU and Federal Government's conflicts in Nigeria. These typologies include the structural, value, relationship, interest and data (Valente, Lourenço and Németh, 2020). In this sense, the structure of the Nigerian educational policies emphasises dichotomies between public and private interests and goods, and politics. The de-prioritisation of educational rights and needs, in terms of budgeting and funding, has continued to widen the gap in access between the haves and the have nots, and by extension, social inequality. These are at the same time embedded in the lack of values attached to education and the clash of interests between the key actors—Nigerian academics, the government, students and parents. An unhealthy relationship exists where stakeholders are at loggerheads. When academics resort to down tools as a way of collectively expressing their displeasure, propaganda is then deployed as a lethal weapon of victimisation, scapegoating and suppression.

In the section to follow, we thematise the narratives of different stakeholders as projected in the mass media in relation to the ASUU/ FG industrial conflicts.

Narratives around ASUU-Federal Government Conflicts: The Media Example

As earlier stated, in the course of its struggles as a stakeholder in the Nigerian university system, ASUU is often vilified by members of the public and even its employer, the government. Relying on media contents (in this instance, the online version of Nigerian national daily newspapers' news stories and editorials between January 2022 and October 2022), we examine the common patterns of general narratives concerning conflicts with regards to ASUU strikes, shedding light on how ASUU and its struggles tend to be projected in a negative light. The period in focus marks the peak of the protracted eight-months-long ASUU strike which generated heavy media coverage and public discourses. As such, it yielded interesting materials to distil themes upon which we anchor our discourses as presented below.

The Reductionist Narrative

The narrative pattern, in the public discourse of ASUU industrial actions, tends to reduce whole issues to the singular act of the declaration of a strike. Strikes are discussed outside the circumstances that led to them and within the context of the Nigerian labour laws. In other words, a strike action is not discussed as an eventual outcome of a failed dispute management process as prescribed by the extant Nigerian labour laws (Giame, Awhefeada and Edu, 2020), but rather it is framed as an isolated arbitrary action on the part of ASUU, thereby diverting attention from the longer process of engagement that failed to resolve disputes which paved the way for strike action. For instance, in discussing the most recent strike which started in February 2022, many commentators failed to recognise that ASUU had, since the middle of 2021, started engaging with the government on the need to sign the renegotiated 2009 agreement that was concluded in May 2021. They equally discountenanced the fact that when appeals failed, ASUU had issued an ultimatum to the Federal Government to sign this document before the end of July 2021 (Lawal, Olayinka and Umeh, 2021). In addition, seemingly overlooked by many public commentators was the fact that the FG had reneged on its commitments made at a reconciliation meeting with ASUU, which included the promise that work would be concluded on the draft renegotiated agreement by a committee set up for that purpose and would be submitted to the government by the end of August 2021, but that nothing was done to this effect weeks after that deadline (Olaitan, 2021). Again, many media contributors to the discourse on the strike failed to consider the three weeks ultimatum issued to the FG by the union in November 2021 to sign this same agreement or risk a strike action (Ezeigbo, 2021). Similarly, many appear to have ignored the fact that the strike would have commenced in December 2021 but was shelved following interventions by some stakeholders including the Nigerian Inter-Religious Council (NIREC) (*Blue Print*, 2022). In summary, the media, in their reporting, failed to represent the strike as a seemingly inevitable outcome of the government's apparent reluctance to follow up on the agreement that had ended the prior strikes.

Instances of this sort of narrative in the discourse of ASUU strike abound. One of them is seen in a comment made to the press by the Minister of Labour and Employment, Dr Chris Ngige, in April 2022. He said: 'there is nothing new about the ASUU strike. It has been a recurrent decimal. In the last 20 years, ASUU has gone on strike 16 times. So, there is nothing new as such' (Olayinka, 2022). While the Minister's observation about the quantity of strikes may have been accurate, the account misled the public. He failed to inform his listeners that these repeated strikes came against the backdrop of perennial failure to permanently resolve disputes by honouring agreements, on the part of the government that he represented. In addition, the Minister was definitely not telling the whole story when, on another occasion, he said of ASUU, 'every time there is a disagreement, it is strike' (*Premium Times*, 2022). In other words, he has failed to acknowledge that ASUU strikes, rather than being abrupt responses to dispute, are usually the last resort following failed attempts at resolution.

Former Minister of State for Education, Hon. Emeka Nwajiuba, was also counted among those pushing this unbalanced discourse. Speaking on a TV programme monitored by *Vanguard* newspaper in May 2022, he said, 'My position has not been that ASUU is talking rubbish. ASUU has a case, they are not making a case for themselves alone. ASUU is making a case for the entire university system. The only point of departure is that we have asked ASUU that strikes can't cure the problem' (*Vanguard*, 2022). Here the Minister appeared to have conveniently overlooked these strikes happening because firstly, the less disruptive means of curing the problem had failed to work, and secondly, the government appears willing to listen only when strikes are activated.

Media houses themselves are not beyond contributing to this discourse. *The Guardian* newspaper—in a feature titled 'ASUU, FG bicker over unfulfilled agreement', published in its August 1, 2021 edition—after giving a statistical breakdown of ASUU strikes which showed that an average of 19.5% of days of every academic year were spent on strike, argued that 'This, perhaps, explains why some stakeholders perceive the activities of ASUU, especially with respect to the industrial actions, as an attempt to frustrate academic pursuits of Nigerian undergraduates' (Lawal et al., 2021, para. 32). There, strikes are presented as 'activities of ASUU', in effect framing strike actions as arbitrary decisions of a single insensitive party, thus diverting attention from the contributory role of the other party (the government). Similarly, in an editorial titled 'ASUU and the Endless Strikes' published in the February 16, 2022 edition of *ThisDay*, the paper noted that 'public disenchantment with ASUU is understandably high because of its bullheaded approach'. The word 'bullheaded' portrays ASUU as being stubborn and uncooperative, a quality the paper sees as justifying the negative public perception suffered by ASUU. No mention was made of the obvious failures of the other party, the government, as seen in its repeated failure to honour agreements—an attitude that equally merits the compliment 'bullheadedness'.

Such portrayals represent a well-known tool employed by the media to demonise a cause and its promoters, especially when they take actions to protest what they want corrected. By employing uncomplimentary words, phrases and negative naming, the media succeed in framing the ASUU promoters in a way that demonises them and the cause of their members. Brown and Harlow's (2019) study reveals this pattern in the US media, where protests related to racial issues were reported as adopting more negative frames, even though an opposite pattern was found in the coverage of protests related to migrants' rights, health and the environment. Through this selective framing, the media promotes a discourse of 'hierarchy of social struggle' (Brown and Harlow, 2019, p. 523) where certain social struggles are glorified while others are demonised.

In all, the reductionist narrative highlighted above—which constructs strikes outside of the circumstances that seemingly made them inevitable—has the effect of portraying the ASUU as an insensitive body that irrationally and recklessly shuts down the nation's universities at will. Such narratives achieve this by failing to engage with those developments that are antecedent to the actual declaration of a strike and which, if critically viewed, may have positioned ASUU more as victims than as troublemakers. Stated differently, there is a clear failure among public commentators to balance the discourse around ASUU's industrial actions by engaging with the history of the strikes which would have brought under equal scrutiny the government and its agencies, who have often created the conditions for strikes by failing to honour agreements.

The Isolation of Strike Episodes

This was another way in which public discourse on ASUU strikes tended to portray ASUU as the problem. In this narrative pattern, each instance of striking was viewed in isolation; in other words, it was seen as an isolated episode rather a phase in a continuing chain of strikes arising from problems that have remained unsolved. Thus, each strike was discussed outside its historical connectedness with previous strikes.

Hence, the following picture is created: an issue arises, ASUU goes on strike, the government attends to the issue, ASUU calls it off, then another issue arises, ASUU goes on strike, the government solves the problem, ASUU calls it off only to return to strike once the next issue arises. This pattern of narrative has the effect of portraying ASUU as instantly invoking strikes once a dispute arises without first giving the government a chance to resolve the issue. However, in reality, each strike—at least in recent years—has practically been a continuation of the previous one. Hence, what is seen as recurring strikes by ASUU within a succession of unconnected industrial actions, are ultimately part of a continuum of struggles over largely the same set of issues. This is evident in ASUU's use of the word 'suspend' whenever it was ending any particular strike action. The import of this choice of word came to the fore when ASUU declared a strike in October 2018 and its leaders were called for a meeting by the Minister of Labour and Employment. The Minister, Dr Ngige, started by blaming the union for not giving him as the conciliator notice, before embarking on the strike as required by law. To this, the union leadership replied that its last strike was never called off but was merely suspended.

However, narratives in the public domain in many instances tend to ignore the connectedness between strikes, treating each strike as an isolated episode. For instance, in an editorial published by *Vanguard* newspaper on April 8, 2020, the newspaper blamed ASUU for being insensitive and always choosing the strike action once any dispute arises. According to the editorial report, 'The Academic Staff Union of Universities, ASUU, returned to its old "hobby" of indefinite strikes on Monday, March 23, 2020 [...] We see the main reason for this indefinite strike [the IPPIS issue] as unnecessary and undue muscle-flexing by ASUU' ('ASUU's insensitive strike', 2020, paras 1 and 9). The use of the language 'hobby' here is telling. *The Punch*, in an editorial titled 'ASUU Can't Be Exempted from the IPPIS' published on November 3, 2019, adopted a similar narrative: 'it is curious', the paper wrote, 'that academics who should know better are opposing innovation and cutting-edge technology to fight corruption at its roots' (*The Punch*, 2019). The phrase 'opposing innovation and cutting-edge technology' conveys the picture of unconnected instances of dispute rather than a protracted dispute over largely the same issues and which resolution thereof has been repeatedly frustrated. Also to be placed in the same league of disjointed narratives is the earlier quoted media statement of the Minister of Labour that 'every time there is a disagreement, it is strike' (*Premium Times*, 2022).

The Narrowed Narrative on the Impact of Strikes

In this instance, narratives around ASUU industrial actions tend to emphasise the immediate disruptive impact of strikes on the university system rather than taking a holistic view of the role of such industrial actions over time. Thus, public commentators tend to dwell on issues such as the delays suffered by students as a result of interruptions of academic activities, and their potential exposure to vices due to idleness. These issues are raised without any care to reflect on the huge impact of the series of concessions which ASUU has, through these strikes, successfully extracted from the government. These concessions include the establishment of the Tertiary Education Trust Fund (TETFund) and National Economic Empowerment and Development Strategy (NEEDS) Assessment, which have seen massive infrastructure development not only in universities but also in Polytechnics and Colleges of Education across the nation—both federal and state-owned—as well as extensive human resources development in these institutions. ASUU's industrial actions have also led to a legislative action to grant autonomy to universities in line with global standards, and have contributed to the quest for accountability in the system by forcing the government to constitute Visitation Panels for universities (Ero, 2022; Ibrahim, 2021).

A typical example of such faulty narratives is found in a feature on the ASUU-Federal Government disputes published in *The Guardian* of August 1, 2021 where the newspaper quoted a news source, one Duro Adebisi, as saying that 'the only thing achieved by these incessant strikes is to keep the system shut down, keep students at home, expose them to social ills, and progressively degrade the quality of learning in our universities' (Lawal et al., 2021). Another source, Priscila Etukudo, who was introduced as a parent, was quoted as saying: 'these strikes only succeed in disrupting the education of these children. Instead of being at school they are at home and may learn bad things in the process. Also, they [the students] risk spending more time than necessary pursuing a degree'. A similar sentiment was expressed just as emphatically in an online opinion piece titled 'Incessant ASUU strike—The devastating effects on Nigeria', by one Emmanuel Ojukwu whose main argument was that ASUU's 'incessant strike action continues to take a huge toll on the academic performance of students' (Ojukwu, 2022, para. 4). The writer went on to list the various ways the system suffers as a result of the strikes, without bothering to reflect on the other side of the story as told by ASUU, regarding the lasting positive impact of the strikes.

Narratives like these are not scarce in newspapers, on radio, television and social media, particularly during times when a strike has been declared. While they dwell on the immediate disruptive impact of strikes, ASUU is usually found to be toiling in isolation in trying to direct attention to the long-term positive impact of such industrial actions—both as already realised and as hoped to be realised in future. The result of this disjunct is that the public space is dominated by a narrative that tends to demonise ASUU by dwelling almost entirely on perceptions of the negative impact of strikes. Scholars of language analysis contend that such an unbalanced approach to discourse has proved to be a strong means of privileging a particular viewpoint over a competing viewpoint (Fairclough, 1989; Hall, 1997; Machin and Mayr, 2012).

The Distorted Narrative about the Beneficiaries of Strikes

This is an emerging pattern in the discourse around ASUU's industrial actions, with potentially serious consequences on the public perception of the union. In this instance, narratives about ASUU strikes tend to revolve around a false premise that the union's industrial actions are self-centred; that the objectives of the strikes are meant to benefit only the members of the union. Thus, in constructing the impetus of the union as about self-interest for the private gains of members, attention is deflected from the broader benefits, including the public good, which ASUU intends for the system in most of its industrial actions.

This sort of narrative has been dominant in the discourse around financial concessions made by the government in response to ASUU strikes. For example, *The Guardian* of March 1, 2022 has a story with the headline 'ASUU Strike: Ngige Updates Buhari, Says FG Paid N92bn to ASUU'. This headline is seriously misleading, if one goes down to read the body of the report. Therein it is reported that only N40bn out of this N92bn went to the university staff, including non-academic staff, as earned allowance (*The Guardian*, 2022). The rest was part of the revitalisation funds that went into the coffers of respective university management. It is interesting to see in this report what has become a regular pattern, where money meant for multiple purposes is framed as going entirely to ASUU, thereby portraying ASUU's demands for better funding of the universities as demands for personal monetary benefit. Similarly, a report in *Business Day* from May 8, 2022 reported that 'President Buhari has approved the sum of 456 Billion for ASUU to end the strike' (Ogwo, 2022, para. 8). The report did not bother to break down this sum to show who would actually benefit from this money and how.

This sort of narrative tends to mix up issues by presenting ASUU strikes as a mission in self-aggrandisement, thereby diluting the altruistic dimension of its struggles over the years. This has been the case even in the face of verifiable evidence of the many gains achieved for the system through these struggles (Ero, 2022; Ibrahim, 2021). ASUU members are, in effect, portrayed as selfish trade unionists who do not mind destroying the system for private gains. Such portrayals are inconsistent with the notion of academics as acting in service of education for the common good, as trustees of knowledge.

Parting Shots: The Way Forward

This chapter has exposed the dominant prevailing perspectives on the incessant ASUU-Federal Government conflicts. From the foregoing expositions, it becomes clear that public discourse on ASUU strikes in Nigeria still falls short of being anchored on balanced and holistic narratives. This, perhaps, explains why the recurrent impasse has defiled all known solutions—at least, at the moment—largely due to the politicisation of the genuine demands to improve the quality of Nigerian higher education in particular. This chapter has focused on the way these narratives are tilted towards diluting the persuasiveness of ASUU's case and in effect projecting them as the villains of the whole situation. Thus, it is common to see from the ontology of the Nigerian industrial conflicts that academics have consistently been doubly oppressed and maligned by the government as the enemy of the university education system in the eyes of the students, parents and other concerned social actors, despite their pitiable realities. While

ASUU remains in the eye of the storm, the principle of the idiom 'when two elephants fight, the grasses suffer' comes into focus. The conditions for the education of students in particular, and national development in general, have been adversely impacted, while public opinion of the professoriate has been tainted.

It is our conclusion that such lopsided narratives have the effect of distorting public understanding of the significant issues involved in these unending industrial disputes. This, in turn, miseducates the public about the institution of the university, and perpetuates the lack of accountability and often unhelpful responses from state stakeholders. The Nigerian Federal Government, therefore, needs to set its priorities right and begin to deliberately implement policies that recognise the voice of academic staff as central to their mutual mandate to promote quality education and knowledge creation for the global common good. As a developing country, the university system plays a significant role as the knowledge base of any progressive nation and must be empowered to function optimally. Although ASUU is not exonerated in the entire decay in the university system, the onus lies on the government to recognise, protect and inspire high standards in line with global best practices.

The above position is reinforced by the issues around which ASUU's struggle revolve, which are largely the same issues that university teachers around the globe have been struggling with, far from being a product of mere self-interest nor the utopian imaginations of a trade union (as some have charged) (see *The Punch*, 2019; Ojukwu, 2022). For example, the challenge of funding of public universities has been an issue of spirited public engagement in Europe and the USA (European University Association, 2022; Lung, Moldovanb and Alexandrac, 2012), and like in Nigeria, universities in these climates have had to contend with reduced government funding in recent years. The same applies to the increased constraints on academic freedom which intellectuals globally have had to engage with for decades (Allen, 2019; Palfreyman, 2007). Similarly, the problem of unbefitting wages for academics has been highlighted in several other countries including China (He et al., 2020), the UK from 2018 to 2023 (as discussed by Hudson-Miles in Chapter 10 in this book; Staton, 2022) and Nigeria's neighbouring country of Ghana (BBC News Pidgin, 2022). All this would tend to vindicate ASUU's position by showing that its demands are in line with the global sentiments as to how universities and their teachers should be treated, and global resistance to neoliberal erosion of the universities.

Against this backdrop, it becomes imperative on the part of ASUU to do more to influence the public opinion around its industrial engagement with the government. Public engagement generally, and with the national press in particular, has not been a central consideration of the union's strategy. A way out of the impasse may be to be more proactive and decisive in public communications, as well as to show more robust recognition of the critical role played by the perceptions of stakeholders such as students, parents and the media. This is indispensable if its voice is to be heard loud and clear, and if its activism is to yield more positive results. There is no more room to be complacent and presume that the public will be sympathetic to the cause simply because ASUU believes it to be a just cause, particularly as both the reputation of academics as trustees of education and the credibility of the union have been put to the test.

Acknowledgements

The first author wedded during the early stage of the 2022 eight-month-long ASUU strike. His new family started off in abject lack since he had no other means of livelihood to take care of his home. His wife stood by him patiently. He, therefore, appreciates his wife, Philippine Ugbo, most sincerely for the genuine love that gave him the peace of mind and sanity he needed at the time to cope. Our special appreciation also goes to the Academic Staff Union of Universities (ASUU) as a body for its resilience, genuine concerns for the members' welfare, and forthrightness in dealing with the Federal Government throughout the eight months in which we remained without salaries. The immediate support ASUU provided went a long way in cushioning the crushing impact of the no-work-no-pay FG policy on academics.

Bibliography

Academic Staff Union of Universities (ASUU). (n.d.). *History and Struggles of ASUU at a Glance.* https://asuu.org.ng/history-struggles-of-asuu/#

Afzal, M. (2020). *From 'Western Education Is Forbidden' to the World's Deadliest Terrorist Group.* Education and Boko Haram in Nigeria. Foreign Policy at Brookings.

Aidelunuoghene, O. S. (2014). ASUU Industrial Actions: Between ASUU and Government Is It an Issue of Rightness? *Journal of Education and Practice,* 5(6), 7–17.

Allen, L. (2019). *Academic Freedom in the United Kingdom.* AAUP Foundation. https://www.aaup.org/article/academic-freedom-united-kingdom#. YyaiInbMLIU

Arowosegbe, J. O. (2023). African Universities and the Challenge of Postcolonial Development. *Africa, 93,* 591–614. https://doi.org/10.1017/S0001972023000785

Atoi, E. N. (2022). Boko Haram Religious Fundamentalism and Western Education in North-East Nigeria. *KIU Interdisciplinary Journal of Humanities and Social Sciences, 3*(3), 14–28.

BBC News Pidgin. (2022, February 22). UTAG Strike update: Ghana University Lecturers Suspend Action. https://www.bbc.com/pidgin/tori-60474818

Bello, M. F., and Isha, M. K. (2016). Collective Bargaining in Nigeria: ASUU and Federal Government Face-off in Perspective. *Sahel Analyst: Journal of Management Sciences, 14*(1), 65–78.

Blue Print. (2022, February 6). *Again, Nigerian Universities Set to Shut Down as ASUU Threatens Showdown, Buhari, Religious Leaders Beg.* Blue Print. https://www.blueprint.ng/again-nigerian-universities-set-to-shut-down-as-asuu-threatens-showdown-buhari-religious-leaders-beg/

Brown, D. K., & Harlow, S. (2019). Protests, Media Coverage, and a Hierarchy of Social Struggle. *The International Journal of Press/Politics, 24*(4), 508–530. https://journals.sagepub.com/doi/full/10.1177/1940161219853517

Bubtana, A. R. (2006). Problems and Challenges in Arab and African Countries. In A. R. Bubtana (Ed.), *Academic Freedom Conference 'Problems and Challenges in Arab and African Countries'* (pp. 6–10). United Nations Educational, Scientific and Cultural Organization.

Duze, C. O. (2011). Falling Standards of Education in Nigeria: An Empirical Evidence in Delta State of Nigeria. *LWATI: A Journal of Contemporary Research, 8*(3), 1–12.

Eme, O. I., and Ike, F. O. (2017). Education Financing in Nigeria: A Comparative Analyses of Pre-SAP and Post-SAP Epochs. *South East Political Science Review, 1*(1), 296–312.

Eneji, C. O., Onnoghen, N. U., Agiande, D. U., and Okon, G. M. (2019). Lecturer's Industrial Actions and Environmental Education Student's Academic Performance in the University of Calabar, Nigeria. *Civil and Environmental Research, 11*(7), 45–55.

Ero, A. (2022, April 22). *ASUU Knocks Okowa over Position on Strike, Alleged Proliferation of State Universities.* TELL. https://tell.ng/asuu-knocks-okowa-over-position-on-strike-alleged-proliferation-of-state-varsities/

European University Association. (2022). *Funding.* https://eua.eu/issues/18:funding.html

Ezeigbo, O. (2021, November 16). *ASUU Issues Fresh Strike Threat, Gives FG 3-week Ultimatum.* ThisDay. https://www.thisdaylive.com/index.php/2021/11/16/asuu-issues-fresh-strike-threat-gives-fg-3-week-ultimatum

Fairclough, N. (1989). *Language and Power.* Addison Wesley Longman.

Ghosh, P. (2017, February 24). *Minister to Enshrine Protection for Research Independence.* BBC News. https://www.bbc.com/news/science-environment-39078281

Giame, B. P. S., Awhefeada, U. V., and Edu, O. K. (2020). An Overview of the Right to Strike in Nigeria and Some Selected Jurisdictions. *Beijing Law Review, 11*, 464–488. https://doi.org/10.4236/blr.2020.112029

Hall, S. (1997). The Spectacle of the 'Other'. In S. Hall (Ed.), *Representation: Cultural Representation and Signifying Practices* (pp. 226–285). Sage.

He, Y., Pei, Y., Ran, B. Kang, J., and Song, Y. (2020). Analysis on the Higher Education Sustainability in China Based on the Comparison between Universities in China and America. *Sustainability, 12*(12), 1–19. https://doi.org/10.3390/su12020573

Ibrahim, Z. B. (2021, September 30). *TETFUND, ASUU and University Interventions.* Premium Times. https://www.premiumtimesng.com/opinion/487474-tetfund-asuu-and-university-interventions-by-zubaida-baba-ibrahim.html

Iyekekpolo, W. O. (2016). Boko Haram: understanding the context. *Third World Quarterly, 37*(12), 2211–2228. http://dx.doi.org/10.1080/01436597.2016.1177453

Lawal, I., Olayinka, C., and Umeh, K. (2021, August 1). *ASUU, FG Bicker over Unfulfilled Agreement.* The Guardian. https://guardian.ng/news/asuu-fg-bicker-over-unfulfilled-agreement/

Lung, M., Moldovan, I., and Alexandra, N. L. (2012). Financing Higher Education in Europe: Issues and Challenges. *Procedia - Social and Behavioral Sciences*, *51*, 938–942. https://doi.org/10.1016/j.sbspro.2012.08.266

Machin, D., and Mayr, A. (2012). *How to Do Critical Discourse Analysis: A Multimodal Introduction*. Sage.

Mojalefa, M. L. (2021). Factors Contributing to Industrial Conflicts within Higher Education Institutions in Lesotho: A Case of the National University of Lesotho. *Business and Economic Research*, *11*(2). https://doi.org/10.5296/ber.v11i2.18550

NUC [National Universities Commission]. (n.d). *ASUU Suspends Eight Months Strike*. https://www.nuc.edu.ng/asuu-suspends-eight-months-strike/

Vanguard. (2022, May 16). *Nwajiuba Apologises for ASUU Strike*. Vanguard. https://www.vanguardngr.com/2022/05/nwajiuba-apologises-for-asuu-strike/

Odey, C. O., Okute, A. L., and Adams, A. P. (2020). Industrial Conflict and University Students' Attitude towards Academic Activities: A Study of the University of Calabar. *European Journal of Social Sciences*, *60*(1), 5–17.

Odiagbe, S. A. (2012). *Industrial Conflict in Nigerian Universities: A Case Study of the Disputes between the Academic Staff Union of Universities (ASUU) and the Federal Government of Nigeria (FGN)* [Doctoral thesis, The University of Glasgow]. Glasgow Theses Service. https://theses.gla.ac.uk/id/eprint/3333

Ogwo, C. (2022, May 8). *ASUU Strike: Group Urges Lecturers to Be Flexible in Negotiation*. Business Day. https://businessday.ng/news/article/asuu-strike-group-urges-lecturers-to-be-flexible-in-negotiation/

Ojukwu, E. (2022, May 4). *Incessant ASUU Strike—The Devastating Effects on Nigeria*. TEKEDIA. https://www.tekedia.com/incessant-asuu-strike-the-devastating-effects-on-nigeria/

Olaitan, K. (2021, September 10). *ASUU to Nigerians: Hold Buhari Responsible for another Academic Crisis*. ThisDay. https://www.thisdaylive.com/index.php/2021/09/10/asuu-to-nigerians-hold-buhari-responsible-for-another-academic-crisis/

Olayinka, C. (2022, April 27). *Why I'm Not Responsible for ASUU Strike, by Ngige*. The Guardian. https://guardian.ng/news/why-im-not-responsible-for-asuu-strike-by-ngige/

Palfreyman, D. (2007). Is Academic Freedom under Threat in UK and US Higher Education? *Education and the Law*, *19*(1), 19–40. https://doi.org/10.1080/09539960701231207

Peters, M. A. (2014). 'Western Education Is Sinful': Boko Haram and the Abduction of Chibok Schoolgirls. *Policy Futures in Education*, *12*(2), 186–190. http://dx.doi.org/10.2304/pfie.2014.12.2.186

Premium Times. (2022, April 12). *ASUU Strike: Ngige Criticizes Education Ministry, Suggests Alternative to Strike*. Premium Times. https://www.premiumtimesng.com/news/top-news/523298-asuu-strike-ngige-criticizes-education-ministry-suggests-alternative-to-strike.html

Salami, U. (2024, August 27). *ASUU Protests Lecturers' Dismissal, Brand VC 'Enemy'*. The Punch. https://punchng.com/asuu-protests-lasu-lecturers-dismissal-brand-vc-enemy/

Salau, S., Worlu, R., Osibanjo, A., Adoniji, A., Falola, H. Olokundun, M. Ibidunni, S., Atolagbe, T., Dirisu, J., and Oguoyungbo, O. (2020). The Impact of Workplace Environments on Retention Outcomes of Public Universities in Southern Nigeria. *Sage Open*, 1–16. https://doi.org/10.1177/2158244020930767

Salihu, M. J. (2019). Agencies Governing the University Education System in Nigeria: An Examination of their Administrative Powers, Conflict and Advocacies. *Journal of Science Technology and Education*, 7(4), 231–239.

Staton, B. (2022, September 12). *College Lecturers in England Call 10 Days of Strike Action over Pay*. Financial Times. https://www.ft.com/content/b637db5b-10e0-4877-9a06-d473f8c1ba3f

The Guardian. (2022, March 1). *ASUU Strike: Ngige Updates Buhari, says FG Paid N92bn to the ASUU*. The Guardian. https://guardian.ng/news/asuu-strike-ngige-updates-buhari-says-fg-paid-n92bn-to-the ASUU/

The Punch. (2019, November 3). *ASUU Can't Be Exempted from the IPPIS*. The Punch. https://punchng.com/asuu-cant-be-exempted-from-the-ippis/

ThisDay. (2022, February 16). *ASUU and the Endless Strikes*. ThisDay. https://www.thisdaylive.com/index.php/2022/02/16/asuu-and-the-endless-strikes/

Ugar, A. A. (2018). ASUU Strike: The Federal Government and Nigerian Educational System. *International Journal of Education and Research*, 6(5), 19–32.

Ugbo, G. O. (2020). Peace Journalism and Conflict Reporting. In C. S. Okunna (Ed.), *Communication and Media Studies: Multiple Perspectives* (pp. 61–83). New Generation Books.

Valente, S., Lourenço, A. A., and Z. Németh (2020). School Conflicts: Causes and Management Strategies in Classroom Relationships. *IntechOpen*, 1–16. http://dx.doi.org/10.5772/intechopen.95395

Waswa, F., and Katana, G. (2008). Academic Staff Perspectives on Operating beyond Industrial Actions for Sustainable Quality Assurance in Public Universities in Kenya. *International Journal of Environment, Workplace and Employment*, 4(1), 45–58.

Wojuade, J. I. (2019). Lecturer' and Students' Perceptions of Impacts of Incessant Strike Action on Academic Performance of Social Studies

Students in Colleges of Education in South West Nigeria. *International Journal of Advanced Academic Research | Arts, Humanities and Education*, 5(8).

Ya'u, Y. Z. (2006). Ever Changing Contest: The Struggle for Academic Freedom and its Repercussion in Nigeria, 1985–2005. In A. R. Bubtana (Ed.), *Academic Freedom Conference 'Problems and Challenges in Arab and African Countries'* (pp. 43–50). United Nations Educational, Scientific and Cultural Organization.

10. The Conflict of the Faculties, Again

Richard Hudson-Miles

Introduction

In this chapter, textual fragments and composite images constitute 'scenes' of university history. They narrate histories of conflict. Perhaps, conflictual histories. They are broadly chronological but are not intended to be teleological. Rather, what follows is a non-linear scenography of the Western university. I prefer 'scene' to analysis, exegesis, exposition, interpretation, and such terms associated with theoreticist critique. My approach is inspired by Jacques Rancière's in his book *Aisthesis* (2013, p. ix). A scene suggests something theatrical, constructed, a stage for encounter. A scene is also a space which foregrounds sensible knowledge. Perhaps, it allows us to recognise the sensible fabric which precedes and delimits intelligible knowledge. Classical philosophy has always been sceptical about the merits of artistic knowledge. In response, Rancière (2003, pp. 45–47) weaponised the Platonic portmanteau 'theatrocracy' (Laws, III, p. 701; 1975, p. 154) to describe the aesthetic effects of political subjectification. In particular, the effects of a subject making itself visible within a discourse which would otherwise render them invisible. My scenography therefore relates to both the politics of aesthetics and the aesthetics of politics (Rancière, 2004). It is a contribution towards deconstructing the logocentric privilege afforded to textual expression above oral or visual, especially within academic writing.

In the chapter, I counter the words spoken on conflict and the university by Derrida (2004), Kant (1979 [1798]) and others, with images of the university invented through visual art. Some of the source images romantically depict a university devoid of conflict. Occasionally,

 https://doi.org/10.11647/OBP.0427.10

they present trivialised forms of university conflict, as if to disguise the always already conflictual character of the university that Kant first identified. At other times, the gaze of these images of the university drifts away from its lofty ideas and celebrated figures, focusing instead upon the sensory effects of prosaic university life. I want to suggest, following Readings (1996), that the contemporary university exists in a state of psychic conflict with its repressed foundational ideals. As an implicit form of base materialism (Bataille, 1985, pp. 20–24), the following scenography demonstrates how such lofty foundational ideals are constantly reworked, even sullied, by the material, sensory and political experience of the university, on a day-to-day basis. Finally, I wish to show that the discursive and aesthetic conditions which make the university recognisable as such are also those which render its conflicts inaudible or invisible.

This scenography also contributes to a tradition of critique. Specifically, concerning the trajectory of the neoliberal university (Brown, 2015; Raunig, 2013; Edu-Factory Collective, 2011; Readings, 1996). To use Marxian terminology, one might describe these as conflict theories. Against corporate mission statements, value for money rhetoric and interpellative university branding, voices of university 'dissensus' (Rancière, 2010) have grown exponentially during the last decade. The title 'university' is derived from the Latin *universitas*, meaning the universe, the whole, the totality or the world. Anyone who has worked in a contemporary university knows that its titular universality is a very bad joke. From my perspective, the university seems narrow and unrepresentational. Rancière's (1995, p. 8) work has taught me that repressive politics always coalesces around the 'rational deployment of the One', whereas emancipatory politics enacts a disidentification, slowly, as the political *universitas* forms outside the ivory tower, or within its undercommons (Harney and Moten 2013). Increasingly, voices of opposition to free market university financialisation (McGettigan, 2013) are coalescing with pluriversal voices of difference (de Sousa Santos, 2018) as a counter-hegemonic multitude (Hardt and Negri, 2005). Within this movement, each articulation of 'the part of those who have no part' (Rancière 1999, pp. 29–30) is a red brick removed from the consensus reality of the neoliberal university. To borrow the words of

Gordon White, the university is an eight-hundred-year project which feels like it is winding down.

I have been asked to define a position; to specify my terms of engagement, to delineate belligerents, weapons, tactics. Furthermore, to make my voice audible. Hesitantly, I write about conflict, from a position of conflict. During this last decade, I have repeatedly argued (Hudson-Miles, 2022, 2021; Hudson-Miles and Broadey, 2019; Miles, 2016b) that the arts and humanities simply do not fit within the HE sector's instrumental logic of economisation (Brown, 2015). With the artistic collective @.ac [www.attackdotorg.com], I have attempted to facilitate ways that the art school can 'write back' to such economisation. By working with the UK alternative art school movement, I have relearned the art school's civic and political function (Hudson-Miles, Goodman and Jones, 2021; Miles, 2016a). If pushed, I would say that I declare, like Herbert Read, for anarchy. Specifically, the an-arkhé of the popular university. I declare, then, for Mondragon, for The School of the Damned, for the Copenhagen Free University, for the Other MA, for the Anti-University London, for the Global Autonomous University, the Lincoln Social Sciences Centre, for the Free Black University. I also declare for the abolition of student debt. My position is forged at the intersection of these struggles, through years of precarious hourly-paid contracts, through redundancy letters, through the 'vampire castle' (Fisher, 2018, pp. 737–746). Through an eight-year struggle to complete a PhD whilst teaching a strictly regimented 37.5 hour working week in a further education (FE) college. Through the oxymoronic identity of the working-class academic. Through a 175-mile commute to work. Through fifteen years of pay suppression. Through unmanageable workloads, rampant managerialism and the infiltration of academic work into everyday life.

I am writing this in late October, watching the autumnal rain bounce off expanding puddles on the ground. The leaves on the oak trees outside have long since turned golden, then russet and now fall to rot. The rain, momentarily, makes me think of Althusser writing his last words in the hospital overlooking the cemetery at Père Lachaise. Althusser used the metaphor of a single raindrop, veering off course, to describe a new philosophy of aleatory materialism. This is the materialism of the encounter, the swerve, the throw of the dice, the chain reaction which sets off a string of unpredictable events. For this unfinished work (Althusser, 2006, pp. 163–207), Althusser turned to Ancient Greek atomism, a comprehensive materialist philosophy which denied teleological or divine theories of historical progress. In any given age, there are always rival epistemic regimes competing for the right to interpret and validate sensible information. In pagan Britain, way before Enlightenment rationality stamped its name over the university, this time was called *Samhuinn*. This was the end of the pagan year, the season of death and finality, the time of no time. Here, the worlds of the living and the dead became interconnected. Rituals were enacted and spiritual forces invoked. During Samhuinn, the glow of reason ceded to darkness and irrationality. This was a time for licentiousness, and for abandoning public personas. In what Bakhtin would later call the carnivalesque (1984 [1965]), men dressed as women, and women as men. Farm gates were unlocked and animals freed (Carr-Gomm, 1994, p. 70). As part of this, Samhuinn represented the renewed hope for change. In contemporary academia, this is the period when the university machinery kicks back into gear. The time of dreams and debts, when the loans which shackle students to the neoliberal system are issued and cashed. Over the last years, the University and College Union (UCU) have launched repeated industrial action in protest over low pay and untenable working conditions. Echoing the chthonic forces summoned during Samhuinn, their most recent campaign was called UCU Rising (UCU 2023). The composite images in the following scenography are partially composed of mobile phone reportage from previous UCU strikes. This conflict photography encounters the pictorialist exorcism of conflict and the university voices which speak, incessantly, of conflict. For my part, I offer these encounters as dialectal images. That is, moments 'wherein what has been comes together in a flash with the now to form a constellation' (Benjamin 1999, p. 462; n2a, p. 3)—encounters, images, memories, which can be retrieved as weapons in service of a struggle renewed.

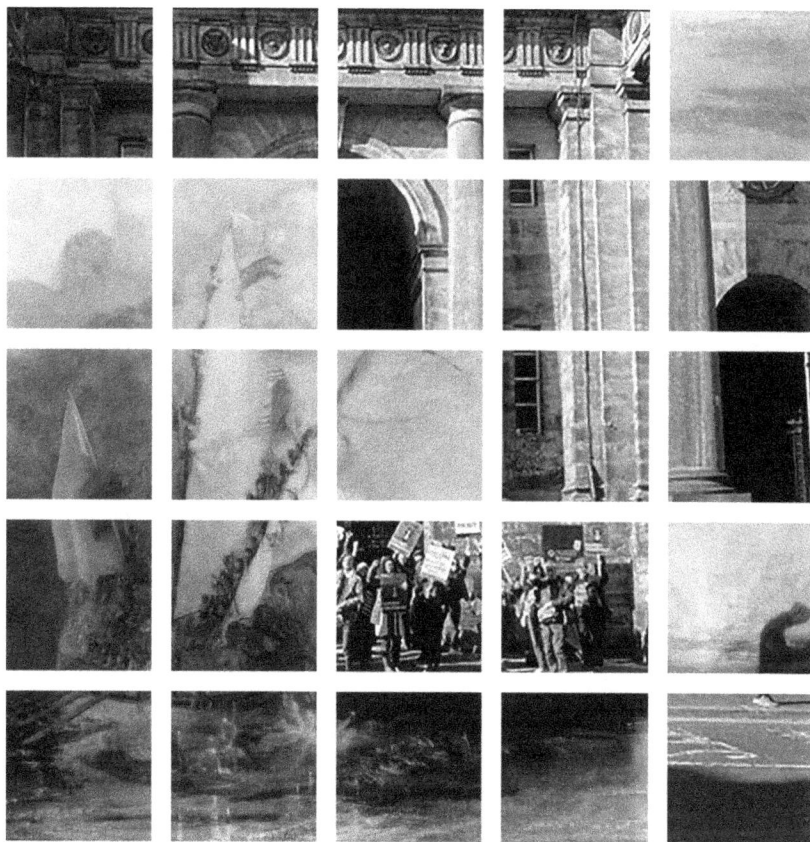

Fig. 10.1 After Samuel Bough (1853), *Snowballing Outside Edinburgh University*. Scene created by the author from images sourced, with permission, from UCU members and the digital archives of Yale's Paul Mellon Centre for British Art', https://photoarchive.paul-mellon-centre.ac.uk/collections

1. Conflict

Composed of texts on the university and the teaching of the humanities written between 1975 and 1990, Derrida's *Du droit à la philosophie* [The Right to Philosophy] (1990) was published in English in two volumes, *Who's Afraid of Philosophy?* (2002) and *Eyes of the University* (2004). These texts are Derrida's most important contributions to the philosophy of education. The second volume includes an influential essay called 'Mochlos, or the Conflict of the Faculties' (2004, pp. 83–113). This concerns the Enlightenment ideals of the university, and the persistent internal and external conflicts which undermine those ideals. From a close reading of Kant's *The Conflict of the Faculties* (1979 [1798]), Derrida builds a discourse on the responsibility of the university in the age of its contemporary techno-political, transnational and bureaucratic institutionalisation. One of his aims, in returning to Kant, is to uncover an original conflict within the foundational university ideal which could be mobilised as a hauntology of the conflicted university of the present.

The Conflict of the Faculties was one of Kant's last published works. It was considered marginal before Derrida's critical resurrection. It analysed the structural dynamic of the early modern Prussian university, which was composed of four interrelated faculties. Of these, Medicine, Theology and Law were understood as 'higher' faculties, given that they directly equipped students with the skills necessary to enter the major graduate professions. The remaining faculty of Philosophy was understood as 'lower'. This was because it was presumed to merely service the other faculties. Kant reverses this understanding, arguing that philosophy was the only autonomous discipline, and therefore the true higher faculty—indeed, that philosophy is the essential and irreducible essence of the university. For Kant (1979 [1798], pp. 33–43), the three higher faculties are heteronomous, meaning that they ultimately answer to some external authority, law or standard. The faculty of Theology, for example, is delimited by, and reproduces, the doctrines of the church. Similarly, the faculty of Law teaches the skills of legal interpretation, logical argument and jurisprudence. However, they still operate within the constraints of state legislation produced by 'the precepts of the legislative power' (p. 39). Furthermore, by proceeding by an oath sworn on a Holy Book, all legislative processes submit to the authority of God and religion. Kant concedes that the medical faculty is freer than the first two. Rather than external laws, medicine is regulated by professional bodies. This reflects the professional autonomy of a self-determining discipline whose practices are so specialist that the state cannot dictate its limits. In the final analysis, however, medical practices are still subject to the laws of the state and what Kant calls the 'medical police'.

For Kant, the faculty of Philosophy is autonomous, meaning that it does not answer to the directives of an external authority. Instead, it inculcates the skills of reason, which allow its practitioners to independently determine truth from falsehood, or right from wrong. Philosophy therefore stands as the critical interlocutor of the supposedly higher university faculties. It pushes them towards disciplinary self-reflexivity whilst mitigating against instrumentalism. For Kant, Philosophy was the true higher faculty of the university. Kant's text therefore doubles as a foundational manifesto for the modern university of reason. As Derrida recognises, Kant's essay also implies that this university is essentially founded within conflict. This conflict is interfaculty, but also fought over divergent interpretations of the ends of education itself. Crudely put, this is a conflict between education as vocational training and education for education's sake.

Kant's reading of the university as an essentially rational institution haunts the contemporary university. Instead of reason, Readings (1996, p. 14) argues that our neoliberal universities are driven by the empty 'techno-bureaucratic notion of excellence'. 'Excellence', which is also the watchword of the modern service industries, has subsumed all preceding paradigms of the university. For Readings (1996, p. 59), this most influential historical model of the university was proposed by the Prussian minister and philosopher Wilhelm von Humboldt (1767–1835). The Humboldtian model emphasised the cultural function of university education. Politically, it was liberal-humanist. Pedagogically, it valorised the synthesis of research and teaching. This philosophy found its physical manifestation in the University of Berlin, 1810, arguably the first modern university. The philosophical 'founding fathers' of this university were the German Idealist philosophers Schelling (1803), Fichte (1794; 1807), Schleiermacher (1808) and Humboldt himself. Collectively, these thinkers figure the university's mission as the development of *bildung*, or national character building. Here, the university operates in a quasi-autonomous relationship with the state. Instead of Kant's dynamic conflict, we have a relationship of benevolent reciprocity. The state authorises the university, which in turn realises national consciousness and cultural unity. The university professor is the living embodiment of this ideal. Intrinsic to this are the concepts of *Lehrfreiheit* and *Lernfreiheit*. In turn, the freedom to teach and the freedom to learn, outside of state interference. These concepts understand education as the disinterested pursuit of truth, achieved through a perfect synthesis of research and teaching. The contemporary concept of 'academic freedom', protected in a very limited sense in legislation, is a diluted version of these Humboldtian ideals.

Ultimately, as Derrida (2004, p. 98, 103) recognises, Kant's model of the university is its own rhetorical front. It depends on the delineation of various university borders, which also serve as battle lines. Firstly, the frontlines between the lower and higher faculties. Secondly, between the university inside and outside. In the name of academic freedom, Kant wished to stage an 'unavoidable conflict' between the 'scholars in the university and businessmen of learning or instruments of government power' (2004, p. 103). Romantic art supplements the frontlines between autonomous rationality and heteronomous commerciality with a third term: sensibility.

Take the example of the nineteenth-century painting of Edinburgh University by Samuel Bough, incorporated within the dialectical image above (Fig. 10.1). A self-taught artist, Bough began his career as a theatrical scene painter. Maintaining a painting practice through this income, he rose to prominence, becoming one of the most influential Scottish landscape painters and eventually being accepted by the Royal Scottish Academy. Given his outsider status, it is perhaps unsurprising that Bough's painting relegates Edinburgh University, high temple of the 'Athens of the North', to the backdrop to a scene of juvenile reverie. Bough's gaze rests on footsteps in the snow, frosted lintels, the hubbub and commixture of the crowd. 'Snowballing Outside Edinburgh

University' was painted at the tail end of the Romantic era, and two years after the Great Exhibition of 1851, arguably the high point of Victorian cultural imperialism. It bears the hallmarks of a reckoning between rival regimes of meaning. Firstly, the classical age of reason, order and idealisation, embodied in the architecture of the University. Secondly, the age of industry, mercantile capitalism and the imperial nation-state, all of which would transfigure the ideal of the university in the centuries to come. Finally, the 'cult of sensibility' which became popular in mid-eighteenth-century Britain. This emphasised emotion and imagination. Here, the capacity to feel and empathise become valued over the capacity to rationalise. Though the second paradigm of marketisation has arguably become preeminent, the others still haunt the university, perhaps as forgotten dreams.

Unfortunately, no ideological or rhetorical university battle line can hold in the face of absolutist state power. Following the publication of *Religion within the Limits of Mere Reason* (1793), Kant was censured by King Frederick William II (1744–1797) for daring to 'distort and disparage many of the cardinal and basic teachings of the Holy Scriptures and of Christianity'. Kant was accused of acting against his 'paternal purpose' and 'duty as a teacher of youth' (1979 [1798], p. 11), and threatened with severe punishment if this irresponsible behaviour continued. As Readings (1996, pp. 59–60) suggests, ultimately the Kantian university of reason is a fiction, which collapses when institutionalised. This is not to suggest that the fiction of the university of reason, nor the university of culture, nor the university of sensibility, should be hastily abandoned as a historical oddity. Especially, when questions of university responsibility, or the ends of university education, are raised.

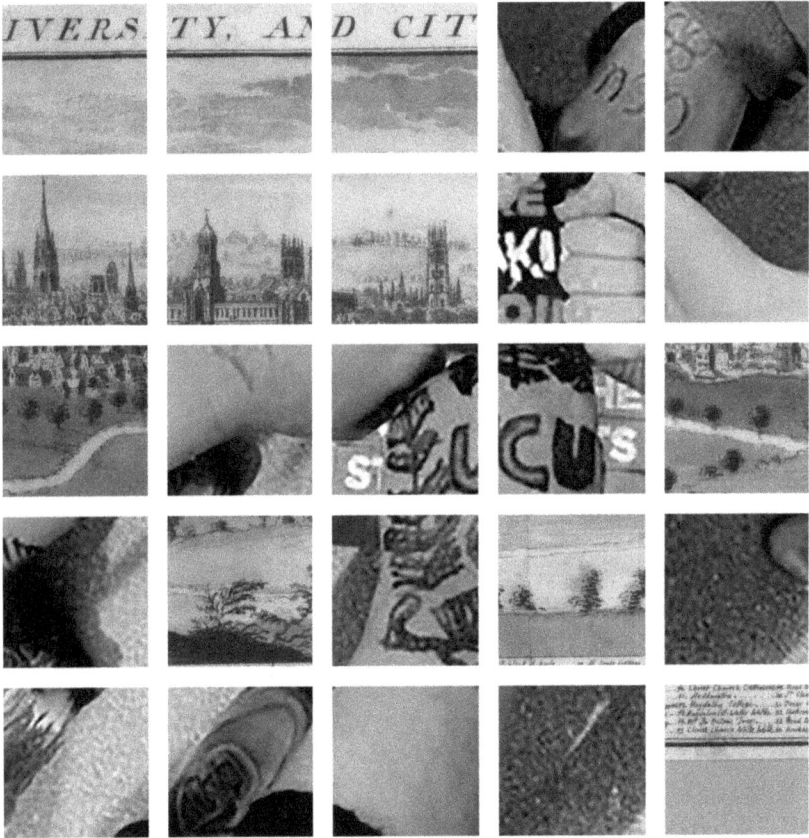

Fig. 10.2 After Nathaniel Buck (1731), *The South West Prospect of the University and City of Oxford*. Scene created by the author from images sourced, with permission, from UCU members and the digital archives of Yale's Paul Mellon Centre for British Art', https://photoarchive.paul-mellon-centre.ac.uk/collections

2. Two Worlds

The battle lines of the university were made apparent in quite a different way during the University of Paris strike of 1229. Active from 1150, and officially recognised by the French monarchy in 1200 and the Catholic church in 1215, this was one of the Western world's earliest universities. Alongside the University of Bologna, founded 1088, the University of Paris was the model replicated by a wave of mediaeval universities established in Europe throughout the thirteenth century. Like Kant's eighteenth-century university at Königsberg, the University of Paris was composed of three higher faculties of Medicine, Theology and Law, and a lower faculty of the Arts. The conflict of 1229, however, did not result from the Kantian frontlines between reason and instrumentalism. Instead, the confrontation erupted from a spatial, cultural and ideological conflict commonly referred to as 'town and gown'.

This phrase is ubiquitous today, frequently used within media reports of anti-social student behaviour. The ancient university town of Cambridge, UK, has a gastropub named after this cultural division. The phenomenon has also been studied repeatedly in the social sciences. Writing in the *American Journal of Sociology* in 1963, Delbert C. Miller analysed the power relations in an American university town, which he referred to pseudonymously as 'Cerebrille'. He noticed a distinct separation between the values of the university and local communities. For him, Cerebrille was a town composed of 'two worlds'. On the one hand, locals who were concerned with community and personal relationships. On the other, academic cosmopolitans who were largely indifferent to the local community and their issues. For these academics, Cerebrille was simply one provincial town amongst many. Deep down, the university workers knew that their personal career ambitions could be realised equally well elsewhere. Indeed, these cosmopolitan academics were more likely to channel their intellectual energies towards political and cultural centres like Washington. Though some university leaders involved themselves with community institutions, the experience of faculty staff would remain largely untapped. Miller sees this as a missed opportunity. He argues that the university and community have settled into a compromised social contract regulated largely by self-interest. For Miller, each of the two communities lives 'in peace with, and contributes to, the other, but neither is able to harness the total potentialities for the good life which is inherent in the people' (Miller, 1963, p. 443).

Miller's Aristotelian conclusion seems almost comically nostalgic today. Only the most ideological or romantic thinkers would argue that the neoliberal university is in any way concerned with promulgating 'the good life', communally nor individually (Aristotle, 1992, p. 187; Politics, 1278b, pp. 15–30). Media representations have done much to integrate the idea of a university with the specifics of a particular locale. The recent British TV show *Endeavour* (2012–2022), about the early life of a young Oxford graduate and fledgling detective, featured the quads of Christ Church so frequently that unfamiliar viewers would be forgiven for assuming that Oxford was nothing more than University Colleges and their estates. The cloisters and dining hall of Christ Church also served as the backdrop to the *Harry Potter* series of family fantasy movies. These simulations, implicitly or explicitly, now precede our experiences of these universities, whose sign-value therefore includes magic, derring-do, the roman-à-clef, alongside academic excellence. Commercial art, designed to appeal to aesthetes, tourists and local sensibilities alike, also has a part to play in this chain of signification. When the Buck Brothers, the eighteenth-century English engravers, created a prospect of Oxford (Fig. 14), they purposely integrated the city and university within a pictorialist landscape designed for mass appeal. Representations like these prefigure and reproduce one another, in a precession of simulacra (Baudrillard, 1994). The consequence is that the university is not just a metonym for its host city but the reality of that city itself. However, despite the work of national research councils, local government initiatives, widening participation departments and student unions, most would still recognise the persistence of the town versus gown dichotomy.

This phrase dates back to the early mediaeval universities, where university students and staff would be visibly demarcated from fellow citizens due to their dress and language. Unlike contemporary universities, they lacked the enclosed campuses which delineate the cultural border separating town and academy. Masters and students would live in city lodgings; teaching spaces would also be rented from the city. This gave the institution certain powers of leverage against their host cities. Students and staff were given privileged status which, if withdrawn, may result in the university decamping to another town. This distinction was performatively displayed through dress. Under the influence of the Catholic church, the students wore monastic robes and shaved their heads in tonsure. The area around the University of Paris was known as the Latin Quarter because of the preponderance of Latin, the language of academic citizens of the time, rather than vernacular French, in this area.

The riot of 1229 occurred during the Parisian mardi-gras celebrations, following Shrove Tuesday. This is still a significant day in the Parisian cultural calendar. Meaning 'Fat Tuesday', it is a Bacchanalian feast of drinking, music and excess. Like the carnivalesque described by Bakhtin, the Parisian mardi-gras was a space where the 'extreme corporative and caste divisions of the mediaeval social order' (Bakhtin, 1984, p. 10) were cast aside. Social hierarchy ceded to familiarity. Bodies intermingled and new identities adopted. Like all mediaeval carnivals, social authority figures were satirised. Bakhtin argues that masquerades allow people to adopt new personalities and social roles. For him, the carnivalesque is a political and aesthetic mode: 'people were, so to speak, reborn for new, purely human relations. These truly human relations were not only a fruit of imagination or abstract thought; they were experienced' (p. 10).

The mardi-gras of 1229 achieved the opposite effect to Bakhtin's carnivalesque. A student fracas erupted after a drunken dispute with a local tavern landlord. After being beaten and thrown out of the tavern, the students returned the following day to take revenge. The tavern was ransacked and a riot ensued, with various shops in the vicinity being damaged. Under the protection of the Catholic church, students were usually protected from the local authorities. However, following the pressure of an appeal to the Pope, the university granted permission to punish the guilty students. Immediately, a gang of armed city guardsmen rounded up the first students they could find, killing several of them.

The university responded by going on strike. Classes were cancelled for two years and students and staff dispersed to other cities. This had a measurable effect on the local area, given that many local businesses relied on university rental incomes. Gorochov (2018) has called this 'the great dispersion'. Today, this might be called a 'brain drain'. Some scholars quit teaching altogether, many moved cities to revitalise the teaching in other European universities. Henry III persuaded some to come to Oxford, which had stagnated since its own dispersion in 1208. Here, scholars fled to Cambridge to form a rival university after persecution from townsfolk.

The two-year Paris university strike was also notable for the role of what contemporary socialists call scab labour. This is a pejorative for workers who cross picket lines, therefore undermining industrial action. According to Demkovich (2013), the teaching roles were filled in part by itinerant Dominican monks, who otherwise 'lived off the alms they begged' (p. 440). Their role as strike-breakers caused wide resentment amongst the university faculty. The Dominicans were harassed and taunted. As well as having mud and waste thrown at them, students turned their name into the pun *Domini Canus*. To emphasise the joke, students would bark like dogs whenever one of the 'begging friars' walked past (p. 440–441).

Self-evidently, the history of the university is marked by incomprehension and antagonism with its local community. However, Miller's lament of missed opportunities needs to be tempered against the dismal reality of recent partnerships between local business and the university. For example, the partnership between Ohio State University and Ford Motors in 1994. Ford had a large car production plant in Ohio. Their ambition for this partnership was to implement the 'Total Quality Management' procedures, which had exponentially increased the productivity of workers at the production, into the university. As a quid pro quo, Ford would receive educated graduates who 'understand quality principles and concepts' and are 'ready to hit the ground running' (Ohio State University, 1994; cf. Readings, 1996, pp. 21–22). The TQM ideology, which has been adopted widely by universities since the 1990s (Meirovich and Romar, 2006), depends upon a singular and unchallenged problematic: that higher education is a business, and that students are its customers.

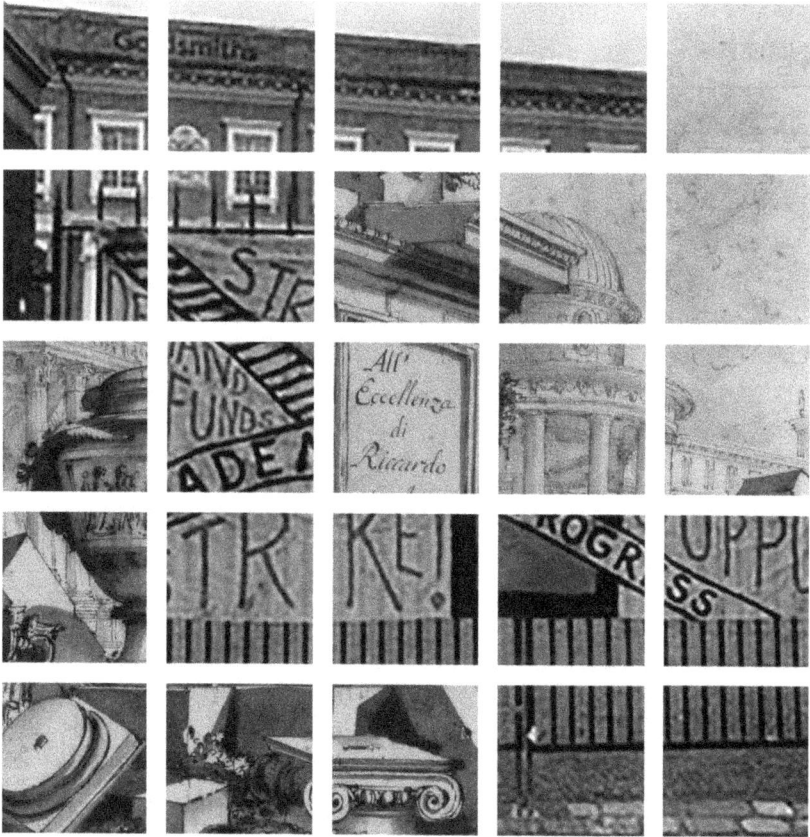

Fig. 10.3 After Filippo Juvarra (1729), *Album of Architectural Fantasies (Frontispiece), Dedicated to Lord Burlington*. Scene created by the author from images sourced, with permission, from UCU members and the digital archives of Yale's Paul Mellon Centre for British Art', https://photoarchive.paul-mellon-centre.ac.uk/collections

3. Excellence

Since its posthumous publication, Bill Readings' (1996) *The University in Ruins* has become a staple text within the field of Critical University Studies. Beyond suggesting the Kantian university of reason was always already a fiction, its central argument is that neoliberal capitalism has permanently destroyed all foundational ideals of the university.

As stated, for Readings, the 'University of Reason' has been subsumed by the 'University of Excellence'. This means that the university, which was formerly the sight of autonomous critical thinking, and the site where national culture was thought through and developed, is now simply one of many sites for the reproduction of corporate logic. The term 'excellence' is directly appropriated from the self-assessments and mission statements of corporate firms. Fundamentally, 'excellence' is the language of 'Total Quality Management' transposed to education. Within the university, 'excellence' serves a bureaucratic function within standardised assessments, customer satisfaction surveys and institutional quality audits. However, the term has become so ubiquitous it has achieved a form of transcendence, operating as the guiding principle of the university, in lieu of the aforementioned lost ideals. This is undoubtedly a reflection upon this increased influence of internal university Quality departments, since the first experiments in university TQM and managerialism in the 1990s. However, it is also a reflection of the financialisation, marketisation and commodification of higher education (McGettigan, 2013) which has rebranded universities as service providers and students as customers.

This is part of a broader neoliberal assault on the socius which Wendy Brown (2015) has simply called 'economisation'. For Brown (2015, p. 17) 'neoliberal reason [...] is converting the distinctly political character, meaning and operation of democracy's constituent elements into economic ones'. For Brown, one of the most important 'constituent elements' of democracy is education. For her, the economisation of education is also its neutralisation and depoliticisation. The term excellence is a superlative. Its intrinsic hyperbole protects it from criticism. Anyone who criticises the aspiration of excellence is de facto rendered a cynic or reactionary. This disguises the limitations of 'excellence' as an objective criterion. Excellence is an empty abstraction, malleable to the point where it becomes almost meaningless. If everything can be understood as excellent, from the service in fast food restaurants, to the management structure of corporations, to the calibre of undergraduate essays, then nothing can. Describing the publicity materials of modern American universities, Readings (1996, p. 12) observes 'they all claim that theirs is a unique educational institution. On the other hand, they all go on to describe this uniqueness in exactly the same way'.

That said, it would be a mistake to dismiss 'excellence' as empty corporate rhetoric. As an institutional principle, it is a mechanism of integration and standardisation (Readings, 1996, p. 29). The global university of today is standardised to the effect that one university curricula is roughly transferable to another. Legislation such as the Bologna Process (1999) was written to achieve precisely this integration within the European Union. The global standardisation of university education disguises the fact that it is ultimately a Western university model which is being expanded aggressively across global markets, as a new form of cultural imperialism. The globalisation of standardised Western business models, also globalises their malpractices and deleterious social effects. Ritzer (2009 [1993]) has referred to this as McDonaldisation, where society increasingly operates according to the principles of a fast-food restaurant. Here, every sector of Western culture becomes standardised and franchised, from food, to entertainment, to sport, to education. To speak of the global university today is really to speak of the McDonaldised university. Just like most metropolitan cities have a McDonald's restaurant, soon they will also have a campus from a leading Western university. One obvious consequence of this is cultural assimilation, through which hegemonic Western culture encloses all of the cultural and epistemological spaces where its subalterns might otherwise flourish. As Readings argues, the Humboldtian ideal of a university of national culture makes no sense in the era of globalisation. Here, 'capitalism swallows up the idea of the nation-state' (1996, p. 44), and formerly national universities become indivisible from the transnational corporations (TNCs) which dominate the globe.

As a TNC in its own right (Readings, 1996, p. 45), the franchising of degrees to overseas private for-profit providers has now become a major activity for Western universities (Healey, 2013). An extension of these practices has been the scramble to open overseas campuses in emerging markets. In the UK, the employers' representational body Universities UK recently announced a new UK University Overseas Campuses Network to facilitate this pedagogical-imperialist expansion. It initially includes seventeen UK universities with twenty-seven campuses located in seventeen countries across the world (Universities UK, 2021). Notable UK examples include the University of Nottingham, Malaysia (est. 2000); University of Reading, Malaysia (est. 2011), University of Birmingham, Dubai (est. 2018) and De Montfort University, Dubai (est. 2021). Reading's Malaysia campus has been a financial disaster, resulting in multi-million-pound losses and staff redundancies. Commenting on this, the Shadow Education Secretary Angela Rayner said that both staff and students were 'victims of a free-market experiment in higher education' (McGettigan and Adams, 2019). Beyond its original university campus in Coventry, West Midlands, UK, the Coventry University Group now has premises in London and Scarborough, North Yorkshire, as well as offices in China, Nigeria, Kenya and Pakistan, and 'global hubs' in Kigali, Rwanda, and Brussels, Belgium and Dubai, UAE.

TNCs are indifferent to national borders, ever since the processes of off-shoring begun by Western economies in the 1970s (Metters and Verma, 2008). Many TNCs move headquarters from state to state chasing tax benefits, cheaper labour and lighter regulations. One consequence is widespread wage suppression and unemployment (Slaughter and Swagel, 1997). This has only accelerated following advances in technology and communication systems which have almost achieved the full integration of the global labour markets. Like 'excellence', mythologies of 'multiculturalism' disguise the processes of domination at work beneath globalisation. The normalisation of online learning in a post-pandemic era has allowed Western universities to recruit even more international students, and to teach those students with significantly lower overheads. Criticisms of hastily constructed 'emergency remote teaching' (Hodges et al., 2020) to serve these new markets might not be enough to preserve the traditional role of the lecturer within these contexts. In the age of online learning platforms, lecture capture software and metaverse integration, the final conflict of the faculties might be fought between the sovereignty of the university worker and the infinitely reproducible, globally scalable, digitally automated, online service model of the university.

Readings' symbol of the university in ruins is the Bard point columns at the State University of New York at Buffalo (1996, p. 169). These neoclassical Ionic columns were formerly located at the entrance to a bank in downtown Buffalo. Fragments were salvaged and reconstructed next to a lake on the SUNY campus. Deliberately, they have been arranged to resemble the ruined temples which young, aristocratic gentlemen would have encountered during their seventeenth- and eighteenth-century grand tours. This aesthetic sensibility is embodied in a book of 'architectural fantasies' (Fig. 10.3) sent by the architect Filippo Juvarra to Lord Burlington as a memento of his own grand tour of Italy. Over a third of these fictitious architectural landscapes depict ruins. The fascination with ruins, real and allegorical, was that for sensitive ears they spoke a lament for lost civilisation. For Ruggero (in Bianchi and Wolf, 2017, p. 258) 'a noble construction reflected the morality and freedom of the society that produced it'. A classical ruin, therefore, also represents morality, freedom and civil society in ruins. As a distant simulacrum of this, the Bard Point columns are mainly used today as a marketing image for the university or as the scenic background for student selfies.

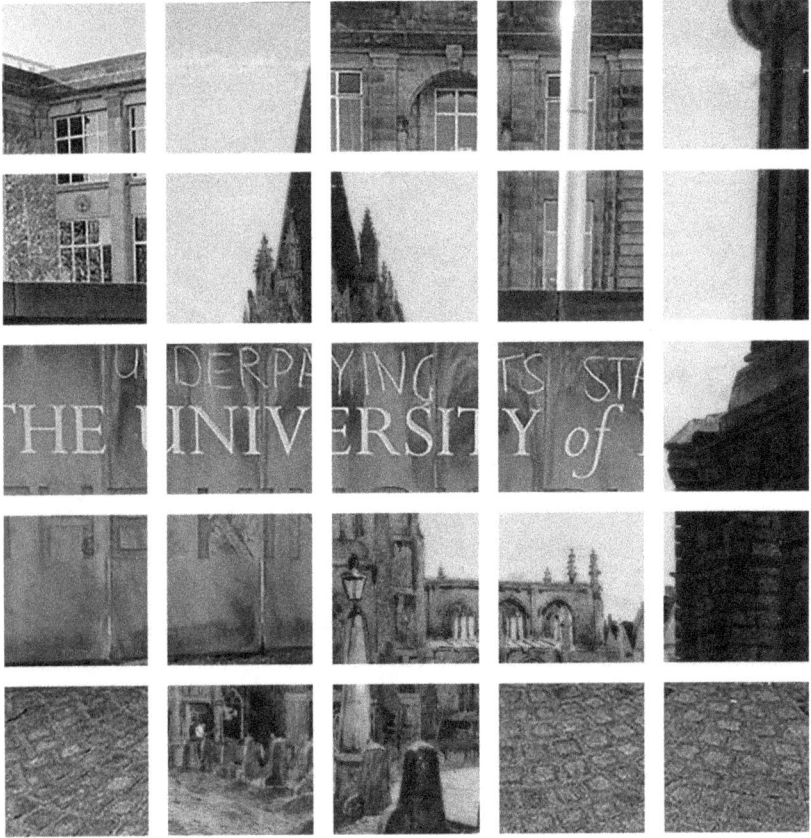

Fig. 10.4 After C. C. Hamilton (1810), *The University Church of St. Mary's Oxford from Beside the Radcliffe Camera*. Scene created by the author from images sourced, with permission, from UCU members and the digital archives of Yale's Paul Mellon Centre for British Art', https://photoarchive.paul-mellon-centre.ac.uk/ collections

4. Rebellion

Harvard University would eventually publish Readings' (1998) *The University in Ruins* on its own university press. Founded in 1636, it is the oldest higher education institution in the United States, and one of the most prestigious universities in the world. It was also the site of the first recorded university protest in North America. This is now referred to as The Great Butter Rebellion of 1766. Ostensibly, this was a protest about the quality of food in the university dining hall. One student leader, Asa Dunbar, climbed upon one of the dining hall tables and shouted 'Behold, our butter stinketh!—Give us, therefore, butter that stinketh not'. This became a protest slogan which echoed around campus in similar demonstrations throughout the next month. University authorities reacted heavy handedly, rounding up groups of students in order to coerce them to disclose the names of protest leaders. At one point, the university suspended almost half of the student body in an ultimately vain attempt to extract this information. Eventually, Harvard's Board of Overseers intervened and provided the canteen with better quality butter. However, the general quality of food remained poor. Buoyed by the success of their initial revolt, protests would resume in the following years. Firstly, the Bread and Butter Rebellion in 1805 and the Cabbage Rebellion in 1807. The latter was triggered specifically by the preponderance of maggots in the student's cabbage soup. These may seem like the inconsequential grievances of an entitled student bourgeoisie. Nevertheless, they represent an origin point for the ideological alignment of university students with anti-establishment struggle which would reach its apotheosis in the North American university protests of the mid-twentieth century.

The triviality of the 1766 Butter Rebellion's central object disguises a subtler connection to the revolutionary sentiment fomenting throughout America at this time. The symbolic epicentre of this was an ancient Elm tree at the heart of campus, which the students referred to as the 'Rebellion Elm'. It was given this name because it was the site where students gathered to protest. Preceding this, in the student imaginary, there was a powerful symbolic motivation for choosing this specific congregation point as mythic. This 'Rebellion Elm' is connected in a chain of signification back to another ancient Elm tree, known as the Liberty Tree of Boston. This tree stood outside the house of Andrew

Oliver, a Boston Merchant and government tax collector. The British parliament had recently imposed a hated Stamp Tax on the American colonies, which many people could not afford. According to Fischer (2015), the Stamp Tax was not just a form of revenue raising for the British imperialists. It was also a tax on liberty. Britain was concerned about the number of independent American lawyers, newspapers and educated citizens, all of which were fostering liberal values and critical opposition to British rule. The Stamp Tax introduced levies on newspaper advertisements, legal decrees, school diplomas or 'any grant of liberty, privilege, or franchise' (p. 21). It therefore explicitly sought to impede the spread of democracy.

Enraged by this oppressive tax, a large protest mob gathered by the tree outside Oliver's house. The crowd grew throughout the day, hanging an effigy of him from the tree's branches. Eventually, Oliver's house was ransacked and his wine cellar drunk dry. He promptly resigned the next day. Subsequently, the tree was adorned with a gold plaque which referred to it as the Tree of Liberty. The leaders of the protests became known as the Sons of Liberty, identifying themselves through specially manufactured medallions with an image of the Liberty Tree. Similar trees were symbolically adopted by other US cities in the years leading up to the American Revolution of 1775. In the War of Independence, the Liberty Tree became a symbol of resistance and could be seen on military flags and other insignia (Fischer, 2015, p. 30). Though apparently trivial, the Harvard protests symbolically aligned themselves with this growing revolutionary spirit. The student protest leaders self-identified as the Sons of Harvard. Their Rebellion Tree was their own metonym for a revolutionary generation.

In countries across the world, the university campus became a recurrent stage of anti-government protests. Each protest fed off and reanimated its antecedents like a dialectical image. The 1960s, 1968 in particular, witnessed an explosion of campus protests globally. Invariably, these were called by the student movement in the name of radical democracy. The Port Huron Statement (1962) was the manifesto of a radical American student movement called Students for a Democratic Society (SDS). They also revealed the hypocrisy of a country which mythologised Jefferson's (1776) Declaration of Independence, which enshrined 'that all men are created equal, that they are endowed by their Creator with certain unalienable Rights, that among these are Life,

Liberty and the pursuit of Happiness'. Against this national-cultural ideology, the SDS pointed to the racial inequality in America's southern states, and 'its economic and military investments in the Cold War status quo'. The American military-industrial complex received exponentially increased governmental funding during the Vietnam War (1955–1975). This was justified by anti-Communist ideologies and national myths of manifest destiny (Fleming, 1968, p. 141). Against US militarism and imperialism, the SDS called for a participatory democracy, where all decisions were made through public gatherings, in the manner of the very earliest democracies of Ancient Athens. They also called for the replacement of 'power rooted in possession, privilege or circumstance by power and uniqueness rooted in love, reflectiveness, reason, and creativity' (SDS, 1962). This confrontation between love, reason and creativity and military-industrial complex would reach its nadir at Kent State University, Ohio. Here, the SDS had an active and militant branch, and were instrumental in organising protests. On May 4, 1970, the Nixon government called in the National Guard to suppress an anti-Vietnam protest. In order to defend American democracy against agitators, Guardsmen fired on these protests which were also called in the name of democracy. Four students were shot dead, nine wounded.

More recently, England saw a wave of university demonstrations opposing the trebling of undergraduate tuition fees in 2010. Like the Liberty Tree of Harvard, the most symbolic university buildings became the key sites of strategic interest for protestors. On November 24, 2010, Oxford University's most picturesque building, the world-famous Radcliffe Camera (Fig. 10.4), was stormed by student-activists wearing animal masks. Subsequently, they occupied its inner rooms and unfurled banners from its windows saying 'Fuck Fees' (The Oxford Student, 2010). This was part of a coordinated 'day of action' by the National Union of Students, following a joint demonstration with UCU on November 10. Alongside a peaceful mass-demonstration of roughly 50,000 people, the central headquarters of the governing Conservative Party were ransacked. Despite this, and subsequent protests, nothing has been done to reverse the commodification of HE enacted by the Browne review of 2010. Despite concerns about the sustainability of the current HE funding structure, the subject has become so politically toxic that politicians have become reluctant to change the status quo.

Fig. 10.5 After Henry William Bunbury (1772), *The Hopes of the Family... An Admission at the University*. Scene created by the author from images sourced, with permission, from UCU members and the digital archives of Yale's Paul Mellon Centre for British Art', https://photoarchive.paul-mellon-centre.ac.uk/collections

5. Representation

Derrida begins the Mochlos essay with the following sentences: 'if we could say we (but have I not already said it?), we might perhaps ask ourselves: where are we? And who are we in the university where apparently we are? What do we represent? Whom do we represent?' (Derrida, 2004, p. 83). These apparently elliptical sentences open on to important questions of representation and university responsibility. Derrida's contention is that, if it is possible to think of a university responsibility, it must begin by posing the questions listed above; questions which increasingly make the universal character of the university creak under its ideological weight.

These questions are made with the most urgency under the banner of 'decolonise the university'. These were initiated by the anti-colonial 'Rhodes Must Fall' protests at Cape Town University, South Africa during March 2015. Here, Black students demanded the removal of a statue of the British colonialist and documented white supremacist Cecil Rhodes. The statue was forged in bronze by Marion Walgate, who was one of the first white female sculptors in South Africa. Unveiled in 1934, it depicts Rhodes in a pensive position, chin in hand, and gazing into the middle distance. In his hand, he clutches a scroll, presumably in reference to the scholarships established in his name. This is a laboured reference to Rodin's (1904) *The Thinker*, a sculpture which has now become the visual metonym for philosophy itself. Rhodes is seated on 'the bench which he caused to be erected for his own use looking over the Cape Flats towards the glorious panorama of the Hottentots Hollands mountains' (Mills, 2024). This composition invites comparisons to the Lincoln memorial made by Daniel Chester French in 1920. Such comparisons are both unfortunate and prescient. Unfortunate, because against Lincoln's steely determination, iron grip and foreboding solemnity, Walgate's Rhodes sculpture looks like a sentimental caricature. Prescient, because the statue of the 'Great Emancipator' Lincoln framed one of the defining moments of US political history. With Lincoln at his back, Martin Luther King Jr. delivered his legendary 'I have a dream' speech, following the March on Washington for Jobs and Freedom on August 28, 1963. The connection between the nineteenth-century emancipation of the slaves and the twentieth-century civil rights struggle was obvious to a national, and international, audience. Similarly, the connections between Rhodes' statue and the history of Apartheid in South Africa were obvious, to the point of affront. For the students of Cape Town University, Rhodes' statue was not just an homage to a white colonialist and racist but also an embodiment of the university's institutional racism. In a series of student protest actions throughout May, the Rhodes statue was covered in human excrement and wrapped in black bin bags (Schmahmann 2016), like a bathetic version of a Christo and Jean-Claude land work. On April 9, 2015, the sculpture was removed, symbolising the democratisation of a newly pluralist university and the first steps towards the fall of white privilege on campus.

The campaign spread to Oxford, where a statue commemorating Rhodes is displayed over the entrance to Oriel College. Rhodes used part of the wealth he personally expropriated from the colonies to establish a scholarship to allow underprivileged students from across the world to study at Oxford. However, as Rhodes believed that Africans were an inferior race, he stipulated that only white students should benefit from these posthumous awards (Keogh, 2016). Following numerous student protest actions, the college's governing body considered removing the statue. However, in May 2021 the college suspended removal plans, citing 'regulatory and financial challenges' (Mohdin, 2021). In June 2021, 150 scholars wrote a letter to Oriel stating that they would refuse to teach in the building adorned by Rhodes' statue (Peltier, 2021). Shortly after, in October 2021, Oriel installed a small white plaque, roughly two feet in length, at the base of Oriel's Corinthian columns. This plaque was installed during Black History Month (October), which originated in the USA as a consciousness-raising event, specifically intended to critically contextualise the tragic legacy of the African diaspora and Black resistance. The Oriel plaque includes only three short paragraphs, which acknowledged that 'some of [Rhodes'] activities led to great loss of life and attracted criticism in his day' but that his statue will not be removed 'following legal and regulatory advice'.

Following protests against similar public monuments, such as the statue of British slave trader Edward Colston on June 7, 2020 by Black Lives Matter protestors in Bristol, the UK government rushed through legislation to protect 'England's heritage' (UK Govt, 2021). These new legal protections insisted that the country's historic statues should be 'retained and explained', rather than defaced or erased from history. The Culture Secretary Oliver Dowden MP said that 'it is our duty to preserve our culture and heritage for future generations' (UK Govt, 2021). Speaking of the Rhodes plaque at Oriel, the Oxford Professor Dan Hicks described the plaque as an embarrassment and reveals the incoherence and futility of the ideology of 'retain and explain' (Clayton, 2021). For him, the plaque simply represents an additional memorial to Rhodes at the college.

Commenting on the contrived, earnest character of election campaign photography, Roland Barthes observed that such images presuppose 'a kind of complicity: a photograph is a mirror, what we are asked to read is the familiar, the known; it offers to the voter his own likeness, but clarified, exalted, superbly elevated into a type' (Barthes, 1993, p. 91). For Barthes, such images function as an 'anti-intellectual weapon' which 'tends to spirit away "politics"' (Barthes, 1993, p. 91). Public sculptures often carry out a similarly ideological function, naturalising historically contentious figures within smooth narratives of national culture and progress. Yet, art and artists have also historically disrupted such national-cultural ideology. Infamously, the critic Ruskin once described the 'art for art's sake' proto-abstraction of Whistler's *Nocturne in Black and Gold: The Falling Rocket* (1875) as 'flinging a pot of paint in the public's face' (Merrill, 1992, p. 1). The apparently reactionary character of Ruskin's dismissal is evidence that Whistler's art forced the critic, unwittingly, to recognise a paradigm shift in the nature of art. A similar paradigm shift, this time moving from the colonial to decolonial mindset, is evident in the shit thrown in Rhodes' face by CTU protesters. Hastily introduced statue-protection legislation, supported by governmental rhetoric and exaggerated outrage amongst the right-wing UK media, are merely knee-jerk attempts to contain a threat to the dominant-hegemonic world view; a threat which the establishment knows is impossible to contain. Herein lies a triple denial: the denial of politics, which is caricatured as mindless vandalism, and the denial of responsibility, through recourse a rearguard defence of the social order, presumed to be uncritically benevolent, through ideological concepts such as heritage, culture and education. Both disguise the more profound denial that the world could be otherwise.

One of the conclusions we can draw from this example is that the institutional structures of imperialism are incapable of reflecting on their legacy, nor reforming themselves within. De Sousa Santos' (2018, p. vii) *The End of the Cognitive Empire* begins by insisting that 'modern ideologies of political contestation have been largely co-opted by neoliberalism'. Therefore, 'the reconstruction or reinvention of confrontational politics requires an epistemological transformation'. For him, Western centric thought, in both radical and conservative form, has formed a fatal alliance which represses the 'epistemologies of the South'. For him, there is a permanent 'abyssal line', which demarcates Western thought from its others, and which Western universities are incapable of crossing without coercion.

If universities are incapable of reflecting on questions of representation and responsibility, then where can critical reason be located, if at all? Harney and Moten (2013) believe that genuinely counter-hegemonic thought still exists within the contemporary university, but only within what they call the 'undercommons'. Against the *universitas*, the undercommons is an endlessly deconstructing procession of intersectional disidentifications. It is composed of 'maroon communities of composition teachers, mentorless graduate students, adjunct Marxist historians, out or queer management professors, state college ethnic studies departments, closed-down film programs, visa-expired Yemeni student newspaper editors, historically Black college sociologists, and feminist engineers (Harney and Moten, 2013, p. 104). Against these, the modern university represents the institutional mechanism for the 'social reproduction of conquest denial'; the logic of consensus.

This is an aspect of the 'University of Excellence'. Excellence is the discourse which dilutes, even co-opts, the specificity of intersectional struggles. For Readings, it is an 'integrating principle that allows 'diversity' (the other watchword of the University prospectus) to be tolerated without threatening the unity of the system' (Readings, 1996, p. 32). Within the university of excellence, dissent can readily become co-opted as the achievement of diversity targets, or as an impact factor on cultural studies research audits. Against this, de Sousa Santos (2018) has called for the 'pluriversity', which subverts the university ideal in the name of a radical and inclusive polyphony. The pluriversity generates the post-abyssal thinking which potentially reverses both the colonial effects of the white Western university episteme and the centripetal effects of globalisation. An emerging example of the pluriversity is rising in the UK. The Free Black University, crowdfunded by the Black activist Melz Owusu, recruited its first cohort in September 2022 and has now concluded, at least in its first iteration. Designed specifically as an alternative to the abyssal University, the FBU focused on the 'multiple and infinite routes to producing knowledge outside of the evidence-based Eurocentric rationalist model' (Free Black University, 2024a). Their self-published 'Radical Imagination Labs' journal includes a mission statement which declares a commitment to 'centering Black radical futures, liberation, abolition and African and Caribbean philosophies about life, time, and linearity'. They cite bell hooks (1994) as a formative theoretical influence, amongst others. Accordingly, their teaching is simultaneously an act of transgression and cathartic love. Owusu claims she founded the institution as a testament to 'the power and possibility of education as a tool of healing and liberation' (Free Black University, 2024b). Furthermore, as a release to 'the knowledges which may have become knotted-up within us and that which we may try and push down and hide because if we allowed it to escape into the light, we would be confronted by a world that denies our truth' (Free Black University, 2024b).

In 1772, the 'gentleman cartoonist' Henry William Bunbury depicted a satirical image of a young man being scrutinised by an Oxbridge don for admission to university. The subtitle reads 'the hopes of the family'. Oxbridge colleges maintain an idiosyncratic, arguably archaic, interview process for undergraduate admissions to this day. However, the intergenerational investment implied by Bunbury's image has now ceded to the capitalist realist acceptance that Generation Z, despite their education, will be significantly worse off than their parents. In 2021, in the face of campaigns to decolonise the university, Oxford accepted a record number of Black students (Yeomans 2021). Despite this, just like Bunbury's cartoon, elite British universities remain demonstrably white.

Fig. 10.6 After John Carter (1790), *The Entry of Frederick into the Castle of Otranto*. Scene created by the author from images sourced, with permission, from UCU members and the digital archives of Yale's Paul Mellon Centre for British Art', https://photoarchive.paul-mellon-centre.ac.uk/collections

6. Revolt

On the morning of Monday May 13, 1968, a wave of militant students poured into the Sorbonne University, placing key buildings under student control. In the weeks before, similar actions by student militants at the University of Paris' expansion campus in Nanterre had inspired a wave of copycat high school occupations. These student protests also inspired a large general strike by the French trade unions, also organised for May 13. In turn, this generated a call for the occupation of all French universities (Fraser, 1988, p. 215). In this vortex of protest, the Sorbonne was occupied by a crowd of 20-30,000 students (Ali and Watkins, 1998, p. 100), who covered its walls with graffiti, revolutionary posters and banners. These proclaimed the death of the Sorbonne and its rebirth as the 'Autonomous People's University' (Kugelberg and Vermès, 2011, p. 78). In the radical newspaper Black Dwarf, Clive Godwin (1968, p. 4) labelled it 'The Sorbonne Soviet'. They quoted a firebrand speech from a young student who declared: 'this revolution is for the red flag of socialism and the worker's state, and for the black flag of anarchy and the individual' (Godwin, 1968, p. 4). To add to the spectacle, a large piano was dragged into the university's main quadrangle and the whole occupation was soundtracked to a live improvised jazz score.

Within twenty-four hours, students then occupied the historic art school of the Sorbonne, L'École de Beaux-Arts. Its print rooms were commandeered to produce propaganda leaflets and posters, which were then distributed around the university to foment the revolution. A manifesto statement on May 14 declared the art school had been renamed to L'Atelier Populaire [The People's Studio]. The Beaux-Arts is an elite and hierarchical institution, highly selective, and indivisible from the historic Prix de Rome—the competition traditionally figured as the golden to route professional success for academic artists. These occupations transformed the school into a space of democracy, horizontality and co-production. By May 15, organised committees for the design and distribution of this agitprop had been formed. These designs were democratically selected by daily assemblies open to the public. These images of revolution inspired a wildcat strike at the

Nantes Sud-Aviation factory, immediately followed by the occupation of the Renault factory at Cléon. Shortly, red and black flags flew over the Doric columns at the entrance to the historic and symbolic Odéon theatre, now hosting a sister occupation of 2,500–3,000 students (Kugelberg and Vermès, 2011, p. 78). Like the Sorbonne, 'l'ex-Théatre de France' was covered with banners proclaiming solidarity between students. By May 16, strikes were erupting across France and significant solidarity actions had taken place at 'Flins, Le Mans, and the 30,000 strong Renault-Boulogne-Billancourt factory' (Kugelberg and Vermès, 2011, p. 79).

Rather than oil paint, these revolutionary occupations were captured in celluloid, via the conflict photography of Marc Riboud, Guy Le Querrec, Henri Cartier-Bresson and other Magnum photographers. However, the spectacle of '68 has archetypal precedents which can be recognised throughout visual culture. In the French revolutionary imaginary, the occupation of university buildings connects directly to the storming of the Bastille at the outset of the revolution of 1789. The defence of student leader Daniel Cohn-Bendit, when arrested for making Molotov cocktails, was that 'violent revolt is in the French culture' (Kurlansky, 2004, p. 226). Another esoteric connection is the Tower card, or La Maison Dieu, from the Tarot de Marseille. This depicts a regal tower exploding, like the Bastille, and its 'crowned jugglers' being cast to the floor. Many siege images relate to this archetype, which in the final analysis probably emerges with the parricidal desires of the Oedipus Complex. This can be recognised in even the most innocuous images, such as John Carter's (1790) *The Entry of Frederick into the Castle of Otranto* (Fig. 10.6). This illustrates a key moment of Horace Walpole's gothic novel, which centres around a dispute about the titular castle and crown of Otranto. The scene, which depicts Frederick's army triumphantly marching into Otranto, actually represents the moment the father reclaims his daughter from the hand of Manfred, potential suitor and would be usurper. The story is underpinned by ancient prophecy. Namely, that the crown should be relinquished 'whenever the real owner should be grown too large to inhabit it' (Walpole, 1996).

This tale of power, hubris and oedipal conflict maps very well onto the scene of '68. The student protests very nearly deposed the government of Charles de Gaulle. He ultimately held on to power through divide and conquer tactics, buying the unions off with unprecedented pay rises. The eventual failure of the May '68 movement should not detract from the world-historic synthesis of revolutionary, artistic and libidinal energy it unleashed. In *Declaration* (2012), Hardt and Negri suggest that 'an occupation is a kind of happening, a performance piece that generates political affects'. For them, the prevalence of 'occupation' as the primary political strategy for the twenty-first-century global resistance movements, results from its effectiveness at communicating an essential political truth. This is that 'the class and the bases of political action are formed not primarily through the circulation of information or even ideas but rather through the construction of political affects, which requires a physical proximity'. For them, 'nothing can replace the being together of bodies and the corporeal communication that is the basis of collective political intelligence and action'. Togetherness, and the solidarity generated through actions which manifest being-together, are the prerequisites for rebuilding the commons.

Ken Knabb's *The Joy of Revolution* (1997), like Bakhtin (1984 [1965]), draws parallels between images of Bacchanalian and revolutionary situations. Here, the strategic differences between wildcat, sit-down and consumer strikes are eroticised into subheadings entitled 'foreplay' and 'climaxes'. Knabb characterises revolutionary situations as 'collective awakenings' energised by 'open-ended public dialogue and participation'. Such situations amplify critical and satirical attitudes to the status quo, resulting quickly in the revelation of the normal as abnormal. Here, qualitative change becomes conceivable and achievable. For Knabb, the revolutionary event is where 'the old order is analysed, criticised, satirised. People learn more about society in a week than in years of academic 'social studies' or leftist 'consciousness raising'. Long repressed experiences are revived. Everything seems possible—and much more is possible' (Knabb, 1997).

Similarly, Gerald Raunig has recently discussed university occupations using Deleuzo-Guattarian concepts of 'deterritorialisation' and 'reterritorialisation' (Deleuze and Guattari, 1988, pp. 3–21), and 'modulation' (Deleuze, 1992). For Raunig (2013, p. 29), an occupation oscillates between 'a striating, standardising, modularising process and at the same time a permanent movement of remodelling, modulating, re-forming and de-forming the self'. In the contemporary neoliberal university, the 'striated space' to which Raunig refers is the space of disciplinary divisions and subdivisions, modular curricular and assessments, performance metrics and institutional league tables. All of these generate behavioural self-regulation and the modular reproduction of institutional subjectivities. The activist Edu-Factory Collective (2011, 2009), with which Raunig is associated, have similarly described the current educational conjuncture as the 'system of measure', underlining its disciplinary character. University occupations, as politics, expose these striations whilst smoothing them into nomadic spaces of becoming. Defined thus, the university 'in occupation' embodies what Deleuze and Guattari call the 'war-machine' (2010).

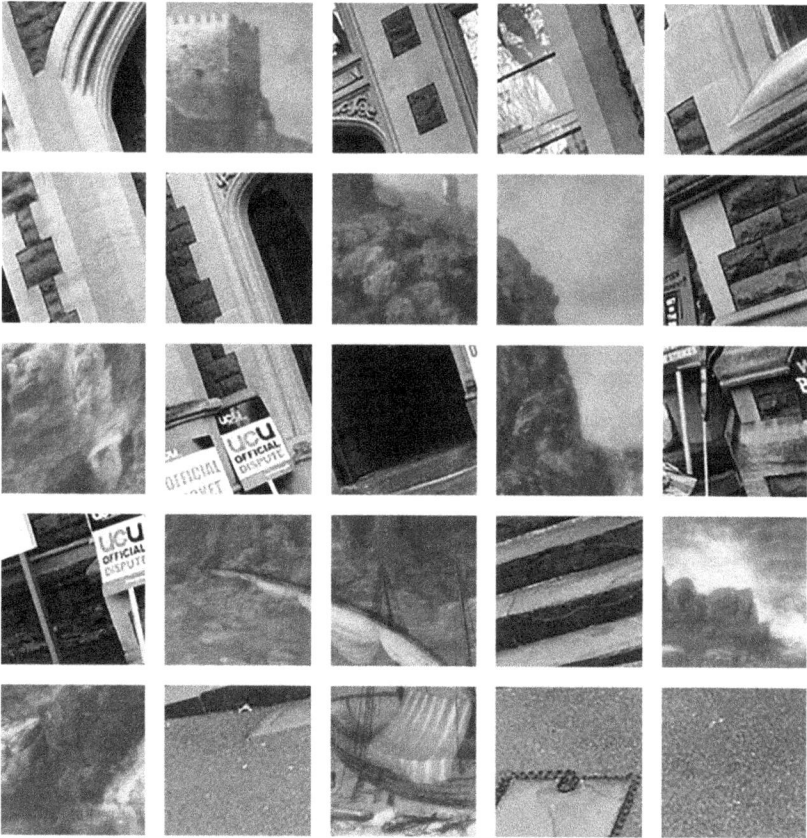

Fig. 10.7 After Sydney Herbert (c. 1870), *The Castle of Ari, with a Distant View of the Cyclops Scropuli or Rocks which Polyphemus Hurled at Ulysses*. Scene created by the author from images sourced, with permission, from UCU members and the digital archives of Yale's Paul Mellon Centre for British Art', https://photoarchive. paul-mellon-centre.ac.uk/collections

7. Strike

On February 21, 2018 UK's higher and further education workers' union, the University and College Union [UCU], commenced strike action. At the time, Bergfeld (2018, p. 233) claimed this as the biggest industrial dispute in the history of UK universities. It involved academic and academic related staff at sixty-one institutions. As Bergfeld noted, the dispute was fought on many fronts simultaneously, but ostensibly it was called in defence of pay, working conditions and pensions. Over the next five years, UCU called a series of increasingly serious industrial actions, culminating in an ultimately unsuccessful five-month long marking and assessment boycott (MAB), called off on September 6, 2023. The fallout from these latest actions has been severe. University staff morale is at an all-time low (Jackson, 2023) and two-thirds of university staff are seriously considering leaving the sector (UCU, 2022d). This protracted dispute, especially the MAB, was costly to UCU members and its lack of success has depleted the spirit of the membership. Consequently, the general secretary of UCU, Jo Grady, faced a leadership challenge which she survived in a narrow victory on March 1, 2024. Grady is a rank-and-file general secretary, elected in a landslide in 2019 on the back of her grassroots branch activism. She comes from the working-class mining city of Wakefield, West Yorkshire. Her father participated in the two-year long National Union of Miners' strike against the Thatcher government in 1984–1985. Nevertheless, in an increasingly dysfunctional and factional union, Grady has become synonymous with counter-revolutionary bureaucracy in the eyes of the union's ultra-Left (Kelly and Ozanne, 2024).

The complexity of the UCU dispute, and UCUs internal politics, results partly from the fractured nature of the UK tertiary education system. This is divided into a sector of traditional 'red brick' universities, a sector of former polytechnics granted university titles in 1992, and a sector of further education colleges. The UCU was founded in 2006, as an amalgamation of two specialist sector interest trade unions, with the aim of representing all post-compulsory education workers with a united voice. Following their formation as a united union, UCU won a historic concession from university employers. Workers were awarded a 13.1% pay rise over three years in 2006 (Smithers, 2006). This appears like a lesson in the efficacy of union organisation, solidarity and class struggle. However, 2006 would also be the last time that university workers won a pay deal above the rate of UK inflation (UCEA, 2022). Most 'pay awards' since that time have been sub-inflationary. UCU introduced pay modelling software in 2021 which calculates that pay suppression in the sector has cost university workers' 20% of their salary in real terms since 2009. This pay suppression is compounded by high rates of inflation, measured at 9.4% by the Office for National Statistics, as of June 2022 (ONS, 2022).

UCU's ambition to be a single voice for all post-compulsory education workers has been made deliberately more difficult by anti-trade union legislation introduced by different right-wing governments. Specifically, the Trade Union and Labour Relations (Consolidation) Act (1992), revised as the Trade Union Act (2006). This legislation made secondary striking unlawful, so workers can no longer take action in solidarity with sister disputes. Also, branch specific turnout thresholds were introduced, alongside time-bound limits on balloted mandates, which complicate the organisation of national disputes. In order to take united national action, UCU must now coordinate multiple ballots for sector-specific disputes. From February 2018, workers at the historic pre-'92 universities acted in defence of their pension, the University Superannuation Scheme. This was in response to severe cuts to the pension scheme's benefits, imposed following a tokenistic consultation process, based upon misleading data (Cumbo, 2022). UCU research (Grant et al., 2022, p. 9) estimates that these cuts could cost workers under 40 up to £200k in lost pension income. Despite widespread scepticism about their necessity (Cumbo, 2022; Smith, 2020; Grove, 2018; Wilkinson and Curtiss, 2018), these cuts were pushed through on April 1, 2022, whilst many institutions were on the picket lines.

The post-'92 members of UCU have a different pension scheme, so were not legally eligible to join their fellow members in this dispute. Instead, in 2019 post-'92 members joined after winning a ballot to strike on pay suppression, unmanageable workloads, anti-casualisation and workplace inequality. This has become known as the 'Four Fights' (UCU, 2022a). Alongside the aforementioned pay suppression, UCU estimates that 68% of the HE workforce is currently on casual contracts. Furthermore, their research indicates that the average university working week is above fifty hours. Depressingly, the same research indicates that there is a gender pay gap of 15%, a pay gap between Black and white workers of 17%, and a pay gap between able-bodied and disabled workers of 9% (UCU, 2022a). UCU's FE members, again, are ineligible to strike in this dispute so have been forced to ballot on FE pay specifically. In July 2022, these members voted for strike action about the most recent pay offer of 2.5%, merely a quarter of current rates of inflation. UCU (2022b) estimates that FE staff pay has fallen 39% in real terms since 2009. Currently, a fully qualified FE Lecturer enters the profession with a starting salary of less than £26,000 p.a. This is less than half the base pay of a Transport for London underground train driver, who earns £55,011 p.a. before bonuses (Herbert 2019).

In *Disagreement* (2009, p. 41), Rancière characterises the political demonstration as a 'polemical scene' which paradoxically 'bring(s) out the contradiction between two logics, by positing existences that are at the same time nonexistences'. His example is the French socialist Jeanne Deroin (1805–1894) who stood in a French legislative assembly, despite being legally prohibited from taking up her seat if victorious. The motivation was to spectacularly demonstrate the hypocrisy of a republic built upon democratic ideals, but whose legislation systematically prevents the realisation of truly democratic equality. Politics, for Rancière, consists of three key elements. Firstly, it is the visible and spectacular demonstration of a 'wrong' (p. 35), the making audible of a voice where previously there was just silence (p. 35). Secondly, it enacts a disidentification from the 'natural order' or presumed social ethos (p. 36). Politics is the force of dissensus against consensus; the paradoxical revelation of 'the part of those who have no part' (p. 65) within the status quo. Finally, it stages a reckoning between the logic of inequality and the logic of equality (pp. 41, 49–51).

Bergfeld's (2018, p. 234) account of the 'creative, large and vibrant picket lines' of the recent UCU demonstrations contains ample evidence of all of these elements. For example, he documents how the Leeds University UCU produced music videos to spectacularly raise awareness of the dispute. The 'Four Fights', criticised by some for its incoherence, actually gained strength through its cumulative revelation of 'parts who have no part'. Indeed, Bergfeld reports how institutionalised divisions between professors and casualised staff were broken down through the act of protest. Furthermore, the placards, aesthetics and banners of the student movement were adopted by striking staff. There are ample documents of various workers' Twitter feeds which show how university campuses were transformed into heterotopic carnivalesques of humour, laughter and liberty. Bergfeld even recalls how picketers sang 'do you believe in life after work?' (2018), reworking a famous pop song by Cher. This is not just a glib pop culture reference. It is a refusal of a world order where workers are only defined by work, the remuneration of that work and the overarching discourses of the workplace (Rancière, 1999, p. 29).

Fig. 10.8 After J. M. W. Turner (1829), *Ulysses Deriding Polyphemus*. Scene created by the author from images sourced, with permission, from UCU members and the digital archives of Yale's Paul Mellon Centre for British Art', https://photoarchive.paul-mellon-centre.ac.uk/collections

8. Mochlos

Derrida's Mochlos essay ends on a quite remarkable deconstructive turn, which seems incongruent from the rest of the essay, and completely lacking the conventional requirements of a conclusion. Derrida's 'inconclusion' is partly an homage to Kant's own tangential conclusion to his Conflict essay. Here, Kant drifts away from the central subject to discuss sleep regimens, eating habits, controlled breathing, 'pathological feelings' and the relationship of all of the above to the mind's capacity for critical thought. In these passages, Kant writes about his conviction that the mind can control any pathological or physiological states, including the impulsive desire for sleep or food. Indeed, Kant believed that the mastery of these 'feelings by sheer steadfast will [is] the superior power of a rational animal' (Kant 1979 [1798], p. 205). Kant even implies that there is a continuity between the rational mastery of one's bodily impulses and the mastery of the logical argumentative structure of a text.

In lieu of a conclusion, Derrida cites two lengthy citations from the final sections of *The Conflict of the Faculties*, without commentary. The first concerns Kant's technique of avoiding stomach cramps by concentrating on 'some neutral object... (for example, the name of Cicero)' (Derrida, 2004, p. 112). The second excerpt discusses military training within the Prussian infantry. Specifically, that physical deficiencies can be corrected with proper training. This ends with the discussion of a specific military technique, where the soldier uses the left foot as a lever to mount an attack with the right. Kant compares this to a hypomochlium, meaning an orbital joint, fulcrum or pivot point. Buried in the final footnote of the essay, after the last sentence has concluded, Derrida introduces the titular theme of the essay. Derrida: 'Let us repeat here the name of Polyphemus' (Figs. 10.7 and 10.8). This was the name of the man-eating cyclops who imprisoned Odysseus (or, Ulysses), the eponymous hero of Homer's *Odyssey*. Derrida continues: 'Mochlos is also the name for the "wedge" or wooden lever that Ulysses [...] puts into the fire before driving it into the pupil of the Cyclops' (Derrida, 2004, p. 289). At the risk of enclosing the signification of Derrida's essay, it is worth underlining that one of Derrida's ambitions is to foreground thought itself as a tool of leverage, or resistance, and also a weapon. Implicitly, the cyclops must also signify the increasingly panoptic, carceral and disciplinary character of the contemporary university, where thought is situated, within and against.

This resonates with the analysis of both Readings (1996) and Brown (2015, pp. 175–200). Brown devotes a whole chapter, entitled 'Educating Human Capital', to the differences between education as discipline and thought as freedom. One conclusion is that the economisation of higher education has not only depoliticised university education but also extinguished the criticality necessary for a free and democratic society. Her central case study is US Liberal Arts education. This saw an unprecedented mass expansion throughout public universities and community colleges in the twentieth century. Like Raymond Williams' (1988, p. 127), Brown recognises that the Liberal Arts are historically rooted in the culture of the ruling class. Their mass expansion is therefore also a form of cultural democratisation. Originating in fourteenth-century England, Williams insists that the Liberal Arts were intended for 'men of independent means and assured social position, as distinct from other skills and pursuits (cf. Mechanical) appropriate to a lower class'. Williams' reference to 'mechanical' is a nod to the Aristotelian distinction between philosopher-kings and 'mechanical men' (*Politics*, 1339a41, p. 463). The latter are merely 'hirelings'. They use their bodies as a means to an end and are therefore not free. In contradistinction, a Liberal Arts education was understood as the means by which free men would come 'to know the world and engage the world sufficiently to exercise that freedom' (Brown, 2015, p. 184).

Brown argues that the postwar expansion of the Liberal Arts was no less than a democratic revolution. Studying these subjects opened 'the door through which the descendants of workers, immigrants and slaves entered onto the main stage of the society to whose wings they were historically consigned' (Brown, 2015, p. 180). Access to the Liberal Arts gave mechanical men the opportunity to think like free men (Rancière, 2013, ix, 2004, pp. 31–34). By disseminating the philosophy of freedom 'this extension importantly articulated equality as an ideal' (Brown, 2015, p. 186). Brown warns that 'we can no longer speak this way about the public university, and the university no longer speaks this way about itself' (p. 187). Within the economised university, the Liberal Arts are routinely attacked as 'expensive and outmoded', irrelevant to the job market, poor value for money or an expensive indulgence (pp. 180–181). This instrumentalism was identified earlier by Jeffrey Williams (in Edu-Factory Collection, 2009, 89–97) as the entirely predictable consequence of the economisation of education.

In 2022, the University of Roehampton, London, announced the closure of nineteen courses, including most of its Liberal Arts provision. The discarded courses include Anthropology, Classics, Creative Writing, Drama, English, Film, History, Literature and Philosophy. These course closures will also come at the expense of sixty-four academic positions. Roehampton is one of the post-'92 universities, historically created as amalgamations of provincial art schools, polytechnics and further education colleges. Their student demographic, in comparison to the elite pre-'92 Russell Group universities, includes more ethnic, cultural and class diversity. In the early twentieth century, Roehampton was a leading site of women's education. Now, Roehampton recruits 97% of its cohort from state schools, which is unheard of at Russell Group universities. The closure of the Liberal Arts at Roehampton represents the closure of a door of access to culture for the unrepresented and socially marginalised.

Roehampton management cite under-recruitment, rising costs and market forces as the reasons for the closures. Jo Grady said that Roehampton were complicit in a governmental agenda 'to restrict access to the arts and humanities—subjects that are well known for encouraging critical thinking' (UCU, 2022b). In response, Roehampton students have set up a lobby group to resist the cuts, inviting figures from across the arts and humanities sector to send letters of support. The British Bangladeshi dancer and choreographer Akram Khan submitted a statement which said 'in a time of real turmoil within our identity as a nation and as a global species, we are cutting the very thing that challenges, guides, nourishes and reminds us to question our actions and to be compassionate and understanding' (Khan, 2020). Khan does not cite Aristotle, but he is speaking directly of the Good Life, eudaimonia, human flourishing.

In an oil painting of 1829 (Fig. 10.8), J. M. W. Turner depicted the moment when Odysseus' crew escaped the island of the cyclops Polyphemus. In vain, the giant hurls rocks at the sailors to prevent their escape (Fig. 10.7). The hero stands on the deck of his Homeric

Galley, triumphantly raising the flaming mochlos to the sky beneath an unfurled red flag. Retrospectively, we can recognise another archetype within this image, connecting Turner's *Odysseus* to Bartholdi's (1876) 'Statue of Liberty', and Mukhina's (1937) 'Worker and Kolkhoz Woman'. In addition, to the scarlet standards and protest songs of workers' struggles. The flame of freedom held aloft; the powerless standing up to the powerful. The vertiginous neoclassical architecture on the façades of university architecture is designed to humble the individual before the weight of intellectual tradition. Nowhere is the chasm between the university's inflated ego-ideal and its attitude to its workers more apparent than on the picket lines. Similarly, Turner depicts Odysseus and his men as so infinitesimally small, so that they appear almost insignificant in comparison to the eternal, tempestuous, seascape behind. This, of course, is the express intention of a romantic art of the sublime. Precisely the opposite to the aggrandisement of heroic workers within socialist realism. During Samhuinn, candles are lit to banish the darkness and guide spirits home. Behind Turner's tempestuous sea, a sunrise guides the sailors away from the dark cave which imprisoned them.

Like Derrida, I eschew formal conclusions here. The university struggles in the UK, though temporarily paused, show no signs of conclusion either. As the academic year turns, so does the pagan wheel of the year, towards the fires of Beltaine, *le rire du mai*, freedom from the cold, death of winter. The sun rising, workers rising. The burning mochlos thrust into the cyclops eye of administration.

Acknowledgements

I would like to give thanks to all the members of the University and College Union, particularly those who allowed me to use their picket line photography as the basis for the illustrations for this essay. I would also like to thank Yale's Paul Mellon Centre for British Art for permission to use their archival images, which I encountered during my Postdoctoral Research Fellowship there. I hope that my composite scenes encourage people to explore this archive and, in turn, develop new perspectives on British art.

I would also like to express solidarity to all those involved in the global university struggles. My essay is dedicated to you all: *la lutte continue*.

Bibliography

Ali, T., and Watkins, S. (Eds). (1998). *1968: Marching in the Streets*. The Free Press.

Althusser, L. (2006). *Philosophy of the Encounter: Later Writings 1978–87*. Verso.

Aristotle. (1992). *The Politics* (T. A. Sinclair, Trans.). Penguin.

Bakhtin, M. (1984 [1965]). *Rabelais and His World* (H. Iswolsky, Trans.). Indiana University Press.

Barthes, R. (1993). *Mythologies* (A. Lavers, Trans.) Vintage.

Bataille, G. (1985). *Visions of Excess: Selected Writings 1927–1939*. University of Minnesota Press.

Baudrillard, J. (1994). *Simulacra and Simulation*. University of Michigan Press.

Benjamin, W. (1999). *The Arcades Project*. Harvard University Press.

Bergfeld, M. (2018). 'Do You Believe in Life after Work?' The University and College Union Strike in Britain. *Transfer: European Review of Labour and Research*, 24(2), 233–236.

Brown, W. (2015). *Undoing the Demos*. Zone.

Carr-Gomm, P. (1994). *The Elements of the Druid Tradition*. Element Books.

Clayton, I. (2021). *'Disrespectful': New Cecil Rhodes Notice at Oriel College Sparks Debate*. The Oxford Mail. https://www.oxfordmail.co.uk/news/19639658. disrespectful-new-cecil-rhodes-notice-oriel-college-sparks-debate/

Cumbo, J. (2022, June 18). *Universities Accused of Misleading Claims over UK Staff Pension Reforms*. Financial Times. https://www.ft.com/content/a7937ee8-d075-414d-a313-429de3b0a7b2

Deleuze, G. (1992). Postscript on the Societies of Control. *October*, 59, 3–7.

—, and Guattari, F. (2010). *Nomadology: The War Machine* (B. Massumi, Trans.). Wormwood.

—, & Guattari, F. (1988). *A Thousand Plateaus: Capitalism and Schizophrenia* (B. Massumi, Trans.). Athlone.

Demkovich, M. (2013, July). The Sound of Barking Dogs: Meister Eckhart & Saint Thomas Aquinas. *New Blackfriars*, 94(1052), 440–455.

Derrida, J. (2002). *Who's Afraid of Philosophy? Right to Philosophy 1* (J. Plug, Trans.). Stanford University Press.

—(2004). *Eyes of the University: Right to Philosophy 2* (J. Plug, Trans.). Stanford University Press.

De Sousa Santos, B. (2018). *The End of the Cognitive Empire: The Coming of Age of Epistemologies of the South.* Duke University Press.

Edu-Factory Collective. (2011). The University Struggles and the System of Measure. *Edu-Factory Journal, 1.*

—(2009). *Towards a Global Autonomous University.* Autonomedia.

Fichte, J. G. (1988). *The Purpose of Higher Education* (J. K. Bramann, Trans.). Nightsun Books.

—(1979). *Addresses to the German Nation.* (R. F. Jones and G. H. Turnbull, Trans.). Greenwood Press.

Fisher, M. (2018). *K-Punk: The Collected and Unpublished Writings of Mark Fisher.* Repeater.

Fischer, D. H. (2005). *Liberty and Freedom: A Visual History of America's Founding Ideas.* Oxford University Press.

Fleming, D. F. (1968). Vietnam and After. *Western Political Quarterly, 21*(1), 141–151.

Fraser, R. (Ed.) (1988). *1968: A Student Generation in Revolt.* Pantheon.

Free Black University. (2024a). *Our Mission.* https://www.freeblackuni.com/mission

—(2024b). *Pedagogical Principles.* https://www.freeblackuni.com/pedagogy-principles

Goodwin, C. (1968, June 1). The Sorbonne Soviet. *Black Dwarf, 13*(1), 4. https://www.marxists.org/history/etol/newspape/black-dwarf/v13n01-jun-01-1968.pdf

Gorochov, N. (2018). The Great Dispersion of the University of Paris and the Rise of European Universities (1229–1231). *CIAN-Revista de Historia de las Universidades, 21*(1), 99–119.

Grant, J. F., Hindmarsh, M., and Koposov, S. E. (2022). *The Distribution of Loss to Future USS Pensions Due To The UUK Cuts Of April 2022.* Cornell University. https://arxiv.org/abs/2206.06201

Grove, J. (2018, October 7). *Universities Superannuation Scheme Rejects Valuation Error Claim.* Times Higher Education. https://www.timeshighereducation.com/news/universities-superannuation-scheme-rejects-valuation-error-claim

Hardt, M., and Negri, A. (2012). *Declaration.* https://antonionegriinenglish.files.wordpress.com/2012/05/93152857-hardt-negri-declaration-2012.pdf

Hardt, M., and Negri, A. (2005). *Multitude.* London: Penguin.

Harney, S. and Moten, F. (2013). *The Undercommons: Fugitive Planning and Black Study*. Minor Compositions.

Herbert, T. (2019, May 16). *London Tube Driver Salary: How Much do Tube Drivers Earn? What you Didn't Know about Working for TfL Underground*. The Evening Standard. https://www.standard.co.uk/news/uk/tube-driver-salary-holidays-working-conditions-a3982211.html

Healey, N. (2013). Why do English Universities really Franchise Degrees to Overseas Providers? *Higher Education Quarterly, 67*(2), 180–200.

Hodges C., Moore, S., Lockee, B., Trust, T., and Bond, A. (2020). The Difference between Emergency Remote Teaching and Online Learning. *Educause.* https://er.educause.edu/articles/2020/3/the-difference-between-emergency-remote-teaching-and-online-learning

hooks, b. (1994). *Teaching to Transgress: Education as the Practice of Freedom*. Routledge.

Hudson-Miles, R., and Broadey, A. J. (2019). Messy Democracy: Democratic Pedagogy and its Discontents. *Research in Education, 104*(1) 56–76.

Hudson-Miles, R., Goodman, J., and Jones, J. (2021). What Artists Want, What Artists Need: A Critical History of Feral Art School, Hull, UK. *International Journal of Art & Design Education, 41*(1), 81–95.

Hudson-Miles, R. (2022). 'Let us Build a City and a Tower': Figures of the University in Gregor Reisch's (1503) Margarita Philosophica. In J. Cruickshank (Ed.), *The Social Production of Knowledge in a Neoliberal Age: Debating the Challenges facing Higher Education*. Rowman and Littlefield International.

—(2021). Experiments in Autonomous Art Education in the UK, 2010-Present. *Educação & Realidade*, Special Edition: Within or Beyond the University? Experiences in Alternative Higher Education. *46*(4), 1–34.

Jackson, L. (2023, August 6). *Staff Morale at 'All-Time Low' in Universities after Talks Break Down*. Yahoo News. https://uk.news.yahoo.com/staff-morale-time-low-universities-040000118.html?guccounter=1

Kant, I. (1979 [1798]). *The Conflict of the Faculties* (M. J. Gregor, Trans.). Abaris.

—(1793). *Religion within the Limits of Reason Alone*. Marxists Internet Archive. https://www.marxists.org/reference/subject/ethics/kant/religion/religion-within-reason.htm

Kelly, J., & Ozanne, A. (2024, January 16). *UCU Left's Trotskyist Politics are Driving UK HE's Perennial Strikes*. Times Higher Education. https://www.timeshighereducation.com/opinion/ucu-lefts-trotskyist-politics-are-driving-uk-hes-perennial-strikes

Khan, A. (2020, October 22). [Twitter/X post]. https://twitter.com/AkramKhanLive/status/1319307605517414400

Keogh, E. (2016, January 14). *What Cecil John Rhodes Said in his Will about Who Should Get Scholarships*. The Conversation. https://theconversation.com/what-cecil-john-rhodes-said-in-his-will-about-who-should-get-scholarships-53172

Knabb, K. (1997). *The Joy of Revolution*. The Anarchist Library. https://theanarchistlibrary.org/library/ken-knabb-the-joy-of-revolution#toc27

Kugelberg, J., and Vermès, P. (Eds). (2011). *Beauty is in the Street: A Visual Record of the May '68 Paris Uprising*. Four Corners.

Kurlansky, M. (2004). *1968: The Year that Rocked the World*. Random House.

Lewis, J. (2024, January 30). *University Strike Action in the UK*. House of Commons Library. https://commonslibrary.parliament.uk/research-briefings/cbp-9387/

McGettigan, A. (2013). *The Great University Gamble: Money, Markets, and the Future of Higher Education*. Pluto Press.

—, and Adams, R. (2019, February 9). *Reading University in Crisis amid Questions over £121m Land Sales*. The Guardian. https://www.theguardian.com/education/2019/feb/09/reading-university-in-crisis-amid-questions-over-121m-land-sales

Meirovich, G., and Romar, E. J. (2006). The Difficulty in Implementing TQM in Higher Education Instruction: The Duality of Instructor/Student Roles. *Quality Assurance in Education, 14*(4), 324–337.

Merrill, L. (1992). *A Pot of Paint: Aesthetics on Trial in Whistler v Ruskin*. Smithsonian Institution Press.

Metters, R., and Verma, R. (2008). 'History of Offshoring Knowledge Services'. *Journal of Operations Management, 26*(2), 141–147.

Miles, R. (2016a). Illustration, Education, Revolution: Lessons from Rancière for the C21st Illustration Student. *Varoomlab, 4*, 25–40.

—(2016b). Indisciplinarity as Social Form: Challenging the Distribution of the Sensible in the Visual Arts. *Message, 3*, 35–55.

Miller, D. C. (1963). Town and Gown: The Power Structure of a University Town. *American Journal of Sociology, 68*(4), 432–443.

Mills, R. P. (2024). *Cecil Rhodes Monument, Cape Town, South Africa*. World History Commons. https://worldhistorycommons.org/cecil-rhodes-monument-cape-town-south-africa

Mohdin, A. (2021, May 20). *Oxford College Criticised for Refusal to Remove Cecil Rhodes Statue*. The Guardian. https://www.theguardian.com/education/2021/may/20/cecil-rhodes-statue-will-not-be-removed-for-now-says-oxford-oriel-college

Ohio State University. (1994). *Ford and Ohio State Form Partnership on Quality*. Ohio State University. https://news.osu.edu/ford-and-ohio-state-form-partnership-on-quality/

ONS [Office for National Statistics]. (2022, July 20). *Consumer Price Inflation, UK: June 2022*. UK Government. https://www.ons.gov.uk/economy/inflationandpriceindices/bulletins/consumerpriceinflation/june2022

Peltier, A. (2021, June 10). *Scholars at Oxford University Refuse to Teach Under Statue of Colonialist*. New York Times. https://www.nytimes.com/2021/06/10/world/europe/cecil-rhodes-statue-oxford.html

Plato. (1975). *The Laws* (T. J. Saunders, Trans.). Penguin.

Rancière, J. (1995). *On the Shores of Politics* (D. Nicholson-Smith, Trans.). Verso.

—(1999). *Disagreement: Politics and Philosophy* (J. Rose, Trans.). University of Minnesota Press.

—(2003). *The Philosopher and His Poor* (J. Drury, C. Oster and A. Parker, Trans.). Duke University Press.

—(2004). *The Politics of Aesthetics: The Distribution of the Sensible* (G. Rockhill, Trans.). Continuum.

—(2010). *Dissensus* (S. Corcoran, Trans.). Continuum.

—(2013). *Aisthesis* (Z. Paul, Trans.). Verso.

Ramsey, A. (2022, June 21). *It's Great to See Mick Lynch Calling out the Media's Anti-Union Bullshit*. Open Democracy. https://www.opendemocracy.net/en/its-great-to-see-mick-lynch-calling-out-the-medias-anti-union-bullshit/?source=in-article-related-story

Raunig, G. (2013). *Factories of Knowledge, Industries of Creativity*. Semiotext(e).

Readings, B. (1996). *The University in Ruins*. Harvard University Press.

Ritzer, G. (2009 [1993]). *The McDonaldization of Society*. Pine Forge Press.

Ruggero, C. (2017). A Homage from Turin: Filippo Juvarra's Sketches for Lord Burlington. In P. Bianchi and K. Wolfe (Eds), *Turin and the British in the Age of the Grand Tour* (pp. 231–245). Cambridge University Press.

von Schelling, F. W. J. (1966). *On University Studies* (E. S. Morgan, Trans.; N. Guterman, Ed.). Ohio University Press.

Schleiermacher, F. (1991). *Occasional Thoughts on Universities in the German Sense. With an Appendix Regarding a University Soon to Be Established* (T. N. Tice and E. Lawler, Trans.). EMText.

Schmahmann, B. (2016). The Fall of Rhodes: The Removal of a Sculpture from the University of Cape Town. *Public Art Dialogue, 6*(1), 90–115.

SDS [Students for a Democratic Society]. (1962). *The Port Huron Statement*. The American Yawp Reader. https://www.americanyawp.com/reader/27-the-sixties/the-port-huron-statement-1962/

Slaughter, M. J., and Swagel, P. L. (1997). *Does Globalization Lower Wages and Export Jobs?* International Monetary Fund. https://www.imf.org/external/pubs/ft/issues11/

Smith, S. (2020, December 11). *University of Cambridge Reps Highlight Serious Concerns Over USS Valuation*. PensionsAge. https://www.pensionsage.com/pa/University-of-Cambridge-representatives-highlight-serious-concerns-over-USS-valuation-approach.php

Smithers, R. (2006, June 7). *Exams Boycott Suspended after Lecturers Agree Deal*. The Guardian. https://www.theguardian.com/uk/2006/jun/07/highereducation.lecturerspay

de Sousa Santos, B. (2018). *The End of The Cognitive Empire: The Coming of Age of Epistemologies of The South*. Duke University Press.

The Oxford Student. (2010, November 25). Students Occupy Radcliffe Camera in Fees Protest. https://www.oxfordstudent.com/2010/11/25/students-occupy-radcliffe-camera-in-fees-protest/

University and College Union. (2021). *University Staff Pay Cut by 20%, New Figures Show*. UCU News. https://www.ucu.org.uk/article/11830/University-staff-pay-cut-by-20-new-figures-show

—(2022a). *Four Fights Dispute FAQs*. https://www.ucu.org.uk/article/11818/Four-fights-dispute-FAQs

—(2022b). *College Staff in England to Join Wave of Strike Action*. UCU News. https://www.ucu.org.uk/article/12419/College-staff-in-England-to-join-wave-of-strike-action

—(2022c). *University Of Roehampton Pushing Ahead with Mass Fire & Rehire in Arts and the Humanities*. UCU News. https://www.ucu.org.uk/article/12424/University-of-Roehampton-pushing-ahead-with-mass-fire--rehire-in-arts-and-the-humanities

—(2022d). *Two-thirds of University Staff Considering Leaving Sector, New Report Reveals*. UCU News. https://www.ucu.org.uk/article/12212/Two-thirds-of-university-staff-considering-leaving-sector-new-report-reveals

—(2023). *UCU Rising FAQs*. https://www.ucu.org.uk/article/13287/FAQs

UK Government. (2021). *New Legal Protection for England's Heritage. Ministry of Housing, Communities & Local Government Press Release*. https://www.gov.uk/government/news/new-legal-protection-for-england-s-heritage

Universities UK. (2021). *New UK University Overseas Campuses Network Announced at UUKi TNE conference*. UUK News. https://www.universitiesuk.ac.uk/universities-uk-international/events-and-news/uuki-news/new-uk-university-overseas-campuses

Walpole, H. (1996). *The Castle of Otranto*. Project Gutenberg, https://www. gutenberg.org/files/696/696-h/696-h.htm

Wilkinson, T., and Curtiss, F. (2018, May 29). *Death by Discount Rate: The Fundamental Flaws of the Accounting Approach to Pension Scheme Valuation*. Professional Pensions. https://www.professionalpensions.com/ opinion/3033124/death-discount-rate-fundamental-flaws-accounting-approach-pension-scheme-valuation

Williams, R. (1985). *Keywords: A Vocabulary of Culture and Society*. Oxford University Press.

Yeomans, E. (2021, February 5). *Oxford University Accepts over 100 Black Students*. The Times. https://www.thetimes.co.uk/article/ oxford-university-accepts-over-100-black-students-cngl73kpw

List of Illustrations

Figures

Fig. I.1   Unnamed artistic intervention marks the absence of the   p. 3
            long shadow once cast by the monument to Cecil John
            Rhodes at the University of Cape Town. Photo taken by
            Dina Zoe Belluigi (Cape Town, 2018).

Fig. 2.1   Black-and-white hand-printed photograph (97 x 157mm),   p. 65
            circa 1986. Identities obscured by the author. Author's
            collection.

Fig. 2.2   The back of a large format Mozambican stamp (1980)   p. 68
            on which a matrix of adhesive gauze, paper fibres and a
            human hair are attached. Photo: Brent Meistre (Belfast,
            2022).

Fig. 2.3   The back of five small Finnish stamps from 1986 that were   p. 70
            cut out. Rearranged by the author. Note the reference to
            'mom' and 'dad'. Photo: Brent Meistre (Belfast, 2022).

Fig. 2.4   The back of a postcard stamp with the hand-written   p. 72
            words 'arrested' and 'without trial', and the front of a 1987
            stamp celebrating 'welfare' and 'dignity' in the democratic
            constitution of the USA. Photo: Brent Meistre (Belfast,
            2022).

Fig. 2.5   The front and back of a UK 1987 stamp with reference to   p. 72
            Anti-Apartheid Movement (AAM) protests. Photo: Brent
            Meistre (Belfast, 2022).

Fig. 2.6   Some publications explicitly indicated censorship by the   p. 74
            state. These two images of the same page show redacted
            words from The Democrat (1986) with the editor's
            handwritten explanation on the right. Photos: Brent
            Meistre (Belfast, 2022).

Fig. 2.7   Two versions of the same edition of *The African Communist*   p. 75
            (1987). The left version with disguised cover for
            distribution in South Africa and the other for distribution
            elsewhere. Photo: Brent Meistre (Belfast, 2022).

Fig. 2.8   Notes on contributors in *Black Theology* (1972) indicating   p. 76
            banned authors. Photo: Brent Meistre (Belfast, 2022).

Fig. 2.9   Editor's note on the Foreword to *Black Theology*. Photo: p. 76
            Brent Meistre (Belfast, 2022).

Fig. 2.10   Pages 118–119 of the banned *ANC Speaks* (Authorship   p. 82
            withheld, 1977), with cellotape traces where the book was
            torn in two halves. Photo: Brent Meistre (Belfast, 2022).

Fig. 2.11   The first page of the illustrations section of Nelson   p. 84
            Mandela's (1978) book *The Struggle is My Life*. Photo:
            Brent Meistre (Belfast, 2022).

Fig. 10.1   After Samuel Bough (1853), *Snowballing Outside Edinburgh*   p. 291
            University. Scene created by the author from images
            sourced, with permission, from UCU members and the
            digital archives of Yale's Paul Mellon Centre for British
            Art', https://photoarchive.paul-mellon-centre.ac.uk/
            collections

Fig. 10.2   After Nathaniel Buck (1731), *The South West Prospect*   p. 296
            of the University and City of Oxford. Scene created by the
            author from images sourced, with permission, from UCU
            members and the digital archives of Yale's Paul Mellon
            Centre for British Art', https://photoarchive.paul-mellon-
            centre.ac.uk/collections

Fig. 10.3   After Filippo Juvarra (1729), *Album of Architectural*   p. 301
            Fantasies (Frontispiece), Dedicated to Lord Burlington.
            Scene created by the author from images sourced, with
            permission, from UCU members and the digital archives
            of Yale's Paul Mellon Centre for British Art', https://
            photoarchive.paul-mellon-centre.ac.uk/collections

Fig. 10.4   After C. C. Hamilton (1810), *The University Church of*   p. 306
            St. Mary's Oxford from Beside the Radcliffe Camera. Scene
            created by the author from images sourced, with
            permission, from UCU members and the digital archives
            of Yale's Paul Mellon Centre for British Art', https://
            photoarchive.paul-mellon-centre.ac.uk/collections

Fig. 10.5 After Henry William Bunbury (1772), *The Hopes of the*   p. 310
           Family... An Admission at the University. Scene created by
           the author from images sourced, with permission, from
           UCU members and the digital archives of Yale's Paul
           Mellon Centre for British Art', https://photoarchive.paul-
           mellon-centre.ac.uk/collections

Fig. 10.6 After John Carter (1790), *The Entry of Frederick into the*   p. 316
           *Castle of Otranto.*Scene created by the author from images
           sourced, with permission, from UCU members and the
           digital archives of Yale's Paul Mellon Centre for British
           Art', https://photoarchive.paul-mellon-centre.ac.uk/
           collections

Fig. 10.7 After Sydney Herbert (c. 1870), *The Castle of Ari, with*   p. 321
           a Distant View of the Cyclops Scropuli or Rocks which
           Polyphemus Hurled at Ulysses. Scene created by the author
           from images sourced, with permission, from UCU
           members and the digital archives of Yale's Paul Mellon
           Centre for British Art', https://photoarchive.paul-mellon-
           centre.ac.uk/collections

Fig. 10.8 After J. M. W. Turner (1829), *Ulysses Deriding Polyphemus.*   p. 326
           Scene created by the author from images sourced, with
           permission, from UCU members and the digital archives
           of Yale's Paul Mellon Centre for British Art', https://
           photoarchive.paul-mellon-centre.ac.uk/collections

Tables

Table 4.1 Quantity of coups d'état and conspiracies (1945–2019).   p.132
Table 5.1 Illustrative examples of contexts for contemporary   p.168
           medical practice in Northern Ireland.
Table 5.2 Illustrations of healthcare legacies of the Troubles.   p.172

Index

academic autonomy 8, 11, 13, 130, 267

academic citizenry 7, 11, 13, 60–62, 76, 85–86, 92, 95, 99, 101–102, 105, 112, 114, 130, 251, 258, 298–299

academic formation 12, 15

academic freedom xix, 11, 13, 18, 98, 108, 211, 267–269, 280, 294

academic practice 11, 13, 18, 104, 270

academic resistance. *See* resistance

access 3, 8, 16, 33, 41, 79, 96, 107, 110, 112, 140, 142–143, 152, 170, 183–184, 211, 220, 271, 329

activism xx, 4, 29, 35, 39, 45, 51, 58, 60, 66–67, 70–71, 77, 79, 82, 85, 98–99, 104, 110, 131, 179, 193, 195, 199–200, 204, 281, 309, 315, 320, 322

Aleppo 218–221, 229, 231, 234–235, 239

anthropology (discipline) 6, 43, 125–126, 131, 133, 136, 141, 143, 150–151, 329

Anti-Apartheid Movement (AAM) 72, 77, 79, 83

Apartheid 4, 11, 57–60, 62, 64, 67, 70, 73, 77–80, 83, 86, 312

Argentina 9, 126–127, 129–130, 132–133, 135–138, 140, 142, 144, 150–151

armed conflict 7, 9–10, 14, 25–27, 29, 31–36, 38–40, 43–46, 48, 50–51, 91, 147

artefact 7, 17, 64, 69, 73

ASUU strike 272–275, 277–279, 281

Australia 73, 185

authoring 13–19, 218, 242

authorisation 30, 106, 294

authoritarianism xx, 18, 132–133, 136–138, 144–145, 212, 217

authority xix, 13, 18–19, 139, 292–293, 299

authorship 13, 81–82

banned works 7, 61, 73, 79–82

Bethlehem 241, 247–248

biography 5, 17, 85, 125, 127–128

blackmail 264

borders 82, 138, 163–165, 194–195, 206, 251, 254–257, 304

brain drain 93, 99, 108–109, 174, 265, 269–270, 300

Brazil 9, 126–127, 130, 132, 134, 144–146, 150

Bread and Butter Rebellion 307

British Empire 9, 58, 164

Buenos Aires 126, 137–138

Cabbage Rebellion 307

Campinas 144–145

Campinas University (UNICAMP) 134, 144–145

Canada 73, 132, 135–136, 174, 183

capitalism 9, 295, 302–303

Caracas 138, 146, 149

Centro de Estudios del Desarrollo (CENDES) 134, 143

Centro de Investigaciones en Ciencias Sociales (CICSO) 136

checkpoint 165, 248–249, 251–253

children 60, 63, 96, 112, 137, 139–141, 149, 217, 220–222, 224–227, 230, 232, 234–237, 277

China 280, 304

civil unrest 114, 161, 165, 169

civil war 8, 95, 100, 107–108, 164, 179, 268

Cold War 9, 11, 13, 17, 57, 64, 130, 136, 185, 309

Colombia xix, 9, 25–26, 28, 30–32, 35, 50, 127, 148–149

colonialism 9–10, 58, 73, 95, 102,
    131, 150, 162, 167, 174, 178–182,
    185–186, 265, 269–270, 311–313,
    315. *See also* decolonisation; *See
    also* post-colonialism
coloniality 9–10, 179
commemoration 7, 18, 110
commitment 11, 17, 28, 47, 99, 176,
    181, 183, 194, 229, 238, 273, 315
common good 17, 279–280
community xx, 4–5, 7, 12, 28–29, 35,
    37, 39–40, 42, 45, 47, 49, 51, 71,
    93–100, 105–106, 109–112, 114, 129,
    136, 163, 165, 167–171, 176–177,
    180, 184–185, 195, 198, 202, 204,
    211, 219, 225–226, 229–230, 264,
    268–269, 297–298, 300, 314, 328,
    345
complicity xx, 11, 13, 67, 313
conscription 66, 78–79, 83
Consejo Nacional de Ciencia y
    Tecnología (Conacyt) 148
constitutional change 11, 196
coup d'état 132–133, 135–136
covert communication 70–71
creative arts 14, 86, 217
critical consciousness 7, 167–168,
    170–171, 174, 176, 181, 186
critical function of academia 9–10,
    13–14
critical pedagogy 168, 182. *See
    also* reparative pedagogy
Critical University Studies 17, 302
curfew 149, 251
curriculum 10–11, 93, 105–107, 113,
    133, 161–162, 166–168, 170–173,
    175, 178–179, 181–182, 185–186,
    243, 268, 303
    hidden curriculum 10–11, 162, 170,
    172, 179, 186
Cyprus 9, 73

decolonisation 28, 108, 174–175,
    178–181, 183, 186, 311, 313,
    315. *See also* colonialism; *See
    also* post-colonialism

Derrida, Jacques 17, 287, 292–294,
    311, 327, 330
detention 31, 46, 60, 66–67, 71–72, 251
diaspora 3, 16, 91, 108, 136, 231, 312
dictatorship 97, 126, 130, 133,
    135–136, 144–145, 150
discourse analysis 6, 264–265, 270,
    272–275, 278–279
discrimination 18, 91–93, 95, 98,
    100, 106, 110–111, 140, 150, 165,
    179–180
displacement xx, 1, 6, 16, 19, 26, 30,
    75, 96, 99–100, 109, 112, 136, 150,
    172, 217, 219, 225–226, 233, 235,
    238
    forced displacement 31, 136
divorce 140, 150, 182, 223
doctors in training 161, 167, 175, 177–
    178. *See also* medical education;
    See also medical learners
duty 27, 30, 61, 99, 211, 222, 228, 230,
    295, 313

Easter Rising 164
economic conflict 264
economic crisis 126, 133
epistemicide 180, 185
ethics 3, 5–7, 12, 92, 96, 110–111
ethnic conflict 94–95, 164
ethnicity 58, 91, 94–97, 99, 106,
    109–110, 174, 178, 181, 195, 329
exile 1, 16, 31, 44, 57, 70, 81, 83, 85,
    126, 128, 133, 136–138, 141, 151,
    202, 217, 219

family xx, 4, 16–18, 67, 70, 99, 111,
    133, 135–139, 143, 149–152, 163,
    165, 176–177, 218, 221–222,
    225–227, 230, 232, 235–238,
    243–244, 254, 281, 298, 315
fine art (discipline) 67
Finland 73, 256
France 73, 142, 318
freedom. *See* academic freedom; *See*
    freedom of expression
freedom of expression 44, 98, 110, 209

funding 18, 40, 101, 108, 131, 133, 165, 169, 196, 213, 263, 266, 268, 270–271, 279–280, 283, 309

gender xix, 16, 43, 94, 100, 127–128, 134, 140, 152, 175, 178, 224–225, 324
Global North 168, 267
Good Friday Agreement 165, 176, 180, 195, 203–206
Grahamstown 58–60, 64, 66, 78–79, 85
Great Butter Rebellion 307
guerrilla warfare 26, 30, 42–43, 81, 130, 135, 138–139, 141–142, 149, 151

harms 9–11, 17–18, 25–27, 29–30, 33, 35, 39, 42–43, 46, 48–49, 84
higher education studies 11–12, 130
homicide 2, 30, 32, 45, 49, 67, 97, 137, 148, 226, 233–235
hope 2, 8, 12, 17, 83, 94, 96, 111, 198, 200–201, 227, 256, 290, 310, 315
humanitarian agents 92
human rights 11, 31, 34, 41–42, 62, 95, 98, 131, 136, 138, 146, 196–197, 199–200, 203–204, 209–212
    violations 26, 31–32, 34, 36, 42, 62, 95, 98, 136, 146
hunger-torture 267

identity 13, 15, 19, 93, 104, 106, 127, 151, 162–163, 165, 171–173, 175–176, 180–182, 184–185, 245, 289, 299, 329
implicated subject 62, 64
India 9, 94–95, 174, 185
industrial conflict 10, 265, 267, 272, 279. *See also* strikes
injustice 2, 6, 10, 77, 98, 134, 165, 182, 198, 258, 265
inside/insider 7, 14, 35, 42, 47, 66, 125, 175–177, 198, 226, 233–235, 256, 294
institutional autonomy 10, 129–130, 267–269. *See also* academic autonomy

Instituto Nacional de Tecnología Agropecuaria (INTA) 137
intergenerationality 19, 47, 182, 184, 315
Internal Security Act 73
Intifada 251–253
Iraq 94, 101, 220
Isle of Man 163, 174
Israel 9, 15, 73

Jaffna University 97–98, 101, 110
Jordan 245, 252, 254–255, 257
journalism 8, 34, 44, 78, 96, 149, 205
justice 2, 4, 17, 26, 28–29, 47, 51, 62, 71, 111, 114, 151, 176, 198
    transitional justice 26, 28–29, 51

Kant, Immanuel 287–288, 292–295, 297, 327

law (discipline) 11, 32, 41, 43, 193–194, 198, 200, 203–204, 209–210, 212, 292, 297
literature (discipline) 126, 220–221, 228, 232, 237, 252, 329
lived experience 111, 114, 161–162, 177, 193, 200, 243, 250, 265
Liverpool 243–245
Majority World 15–16

Makhanda 58, 85
Manchester 246, 248–249
Mandela, Nelson 69–70, 83–84
marriage 16, 133, 140, 180, 219, 221–224, 227–228
Medellín 32, 34, 41, 46
media 14, 47, 83, 96, 138, 176, 198–199, 205–207, 214, 226, 264, 272–274, 276, 278, 281, 297, 313
medical education 10, 161–162, 166–168, 170, 172, 174, 177–178, 181, 184, 186
medical learners 161, 166, 168, 170–171, 174, 185. *See also* doctors in training

medicine (discipline) 161, 163, 166–167, 172, 175, 178–180, 182, 185, 292–293

memory xix, xx, 3–8, 17, 33–35, 38–39, 43, 45, 51, 63–64, 84–85, 144, 179, 205, 217–218, 227, 236, 257, 290

México 9, 125–126, 130, 132, 137, 148–150

Michoacán 148–149

migration 99, 108, 126–128, 136, 138, 147, 151, 171, 174, 230

minority communities 94–95, 97, 106, 195, 230

Minority World 15

mobility 13, 15, 99, 126, 246

narcotraffic 126, 148–149

narrative 7, 9, 12, 15, 17, 29, 33, 44, 48–49, 64, 85–86, 106, 126, 128, 152, 166, 193, 197, 202, 212–213, 241–242, 244, 252, 257–258, 264, 272–273, 275–280, 313

neoliberalism 10, 12, 102–103, 109, 114, 132, 147, 162–163, 201, 268, 281, 288, 290, 293, 298, 302, 314, 320

Nigeria xix, 9, 263–266, 268–271, 277, 279–280, 304

Nigerian universities 14, 263–265, 267–270, 272

North America 138, 185, 307

Northern Ireland 1, 9–10, 14, 93, 161–171, 173–184, 186, 193–196, 198–199, 203–207, 209

occupation 150, 246, 251, 317–320

oppression 1–3, 6–9, 17, 57, 93–94, 96, 98, 109, 113, 136, 185–186, 204, 250, 258, 279. *See also* suppression

outside/outsider 14, 18–19, 35, 39, 47, 58, 63, 66, 75, 97, 101, 105, 130, 148, 170, 175–178, 180, 208, 226, 233–235, 243, 248–249, 253, 264, 272, 275, 288–289, 291, 294, 307–308, 315

Palestine xix, 1, 6, 9, 15, 242–246, 249, 251–257

paramilitaries 29, 31–32, 42, 46, 169, 172–173, 177, 205

patriarchy 140, 163, 222

peace xx, 5, 8–9, 12, 26, 35, 38, 50, 52, 92–93, 100–101, 104–107, 112–113, 131, 165, 194–196, 205, 281, 298

peace wall 170

philosophy (discipline) 126, 292–293, 329

photography 14, 62–63, 65–67, 73–75, 83–84, 290, 313, 318, 330

poetry 6, 15, 77, 219, 241, 243–244, 246, 249–250, 256–258

political conflict 1, 10, 126–127, 151–152, 164

political repression 41, 146, 150

political violence 30, 48–49, 194

politicisation 82, 91, 107, 109–111, 265, 279, 302, 328

post-colonialism 178–180, 185–186, 270. *See also* colonialism; *See also* decolonisation

post-conflict pedagogy 172, 174, 180–187

post-conflict society xx, 102–104, 106, 114, 170, 176, 180, 185, 194, 205, 210

protest xix, 2, 31, 36, 41–43, 49, 71–72, 114, 130, 146, 199, 233–234, 274–275, 290, 307–309, 311–313, 317, 319, 325, 330. *See also* rebellion; *See also* revolt; *See also* strikes

psychology 42, 64, 92–93, 95, 109–114, 169, 173, 177, 183, 209, 267

public good 2, 91, 105, 114, 278

rebellion 12, 41, 202, 307. *See also* protest; *See also* revolt

reflexivity 179, 242, 293

religion 16, 18, 91, 181, 223, 293, 295

reparation xx, 25–26, 29, 32, 34, 37, 40, 44, 47, 52, 183

reparative pedagogy 182, 185. *See also* critical pedagogy

representation 2–3, 6–8, 13–15, 17–18, 47, 49, 63, 72, 86, 139, 250, 298, 311, 314

Republic of Ireland 9, 161, 163–165, 169, 175, 178, 193

resilience 14–15, 219, 250, 263, 281

resistance xx, 5, 13, 15, 26, 31, 33–35, 42, 45, 51, 57–58, 81, 109, 140, 162, 164, 250–251, 281, 308, 312, 319, 327

revolt 12, 307, 317–318. *See also* protest; *See also* rebellion

revolution 30, 129, 141–142, 233, 265, 307–308, 317–319, 322, 328

Rhodes, Cecil John 3, 311–313

Rhodes University 58–61, 67, 79, 85

Rhodesia 81–82

Santiago del Estero 136

scapegoating 10, 264–265, 272

Scholars at Risk 113, 203, 213–214

sectarianism 113, 164–165, 173

Security Police 57, 59–60, 66–67, 69, 71, 78, 82, 85–86

segregation 58, 108, 163, 168–169, 198, 251

shame 62, 177

social conflict 127, 147, 150

social movement 43, 130–131, 196

sociology (discipline) 43, 128, 143, 163, 181

sociology of science (discipline) 133–135

soldier 183, 248–249, 251–253, 256, 327

South Africa xix, 1, 7, 9, 11, 13, 57, 64, 66, 70, 74–75, 77–78, 80–81, 83, 86, 250, 311

spies 59, 62, 67, 74, 85

Sri Lanka xix, 7, 9, 13, 91–92, 94–100, 102–103, 105–109, 111–114

strikes 12, 14, 49, 200, 205, 263–264, 266, 272–279, 290, 297, 299, 300, 317, 319, 322–324. *See also* ASUU strike; *See also* protest; *See*

also University and College Union (UCU)

subjectification 287

subjectivity xix, 5, 8, 12–13, 15–16, 105, 125, 127, 182, 184, 193, 197, 244, 320

subject, the 242

Sudan 11, 185

suicide 96, 173, 226

suppression 57, 80, 110, 264, 267, 272, 289, 304, 309, 323. *See also* oppression

Suppression of Communism Act 73

surveillance 11, 14–15, 73, 86, 97, 100, 201. *See also* spies

Syria 1, 9, 94, 184, 217–219, 221–222, 226–227, 229–232, 235–237, 239

terrorism 61, 69, 74, 100, 161, 233, 235, 269

trauma 6, 10, 61, 63–64, 92, 111, 161–162, 165, 167, 169–170, 172–173, 177, 179–186, 267

cultural trauma 161

historical trauma 6, 167, 185

trauma-informed practice 162, 167, 181–183, 185–186

Troubles, the 161–162, 165, 169–174, 176–180, 182–184

truth xx, 2, 4, 7–8, 10–11, 14, 17, 26, 28–29, 32–37, 39–42, 49–51, 62–63, 93, 106, 162, 165, 186, 203, 242, 258, 293–294, 315, 319

truth commission 26, 41, 50, 62

Turkey 217, 239

united Ireland 196–197, 201–202

United States of America 16, 71–72, 178, 183, 185, 217, 220–222, 224, 226–227, 229, 231, 252, 275, 280, 307, 312

Universidad Central de Venezuela 145

Universidad de Antioquia (UdeA) 28, 32, 34–35, 37–38, 40–44, 47–49, 51

Universidad Nacional Autónoma de México (UNAM) 148
Universidad Nacional de Colombia (UNAL) 32, 35, 40, 43–46, 49
Universidad Pública Nacional 140
University and College Union (UCU) 290, 309, 322–324, 329
university autonomy. *See* academic autonomy; *See* institutional autonomy
University of Cape Town 3
University of Chester 246
University of Oxford 126, 131, 135, 296, 298, 300, 309, 312–313, 315

Venezuela 9, 125–128, 130, 132–134, 137–143, 145–147, 149–151
Venezuelan Institute of Scientific Research (IVIC) 128, 134
victimisation 27–28, 30–31, 38–39, 48, 264, 272
victims 2, 5, 25–27, 30–32, 34–38, 42–45, 47, 50, 62–63, 86, 149, 173, 275, 304
Vietnam War 72, 130, 309

violence 3, 9–10, 18, 27, 32–33, 35, 39, 42–43, 47–48, 50–51, 57, 59, 63, 91–93, 95–98, 104, 109, 126, 137, 147–150, 165, 168–169, 176, 185, 198, 208–209, 233. *See also* armed conflict; *See also* political violence; *See also* violent conflict
violent conflict 14, 111, 113, 139, 165, 174, 185, 205
voice 6, 16, 28, 39, 50, 61, 64, 110, 114, 167, 179–180, 186–187, 193, 199, 212, 241–242, 244, 246, 250, 258, 263, 265, 280–281, 288–290, 322–324

war 9, 26, 44, 57, 72, 91–92, 95–96, 98–100, 102–114, 131, 148–149, 182–184, 217–219, 225–226, 231, 233, 236, 309, 320
witnessing, act of 3, 5, 61–63, 67, 86, 98, 114, 126–127, 133, 169, 177, 180, 217, 226, 233–234

Yemen 185, 249, 314

About the Team

Alessandra Tosi was the managing editor for this book.

Annie Hine and Adèle Kreager proof-read this manuscript. Adèle compiled the index.

Jeevanjot Kaur Nagpal designed the cover. The cover was produced in InDesign using the Fontin font.

Cameron Craig typeset the book in InDesign and produced the paperback and hardback editions. The main text font is Tex Gyre Pagella and the heading font is Californian FB.

Cameron also produced the PDF and HTML editions. The conversion was performed with open-source software and other tools freely available on our GitHub page at https://github.com/OpenBookPublishers.

Jeremy Bowman created the EPUB.

Raegan Allen was in charge of marketing.

This book was peer-reviewed by Dr. Staci B. Martin, Portland State University, and an anonymous referee. Experts in their field, these readers give their time freely to help ensure the academic rigour of our books. We are grateful for their generous and invaluable contributions.

This book need not end here...

Share

All our books — including the one you have just read — are free to access online so that students, researchers and members of the public who can't afford a printed edition will have access to the same ideas. This title will be accessed online by hundreds of readers each month across the globe: why not share the link so that someone you know is one of them?

This book and additional content is available at
https://doi.org/10.11647/OBP.0427

Donate

Open Book Publishers is an award-winning, scholar-led, not-for-profit press making knowledge freely available one book at a time. We don't charge authors to publish with us: instead, our work is supported by our library members and by donations from people who believe that research shouldn't be locked behind paywalls.

Join the effort to free knowledge by supporting us at
https://www.openbookpublishers.com/support-us

We invite you to connect with us on our socials!

BLUESKY	MASTODON	LINKEDIN
@openbookpublish .bsky.social	@OpenBookPublish @hcommons.social	open-book-publishers

Read more at the Open Book Publishers Blog
https://blogs.openbookpublishers.com

You may also be interested in:

Migrant Academics' Narratives of Precarity and Resilience in Europe
Olga Burlyuk and Ladan Rahbari (Eds)

https://doi.org/10.11647/obp.0331

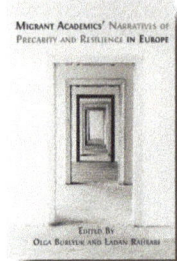

Higher Education for Good
Teaching and Learning Futures
Laura Czerniewicz and Catherine Cronin (Eds)

https://doi.org/10.11647/obp.0363

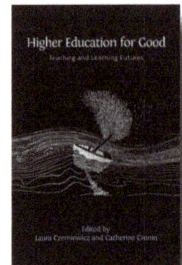

Democratising Participatory Research
Pathways to Social Justice from the South
Carmen Martinez-Vargas

https://doi.org/10.11647/obp.0273

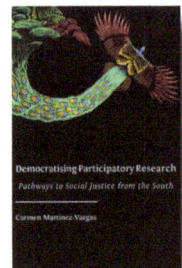

www.ingramcontent.com/pod-product-compliance
Lightning Source LLC
Chambersburg PA
CBHW051441270326
41932CB00025B/3394